Street's Cruising Guide to the Eastern Caribbean

Anguilla to Dominica

In the beginning was the word and the word came from Street. In the first of his **nine** guides to the Eastern Caribbean Don Street chartered the rocks and shoals, sent cruisers to the local bakeries, introduced them to the islands characters and thereby helped to make the world of bareboat chartering possible. Since 1964 all other guide authors have followed in Street's and Iolaire's wake, avoiding the rocks and shoals Street and Iolaire discovered.
Patience Wales—Editor, Sail magazine.

If you want a quiet anchorage buy the other guides, circle in red in Street's Guides the anchorages not described in the other guides. Visit them, and if you do not have a deserted anchorage, you will at least have a quiet one.
Dick Johnson, Former Editor Yachting World.

Experience counts, and no Caribbean cruising guide author has more than Don Street. Don arrived in the Caribbean in 1956, wrote his first guide in 1964, and both Don and his guides are still going strong!
Sally Erdle, Editor, Caribbean Compass

Don Street deserves his reputation as the "best God-damned rock pilot" in the Caribbean. If Don says there's a rock there—there is a rock there. (And he probably found it the hard way!)
**Captain Fatty Goodlander, Author: Chasing the Horizon
And other books about the Caribbean sea gypsy lifestyle.**

Books by Donald M. Street, Jr.

A Cruising Guide to the Lesser Antilles
A Yachting Guide to the Grenadines
The Ocean Sailing Yacht, Volume I
The Ocean Sailing Yacht, Volume II
Seawise

Street's Cruising Guides to the Eastern Caribbean:

Transatlantic Crossing Guide

Puerto Rico, Spanish, U.S. and
British Virgin Islands

Anguilla to Dominica
*Including ANguilla, St. Martin, St. Barthélemy, Saba,
Sint Eustatius (Statia), St. Kitts, and Nevis,
Antigua, Barbuda, Montserrat, Redonda,
Guadeloupe, and Dominica*

Martinique to Trinidad
*Including Martinique, St. Lucia, St. Vincent, Barbadoes,
Northern Grenadines, Southern Grenadines, Grenada,
and Trinidad and Tobago*

Venezuela
*Including Isla Margarita and Adjacent Islands, Los Testigos,
La Blanquilla, La Tortuga, La Orchila, Los Roques, Las Aves,
Aruba, Bonaire, and Curaçao*

Street's Cruising Guide to the Eastern Caribbean

Anguilla to Dominica

Donald M. Street, Jr.

Sketch charts by Morgan B. MacDonald III
Imray-Iolaire harbor charts courtesy of
Imray, Laurie Norie, and Wilson Ltd.

AN AUTHORS GUILD BACKINPRINT.COM EDITION

Anguilla to Dominica
Including Anguilla, St. Martin, St. Barts, Saba, Statia, St. Kitts, Nevis, Antigua, Barbuda,
Montserrat, Redonda, Guadeloupe, and Dominica

All Rights Reserved © 1974, 2001 by Donald M. Street, Jr.

No part of this book may be reproduced or transmitted in any form
or by any means, graphic, electronic, or mechanical, including photocopying,
recording, taping, or by any information storage or retrieval system,
without the permission in writing from the publisher.

AN AUTHORS GUILD BACKINPRINT.COM EDITION

Published by iUniverse.com, Inc.

For information address:
iUniverse.com, Inc.
5220 S 16th, Ste. 200
Lincoln, NE 68512
www.iuniverse.com

Originally published by W.W. Norton & Company

Credit for Graphics: Gail Anderson, Cheryl Tennant, Morgan MacDonald III and Nigel Pert

ISBN: 0-595-17357-8

Printed in the United States of America

Dedication

I first conceived of this cruising guide in 1963, and it was only through the hard work, perseverance, courage, and self-sacrifice of my late wife, Marilyn, that the original book got off the ground.

Fortunately for myself and my daughter, Dory, I met Patricia Boucher, now my wife, on the beach in Tyrell Bay. She has presented me with three active sons yet has had time to help in business, sailing *Iolaire*, and exploring. Although she had hardly sailed before our marriage, she has taken to sailing like a duck to water. Her love of sailing was largely instrumental in my decision to keep *Iolaire* when I was thinking of selling her to reduce expenses.

It is only because of Trich's hard work keeping our various enterprises going in my absence that I have been able to keep the third love of my life, *Iolaire*.

Iolaire has been my mistress for more than 30 years; at age 88, she is still the type of boat Michel Dufour would appreciate. She is "fast, beautiful, and responsive." She first arrived in the islands in 1947, remained for a few years, and cruised back to Europe in 1949, directly from Jamaica to England. In 1951, under the ownership of R.H. Somerset, she won her division's RORC Season's Points Championship at the age of 45. In 1952, she sailed from the Mediterranean via the Azores to New York to take part in the 1952 Bermuda Race. She then cruised back to Europe and the Mediterranean. In 1954, she returned to the islands, where I purchased her in 1957.

In 1975, we celebrated *Iolaire*'s seventieth birthday by cruising to Europe via Bermuda, New London, New York, Boston, Halifax, and then a 15-day passage to Ireland. We cruised on to Cowes, took part in the fiftieth anniversary of the Fastnet Race, and then raced to La Rochelle, La Trinité, Benodet, and back to the Solent—four races, totaling 1,300 miles, in 21 days.

After Calais, we went up the Thames to St. Katharine's Dock in the Pool of London under Tower Bridge, then back down the Thames and up the Colne River in Essex, where we lay alongside the dock in Rowhedge—where *Iolaire* had been built 70 years earlier. Then we went to Plymouth, Glandore (Ireland), Madeira, the Canaries, and back across the Atlantic to Antigua in 18 1/2 days.

We arrived in Antigua seven months and seven days after our departure, having sailed 13,000 miles and raced 1,300 miles—all without an engine—and having visited all the places people had said we would never get to except under power.

We decided that *Iolaire* should celebrate her eightieth birthday in 1985 by retiring from round-the-buoys racing. Her swan song in that year's Antigua Sailing Week was wonderful—third in the cruising division (17 boats), first in the division of boats 20 years old or older.

Then we took *Iolaire* on a 12,000-mile, seven-month, double-transatlantic jaunt. In seven months, we visited Bermuda, five of the Azores islands, Ireland, Vigo (Spain), the Salvage Islands and the Madeiran archipelago, five of the Canary Islands, and three of the Cape Verde Islands. Then we rolled on home to the Caribbean in 14 days and four hours from the Cape Verdes to Antigua—not a record, but a good, fast passage for a heavy-displacement cruising boat.

We spent the winter of 1989-90 exploring Venezuela and crisscrossing the Caribbean, double-checking information for revisions of all volumes of this guide. After that, we sailed from Antigua directly to the Azores, then on to Ireland, down to Vigo, the Canaries, and the Cape Verdes—visiting all the islands we had not visited before in order to eliminate all secondhand information from *Street's Transatlantic Crossing Guide*. Again we did 12,000 miles in 12 months, without the aid of an engine. We did the Cape Verdes-to-Antigua leg of the trip in 14 days and 12 hours—with the spinnaker up the last five-and-a-half days. Not bad for an old girl of 85!

In 1990, *Iolaire* came out of retirement to sail in the new Classic Regatta and won her division! She is not about to race against her younger sisters, but she is still ready, willing, and able to take on the classic boats.

Iolaire has 11 transatlantic passages under her belt. I have sailed her at least 140,000 miles. Who knows how many miles she has sailed during her lifetime? There is little of the Caribbean that has not been furrowed by her hull—and, as some of my good friends will point out, there are few rocks that have not been dented by her keel!

To my three loves—Marilyn, Trich, and *Iolaire*—I dedicate this book.

Iolaire at age 95 is still going strong. For her 90th birthday in 1995 we gave her a rebuild and she is like a new boat—for the update on *Iolaire's* activities see the Publishers Notes.

Contents

	Publisher's Preface	ix
	Preface	xi
	Foreword	xv
	Acknowledgments	xxiii
	List of Charts/Sketch Charts	xxvii
	Charts	xxviii
	Prologue	xxxiii
1	Sailing Directions	1
2	Anguilla	9
3	St. Martin	25
4	St. Barthélemy (St. Barts)	45
5	Saba, St. Eustatius (Statia), St. Christopher (St. Kitts), and Nevis	55
6	Antigua and Barbuda	73
7	Montserrat and Redonda	121
8	Guadeloupe	129
9	Dominica	161
	Index	171

Publisher's Preface

Donald M. Street, Jr., a veteran Caribbean sailor, is also known as an author and the compiler of Imray-Iolaire charts of that area, and as a worldwide yacht insurance broker who places policies with Lloyd's of London.

Mr. Street also serves as a design consultant on new construction, most notably recently on *Lone Star*, a 54-foot wooden ketch built by Mashford Brothers of Plymouth, England. He also acts as design consultant on rerigging existing yachts and finding good cruising boats for people who want a proper yacht. His latest project is a sailing and seamanship video series with *Sailing Quarterly*.

Street is known mainly as a cruising skipper, but he has raced successfully on *Iolaire* and other boats. *Iolaire* retired from round-the-buoys racing at age 80, during 1985 Antigua Week. Her swan song was impressive, as she placed third in the cruising class and first among the boats 20 years or older. Her skipper still races in the various Caribbean regattas as an elder statesman—usually as "rock pilot." It is said he is excellent at this, as he has bounced off every rock in the Eastern Caribbean that is slightly less than *Iolaire*'s draft of seven feet six inches.

His contributions to sailing in the Eastern Caribbean consist of his multi-volume cruising guide and the Imray-Iolaire charts. Fifty Imray-Iolaire charts have replaced roughly 200 French, US, British, Dutch, and a few Spanish charts and are all that are needed to cruise the Eastern Caribbean and the Atlantic island groups of the Azores, Madeiran Archipelago, Canaries, and Cape Verdes. These Imray-Iolaire charts have become standard in the Eastern Caribbean, where both the US Coast Guard and the coast guard units on the ex-British islands use Imray-Iolaire charts rather than the ones published by the British Admiralty or the Defense Mapping Agency.

As an author, Street is prolific. His original *Cruising Guide to the Lesser Antilles* was published in 1966, *A Yachting Guide to the Grenadines* in 1970, and an updated and expanded *Cruising Guide to the Eastern Caribbean* in 1974, with continual expansions and updates since then. This has now become *Street's Cruising Guide to the Eastern Caribbean*, which covers a 1,000-mile-long arc of islands, plus the Venezuelan coast and the Atlantic islands. In 1985, Street and *Iolaire* made two transatlantic trips (their sixth/seventh and eighth/ninth, respectively). These trips provided a wealth of information that was incorporated into his rewrite of *Street's Cruising Guide to the Eastern Caribbean, Volume I*. This revision, renamed *Street's Transatlantic Crossing Guide and Introduction to the Caribbean*, contains detailed information on islands and harbors in the Atlantic islands group, plus general information on those islands as well as the Eastern Caribbean. It is the essential companion volume to any and all individual volumes covering the Eastern Caribbean. In 1989, *Iolaire* again did a double-transatlantic crossing. As a result, a supplement was issued to this book, eliminating almost all secondhand information. The Venezuela volume was completely updated and rewritten in 1991. The *Martinique-to-Trinidad* volume was rewritten and updated as a result of explorations in 1991-92, while the *Anguilla-to-Dominica* volume was completely rewritten after extensive exploration during the winter of 1992. In the winter of 1992-93, *Iolaire* began re-exploring the Puerto Rico and Virgin Islands area in order to completely update and rewrite that section of the guide.

The Street guides cover a vast area—equivalent to Eastport, Maine, to Cedar Keys, Florida; or Norway's North Cape to Gibraltar. No other yachting author has ever covered so much territory in such detail.

Street has also written *The Ocean Sailing Yacht, Volume I* (1973) and *Volume II* (1978). *Seawise*, a collection of articles, came out in 1976. He is also working on a series of books—*Street on Sails, Street on Seamanship and Storms*, and *Street on Small-Boat Handling*—as well as *Iolaire and I*, the story of *Iolaire* and Street's lifetime of adventures and misadventures in the yachting world.

Street writes regularly for *Sail, Cruising World, Sailing, WoodenBoat, Telltale Compass, Yachting, Yachting World*, and *Yachting Monthly*, as well as for publications in Sweden, Germany, Italy, Ireland, Australia, and New Zealand.

For more than 20 years, Street owned land and two houses in Grenada, but, unfortunately, the houses are no more. They were taken over by the People's Revolutionary Army (PRA) in May 1979 to be used as part of its military base. The houses did not survive the United States liberation in 1983, when helicopter gunships targeted both of them. He hopes someday to rebuild on the old site. During the winter, he crisscrosses the Caribbean.

Since Street's main occupation is yacht insurance, he and *Iolaire* appear at all the major gatherings of yachts in the Eastern Caribbean. In the fall, he is always at the St. Thomas and Tortola charter-boat shows. Then he proceeds eastward via St. Martin and St. Barthélemy en route to the Nicholson's Agents Week. Spring finds him at the Rolex and BVI regattas, after which he heads to Antigua for the Classic Yacht Regatta and Antigua Week. Then it is south to lay up *Iolaire* beyond the hurricane belt.

Formerly, *Iolaire* was laid up in Grenada, but her berth has been moved south and west to Centro Marina de Oriente in Puerto La Cruz, Venezuela. In July and August, Street is usually in Glandore, County Cork, Ireland, skippering the family's 61-year-old Dragon, *Gypsy*, or trimming her sheets for his sons.

Street claims to be 38 and holding—as long as he can climb the mast without the aid of a bosun's chair; his wife looks young enough to be his daughter (she's the bikini-clad skipper on the cover of the Puerto Rico volume). Street and his son Richard (plus a friend, Niall McDowell) took *Gypsy*, an open day racer, to France in the summer of 1992 for the Classic Boat Festival in Brest. They sailed from Glandore (near Fastnet Rock) across the Irish Sea to the Isles of Scilly, then across the English Channel and on to Douarnenez. After the festival, they returned to Ireland—completing 700 miles in an open boat.

As mentioned, Street is an insurance broker—and, in fact, it is his main source of income. He has pointed out that many boats are having trouble obtaining insurance coverage while in the Caribbean (and especially in Venezuela), so if you are having such difficulties, contact the author, c/o David Payne, Morgan Wright & Coleman, 6 Alie Street, London E1 8DD, England (telephone: 071-488-9000; fax: 071-480-6917). (David sends a weekly courier package to *Iolaire* wherever she is in the Caribbean.)

Preface

When I first bought *Iolaire* in 1957, I found on board what was then the only straight cruising guide to the Lesser Antilles—a mimeographed publication produced by the Coast Guard Auxiliary and edited by a Lieutenant Commander Buzby. Carleton Mitchell's *Islands to Windward*, published in 1948, was generally regarded as a good cruising yarn rather than as a cruising guide, but it did have some basic cruising information in the back of the book. Unfortunately, by the time I started sailing outside the Virgin Islands in 1959, *Islands to Windward* was out of print. In 1960, *The Virgin Islands* by George Teeple Eggleston was published, the result of a one-month cruise aboard Eunice Boardman's 55-foot ketch *Renegade*.

In 1961, Percy Chubb III, after a cruise through the Lesser Antilles, produced the small, privately printed *Guide to the Windward and Leeward Islands of the Eastern Caribbean*. In 1964, Linton Rigg wrote *The Alluring Antilles*, a combination guide and cruising adventure of a half-year sail from Puerto Rico to Trinidad aboard the 45-foot ketch *Island Belle*.

These seemed to suffice for the small amount of Caribbean cruising done in those days, but starting in the early 1960s, the charter-boat business suddenly began to expand, and many new boats arrived. It was Frank Burke of Island Yachts who inspired my entry into cruising-guide writing. Figuring that too many of the charter parties were missing the best spots in the Virgins because their skippers had not been in the islands long enough to get to know them intimately, he asked me to write a cruising guide to the Virgin Islands. I did so, and he had it privately printed. I received the magnificent sum of $100—which was a veritable fortune for me in those days.

This small volume later formed the basis of the Virgin Islands section of my *Cruising Guide to the Lesser Antilles*, published in 1966, after I showed it to Phelps Platt of Dodd, Mead, who encouraged me to expand it to cover the whole island chain. This was followed two years later by Tom Kelly and Jack van Ost's *Yachtsman's Guide to the Virgin Islands*, and then by Al Forbes's excellent *Cruising Guide to the Virgin Islands*—notable in that, unlike many guide authors, he had sailed the area for many years before he wrote his.

In 1970, following eight years of cruising the Grenadines, I produced *A Yachting Guide to the Grenadines*, after which, in 1973, came Julius M. Wilensky's *Yachtsman's Guide to the Windward Islands*, which covered largely the same territory as mine. Also in 1973, Gordon C. Ayer produced an interesting small guide covering an island group that had never been detailed before—namely, the Passage Islands.

During the late 1970s and early 1980s, numerous guides to the Eastern Caribbean appeared. They covered individual areas such as the Virgin Islands, the northern Windward Islands, Anguilla, St. Martin, St. Barthélemy, St. Kitts, Nevis, and the Leeward Islands. Others keep popping out of the woodwork like mushrooms out of an old log.

At the southern end of the islands, Chris Doyle first produced his *Sailor's Guide to the Windwards*, then went to Venezuela to write a guide to the eastern Venezuelan coast. Next he headed north and did his guide to the Leewards. He seems to be following my footsteps!

If, in all this, you find that one guide reads surprisingly like another, I ask only that you refer back to my original works to see who said what first. If nothing else, it's a matter of pride. It is very easy to write a guide to an area if someone else has previously done all the hard work—i.e., extensive exploring, producing charts, and bouncing off uncharted rocks.

Most of the other guides have been written with an eye on the bareboat-charter market, so they concentrate on the well-known, popular anchorages and skip a tremendous number of excellent anchorages that are a bit out of the way.

When people ask, "Why would you need a multi-volume guide to the Eastern Caribbean?" I point out that the area covered is the same as from Eastport, Maine, to Cedar Keys, Florida, or from the North Cape in Norway to Gibraltar! That's a lot of territory to explore!

As each year goes by, and more and more yachts cruise the Caribbean, the bareboat charter organizations are expanding exponentially. The area is now flooded with boats. But if you are willing to go off the beaten track, you can still have anchorages completely to yourself—or almost so.

My suggestion for finding this idyllic world of deserted (or almost-deserted) anchorages is to buy the rival guides. (I know—why am I promoting people who have benefited from my earlier guides? But heed my advice.) Then circle in red in my guide all of the harbors that are not listed in the other books. If you head for the anchorages circled in red, you will be able to avoid most of the other boats cruising the Eastern Caribbean.

To illustrate this, I would like to quote from a letter I received: "My thanks to you for your cruising guides. I have enjoyed my season down here in the Caribbean and the myriad of information in your books has really been a pleasant and informative education and made my cruise more safe, interesting, and fun. Just a brief example: I've begun to seek out the less crowded anchorages, and armed with your guides and eyeball navigation have visited Sandy Island, Grenada; Grand Bay, Carriacou (caught 10 lobsters there in 1 1/2 hours); Petit St. Vincent, north side (6 lobsters); Grand Bay, Canouan; World's End (some help from other sources). Always we were the only vessel anchored. Nifty—we loved it. Soon I'll be going around to Antigua with your guide in hand. Thank you for an excellent job. Great sailing and best wishes, Ray Bachtle, *Alchemist*."

In *Street's Cruising Guide to the Eastern Caribbean*, I have tried to include all the information I have gleaned in some 35 years of cruising these islands. I have drawn not only from my own experiences, but, as you can see from the accompanying Acknowledgments, also from the experiences of old friends who are, in addition, good sailors. Thus, I feel I have described probably every cove in the Eastern Caribbean where one could possibly think of anchoring.

If you find one I may have missed, please let me know. I boldly asserted in my 1966 guide that the book would never become dated because rocks do not move. Little did I realize how eagerly island governments would actually start moving them, along with creating new islands, making islands into peninsulas, building low bridges, and so forth, as the development of the Eastern Caribbean boomed. Further, any guide is destined to go out of date simply because the idyllic, uninhabited spot of one year becomes a thriving hotel and cabaña settlement the next. Indeed, one of my readers once took me to task because he was using my original guide and expected to anchor off an island described therein as uninhabited. As he rounded between Pinese and Mopion, he was greeted by a brand-new hotel ablaze with celebration, and he counted no fewer than 45 boats moored in the lee of Petit St. Vincent! Please . . . don't blame me!

I have largely stayed away from recommending restaurants and bars in the Eastern Caribbean, because these establishments—especially their cooks and bartenders—do change. A superb restaurant or bar one week can become rotten the next when the cook or bartender decides to move on to another challenge.

It is impossible for anyone to say he knows the Eastern Caribbean perfectly; even after three decades, I was still discovering new little anchorages. But then the time came to look to new fields—namely, Venezuela.

At various times, Venezuelan yachtsmen extolled the virtues of Venezuela and the offshore islands. I originally went to Venezuela to give a slide lecture to a yacht club and take part in a race. I then took *Iolaire* to eastern Venezuela for six weeks and later visited western Venezuela on *Boomerang*. There followed a month's cruise in 1978 and a two-week cruise in 1979. In the early eighties, we seldom visited Venezuela, as it was the most expensive place in the Eastern Caribbean. In fact, Caracas was rated as the most expensive city in the world.

But then came the collapse of the oil market—and the devaluation of the Venezuelan bolívar—in the 1980s. Venezuela became the cheapest cruising area in the Eastern Caribbean. At first we were unable to take advantage of this, but since 1986, we have spent six to eight weeks (sometimes 10 weeks) each winter cruising there. The result is *Street's Cruising Guide to the Eastern Caribbean—Venezuela*, published in 1991 and covering the Venezuelan coast, its offshore islands, Aruba, Bonaire, and Curaçao.

With the aid of many veteran Venezuelan yachtsmen, plus yachtsmen from the Eastern Caribbean (see Acknowledgments)—and as a result of all my own cruises—I think the area is now superbly covered. I defy anyone to find a good, safe anchorage suitable for boats drawing seven feet that I have not mentioned in my Venezuelan guide. In fact, I will buy drinks for the evening for anyone who does.

During the summer of 1985, *Iolaire* visited and explored the Azores, the Madeiran archipelago, the Canary Islands, and the Cape Verde Islands. The information gained—combined with the information already in the first volume of *Street's Cruising Guide to the Eastern Caribbean*—came out under a new title: *Street's Transatlantic Crossing Guide and Introduction to the Caribbean*, the essential companion to my guides to the Eastern Caribbean. Not only does it contain transatlantic crossing information—plus cruising information on Bermuda, the Azores, the Madeiran archipelago, the Canaries, and the Cape Verdes—but it also has important background information on the Eastern Caribbean: preparation; wind, weather, and tides; universal tide tables; sailing directions; communications; provisioning and services; chartering; yacht clubs and racing; and lists of navigational aids for the Eastern Caribbean and the Atlantic islands. (*Street's Transatlantic Crossing Guide and Introduction to the Caribbean* should be used in conjunction with the volume that covers the area where you are planning to cruise.)

In 1989, *Iolaire* again crossed the Atlantic and did a double-transatlantic—*Iolaire's* tenth and eleventh such trips, my eighth and ninth. With the aid of my two sons Donald III and Richard, plus other friends, we did extensive explorations of the Canaries and Cape Verdes. The information gleaned on that trip has been included in *Street's Transatlantic Crossing Guide and Introduction to the Caribbean*.

Now I am extending the bet I have offered for a number of years: If you can find any anchorage safe for a boat that draws seven feet in the Eastern Caribbean, the Atlantic islands, or along the Venezuelan coast that I have not mentioned in my guides, I will happily pay for an evening's drinks in exchange for the information on that unmentioned harbor. Also, I greatly appreciate the assistance that yachtsmen have been so willing to provide, so please do send suggestions for corrections, additions, or deletions to: D.M. Street, Jr., c/o David Payne, Morgan, Wright & Coleman, 6 Alie Street, London E1 8DD, England. Telephone: 071-488-9000; fax: 071-480-6917. (Needless to say, this is also valid for anyone requiring marine insurance.)

Many cruising friends who knew the Eastern Caribbean in the early days have headed west to Belize, the Bay Islands, the River Dolce. They have been urging me to base *Iolaire* in that area for a few years and then write a cruising guide. I refuse to do that, as I do not feel you can cruise an area for a total of six to twelve weeks and then write a guide to it. It takes years to explore a cruising area adequately, and exploring is a young man's game. Those days are over for me, the "Old Tiger" has retired. It is time for one of the "Young Tigers" (daughter Dory or one of her three brothers, Donald, Richard, and Mark) to take over *Iolaire* and explore new territory.

— D.M.S.

Foreword

The Lesser Antilles stretch southward from St. Thomas to Grenada in a great crescent 500 miles long, offering the yachtsman a cruising ground of unequaled variety. Some of the islands are flat, dry, and windswept, their shores girded by coral reefs and their land barely arable. Others are reefless, jagged peaks jutting abruptly up from the sea, where they block the ever-present trades and gather rain clouds the year round; water cascades in gullies down their sides, and their slopes are well cultivated. The character of their peoples likewise varies—from the charming and unspoiled but desperately poor Dominicans to the comparatively well-to-do and worldly wise Frenchmen of Martinique.

Unless you have a whole season at your disposal, it is foolhardy to attempt all the islands in a single cruise. Not only will you not make it, but you will fail to enjoy the slow, natural, and relaxed pace of life in these tropical islands. The first measure of a successful cruise is how soon your carefully worked out timetable gets thrown away.

Rule number 1 in the Antilles is: Don't make any plan more than a day in advance, since you will frequently—in fact constantly—alter your intentions to suit the pace and attractions of the locale.

Rule number 2: Each night before turning in, read the sailing directions covering your passage to the next area, and study the detailed description of your intended anchorage. In some cases, this will seriously affect the next day's plans—particularly the hour of departure. Remember, for instance, that when you are on the east coast of Martinique, Guadeloupe, Antigua, and Grenada, you must be in the anchorage by 1400 hours. Otherwise the sun is in the west, directly in your line of vision, making it impossible to see any reefs until it is too late.

Rule number 3: Do not enter a strange harbor at night if at all possible. If necessary, stand off, heave-to, and wait for dawn!

Rule number 4: No chart can be absolutely accurate. In the Caribbean, knowing how to read the water is as important as knowing how to read a chart. Eyeball navigation is the key to safe and satisfying sailing in the islands.

Whether or not Puerto Rico to the north or Trinidad and Tobago to the south should be considered part of the Lesser Antilles is a question for the gazetteers to squabble over. For the purposes of this guide, we welcome all three into the fellowship of proximity. (And, of course, the guide also covers Venezuela and the Atlantic islands.) Taken as such, the Antilles conveniently break up into a number of areas suitable for two- or three-week cruises. The starting and end points of a cruise will be governed by your own tastes and the availability of air transportation. The air services into San Juan and Trinidad are excellent, for example, but neither of these places is a particularly good spot to begin a cruise. San Juan is dead to leeward of the rest of the chain, against a strong current—unless, of course, you are planning to cruise the wonderful undiscovered Passage islands of Culebra and Vieques, or the south coast of Puerto Rico.

Trinidad used to be a poor starting point, as the anchorage off the yacht club was so bad you would get seasick. Now, however, all this has changed; the yacht club has established a marina with a number of berths reserved for visiting yachts, plus there is a good, sheltered anchorage at Chaguaramus, where you will also find hauling facilities. Trinidad Customs and Immigration used to be the most difficult in the entire Caribbean, but now they are very helpful.

To get to most of these places, you must often rely on secondary local airlines with shuttle services.

These vary from being fairly good from San Juan to St. Thomas and Tortola and the Venezuelan airlines, to downright disastrous with LIAT. LIAT's aircraft, pilots, and maintenance personnel are first rate, but the office staff has elevated the art of losing baggage and double-booking reservations to an exact science. There are various jokes about what LIAT actually stands for—some people claim it is an abbreviation for "Leave Islands Any Time," while others insist that it means "Luggage In Another Terminal." (In fact, it's Leeward Islands Air Transport.) Still, it's all part of the adventure of a Caribbean cruise.

Which starting point you choose will say something of your tastes in cruising. If you prefer gunkholing and short jaunts between many little islands only a few miles apart, if you like snorkeling and little in the way of civilization, then it's the Virgins or the Grenadines for you. But you'd best hurry down, because real-estate developers and other sailors are fast making this situation a thing of the past. Mustique, for one example, was until recently a private estate in the hands of the Hazel family. But it was sold to a developer, who has worked it over at a pretty fast rate. Well-to-do Europeans have bought land and built houses, creating many new jobs for local labor but depriving the yachtsman of a wonderful hideaway.

For those of you who want to give boat and crew a good tuning-up for offshore racing, set out from St. Thomas up through the Virgins, then work your way across Anegada Passage to St. Martin or Anguilla, and finish with a final leg up to Antigua. In doing so, you will gain a fair sampling of island diversity and of French, Dutch, and English colonial temperaments. The Anegada Passage is a nice, hard drive to windward, which should uncover any weak points in rig or crew.

Those interested exclusively in the pursuits of diving, treasure hunting, or snorkeling should steer for the low-lying islands of Anguilla, Barbuda, Anegada, Los Roques, and Las Aves. The reefs in these areas are vast and inexhaustible. Fortune hunters still flock to these islands, where innumerable offlying wrecks date back hundreds of years, some presumably undiscovered. Consult the source books—but remember that these islands are low, flat, encircled by reefs, and hard to spot. The charts are based on surveys done mainly in the middle of the nineteenth century. Coral grows, and hurricanes have moved through the area a number of times; earthquakes have shaken the islands, and sand bars have moved. In short, you must be extremely careful. Do not let your boat become the next curiosity for inquisitive divers!

Saba and Statia (Sint Eustatius) are two attractive islands that are too seldom visited. Their anchorages are exceptionally bad, but when the conditions are right, they certainly are worth a go. Their close neighbors, St. Kitts and Nevis, are of historical interest, figuring as they do in the lives of Alexander Hamilton, Admirals Nelson and Rodney, and Generals Shirley and Frazer. St. Kitts is well worth a visit to see the beautiful restoration of the old fortress of Brimstone Hill. A number of the old plantation great houses have been restored and opened up as hotels and restaurants. Renting a car to tour St. Kitts is a good scheme.

If you like longer sails, the bright lights of civilization, and a variety of languages and customs, the middle islands—from Antigua to St. Lucia—should keep you happy. The French islands of Guadeloupe and Martinique afford the finest cuisine in the Antilles. The local merchants offer an excellent selection of cheeses and meats from Europe and the best wines available outside France. The tourist shops are a woman's delight, and the perfumes are at about half the price in the States. Up until a few years ago, bikinis were so inexpensive (two for US$5.00) that the women bought them by the dozen. Regrettably, those days are gone—probably forever. There is still a fabulous collection of bikinis in Martinique, but the prices have gone up so much in France that the savings for an American no longer are substantial. Rough rule of thumb: The smaller the bikini, the more expensive it is. The string has arrived: its size—minuscule; its price—astronomical. One solution frequently used by the always economical French women was to buy only half the string at half the price. Others felt that even that was too expensive and sailed *au naturel*—not really showing off, just economizing!

The universal pastime of watching members of the opposite sex is alive and well in Martinique, and the visiting seafarer soon gets into the spirit of things. This pastime can be enjoyed in many ways, but the two most popular methods are strolling around the streets of Fort de France and rowing around in Anse Mitan (which today is likely to have 40 or 50 boats in it) and pretending to admire the boats while admiring the crews. An added bonus here is that at Anse Mitan, going topless seems to be *de rigeur*.

The women in Fort de France may not be the prettiest in the Caribbean, but they are far and away the most stylish. And the men, sitting at sidewalk cafés sipping their coffee or *punch vieux*, cut figures worthy of the boulevardiers of Paris. Newcomers, however, should take note: The punch will make a strong man weak-kneed and the coffee tastes not unlike battery acid.

The French and their chicory-laced coffee have distressed visiting foreigners for a great many decades. A story is told of Count von Bismarck touring France after the Franco-Prussian War. At the close of a fine meal in a country inn, he called for the maître d'hôtel and offered to buy all his chicory at 10 percent over the market price; the maître d' agreed and sold him what he claimed was all he had. Again the count offered to buy any remaining chicory, this time at 50 percent over the market price; the maître d' managed to produce a second quantity of the plant. For a third time, the count offered to buy any that remained—at *double* the market price—and the maître d' surrendered an additional small amount, insisting that this was indeed all that remained. Satisfied at last, the count concluded, "Very well, now you may prepare me a cup of coffee!"

H.M.S. Diamond Rock, off the south coast of Martinique, is the basis for many stories in folklore, most of them inaccurate. The story of Diamond Rock (now called Rocher du Diamant) is contained in *Her Majesty's Sloop of War Diamond Rock*, by Stuart and Eggleston.

Dominica is for the adventurous. A ride into the mountains by Jeep and horseback will take you to the last settlement of the Carib peoples. Here the natives fashion the distinctive Carib canoes that are also seen in Guadeloupe, Martinique, and St. Lucia. With nothing but a flour sack for a sail and a paddle for a rudder, the islanders set out in these boats against the wind to fish in the open Atlantic. Not an easy way to earn a living. Prince Rupert Bay, at the northern end of Dominica, should be one of the most popular anchorages in the Eastern Caribbean. It is well sheltered, has numerous small, shorefront bars and restaurants, has a splendidly restored old French fort, and is a good jumping-off place for exploring the island. Also, it is the first good harbor north of Martinique for boats heading northward. In fact, it has everything going for it except that it has probably the most miserable group of boat boys (or perhaps I should say boat bums) in the entire Eastern Caribbean! I hope that by the time you read this, the government will have stepped in and sorted out the situation. If they have, I would certainly advise stopping there. Check locally to find out the current situation.

St. Lucia provides some superb anchorages at Pigeon Island, Marigot, and Vieux Fort, and the truly unbelievable one beneath the Pitons at Soufrière. The volcano and sulfur baths are an impressive spectacle, and it is well worth the expense to explore the island by car or Jeep, an adventure vividly recounted by George Eggleston in *Orchids on the Calabash Tree*.

St. Vincent, at the northern end of the Grenadines, is a high, lush island richly and diversely cultivated. The island has an intriguing history, highlighted by the almost continual warfare among French, English, and Caribs that lasted from 1762 until 1796, when the Caribs were expelled to Central America.

Bequia is the home of fishermen and whalers, an island where any sailor can explore, relax, and "gam" for days on end. The harbor is beautiful and life is relaxed.

After cruising the entire Caribbean and getting to know all the islands intimately, many experienced yachtsmen declare Grenada to be "the loveliest of the islands." The highlands produce enough rain to allow the farmers to grow a large quantity of fresh fruit and vegetables, but the south coast is dry enough to allow the yachtsman to live and work on his boat. The island also has a dozen different harbors, providing 60 separate anchorages. Most of these harbors are only short, one- or two-hour sails from each other.

The town of St. Georges is picturesque; the main anchorage, in the lagoon, is only a short dinghy ride from supermarkets, cable and telephone offices, banks, and other services. The island has yacht yards and a yacht club, providing slipways, a good stock of marine supplies, and—most inportant—a large stock of friendly people. In short, after some years of a topsy-turvy political situation, the island should, in years to come, reassert itself as the capital of Eastern Caribbean yachting.

Unfortunately, this will happen only if the government gets organized and persuades someone to buy out Grenada Yacht Services. Someone needs to bulldoze everything and completely redo the docks. Because of its harbor and location, GYS should be a major yacht yard, but political problems and poor management have thrust it into a state of utter disrepair. The economy of Grenada will never recoup unless GYS is rebuilt and the island again becomes a yachting center.

Barbados is relatively remote and seldom visited by yachts, except those that are coming downwind from Europe. If your plane stops there en route to another island, arrange for a layover of a day or two. It is undoubtedly the best-run island in the entire Caribbean and everything is clean and neat (by West Indian standards). The people are charming, speak with the most wonderful accent, and are solicitous and helpful to visitors. The old Careenage in Bridgetown should not be missed.

It is a shame that Tobago is seldom visited by yachtsmen. It is dead to windward of Trinidad, and from Grenada it is 90 miles hard on port tack. Even if you manage to lay the rhumb line from Grenada, it will be a long slog, hard on the wind. Current and sea will drive you off to the west. It is fairly inaccessible except from Barbados, from where it is an easy reach southwestward.

The American and British Virgin Islands have been described laboriously in the various tourist guides, but whatever the evaluation of shoreside life, a sailor can pass a very pleasant month cruising in this area.

The Virgin Islands are only a few miles apart, and if you enjoy snorkeling and short sails, head for the Virgins or the Passage Islands. (The Grenadines and Puerto La Cruz, Venezuela, are also good locales for these pursuits.) If you are cruising the northern Virgins, take a side trip over to St. Croix. With luck, it will be a glorious, 35-mile beam reach. Christiansted is without doubt the most attractive town in the Caribbean, and you can make side trips out to Buck Island, which divers consider one of the finest dive sites in the world.

The character of the various island peoples is apt to vary broadly within a very small area. Even among the former British islands, each has its own peculiar flavor, its own outlook and accent. (In fact, natives are known to complain that they can't understand the English spoken on neighboring islands.) For the most part, the people are quiet and law-abiding. Actually, the sort of racially inspired violence that periodically has troubled St. Croix and St. Thomas has been far less of a problem in the islands farther south.

As the years go by, the Eastern Caribbean becomes more crowded; hence, yachtsmen are beginning to head west to Venezuela. In the 1950s and 1960s, cruising in Venezuela was looked on as a hazardous pursuit—not because of unfriendliness to yachtsmen but rather because Fidel Castro was smuggling guerrillas ashore in small fishing boats. The Guardia Nacional and the Navy frequently were guilty of shooting first and asking questions later, with the result that a number of yachts were ventilated by Venezuelan government agencies. All that is now a thing of the past. Although you may have to fill out a lot of documents, everyone is extremely friendly, and, to the best of my knowledge, there have been few nasty incidents involving yachts in Venezuela in recent years.

Venezuela is a land of contrasts. The coast, with its mountains that rise directly from the sea to 9,000 feet, in some parts is dry and desolate like a desert; other sections, like the eastern end of the Peninsula de Paria, are covered with dense jungle. The easternmost tip of the peninsula rises 5,000 feet, with vertical slopes spilling into the Caribbean on one side and into the Golfo de Paria on the other. From the Golfo de Paria, one can visit Angel Falls and the Orinoco Delta, take excursions into the jungle, and see unbelievable wildlife right from the boat. This area is the original primeval jungle, occasionally visited by powerboats but seldom by sailing yachts. The windswept offshore islands provide some of the finest fishing, snorkeling, and diving in the Eastern Caribbean. They have not been fished out and they are generally uninhabited.

The north coast of Venezuela, as one progresses westward, begins with heavy jungle that tapers out to brush and ends up finally in Laguna Grande del Obispo. In the Golfo de Cariaco, one finds a fantastic harbor—the scenery ashore is like a lunar landscape, and it looks as though it hasn't rained here in 20 years!

Continuing westward, the mountains of Venezuela are always close to the coastline and always barren. The cities are exploding rather than simply growing. Side by side are sophisticated new marinas and tiny fishing villages. Offshore are low, deserted reef and uninhabited islands. After Puerto Cabello, you can pretty much forget the rest of the Venezuelan coast.

Los Roques, a 355-square-mile cruising area off the north coast, is almost as large as the American and British Virgin Islands, and at least 50 percent of it is unsurveyed. Venezuelan yachtsmen and a few Americans (such as Gordon Stout) have crisscrossed this wonderful place and spent as long as a week cruising here. This area would be ideal for a bareboat organization, and perhaps one will expand into this region. It will be interesting to see what develops here in years to come.

Yachting has taken hold in Venezuela, and modern marinas now can be found at Caracas (five, in fact), Cumaná, Puerto La Cruz (three), Puerto Cabello, and in Morrocoy National Park. Furthermore, there are hauling facilities in all of these harbors. In addition, at Centro Marina de Oriente, in Puerto La Cruz, you will find a brand-new yacht yard, repair facility, and marina—specifically built to cater to the needs of cruising yachtsmen. Without a doubt, it's the most modern facility east of Miami.

Because of the devaluation of the bolívar, most things in Venezuela are inexpensive. Hauling and repair costs, for example, are considerably less than in the Eastern Caribbean, so more and more yachtsmen now are sailing to Venezuela for repairs and refits. This is especially true in summer, when boats head there for refitting and at the same time escape from the hurricane belt. Everyone remembers the devastation caused by Hurricane Hugo in 1989, and one way to avoid being "Hugoized" is to head for Venezuela. (See "Reflections on Hugo," below.)

Once you get away from the major population areas, you will seldom have more than one or two other yachts in your anchorage—and the only time you are likely to find many boats in the anchorages is on the weekends.

One cruising technique used by yachtsmen in Venezuela is to arrive at a marina on Friday night as the Venezuelans are all departing and berths become available. Stay for the weekend, enjoy sightseeing, etc., on Saturday, go out on the town Saturday night, sleep late Sunday morning, and depart Sunday afternoon prior to the arrival of the returning Venezuelan yachts.

Unfortunately, the great welcome that the Venezuelan private clubs used to give visiting yachtsmen has cooled. As more and more sailors go to Venezuela, the behavior of some has been such that the door has been slammed shut against the rest of us in most private Venezuelan clubs. If you know a Venezuelan yachtsman, write to him ahead of time and he probably can get the door opened specifically for you.

Close to Venezuela are the ABC islands of Aruba, Bonaire, and Curaçao. Low and windswept, they vary from the quiet, simple, and slow-moving Bonaire to the hustling, bustling, and very cosmopolitan Curaçao.

Fighting your way eastward along the north coast of South America is rough—especially once you pass Cabo de la Vela. By the time you reach the Golfo de Maracaibo, you are dead exhausted and would love to stop. It used to be a matter of pushing on to reach Aruba, but a few years ago I discovered (via the Venezuelan Hydrographic Office) that there is a small naval base at Los Monjes with a passable anchorage between the islands. Here you can stop, rest for a day or so, and then fight your way to Aruba.

Aruba used to be just a low, flat island covered with oil refineries, but now the refineries have been dismantled, tourism has taken hold, and the island is covered with hotels. A new marina in Oranjestad offers all the amenities a yachtsman could want, although it is very crowded, and dock space must be reserved in advance.

Bonaire is low, flat, and sparsely populated. Its shores rise so steeply from the sea bottom that it is almost impossible to anchor in its lee. But the anchorage problem has been solved with a new marina. Adequate supplies—fresh, frozen, and canned—are available. The people are very friendly and Bonaire has some of the best diving in the world—with topnotch support facilities right at hand.

If you want to connect up with the outside world from the ABC islands, go to Curaçao, which has excellent air communications and first-class hotels. Curaçao also has superb harbors and all kinds of supplies.

I hope that with the aid of these books, you will enjoy the Caribbean islands and the Venezuelan coast as much as I have for more than three decades. Anyone contemplating a cruise aboard a charter boat is well advised to read the supplementary chapters, found in *Street's Transatlantic Crossing Guide and Introduction to the Caribbean*, which contain the general information not included in the individual volumes on the island groups. Preparations; Charts; Getting There; Wind, Weather, and Tides; Sailing Directions; Entry and Communications; Provisions and Services; Chartering; and Yacht Clubs are all covered. The *Crossing Guide* is the essential companion to any of the guides you have on board and provides much background information. Not only will it explain why perhaps your charter skipper looks tired (he probably spent the last two days fixing his generator under sail while he was deadheading to pick you up), but it will also offer a better idea of what you can expect upon arrival in the islands. A host of important tips and facts that are not included in the average tourist or charter-boat broker's brochure will, I trust, be found in this book. And, needless to say, if you are planning to bring your own boat to the islands, you should read the whole book carefully with pencil in hand to make notes on what is applicable.

One caution in particular: In May, June, and July, the Caribbean is usually 12 to 18 inches lower than it is in the winter. Thus, at the time of a low-water spring tide in those months, the water is a full three feet lower than it is at high-water spring tide in the winter. Although the soundings on the Imray-Iolaire charts are based on the lowest-level datum, not all charts or local knowledge take the difference into account. If you have any doubt about your situation, take soundings before you venture into questionable waters.

Probably the most important chapter in this book is chapter 1—Sailing Directions—and you should read and study it. Consult it regularly before finalizing the day's plans. While the navigational features and anchorages of the individual islands are described in the chapter concerned with that island, the routes between the islands are detailed in chapter 1.

Remember: Always be alert and cautious. Almost every place in the Eastern Caribbean where a yacht can anchor has been described or at least mentioned in the Street guides, but not all are easy to enter. Many of these anchorages can be used only in good weather and perfect visibility. Besides, some boats are handier than others and some sailors are more skilled than others. Thus, you must evaluate each anchorage for yourself before entering. The time of day, the weather, your abilities, the weatherliness of your boat—all influence the final decision.

Some advice to readers who operate bareboat charter fleets: Study this book carefully, make your judgments, and mark on the charts in the book the anchorages you want your charterers to avoid.

Finally, before you sail anywhere in the Eastern Caribbean (and particularly if you are going during hurricane season), I advise you to read and take to heart the advice that appears below.

Reflections on Hugo

The Eastern Caribbean is basically overpopulated with boats. All of the hurricane holes are so overcrowded that all you need for disaster is one or two boats that are anchored improperly and start dragging. (Of course, I well remember being told in prep school that all general statements are suspect, and even the statement—"all general statements are suspect"—is suspect!) Undoubtedly, there are a few hurricane holes that are not overcrowded or that people do not know about. Witness Ensenada Honda Vieques off Puerto Rico. To the best of my knowledge, almost no boats went to Vieques in 1989 during Hurricane Hugo; like lemmings, they all poured into Ensenada Honda Culebra—whereas Ensenada Honda Vieques, which is a better hurricane hole, had relatively few boats tucked up into the mangroves.

Further, throughout the Caribbean, anywhere there are bareboat fleets, the hurricane season creates what the local yachtsmen refer to as "bareboat bombs"—so called because the bareboat operations do not have enough labor to put a crew on every boat to ride out the hurricane, tend lines, or shift anchors, and the vessels become potential lethal weapons! Few bareboats are equipped with more than two anchors, and those may be sufficient for a 30-to-40-knot blow, but nothing more. Once one of the "bareboat bombs" starts dragging down on you, you have a problem. You may be lucky, and he will just bounce off you and do no damage, but it could be a disastrous situation: The bareboat hooks your anchor, pulls you loose, and you both end up on the beach, high and dry.

One of the tragedies of this sort of situation is that the bareboat companies are all insured. The underwriters pay off the damage done to bareboats, but all of the courts consider the hurricane as an "act of God." If you are insured and a "bareboat bomb" drags down on you and your boat is damaged or lost, it is not fine and dandy, but at least it is not a complete disaster, as your insurance company will cover your loss. If, however, you are NOT insured, your chances are minimal of finding an admiralty lawyer who will entertain a case against a boat dragging down on you in a hurricane. Even if you find one, you will need to put up $US5,000 or $6,000 before he will even consider taking the case. This is just another good reason why cruising yachts should be insured. Insurance is particularly essential for cruising yachtsmen who have retired and are living aboard, with everything wrapped up in their boat. (See *Street's Transatlantic Crossing Guide and Introduction to the Caribbean* for information on insurance.)

In light of the damage done by Hugo, what is the solution to the hurricane problem? Go to sea! This sounds very drastic—going to sea in the face of a hurricane—and it is if you do it at the last minute. But it is a viable option if you do it 48 to 72 hours before the expected arrival of the hurricane.

The situation with hurricanes has changed radically over the years. Until the early 1950s, the hurricane warning system in the Caribbean was very poor. Hurricanes originated out in the Atlantic, and unless they were spotted by a passing ship that sent in a report, the Eastern Caribbean did not realize a hurricane was en route until the barometers started falling. And then the barometers usually dropped so fast that the bottom fell out, and there was little time—perhaps 18 to 24 hours—to prepare. Seamen could only hunker down in the nearest hurricane hole, lash everything down, and hope for the best.

In the early 1950s, however, the old B-36s were converted to weather planes and became hurricane hunters. For more than a decade, they spotted most of the hurricanes, tracked them, and provided fairly good warnings. But they did not find them all. Once, when one popped up just east of St. Barthélemy, the St. Barts people called St. Thomas to tell them a hurricane was on the way. St. Thomas said they had received no warning, and how did St. Barts know it was a hurricane? St. Barts replied, "Because our radio tower is about to blow down," and then they went off the air. Recognizing the danger, St. Thomas went into action and the warnings went out. The St. Thomas charter fleet (which, luckily, was quite small in those days) tried to get out and head to Hurricane Hole in St. John—a dead beat to windward. A few of them made it, but most of them were blown back into the harbor in St. Thomas, where they rode out the hurricane.

Each year, the hurricane tracking system has improved, and now, with sophisticated satellites, it's well nigh perfect. Normally, there is plenty of warning; it is only the freak hurricane, such as Klaus in late 1984, that catches the islands unaware. Klaus popped up just south of Puerto Rico, went northeast, and was very late in the year. Klaus was one of only three hurricanes in 100 years that tracked northeast below 22°N! Today, there is at least a three- or four-day warning of an approaching hurricane. The US government publication *Tropical Cyclones of the North Atlantic Ocean* (US Department of Commerce—NOAA—1871 to 1980, with an update to 1993) shows the tracks of all the known hurricanes in the last 120 years. You'll notice that, with very few exceptions, hurricanes follow a definite and predictable pattern as they approach the islands of the Eastern Caribbean. Admittedly, once they reach Puerto Rico, Haiti, and the Dominican Republic, they can execute a 180-degree turn, or a 360-degree one, or a right angle, or anything in between. They are not predictable once they pass through the islands. Thus, many experienced seamen have concluded that if you have a decent boat of 40 feet or more, well equipped, with an engine so you can power, and if there are light airs in front of the hurricane, the thing to do is pull up the anchor and go to sea. (In any case, if you don't have a boat that can handle 40 knots of wind, you should not be out sailing.)

The boats in English Harbour, Antigua, survived Hugo with relatively little damage, but many seamen figure they were just lucky. If the hurricane had followed a route 30 or 40 miles farther north, English Harbour would have been a disaster area, because even though it is a beautifully sheltered harbor, there were plenty of untended, poorly moored boats that could have become absolute bombs and destroyed the other yachts.

Three days before Hugo passed south of Antigua, it was easily predictable that the hurricane would hit Guadeloupe or Antigua or pass close to the north of Antigua. Thus, any boat in Antigua could have hoisted anchor and headed due south 48 hours before the storm was supposed to hit. They could easily have been 300 miles to the south, down near Grenada, by the time the storm arrived in Antigua, and they would have experienced nothing more than 30 knots of wind.

Similarly, the United States and British Virgin Islands, Puerto Rico, and the Passage Islands had plenty of warning. It was obvious that the hurricane was going to pass south of or through the Virgins, and the boats could have hauled anchor and headed due north (or, possibly better, northeast), thus being 300 miles from the brunt of the storm.

Bill Skokl of the 42-foot double-topsail gaff-rigged schooner *Media* took off southward, singlehanded, from Isleta Marina, Fajardo, on the east coast of Puerto Rico, 48 hours before Hugo hit. He experienced no more than 30 to 40 gusts of wind, huge but long swells, and no damage whatsoever to his boat. When he returned to Isleta Marina, he found nothing but utter destruction. Go to sea; don't try to ride out a hurricane in an overcrowded harbor!

Having seen the havoc caused in harbors by "bareboat bombs" and other poorly moored boats dragging through the fleet, I think that if *Iolaire* and I are ever in the path of a hurricane, we will go to sea rather than look for a hurricane hole.

Another solution to the hurricane problem is to sail south to Grenada and spend the hurricane season doing your repairs and refitting there. Grenada has only been hit three times by hurricanes, and even though many of them have passed fairly close to the north, the hurricane holes on the south coast are so sheltered (until yachting increases even more and produces the same kind of crowded conditions that exist in the Virgin Islands) that you would be safe in any of the hurricane holes there. If it appears that a hurricane is going to pass too close to Grenada, you can always pick up anchor and head a hundred miles south to Trinidad, thus avoiding even the edges of the storm.

To be absolutely safe, of course, go to Venezuela, which is out of the hurricane area. Just north of Venezuela, a few lows have developed, blowing 40 to 50 knots, that later turned into hurricanes when they reached the Western Caribbean, but, to the best of my knowledge, Venezuela has never had a bad hurricane and has only suffered heavy rain and massive ground swells from storms passing through the region.

But what about boats stored ashore? Yacht yards that have onshore storage facilities in the Eastern Caribbean are doing very well. People are storing boats on shore for a number of reasons: to avoid having their boat stolen by someone who wants to make a quick drug run and then pull the plug; to allow the bottom to dry out, thus minimizing the chance of osmosis. Finally, some boats are stored ashore on the misconception that a boat is safer there in a hurricane. This is a very erroneous assumption. Admittedly, if a hurricane just brushes an island, relatively few boats are damaged ashore. If it comes close, there is considerable damage. But if the hurricane hits dead-on, the boats all topple like pins in a bowling alley—a few on a near miss and almost all in a direct hit. The marinas on the east coast of Puerto Rico were pretty well cleaned out by Hugo, with the exception of Puerto del Rey, which survived with an acceptably low level of damage.

As a result of Hugo, not only have boat owners who had their boats stored ashore suffered, but the underwriters have been taken to the cleaners. The only ones that came out on top were the boatyards doing the repairs (often the same yards that made money by storing the boats).

It has been recommended that underwriters should not cover boats stored ashore north of Grenada unless the mast is removed. Further, if the boat is a deep-keel, fin-and-separate-rudder configuration, you should dig two holes and chock up the boat a foot or two off the ground, with the rudder and the keel in the holes. Chocked up this way, with the rig out, the boat should survive the hurricane. I realize this is an expensive procedure, but it is a hell of a lot cheaper than rebuilding your boat.

The entire Caribbean is hurricane territory, and hurricanes are more frequent than most people realize. The Virgins have been hit or sideswiped by 32 hurricanes since 1871. In 1916 alone, there were three hurricanes. In 1889, 1891, and 1979, there were two hurricanes in the same year.

Eastern Puerto Rico has been hit by 37 hurricanes, three in 1916. The Antigua/Guadeloupe area has had 32 hurricanes (three in 1933), plus the area has been sideswiped by 10 or 12 tropical depressions.

The Martinique/St. Lucia area has had 44 hurricanes, plus about a dozen tropical depressions.

The frequency of hurricanes in St. Vincent and the Grenadines is much lower than farther north, BUT there are really no hurricane holes in the area. The first hurricane hole south of St. Lucia is all the way down the south coast of Grenada—an area that has had only about five hurricanes in its history.

Amazingly, Isla Margarita in Venezuela has been hit by two hurricanes in the last 120 years, but no hurricanes have hit mainland Venezuela.

In light of the above, one must figure on a hurricane every four to five years, no matter where you are in the Caribbean. For the best odds, head for Grenada, Trinidad, or mainland Venezuela—and I urge that underwriters give discounts to boats that arrange to be in those areas between 1 July and 1 November.

Acknowledgments

Yachtsmen who cruise the Caribbean should be thankful to Phelps Platt of Dodd, Mead, who saw my original draft of what was then going to be a privately printed guide to the Virgin Islands and liked it enough to encourage me to write a complete guide to the other islands. Yachtsmen should also thank Bernard Goldhirsh, founder of *Sail* magazine, who published the 1974 updated and expanded cruising guide.

Thanks are now due to Eric Swenson of W.W. Norton and Company, who not only agreed to publish a completely updated guide but also agreed that it should be expanded to include Venezuela, its offlying islands, and Aruba, Bonaire, and Curaçao, plus tremendously enlarged sections on "Getting There" and "Leaving." The guide has become so comprehensive that we have produced it in an ever-expanding series.

Special thanks should go to Harvey Loomis—a good literary editor and an excellent sailor. Finally, I had an experienced editor who has cruised in the Caribbean and understands the problems of sailing—and racing—in the Caribbean. For eight years he labored hard as editor of these guides, and he was a tremendous help in rewriting the sailing and piloting directions to make them clear to the reader. Both I, the author, and you, the reader, owe Harvey a vote of thanks.

I must also thank the many yachtsmen who have helped me with valuable information. Augie Hollen of *Taurus* (the only person I know who cruises in a genuine Block Island Cowhorn), Carl Powell of *Terciel*, and Ross Norgrove, formerly of *White Squall II*, all deserve a special vote of thanks for helping me update the Virgin Islands section. Jon Repke of Power Productions—a refrigeration expert, electrician, mechanic, sailor, and pilot—solved many of the mysteries of St. Martin/St. Barthélemy/Anguilla by spending the better part of a day flying me through that area. Carl Kaushold supplied an excellent chart and information on the Salt River. Ray Smith of Grenada was most helpful in his suggestions on tides and weather patterns in the Caribbean, and in compiling the list of radio stations and radio beacons. His brother, Ron, solved the mystery of the whereabouts of Tara Island, off the south coast of Grenada, which is marked improperly on the chart. Carl Amour of the Anchorage Hotel solved the great mystery of the rocks off Scotts Head, Dominica. Dr. Jack Sheppard of *Arieto*, the late Dick Doran of *Laughing Sally*, and Carlos Lavendero of several boats made possible the inclusion of the Puerto Rico and Passage Islands information. Gordon Stout of *Shango* and Peter Lee of *Virginia Reel* made possible the inclusion of Tobago. Jerry Bergoff of *Solar Barque* and Sylver Brin of St. Barthélemy were most helpful in clearing up some of the mysteries of the eastern end of St. Barts.

Pieter van Storn, formerly of Island Waterworld, and Malcolm Maidwell and Peter Spronk, both of Caribbean Catamaran Centre, were most helpful in the Sint Maarten area. Hans Hoff, from the 90-foot ketch *Fandango*, is one of the few people who has won a bet from me on anchorages. The standing bet is that I will buy a drink for anyone who can find a good, safe anchorage with six feet of water in it that has not been mentioned in this cruising-guide series. I expect to be nabbed once in a while by a small boat, but not by the skipper of a 90-foot ketch! Hans found an anchorage inside the reef on the north coast of Anguilla. Where the chart showed nothing but solid reef, Hans managed to find himself inside the reef with 40 feet of water!

John Clegg, formerly of *Flica II*, Dave Price, formerly of *Lincoln*, and Gordon Stout have popped up continually with wonderful odd bits of information that they have gleaned on their cruises from one end of the Lesser Antilles to the other.

Numerous other skippers have, over the years, given me a tremendous amount of help. They include, in the Antigua area, Desmond Nicholson, of V.E.B. Nicholson and Sons, English Harbour, and Joel Byerly, skipper of *Morning Tide* (and former charter skipper on *Ron of Argyll*, *Mirage*, *Etoile de Mer*, and *Lord Jim*), to name but two. For finer points on the exploration of the east coast of Antigua, I am deeply indebted to David Simmons of the little cruising/racing sloop *Bacco*. David is former head of Antigua Slipways and the senior marine surveyor in the Eastern Caribbean. Thanks should also go to Simon Cooper and David Corrigan, both of whom unfortunately have left the islands; Morris Nicholson of *Eleuthera*; Simon Bridger of *Circe* and other boats; Peter Haycraft and George Foster, harbor pilots and yachtsmen based in Tortola; Martin Mathias of the sportfisherman *Bihari*; Bert Kilbride, diver extraordinary of Saba Rock, Virgin Islands; and the Trinidadians Doug and the late Hugh ("Daddy") Myer of *Rosemary V* and *Huey II*. I want also to thank Arthur Spence of *Dwyka*, Marcy Crowe of *Xantippe*, Andy Copeland of various boats, Mike Smith of *Phryna*, Ken McKenzie of *Ti*, Dave Ferneding of *Whisper*, Chris Bowman of *Water Pearl of Bequia*, and others whose names I may have forgotten to include.

The Venezuela section of the guide has been made possible with the help of a tremendous number of Venezuelan friends and yachtsmen—most particularly Dr. Daniel Camejo of *Caribaña*, Rolly Edmonds, Otto Castillo (port captain of Sinclair Oil), Humberto Contazano, Daniel Shaw, Peter York, Pedro Gluecksman of *Bayola*, and especially Peter Bottome, who at various times lent us aircraft so we could fly over the areas we describe in the guide. Sailing is a wonderful way to explore, but a plane allows vast areas to be covered in a matter of hours. This was particularly true for the Los Roques area, a huge archipelago that is mostly listed as UN-SURVEYED. Trying to explore it in a yacht would be almost impossible, but from the air we were able to obtain a very clear view of the layout of the unsurveyed area.

Jim Young of Dive Tobago provided reams of information on Buccoo Reef at the southwest corner of Tobago, on Tyrrels Bay at the northeast corner, and on many coves in between. The Tobago charts in this book could not have been done without his help. Molly Watson, her son Eddie, and all the members of the Trinidad Yachting Association have done a great deal to help get out the word on Trinidad. Curaçao yachtsman Dick Nebbling was most helpful with the Netherlands Antilles section.

Other yachtsmen in the Eastern Caribbean who helped with Venezuela information were Hank Strauss of *Doki*, Richard and Barbara Weinman of *Narania*, and Mike Jarrold of *Lily Maid*.

It is only with the help of experienced yachtsmen such as these that a book of this type can be written.

A special vote of thanks must go to my nephew Morgan B. MacDonald III, who labored hard for three months in Grenada putting together the sketch charts contained in two of the volumes in this series. Thanks to the staff of Imray, Laurie, Norie & Wilson, especially the late Tom Wilson, who decided to produce the Imray-Iolaire charts; his son, Willy Wilson, who is carrying on his father's efforts; and Alan Wilkinson, their cartographer, who has labored long and hard to draw the charts for all of the volumes of the Street guides and who also draws all of the Imray-Iolaire charts of the Eastern Caribbean. Thanks to Jim Mitchell, who has done a superb job of drawing the local watercraft and preparing topographical views.

Admiral Sir David Haslam, retired head of the British Hydrographic Office, and his successor, Rear Admiral R.O. Morris, have been most helpful in supplying information and giving permission for material from the British Admiralty charts to be incorporated in this book. These appropriations have been made with the approval of the controller of Her Majesty's Stationery Office and the Hydrographer of the Navy.

I want to thank Patricia Street, my sister Elizabeth Vanderbilt, her husband Peter, and their son Jay, for their help in rechecking many facts.

Finally, a special round of thanks:

Maria McCarthy of Union Hall, County Cork, Ireland, labored long and hard during the summer of 1978 typing up corrections and inserts on a previous edition of the *Martinique-to-Trinidad* volume. Audrey Semple spent the winter of 1978-79 doing a magnificent job of cutting, gluing, correcting, typing, and fitting it all back together again. Geraldine Hickey, my secretary during the winter of 1979-80, did similar work under times of trying circumstance.

Aileen Calnan of Glandore, County Cork, not only worked with me in Ireland but also came on board *Iolaire* in the winter of 1983 as typist, secretary, crew, sometime babysitter, and sometime cook. She stayed through the summer of 1988, then went on to

Acknowlegements

bigger and better things, working in a bank in New York. Her replacement came on board, started learning the ropes, and was beginning to do a very good job when she fell in love with our Venezuelan interpreter/expediter and departed in January 1989 with 24 hours notice. Needless to say, we were up a creek without a paddle, but we were saved by Nick Pearson, an ex-British Army telegrapher who was wandering through the Caribbean on boats. He became our "hairy legged" secretary and labored hard through the winter of 1989. Not only did he bang away at the typwriter, but he also was our number-one man for jumping overside in shoal water, grabbing the anchor, carrying it onto the beach, and burying it.

In January 1990, Cheryl Tennant came on board, worked extremely hard as secretary and also helping train Venezuelan crew, but, unfortunately for the skipper, she fell in love with a crew member and got married.

Aileen Calnan returned in the summer of 1991 to help me put together the complete rewrite of the *Martinique-to-Trinidad* volume.

Nancy White labored hard during the winter and spring of 1992 and helped me put together the revision of *Anguilla-to-Dominica*.

The help of all these doveted friends of the Street family and of *Iolaire* has been invaluable to the production of this book.

Thanks should also go to Diane O'Connor, production editor at Norton, who has fought all the guides through the editors, copyeditors, and printers. Finally, when she could no longer stand my bad typing, an manuscripts glued together with last-minute additions, she recruited Kathleen bandes to do a combination job---copyediting and keyboarding all the guides on computer. Kathleen has done a wonderful job, as not only has she put the books on discs, but she has also copyedited them at the same time. And, unlike other copyeditors I have suffered through and fought with, Kathleen knows and understands both sailing and the Caribbean, so she can do both editing and copyediting. The Street guides have finally entered the computer age!

For the latest update of the guide thanks must go to Hal Roth fellow yachting author, and sailor who convinced me to join the Author's Guild about twenty years ago. through the Author's Guild and the wonderful help of Julie Kaufmann out of date books published by Author's Guild members are being electronically published by iUniverse.com. Lori Brown of iUniverse.com has been extremely helpful in putting together this guide and by bending the rules a little bit.

Thanks must also go to my secretary Frances MacMahon who with the aid of her computer has transcribed my taperecordings, with the updates, and with the aid of my son Richard who edited them into shape so they would fit the space available.

Thanks must also go to my son Richard for correcting, updating and altering the various charts in the various guides.

Last and not least I really want to thank my long suffering wife Trish who has sailed with me this past 33 years, largely raising our family of four children on the boat or holding the fort down in Glandore and raising the children while I have been out sailing and exploring on *Iolaire* and *Li'l Iolaire*.

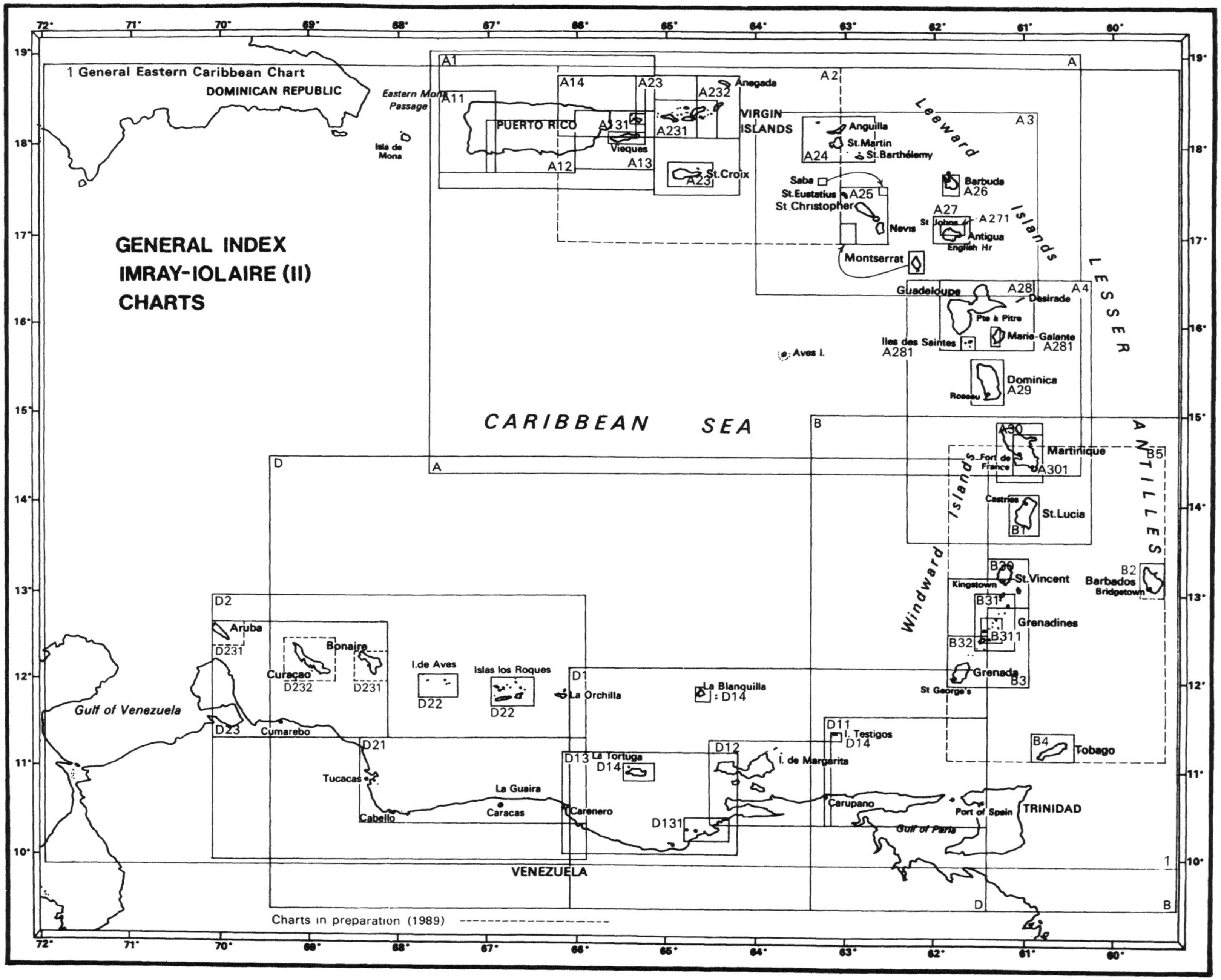
GENERAL INDEX
IMRAY-IOLAIRE (II)
CHARTS
1 General Eastern Caribbean Chart
DOMINICAN REPUBLIC
Eastern Mona Passage
Isla de Mona
PUERTO RICO
Vieques
VIRGIN ISLANDS
Anegada
St.Croix
Anguilla
St.Martin
St.Barthélemy
Saba
St.Eustatius
St.Christopher
Nevis
Barbuda
St Johns
Antigua
English Hr
Montserrat
Guadeloupe
Désirade
Pte à Pitre
Marie-Galante
Iles des Saintes
Dominica
Roseau
Aves I.
Martinique
Fort de France
St.Lucia
Castries
St.Vincent
Kingstown
Grenadines
Grenada
St George's
Barbados
Bridgetown
Tobago
TRINIDAD
Port of Spain
Gulf of Paria
Carupano
I. Testigos
I. de Margarita
La Blanquilla
La Tortuga
La Orchilla
Islas los Roques
I.de Aves
Bonaire
Curaçao
Aruba
Gulf of Venezuela
Cumarebo
Tucacas
Cabello
La Guaira
Caracas
Carenero
VENEZUELA
Leeward Islands
Windward Islands
LESSER ANTILLES
CARIBBEAN SEA
A1
A11
A12
A13
A14
A2
A23
A231
A232
A24
A25
A26
A27
A271
A28
A281
A29
A3
A30
A301
A31
A4
A
B
B1
B2
B3
B30
B31
B311
B32
B4
B5
D
D1
D11
D12
D13
D131
D14
D2
D21
D22
D23
D231
D232
1
Charts in preparation (1989)

List of Charts and Sketch Charts

ANGUILLA

1. Road Bay — 13
2. Crocus Bay — 15
3. Shoal Bay and Island Harbour — 17
4. Cove Bay to Blowing Point Harbour (sketch) — 18
5. Forest Bay (sketch) — 19
6. Sandy Hill Bay (sketch) — 20
7. West End of Scrub Island (sketch) — 21
8. Prickly Pear Cays — 22
9. Dog Island (sketch) — 24

ST. MARTIN

10. Ranges for Proselyte Reef — 29
11. Groot Baai and Philipsburg — 30
12. Grand Etang de Simsonbaai and Baie de Marigot — 32
13. Grand Etang de Simsonbaai (sketch) — 33
14. Baie Grand Case (sketch) — 36
15. Northeast Coast of St. Martin — 38
16. Baie Orientale and Baie des Flamands (sketch) — 40
17. Oyster Pond — 42

ST. BARTHELEMY (ST. BARTS)

18. Gustavia — 50
19. Baie St. Jean (sketch) — 51
20. Anse de Marigot (sketch) — 52

SABA, ST. EUSTATIUS (STATIA), ST. CHRISTOPHER (ST. KITTS), AND NEVIS

21. Fort Baai, Saba — 57
22. Oranjebaai and Oranjestad, St. Eustatius — 61
23. Basseterre and Basseterre Bay, St. Christopher — 65
24. The Narrows, St. Christopher and Nevis — 67

ANTIGUA AND BARBUDA

25. Ranges for Antigua (sketch) — 78
26. Falmouth and English Harbours — 80, 90
27. Mamora Bay (sketch) — 92
28. Willoughby Bay — 93
29. Nonsuch Bay — 95
30. Belfast Bay and Guana Bay — 99
31. Northeast Coast of Antigua — 101
32. North Coast of Antigua — 102
33. Saint Johns Harbour — 108
34. Antigua, West Coast St. Johns to Old Road Bluff — 110
35. Five Islands Harbour and Jolly Harbour — 111
36. Cocoa Point to Spanish Point, Barbuda — 117

MONTSERRAT AND REDONDA

37. Montserrat — 122
38. Plymouth, Montserrat — 123
39. Old Road Bay, Montserrat — 124
40. Redonda (sketch) — 126

GUADELOUPE

41. Marina de Rivière Sens, Basse Terre (sketch) — 132
42. Anse Deshaies — 134
43. Rivière Salée, Northern Entrance — 135
44. Port Louis — 138
45. Port du Moule — 139
46. Sainte Marie — 141
47. Pointe-à-Pitre — 142
48. Gozier — 145
49. Petit Havre — 146
50. Anse Accul and Sainte-Anne — 147
51. Saint François and Marina de la Grande Saline — 149
52. Grande Anse, Désirade — 150
53. Iles de la Petite Terre — 151
54. Terre d'en Haut, Iles des Saintes — 153
55. Anse Fideling, Iles des Saintes — 156
56. Marie-Galante — 158
57. Grand Bourg, Marie-Galante — 159

DOMINICA

58. Woodbridge Bay and Roseau Roads — 165
59. Prince Rupert Bay — 167

All the Imray-Iolaire Harbour Charts are to WGS 84. However,
Many of the other harbour charts are not to WGS 84.
Therefore, do not use GPS for final approach, use visual
navigation. ie. Bearings, soundings by lead line, fathometer,
or colour of the water.

Charts

REMEMBER: DO NOT ENTER STRANGE HARBORS AT NIGHT!

I used to carry on board *Iolaire* about 200 United States, British, French, Dutch, and a few Spanish charts—all of which were out of date; that is, even though they were new charts, the various government offices had not accurately corrected and updated them. The British Admiralty will correct charts of a foreign area *only* if the government concerned officially notifies the BA. Much worse, US charts are corrected only when a whole plate is corrected; if you buy a new chart of Puerto Rico and it is a 12-year-old edition, no corrections will have been made on that chart since the date of the edition 12 years earlier!

Furthermore, BA and US charts often are on the wrong scale for inshore navigation by a yacht. The charts covering Grenada, the Grenadines, and St. Vincent are 1:72,000, while the famous old Virgin Islands chart is 1:100,000, which is even worse. You need a magnifying glass to find small anchorages and coves. In addition, it cuts Virgin Gorda in half. Several of the US and British charts break up the St. Vincent and Grenadines area in odd splits not conducive to use by the average yachtsman. The US chart of the Grenadines has an excellent enlarged insert for the Tobago Cays, but it does not have tidal reference points. The British chart does have this valuable information. Furthermore, the US and BA charts are based on surveys made in the 1890s. The latest NOAA and Admiralty charts have new deepwater information but retain the old inshore errors.

As a result of all these difficulties, I signed a contract with Imray, Laurie, Norie & Wilson (usually known simply as Imray)—which traces its ancestry back to 1670—to do updated and accurate charts specifically tailored to the needs of the yachtsman. Our information has been gathered from US National Ocean Survey (NOS) and Defense Mapping Agency (DMA) charts, British Admiralty charts, French and Dutch charts, plus unpublished US and British Admiralty surveys, topographical maps, and aerial photography, backed up by the information I have gathered in more than 35 years of exploring the Eastern Caribbean. Information also has been supplied to me by other experienced yachtsmen. Although it may be true that I know the Eastern Caribbean as a whole better than any other yachtsman, there are people who know individual islands and areas much better than I do. These yachtsmen have been tremendously helpful in sharing their knowledge.

Our charts come in one standard size, 25 inches by 35 1/2 inches, and three colors. Blue denotes deep water; white denotes water five fathoms or less; yellow indicates one fathom or less. Detailed harbor charts are inserted in the margins of the general charts. Useful ranges (transits) are shown to guide the mariner clear of dangers. Various overlapping coverages and often contradictory information found in the various French, US, Dutch, and British Admiralty charts have been eliminated.

Imray-Iolaire charts are kept up to date through careful attention to the British Notices to Mariners, my own observations, and comments sent by users of these charts and readers of these cruising guides. Important corrections are inserted by hand at Imray prior to shipment; all corrections are logged in on the master sheet so that even minor corrections are included in new editions. Seldom do we go more than six months between printings of a chart. (The most popular Imray-Iolaire charts—those of the US and British Virgin Islands, and Anguilla, St. Barthélemy, St. Martin, and Antigua—are available on waterproof paper.)

As of this writing, 50 Imray-Iolaire charts cover the entire Eastern Caribbean, replacing the 200-

plus government charts (which had numerous inaccuracies) I formerly carried on *Iolaire*. Further, we have expanded the charts to cover the Atlantic Island groups: Azores, Madeiran archipelago, Canaries, and Cape Verdes. Each group is covered by a single chart, with the detailed plans of the major harbors shown on each chart as insets.

The Imray-Iolaire charts have become the accepted standard; the US Coast Guard, as well as the St. Vincent and Grenada Coast Guards, use Imray-Iolaire charts rather than government charts. Very few chart agents in the Eastern Caribbean continue to stock the government charts.

In short, I strongly recommend that yachtsmen use the Imray-Iolaire charts instead of British Admiralty or US government charts.

Most of the harbor charts in this volume have been taken from the relevant Imray-Iolaire charts. The few sketch charts included here are just that—sketches. They are as accurate as I can make them, but they are *not* official publications, so they should be used only in conjunction with *reliable* navigational charts, common sense, and eyeball observations.

NOTE: Keep in mind that the sea level in the Eastern Caribbean is roughly 12 to 18 inches lower in May, June, and July than it is the rest of the year. Imray-Iolaire chart soundings are based on this low, low datum. Other charts may not be.

Electronic navigation is becoming more and more important, and it is much more accurate than the charts, because many islands are improperly located, even on the best charts. Your electronic navigation will be correct, but an island may be anywhere from 1/2 to 1 1/2 miles out of position. Thus, once you get within four or five miles of an island, you must switch from electronic navigation to visual navigation and watch the fathometer. Reports often refer to collisions of ships as "radar-controlled collisions"; don't have an "electronic-controlled grounding."

Negotiations are underway at the moment for electronic companies who produce charts to use Imray-Iolaire charts rather than the NOS, DMA, or BA charts. The yachtsmen and the US Coast Guard do, why don't the manufacturers do so? Two companies said, "We can't use your charts because they are not guaranteed to be correct; we use the government charts because they are absolutely accurate." I pointed out to them that nothing could be further from the truth. In years to come, you should be able to look at a video screen and see the Imray-Iolaire charts.

As each year goes by, more and more people rely on electronic navigation, especially since the prices have come down on Global Positioning Systems.

This is a mixed blessing. A GPS is extremely accurate, but in the Caribbean east of the Virgin Islands, for example, all of the islands are out of place on the charts. So you can sit and watch your GPS run your boat hard aground!

Even though GPS manufacturers advertise that their systems are accurate to within 100 feet (300 feet is in fact more realistic), all of these devices are not absolutely dead-on, as they are subject to human error during assembly. This is illustrated by the following story.

In 1991, I was in Grenada, driving a borrowed car, when I spotted an obvious "yachtie" walking toward Grenada Yacht Services. I stopped and gave him a lift. He recognized me, congratulated me on the quality of our charts, but complained that the latitude and longitude of the Imray-Iolaire chart of Grenada were off by half a mile. He said he could prove this with a GPS. After I dropped him off, I ran into the British naval commander who has been seconded to the Grenada Coast Guard to try to keep them out of trouble. He informed me that the Grenada Coast Guard had just had installed (and checked out by the Royal Navy) a GPS unit in its patrol vessel. According to his GPS, Grenada is one-third of a mile east of its charted position.

Later the same day, I was visiting Gordon Braithwaite, who has established a development at L'Anse aux Epines. He has also owned boats, all of which we have insured. He told me that he had purchased one of the Moorings boats in St. Martin and sailed it to Grenada. Because he ran into low visibility and had to use dead reckoning all the way, he used eyeball navigation. His son-in-law then presented him with a GPS.

At that point, I warned him about the islands being misplaced. He responded, "No, Grenada was exactly where it was supposed to be." We discussed this for a while; then we took his GPS, set it out on his lawn, and went back to drink coconut water. (Gordon is a teetotaler and I was on the wagon while recovering from hepatitis.) After a time, we checked the GPS when it recorded that it had a good fix. I picked up my Imray-Iolaire chart where I can see the location of Gordon's house, and lo and behold, according to Gordon's Magellan GPS, Grenada was exactly where it was supposed to be.

So . . . there are three separate GPS units giving variations of position of half a mile. The electronics experts say this is impossible, but how to explain it? Is it human error in reading the GPS, human error in assembling it?

Some yachtsmen have said, "We must use the government charts, as their latitudes and longitudes are correct. The Imray-Iolaire latitudes and longitudes are not." Nuts! Imray-Iolaire, NOS, DMA, and BA all use the same data, and all the islands are mislocated by the same amount.

Their response usually is, "If this is a known fact, why don't you correct the Imray-Iolaire charts?" We have not done so because we are a private company, and changing the latitudes and longitudes of islands on our own, when neither the US nor British governments are willing to do so, would leave us open to liability suits

I went to Landfall Navigation in Greenwich, Connecticut, and with the help of Erica Kenny went through every US chart from Mona Island to Grenada. In eight cases, we found substantial differences between the Imray-Iolaire chart and the NOAA/DMA chart In every case where there was a discrepancy, I knew that the Imray chart was correct, the government chart wrong. In each case, I had informed NOAA or DMA of the errors anywhere from 10 to 20 years earlier. Yet the charts are still uncorrected. If you find any discrepancy between the Imray-Iolaire and the government charts, I am quite sure you will discover that Imray is correct.

I feel confident that the Imray-Iolaire charts are the most accurate ones available. They can be kept that way only if experienced yachtsmen continue to fee information and corrections to us to correct the small errors that may still exist or to update charts where the topography has been changed by hurricanes, earthquakes, or dredging.

Please send information regarding chart corrections to me

By Post: Rock Cottage, Old School Road, Glandore, Co. Cork, Ireland. Fax: +353 28 33927

Or, by E-mail: streetiolaire@hotmail.com

Since the above was written much has happened. In 1994 Imray turned over to me the job of trying to get all the Imray Iolaire Charts to the single WGS84 datum. I succeeded in doing this over the next eight months People ask me am I trained cartographer and I reply "No". Then they ask how could I get all the Imray Iolaire Charts to WGS84.

I point out to people that I Majored in History (to the English, I read History) at Catholic University, Washington DC. With the library at Congress in the city, as a student often you were often forced out of the Catholic University Library down to the Library at Congress if the University Library did not have enough information.

Hence I learned how to do research. I learned that if you don't know the answer to something, research hard enough and you will find out who does have the answer.

The aeroplanes obviously know where their runways are, so I bought an aircraft chart. No good. The scale was so poor that a pencil line was 600 yards wide.

I then contacted NOAA's aeronautic division and discovered that they had a book which gave the centre line of every runway in the entire Caribbean and South America. By locating the centreline of a runway we could then move the whole island.

I also discovered that NOAA had redone the Puerto Rican charts to WGS84, the DMA had redone the Venezuelan charts to WGS84 and the British had done some of the islands of the Eastern Caribbean to WGS84, but not all and had some off sets of some of the others. I also discovered that the French had re-established Martinique and Guadeloupe to WGS84.

With the aid of all these charts and all this information spread out on the living room floor for the summer of 1994 it became a gigantic jigsaw puzzle. But by the end of the year all the information was collated, cross checked. Alan Wilkinson of Imray then began the process of putting all Imray Iolaire Charts to WGS84 or noting on the charts an off set originally expressed to bring your GPS position to it's correct place on the chart.

Originally this off set was expressed in degrees and minutes and tenths of minutes, in latitude and longitude. This is difficult to plot when doing a series of positions. In 1998 I finally recalculated all the off sets (with the aid of my sons, Richard and Mark, cross checking all my calculations). The offsets are now all expressed in not only latitude and longitude, but also in bearing and distance. This makes it much easier to plot.

Some of the very fancy units will not only say how many satellites are being tracked, but also state the degree of accuracy This will of course vary as to the lay out of the satellites. There are some fancy GPS where the accuracy is continually reported and often it is down to ten or twelve feet.

All the charts from Grenada to U.S. & B V.I. have on the back, sailing and piloting directions pulled from Street's Guides. A chart and a guide in one. By the time you read this the Puerto Rican charts will probably be the same. Not only that but the Puerto Rican charts will have the sailing and piloting directions in both English and Spanish.

Hopefully by the end of 2001 the Venezuelan coast, the off shore islands will have sailing and piloting instructions on the back of the charts and will also be in Spanish and English.

[The Islands] are accessible in every part, and covered with a vast variety of lofty trees, which, it appears to me, never lose their foiage, as we found them fair and verdant as in May in Spain. Some were covered with blossoms, some with fruit, and others in different stages, according to their nature. The nightingale and a thousand other sorts of birds were singing in the month of November wherever I went. There are palm-trees in these countries, of six or eight sorts, which are surprising to see, on account of their diversity from ours, but indeed, this is the case with respect to the other trees, as well as the fruits and weeds. Beautiful forests of pines are likewise found, and fields of vast extent. Here is also honey, and fruits of a thousand sorts, and bird of every variety. The lands contain mines of metals, and inhabitants without number. . . . [Their] harbors are of such excellence, that their description would not gain belief, and the like may be said of the abundance of large and fine rivers, the most of which abound in gold.

—Christopher Columbus, on his return to Spain from the Caribbean, 1494

Prologue

If this guide does not read smoothly at all times please remember it was written many years ago, but luckily rocks don't move—unless a new harbour is created or breakwater built. Electronic printing has made it possible to re-publish these guides but the amount of new material that could be included is strictly limited.

For navigational dangers and sailing directions these guides are completely up to date to year 2001. As to the marine oriented infrastructure, no guide can be completely up to date. However, all the islands that have a real marine industry put out each year a free marine guide. Immediately upon clearing customs and immigration pick up the marine guide and you will be all set. On islands that do not produce a marine guide I refer the reader to an Old Timer in the business that will know the answers to the questions you ask as to where things can be bought or repaired.

For bars, restaurants and hotels pick up the free yearly printed tourist guide. It is impossible for a marine guide to cover the marine scene and also the bars, restaurants and hotels. The author would have to eat three meals a day each one at a different restaurant 365 days of the year to cover the restaurants. To cover the bars, to do a decent job, the author would certainly either become an alcoholic or die of cirrhosis of the liver.

Immediately upon arriving at any island pick up the FREE Marine Trade Guide locally produced every year. Also there is a FREE tourist guide—These will be much more up to date than any cruising guide can possibly be.

Every two years a supplement will be available through Imray with whom I published the Imray Iolaire charts. Cost of the update will vary as to the size of the update and the amount of work I have to do to gather the information.

These guides should be used in conjuction with the latest Imray-Iolaire charts. Free updates of the Imray-Iolaire charts are issued every six months and are available from Imray Chart Agents or direct from Imray (Imray, Laurie, Norie & Wilson Ltd., Wych House, The Broadway, St. Ives, Cambridgeshire PE17 5BT, England.
Tel: +44 (0)1480 462114; *Fax* +44 (0)1480 496109.

People always ask when did I get to the Caribbean and how did I end up in the writing business. The short and brief of it is After spending some time in Uncle Sam's navy in a submarine, during the Korean war, I finished Catholic University DC in 1954 where I majored in American History. I landed a job as paid hand on Huey Long's Ondine. A beautiful 53 foot Aberking and Rasmussen Yawl. I was hired as paid hand and a month later they fired the skipper. I ended up as skipper, with no increase in wages! An interesting couple of years followed included racing in Europe.

Our parting of the ways came just before the Fastnet Race when I made a Pier Head jump onto Lloyds' Yacht Club boat *Lutine*, a 57 foot. J Laurent Giles designed yawl built by Camper Nicholson in 1953. I sailed the rest of the season on her, bounced around Europe for about nine months, and sailed back across the Atlantic on Arabella, a 46 foot yawl, as cook and apprentice navigator.

The summer of 1956 I spent sailing delivering boats, helping friends out in boat yards doing odds and ends. Everyone was after me to take a real "job". I asked "Why?" I had money in the bank, did not owe anything on my car, I was making more than I was spending. But, the pressures mounted and I ended up in the job market. I landed a job, at Frank B. Hall & Partners, big ship Marine Insurance brokers on John's Street—in the canyons of New York.

One of the conditions on taking the job was that I had to shave—the weekend before I was to start, I shaved off my beard. We were racing frostbite dinghies in Larchmount and Dick Ronan said, "my God, Don you are the only person in New York who has chap stick on your entire face." I thought about it, and decided I didn't like cold weather.

At the age of 55, after three cases of ulcers and two minor heart attacks, fighting the canyons of New York and commuting my father had to retire—living in that atmosphere my mother had minor cases of ulcers—At the age of 70 I haven't had an ulcer or a heart attack, I give them!!

You can't change the weather, but you can fly to where the weather is good. A friend had just come back from the Virgin Islands and told of the wonderful climate, the good sailing and an evolving economyin the Virgin Islands.

So, for $45.00 I bought myself a ticket on the "Vomit Comet" a Pan-American DC6—so called because in those days the propeller planes couldn't fly over the storms they flew through them! They didn't really take off from Idlewild (now Kennedy) they just flew down the runway, the runway ended, they pulled up the wheels and staggered off across Jamaica Bay. The rate of climb predicated by how

xxxiii

fast the fuel was used up. When they hit an air pocket the plane would drop around 500 feet, the "barf" bags would come out, and the Puerto Ricans would have their rosary beads going round like a bicycle chain.

I landed in San Juan in the wee hours of the morning—and picked up for $10, the Carib Air flight to St. Croix. A few days later I ended up in St. Thomas, and landed a job as a land surveyor.

People ask how did I do that, having graduated with a History Major. On Friday I borrowed a book on basic surveying. Monday and Tuesday were bank holidays. By Wednesday morning I convinced them I was a surveyor—in the land of the blind the one eyed are king.

Not too long after I arrived in St. Thomas I met the late Captain Bob Crytzer who owned three boats. *Little Electra*, a sister ship to the 44 foot academy yawls, big *Electra* a 56foot Camper Nicholson ketch (Owen Aischer's original *Yeoman*) and *Iolaire*, 45foot engineless cutter—owned for many years by Bobby Sommerset. *Iolaire* had been across the Atlantic five times and was presently engineless (that is a story you can read in *Caribbean Capers*). Glenda Crytzer was trying to convince her husband that he really didn't need three boats. Bob took a liking to me, one thing led to another and I purchased Iolaire for $3,000 down, $1,000 a year for four years, with no interest and no repossession clause!

I slowly drifted into the charter business. Then the exploratory business and then the writing business and all of that is described in great detail in *Iolaire and I*.

Those who like my writing can thank John Steinbeck, John Fernly and Burt Cheveleaux.

My first charter after rebuilding *Iolaire* when she had been wrecked in Lindberg Bay was John Fernly (He had been casting director for Rogers & Hammerstein for many years) and his good friend Burt Cheveleaux who had just written *Something Funny happened on the Way to the Forum* (one of the most amusing characters I have ever met in my life). We stopped at Caneel Bay to have cocktails, then dinner with John Steinbeck—very good friends of John Fernly.

A week or so later on the charter we came back and had another evening with cocktails and dinner. The subject came up on writing and talent. It was kicked around for quite a long time, until finally Steinbeck said, "Hell forget all the B.S. on talent, becoming a good writer depends on your ability to put your ass on a hard wooden chair and look at the G.D. typewriter for six hours a day, seven days a week and pound something out. Eventually an editor will accept your work."

Later that evening he turned to me and said, "Kid you tell a good story. Why don't you try writing?" To which I replied, "But Mr. Steinbeck," "Never mind Mr. Steinbeck, call me John," "John, I can't spell." To which Mr. Steinbeck replied, "What the hell do you think secretaries and editors are for? Try writing. Go get me a drink." I went to the bar to get Steinbeck a drink and had to report that despite it being only 10.00 p.m., the bar was closed. Steinbeck said, "My God, this is a great place for newly weds and nearly deads. I don't know what you characters are doing, but I'm going back to my room to wrap myself around my bottle of scotch. Good night."
That started my writing career.

Carlton Mitchell had done a cruise through the islands on "Carib" in the late 1940's and written a book *Islands to Windward*. It was the story of his cruise, not really a cruising guide and long since out of print when I arrived in the islands.

Eggleston wrote a book in 1960 on the Virgin Islands as the result of a one month cruise. Also Linton Rigg was writing a book *The Alluring Antilles*—a cruise through the islands, and not a cruising guide.

I have always had an exploratory instinct and began to think about writing a guide. I had started on the Virgin Islands about the time Frank Burke of Island Yachts, (also known as "Frank Lurk the friendly Chinaman" count your fingers after you have shaken hands with him), approached me complaining that the new charter skippers didn't know the islands well enough and were missing a lot of the good spots—would I write a guide for them.

I said I would sell him the Virgin Island section of my proposed guide but no copyright. He mimeographed it off and sold it, (note mimeograph this was the days before the photocopying). Frank paid me the magnificent sum of $100.00 (remember this was in the days of 25¢ beer), for the manuscript. Subsequently after printing a couple of hundred I discovered he was selling them at $10.00 a piece. He made a fair piece of change on it.

A couple of years after I wrote the V.I. section of the guide and was working on completing the guide, I met Carlton Mitchell who was in the Eastern Caribbean with Finisterre—his little 39 foot centreboarder with which he won three Bermuda races. He was doing a cruise through the islands to write a series of articles for National Geographic. At this point Carlton Mitchell was probably yachting most famous writer and certainly the most highly paid yachting author in the world.

He looked me up in Grenada to pick my brains. We had a pleasant evening and I told him about my Virgin Island guide. About two years later I ran into Mitch. and he told me a most amusing story.

He arrived in the Virgin Islands and went in to see Frank Burk at Island Yachts. He said he had heard there was a young guy named Street who had written a Virgin Island guide. Frank said "yes he certainly has" and handed him a small mimeographed guide with the price on it of $10.oo. Mitch. looked at the $10.oo price tag and said, "Gee this is expensive."
To which Burk replied, "Look that is really good

solid information. This Street has written a guide that is a hell of a lot better than anything Carlton Mitchell has written in Islands to Windward or in Eggleston's Virgin Island guide, and it is worth the $10.oo Mitch thumbed his way through and decided he liked it. It was worth the $10.oo. He handed over the money and as Frank took it he looked up and said, "By the way, I'm Frank Burk." To which Mitch. replied, "I'm Carlton Mitchell." Burk didn't blink an eye, just said, "I still say the information is better than *Islands to Windward* or Eggleston's book." Mitch walked out the door and related the story to me much later. Luckily Mitch. has a good sense of humour.

I took the bare bones of the book with me to New York on a delivery. I visited eight or ten publishers, and got thrown out on my ear by all of them. I am a persistent soul and I started going back again. Phelp Platt of Dodd Mead, just to get rid of me, said he'd publish the book—*Cruising Guide to the Lesser Antilles* 1965. Also known as "the Cruising Guide tothe Lesser Ant Hills" when a boat hit an "*anthill*" that I had not found!! In those days we were definitely exploring

It is worth noting that as long ago in my first cruising guide (1966), I pointed out that the best sailing of the year occurs in May, June and July—when the wind blows at a steady 12 to 15knots day after day, and no fronts come blasting on through.

June and July are the beginning of hurricane season so you must be wary. After mid-July I would not think of cruising in the Caribbean, north of Martinique. I say this because if a hurricane is approaching and you are in Antigua and decide to head south, unless you have a very large boat and can turn on the engines and head south at 8- or 9-knots you have a long way—300 miles from Antigua to Grenada—to go to get out of the hurricane belt. If you are in the area of Martinique or south, and a hurricane approaches you only have 150 miles to get all the way down to the south coast of Grenada and the various anchorages completely sheltered other than when a hurricane runs right over the top of Grenada—a very unlikely occurrence in the light of past history.

WHEN TO COME AND WEATHER
The weather patterns in the Caribbean—and especially the northern end of the Caribbean—have changed drastically in the last three or four decades. When I first came here some 40 years ago, the fronts coming out of the Bahamas would stall in Hispaniola. We heard about them, but they didn't affect our weather. Come the 1960s, they pushed on through the western end of Puerto Rico, and the main effect in the Virgins was that the trades would die out once in a while and come in very light from the northwest. In recent years, fronts have pushed farther and farther east—through Puerto Rico and down to the Passage Islands. in 1993, when we were anchored at Buck Island in St. Croix, the wind was blowing 15 knots from the west!

From November to July, winds will be 15 to 20 knots from the east. These are referred to as the northeast trades, but that is a misnomer. In early winter, they are generally east to east-northeast, sometimes crawling around to northeast or north-northeast. Traditionally, the weather report reads, "East-northeast to east-southeast, 10 to 15 knots, higher in gusts." Some of us feel that this is a recording put on in early November and played until April. Then it is replaced by a recording that reads, "East to southeast, 10 to 15 knots, higher in gusts." When fronts come through, it will blow 20 to 25 knots, sometimes for a week or more.

The above is that all charter brokers and dreamers speak of as the Eastern Caribbean weather. However, at various times it can pipe way up to where it will be blowing for days on end 20-25 knots with stronger gusts. Those gusts, i.e. small squalls easily go up to 30 to 35 knots. These periods of heavy weather normally last 2/3 days but can last for weeks, as they have done a couple of times. In the extreme weather of 1998, when for almost all of January and the first week of February in the Antigua area it was exceptional when the wind dropped BELOW 25 knots.

Carrying a barometer in the Caribbean it is not much use, as if a hurricane is approaching by the time the barometer shows it, it drops so precipitously that it is too late to do anything. Outside hurricane season "the higher it goes, the harder it blows."

A further example of the changing climate is in 1957, sailing from St. Thomas to Caneel Bay, inside the Caribbean you occasionally ran into patches of Sargasso Weed, the size of a football field. In 1958 they were down to the size of tennis courts. In 1959, only small patches of Sargasso weed could be seen, then it completely disappeared from the Eastern Caribbean until 1989 when small patches of the weed reappeared. Not only that but the Caribbean was warmer than usual. People regularly quoted water temperatures as high as 81° and occasionally 82° instead of the normal 77°

Needless to say, everyone was very worried that hurricanes might be generated. yet only one hurricane came into the Caribbean that year—Hugo. Hugo the single hurricane did a huge amount of damage. See Reflections of Hugo.

In 2000 we have again seen small patches of Sargasso weed within the Caribbean, what does that mean???

It is worth noting that as long ago as my first cruising guide (1966), I pointed out that the best sailing of the year occurs in May, June, and July—when the wind blows at a steady 20 to 25 knots day after day, and no fronts come blasting on through.

UTC	LOCAL	STATION & REPORT DESCRIPTION	FREQ		MODE	
0930	0530	NMN Offshore Forecast	A		Voice	USB
1000	0600	WAH VI Radio Repeat NMN Offshore Forecast	4357		Voice	USB
1035	0685	Antillies Emergency & Weather Ham Net(Eric)	3815		Voice	LSB
1100	0700	Caribbean Maritime Mobile Ham Net	7241		Voice	LSB
1100	0700	Albatross Weather Report (Alex)	4054		Voice	USB
1115	0715	Caribbean Maritime Mobile Ham Net(George)	7241		Voice	LSB
1130	0730	Caribbean Maritime Mobile Ham Net(George)	7086		Wefax	LSB
1145	0745	Albatross Weather Report(Alex)	8155		Voice	USB
1200	0800	Trop Pred Ctr 0600 Tropical Surface Analysis	C		Wefax	USB(Note 1)
1205	0805	ZBVI Morning Marine Report Mon-Fri (David)	0780		Voice	AM(Note 2)
1230	0830	Caribbean Weather Net David)	8104		VoicE	USB(Note 3)
1230	0830	Trop Pred Ctr 24/36hr Winds/Seas Forecast	C		Wefax	USB(Note 1)
1250	0850	Trop Pred Ctr 1200 High Seas Forecast	C		Wefax	USB(Note 1)
1350	0950	Trop Pred Ctr 1145 Goes-8 Trop Sat Image	C		Wefax	USB(Note 1)
1600	1200	NMN Offshore Forecast	B		Voice	USB
1915	1515	Trop Pred Ctr 00 12hr Winds/Seas Forecast	C		Wefax	USB(Note 1)
1950	1550	Trop Pred Ctr 1745 Goes-8 Trop Sat Image	C		Wefax	USB(Note 1)
2000	1600	Southbound II (Herb)	12359		Voice	USB
2030	1630	Cocktail & Weather Net	7086		Voice	LSB
2045	1645	Cocktail & Weather Net (George)	7086		Wefax	LSB
2200	1800	NMN Offshore Forecast	B		Voice	USB
2235	1885	Antillies Emergency Weather Net*	3815		Voice	LSB
0028	2028	V.O.A. Windwards/Leewards Forecast	9945		Voice	AM
0330	2330	NMN Offshore Forecast	A		Voice	USB

WWV has World Marine Storm Warnings (Voice) at 8 min., and Solar Flux (Sunspot) number at 18 minutes after each hour on:
2 500, 5.000, 10.000 15.000, 20.000 MHz (USB)

Frequencies:
A. 4426 6501 8764
B. 6501 8764 13089
C. 4316.0 8502.0 12788
    4817.9 8503.9 12789.9

Notes: (Note 1) Tropical Prediction Center via US Coast Guard, New Orleans Louisiana.
USB. Tune 1.9 kHz below listed frequency. 120 LPM. 576 IOC,
(Note 2) ZBVI Morning Marine Report with David Jones, Mon-Fri 8:05am. Sat 7:45am, Sun 9:45am.
Hourly weather forecasts every hour on the 1/2 hour 7:30am - 9:30pm.
(Note 3) Annual subscription. required for custom forecast,
* temporarily off the air

As well as 4357. WAH also does a simultaneous broadcast on VHF 85. in range. Also included besides the NMN repeat is a weather summary, the east Puerto Rico and Virgin Islands local forecast, the Tropical Weather Outlook, and hurricane co-ordinates as appropriate. Updated broadcasts are also at 1400 and 2200 AST. A continuous broadcast can be heard on VHF WX 3 in range. The Antilles Emergency and Ham Weather Net does the same at 0645 AST on 7163 LSB.

In St Vincent, there is a local forecast on VHF 06 at 0900.
The Safety and Security Net now begins at 0815 AST on SSB 8104.

Thanks to William Mills of Toucan I and John and Melodye Pompa of Second Millennium and Compass Publications for radio information.
Note: NMN = US. Coast Guard Station, Chesapeake, Virginia.

WEATHER REPORTS - ISLAND BY ISLAND
South bound to Herb   12359Khz.   16.30
Amateur Weather   3815Khz.   06.30 + 18.30
Amateur Marine Mobile Net 7230Khz. 07.00

British Virgin Islands.
Because of the volcano eruption on Monserrat Radio Antilles is no more. However, there is a new weather report from Tortola done by a private weather forecaster by the name of David Jones Z.B.V.I. at 0805 Monday to Friday, 0745 on Saturday and on Sunday at 0945. Then there is a forecast every hour on the half hour—0730 to 2130. Further you can receive a customer weather forecast payable by the month.

Contact Dave at Z.B.V.I., Roadtown, Tortola, B.V.I. Caribbean weather Centre Ltd.,:
www.caribwx.com; e-mail: weather@caribwx.com
Tel: 284 494 7559; Fax: 284 494 5358.

Anguilla - not much use above listed stations.

St. Barts - At the Harbour Office there is a weather report produced from the French Meteorological

Office. This is not only a weather report, but also a weather map so that you can do your own predicting.

St. Martins - A continuous weather broadcast is given on Weather Channel VHF. But my experience has been that it is worse than useless as the information comes from Curacao and is about 24 hours out of date.

Antigua - 09.00 Jol Byerly presents a weather report based on information pulled in from many sources. He does a good job of interpreting the information he gathers. But, he is dealing with a commercial broadcast of weather information which is sometimes not all that accurate. The result are not 100%. Jol admits it and more than once he has come on the radio and apologised for the weather prediction of the previous day, saying it had obviously missed. It is not Jol's fault he is doing an excellent and time consuming job. He does a good job with the information supplied to him.

Guadaloupe - At the Harbour Office there is a weather report produced from the French Meteorological Office. This is not only a weather report, but also a weather map so that you can do your own predicting.

Dominica - If you listen to the commercial weather reports which are generally so inaccurate all you do is get very frustrated.

RAIN

The rainy season is the same as the hurricane season—roughly July to October (although hurricanes have occurred in June and November). Even then, it very seldom rains day after day but rather a maximum of three hours a day. The rest of the day is sunny. However, at times the rainy and dry seasons reverse themselves, confusing everyone. In 1993, for example, during the "dry season", our longest stretch without rain was only 36 hours. So be sure to have

on hand a raincoat or a foul weather jacket. Trousers and boots are not really necessary, as the air is warm enough, but you will get tired of having a wet tail, so if you have a full-length raincoat with a hood, you won't be sorry.

Amazingly, however, the best months for sailing the Eastern Caribbean are May, June, and July—the weather patterns tend to be more stable.

SUN

Despite the fact that you might have spent time in Florida or the Bahamas and not suffered from sunburn, that does not mean that you will be safe when you get to Puerto Rico and the Virgins. Remember that Florida is 26°N; the Virgin Islands are 18°30'. You will get a tan in the Virgins even if you keep all your clothes on. Be sure you have a broad-brimmed hat, at least one long-sleeved white shirt, long cotton trousers, and plenty of sunblock. And use it all! If you have a tiller-steered boat, be especially careful to put sunblock on the tops of your hands and the tops of your feet. Men's cotton pyjamas or doctors' scrub suits make good cover-ups to keep you from getting too much sun.

If you intend to spend a large portion of your life sailing in the tropics, it is essential that you cover up and use the strongest sun block you can find on your hands and face. I have done that most of my life. Although I am known as "Squeaky" I could be known as "Swiss Cheese" due to all the holes made in me by doctors removing skin cancer. At times I' come out of the skin specialists feeling like a blown out Genoa rather than a sailor. Cover up and use the sun block.

WHAT TO WEAR

Travel light. If you can't fit everything into the standard duffel (generally measuring 26 inches long by 12 inches in diameter), you have too much gear. Dress in most places is casual. In town, women should wear a skirt and blouse or long shorts and a blouse; bare midriffs and bikinis are not acceptable. For a fancy night out, women may want a long dress and men may want a jacket and tie. Plus, if you go to any of the mountain top restaurants in Puerto Rico, St. Thomas, or Tortola, be sure to take along a jacket or light sweater; you lose a degree of temperature for every 150 feet of altitude. The temperature can easily be in the upper 60s (and feel quite chilly) at one of these areas. On the south coast of Puerto Rico, where the cold air comes down off the mountains at night, the temperature drops quickly to the 60s. On any of the really high islands like Guadeloupe or Dominica the cold air comes down off the mountains at night and the temperature drops quickly to the upper 60s.

On the trip down, carry some clothing in your hand luggage—a bathing suit, a hat, and a change of clothes— incase your baggage doesn't arrive at the same time you do. There is nothing worse than walking around San Juan or St. Thomas or Tortola wearing your winter duds.

To beat the heat in the airports most of which are not air-conditioned, my technique is to change out of my winter duds and into my tropical clothes before the plane lands. Then when standing in the Immigration & Customs line you don't die of the heat and perspiration. Similarly when flying out of the islands, I go through the airport and on board the aircraft wearing tropical attire carrying my winter duds in my bag. Once in the aircraft I change and all is well. I haven't climbed on the aeroplane in a pool of sweat.

DINGHIES

In the eastern Caribbean one finds all sizes of Dinghies and tenders. Varying from small dinghies like our six foot clinker pram that we use on Li'l Iolaire through to nice rowing dinghies like those we carry on Iolaire, or inflatables, very small soft bottom ones, which are willing, eager and desirous of running out from under you when you step into them and dumping you in the drink. I have fallen out of a dinghy twice in my life both times were from one of those soft bottomed tiny inflatables. Then there are those big RIB's thirty feet long, and valued at $40,000 and RIB's of all sizes in-between.

Losing dinghies or the larger boats, called launches, is endemic in the Caribbean. However, it is not all down to the locals. One third of the ships boats that are lost are just not tied up properly. For that reason on Iolaire or Li'l Iolaire, when ever we are anchored in a harbour that is open to the west, I insist that the dinghy be tied on with two separate lines, going on the supposition that a person may miss tie one line, but is unlikely to miss tie two lines. Another third of dinghies are stolen by the locals. Another third stolen by a "fellow" yachtsman. More than once a culprit has been caught stealing a dinghy and when his boat is visited by the police they have found five or six deflated dinghies inside the boat.

The normal safety precaution is to shackle a wire onto the dinghy, and padlock the dinghy to the dock or the boat with the other end of the wire. However, quarter inch 1/19 is not good enough. The thieves come around with wire cutters and slip right through ¼ inch. If you have a valuable ships tender/launch my advice is to use a piece of $5/16^{ths}$ of 1/19 as cutting through that requires more effort and a bigger cutter than the average thief is likely to have. However, the only way you can be absolutely sure of not losing your dinghy at night is to have it sling rigged attached to your halyard and haul it clear of the water. That is the only reliable way. In some areas, there is little or no dinghy stealing, and in other areas it is rife. Thus the prudent mariner asks among his fellow yachtsmen, especially from the bareboat managers, about the dingy stealing situation locally.

SECURITY

If you are flying down and chartering a boat with a skipper and crew they will know what the security situation is and keep you advised so you can sit back and relax. If you are bareboat chartering, check with the bareboat managers and they will advise you of any security problems. Generally there are very few security problems from Guadaloupe north. From Guadaloupe south, i.e. Dominica south, St. Lucia, St. Vincent, the Grenadines, the security problems do arise.

Again if you are cruising through the islands in your own boat, check with the bareboat managers and skippers. They are very friendly and they will keep you advised as to security problems.

People who cruise through on boats ask about guns—forget about them, leave them ashore. They are more hassle than they are worth. The thing to remember is that in my entire yachting life, I have never ever heard of a boat being robbed that has had a barking dog on board. A small barking dog is enough to keep the thieves away. There is no need for a great big huge guard dog

FISH POISONING

Fish poisoning is a major problem in Anguilla, St. Martins, St. Barts area. Occasionally fish poisoning has been reported to Antigua Barbuda area, but I have never heard of an authentic case of fish poisoning from Guadaloupe south.

I have no idea how to avoid the fish poisoning known as ciguatera, although it's easy to find people who will give you advice on the matter. I have never heard reports of anyone dying of ciguatera, but people have said that it makes you feel so terrible you wish you were dead!

One of the problems is determining what fish are likely to be poisonous. What's poisonous in one area is not necessarily so in another area. In St. Croix, barracuda is consumed by the ton. In the northern Virgins, on the other hand, no one eats barracuda because it is alleged to be poisonous if found on the northern side of the islands and non-poisonous if found on the southern side of the islands. How do you tell whether you have caught a travelling barracuda?

One recommendation is to cook fish with a silver spoon; if the spoon stays shiny, the fish is fine. Well, we tried that once on *Iolaire*. Four of us ate the fish, with mixed results. Our West Indian cook ate a lot and was very sick; two American friends, Marv and Carol Bernning, ate a moderate amount and were moderately sick; I at a little and did not get sick. On another occasion, when we were given a fish, part of the crew went to a friend's house and cooked half of the fish. Some of them were fine, some slightly sick, some violently ill. Aboard *Iolaire*, where five of us ate the other half, we were all fine. Who can figure it out?

In St. Barts, the advice is to cut out the fish's liver and put it down for the ants; if the ants eat the liver the fish is fine. If they don't eat it, you shouldn't either. some suggest offering some of the fish to a cat and waiting 24 hours. If the cat is fine, go ahead and eat the fish; if the cat gets sick, throw out the rest of the fish.

The best advice is to check with the locals. In general, if they would be willing to eat it, you should be too.

COMMUNICATIONS

Communications are expanding so rapidly that whatever I write to day would be out of date by the time it is printed. In the big fancy yachts they can pick up a phone and call anywhere in the world and in the medium sized yachts there is the SSB. With this you can get patched through to a shore side station to enable you to make phone calls. Ashore on all the islands, with the aid of a credit card, you can call anywhere in the world

On the French islands it is sometimes difficult to get an English speaking operator to explain what you should do. On St. Martins I think I can say, without fear of contradiction, that the Dutch side of St. Martins historically has had the worst and most expensive phone system in the world. The U.S.A. direct phones seem to work pretty well, but for calling anywhere else, my advice is that if you are in Phillisburg, go to Dockside and use their phones and pay them. If in Simpsons Bay or Simpson Lagoon go to Mailbox and avail of their services. Both organisations also have photocopying, fax, secretarial services—the works.

On Anguilla, Antigua and Dominica with the aid of a credit card you can more or less call anywhere in the world. The only problem is that Cable & Wireless change their procedures and they don't change the new directions in the phone booths.

Mobile phones are coming in on the islands. At the time of writing each island has their own mobile phone system so when travelling from island to island, your mobile phone is useless. However, I am told by 2001 and certainly by 2002 you will be able to have a chip put into your mobile phone, that will enable you to use your mobile phone up and down the eastern Caribbean.

Mail and general delivery is not too hot an idea on most of the islands. It is better to look at the guide, check with the marina or yacht yard. Write to them and make arrangements with them to hold your mail when you arrive.

RENTAL CARS

Rental cars are available everywhere in the eastern Caribbean. You should shop around as the rates vary widely. Also you should drive very defensively as the accident rate on many of the islands is right out the window.

TIDES

You can try to predict the tides on the islands if you refer to Street's Transatlantic Crossing Guide and the information shown on the back of Imray Iolaire charts. It should be noted at the spring and autumn equinox the tide will be extremely high, as much as two feet, sometimes as much as two and half feet in areas that normally have no more that eighteen inches rise and fall of tide. Also a most important thing, for deep draft vessels, or even moderately drafted vessel, THE CARIBBEAN IS EIGHTEEN INCHES TO TWO FEET LOWER IN MAY, JUNE, JULY AND EARLY AUGUST than it is the rest of the year. Thus the channels that you can go up and down all winter long with no trouble, often with 6 inches of clearance, may have you wedged like a cork in a bottle in these months, at spring tides and may have to wait 6 hours to float off. For this reason for the past thirty years I have been urging installation on of tidal guages in channels where depth is a problem. As each year goes by the yachts bet bigger and bigger, and it becomes more and more essential to have tidal guages installed. They should be installed Nanny and Wickhams Cay, Tortola, Simson Bay entrance to Simson Lagoon, St. Martins, Jolly Harbour, Antigual. Rodney Bay, St. Lucia, Blue Lagoon, St. Vincent, the Lagoon St. Georges and Secret Harbour Grenada. With a proper tidal guage installed, one can tell at a glance exactly what the controling depth is in the channel at any moment.

GROUND SWELLS

Ground swells are produced by storms in the North Atlantic and have absolutely nothing to do with local weather. They used to arrive completely unannounced, but now the weather reports from Puerto Rico usually predict them. Each year, ground swells put at least one boat up on the beach. Anytime you see an especially beautiful sandy beach, you know the ground swells have done their bit to create it. When in any volume mention is made of an anchorage subject to ground swells be sure to use a Bahamian moor (see *Street's Transatlantic Crossing Guide and Introduction to the Caribbean*), or your boat may be the one up on the beach.

BUOYAGE

The French islands buoyage system is excellent as they have always had a buoy tender based in Guadeloupe. When a French buoy comes adrift it is replaced almost immediately. On the other islands if a buoy comes adrift it may be years before it is replace.

In the ex-British islands, they are often not buoys but booby traps that catch the unwary yachtsman. Throughout the islands the privately maintained buoys frequently go adrift and are frequently altered. The privately maintained buoys are not marked on the charts, because they are too subject to change. Basically, anywhere there is likely to be a buoy, you should be able to use eyeball navigation. Judge depths by the colour of the water: Brown is reef, white is shoal water, light green usually is deep enough to sail in, and blue is deep water. A good test of your skill is to try to guess the depth of the water and then turn on the fathometer to check.

Don't sail at night; enter all harbours when the sun is still fairly high. When heading eastward, you can enter as late as 1700, because the sun is behind you, but if heading westward, you should be in harbour by 1600 at the very latest. Similarly, before leaving a harbour in the morning, take a good look around. Check the access to the channel and the bearing to the sun. In the morning, the sun may be right in your eyes, making it hard to see anything, so you may have to delay your departure until 1000 or 1100.

LIGHTS

Despite what other guides say, the lights in the Caribbean are NOT all reliable. In the French islands, the lights are excellent and reliable; in the American islands, they are good and fairly reliable, but not absolutely; in the British (and ex-British) islands, it looks as though the lighting and buoyage system was established to keep harbour pilots, ship wreckers and salvagers from starving to death. DO NOT RELY ON THESE LIGHTS.

DIVING

Throughout the islands there are diving organisations. If you wish to do any diving it is best to make contact with the diving organisations as they know the area, the best diving sites, have the equipment and they take all the hassle out of diving. There are a few exceptions.

Many charter skippers do not conduct diving tours as the local divers know the areas so much better than they do and are so much better equipped with suitable boats. Diving from a charter boat, except for those specifically built to cater for it, is pretty much a no no. Further, immediately on checking in with Customs & Immigration you should check what the local regulations are regarding diving, fishing and anchoring as in many of the islands, as of 2001, diving from your boat is NOT LEGAL. It is also very very important that as soon as you have checked in with Customs & Immigration you check what the local regulations are regarding anchoring, fishing with hand lines off the end of a boat and rod and reel fishing. The regulations are regularly being changed and I cannot summarise it here.

In many areas spear fishing is prohibited. In other areas even trolling from a boat is prohibited.

CUSTOMS AND IMMIGRATION

The situation is on arrival on most of the islands, Customs and Immigration is fairly lenient. When you arrive you should hoist the Q Flag and the skipper should go ashore to clear customs and immigration. However, in most islands if you arrive outside office hours, no one will object to the crew going ashore for drinks and dinner with the skipper clearing the next morning.

The trouble comes when you are flying in to join a boat, sailing off the island and flying back from another island, or joining the boat and not flying out. Immigration at the airport will immediately insist on seeing you flight ticket to get out of the island. If you don't have a ticket out all sorts of problems ensue. The way around this is to have a letter from the owner or captain of the boat, addressed to the immigration officer, stating that you are joining the boat and leaving the island on board the yacht. If worse comes to worst, and you have not received a letter sit down and write a letter to yourself. Forge the skipper's signature—it works everytime.

The exact location of the Customs & Immigration on each island is noted on the Imray Iolaire charts.

HURRICANES

See reflections on Hugo in the Foreword page *xx*.

Finally, before you sail anywhere in the Eastern Caribbean (and particularly if you are going during hurricane season), I advise you to take to heart the advice that appeared above.

The entire Caribbean is hurricane territory, and hurricanes are more frequent than most people realise. The Virgin Islands, for example, have been hit or side-swiped by 32 hurricanes since 1871. In 1916 alone, there were three hurricanes. In 1889, 1891 and 1979 there were two hurricanes in the same year.

Puerto Rico has been hit by 34 hurricanes, of which three were in 1916 and two were in 1891, 1898, 1899, 1901 and 1979. The Antigua/Guadeloupe area has had 32 hurricanes (three in 1933), plus the area has been sideswiped by 10 or 12 tropical depressions.

The Martinique/St. Lucia area has had 44 hurricanes, plus about a dozen tropical depressions.

Normally, there is plenty of warning; it is only the freak hurricane, such as Klaus in late 1984, that catches the islands unaware. Klaus popped up just south of Puerto Rico, went north east, and was very late in the year. Klaus was on of only five hurricanes in 100 years that tracked northeast below 22°N!

Today, there is at least a three- or four-day warning of an approaching hurricane. The US government publication *Tropical Cyclones of the North Atlantic Ocean* (US Department of Commerce, National Climatic Data and Information Center, Ashville, North Carolina 28801, U.S.A.—NOAA—1871 TI 1980, with an update to 1993) shows the tracks of all the known hurricanes. You'll notice that, with very few exceptions, hurricanes follow a definite and predictable pattern as they approach the islands of the Eastern Caribbean. Admittedly, once they reach Puerto Rico, Haiti, and the Dominican Republic, they can execute a 180-degree turn, or a 360-degree one, or a right angle, or anything in between. They are not predictable once they pass through the islands. Thus, many experienced seamen have concluded that if you have a decent boat of 40 feet or more, well equipped, with an engine so you can power, and if there are light airs in front of the hurricane, the solution is to pull up the anchor and go to sea. With a two-day head start, you certainly can be 250 to 300 miles from the storm centre. Thus, you could expect a large (possibly huge) ground swell, but no more than 40 knots of wind. (In any case, if you don't have a boat that can handle 40 knots of wind, you should not be out sailing.)

The frequency of hurricanes in St. Vincent and the Grenadines is much lower than farther north, BUT there are really no hurricane holes in the area. The first hurricane hole south of St. Lucia is all the way down on the south coast of Grenada—an area that has had only about five hurricanes in its history.

Amazingly, Isla Margarita in Venezuela has been hit by two hurricanes in the last 120 years, even though no hurricanes have struck the Venezuelan mainland.

In light of the above, one must figure on a major hurricane every four to five years, no matter where you are in the Caribbean. For the best odds, head for Grenada, Trinidad, or mainland Venezuela—and I urge that underwriters offer discounts to boats that arrange to be in those areas between July and November.

Nowadays, the Eastern Caribbean is overpopulated with boats. The hurricane holes are so over-crowded that all you need for disaster is one or two boats that are anchored improperly and start dragging. (Of course, I well remember being told in prep school that all general statements are suspect, and even the statement—"all general statements are suspect"—is suspect!) Undoubtedly, there are a few hurricane holes that are not over-crowded or that people do not know about. Witness Enseñada Honda Vieques, off Puerto Rico. To the best of my knowledge, almost no boats went to Vieques in 1989 during Hurricane Hugo; like lemmings, they all poured into Enseñada Honda Culebra—whereas Enseñada Honda Vieques, which is a better hurricane hole, had relatively few boats tucked up into the mangroves.

Puerto del Rey Marina has been very well thought out they have learned from the early hurricanes and various hard north east blows. They have established a secure basin by building a break water which completely shelters the harbour from the north east. They have also worked out an excellent method, too complicated to describe here, for tying boats down in their dry storage. As a result of all this work, during hurricanes in 1999, the hurricane damage was minimal. Although there was some damage to boats in the marina, losses are note extected.

If you are going to keep your boat in the Caribbean during hurricane season, I feel it is essential that you buy what I call "the hurricane book". It is put out by the National Climatic Data and Information Centre, Ashville, North Carolina 28801, U.S.A. The book has a list of all the hurricanes and tropical storms that have occurred since the keeping of records in 1878.

A study of the book reveals my contention that hurricanes approaching the Caribbean and passing through the Lesser Antilles basically never change track more than 10^0 in 24 hours. BUT having passed through the Lesser Antilles they can do absolutely anything. Especially when they approach the land mass of Puerto Rico and Santa Domingo.

Despite what I have said above, remember the old story of "Any generalised theory is wrong—including the general statement that a general statement is wrong." There have been exceptions. It is generally thought that November 1st is the end of hurricane season. However, since the late 1980's there have been a number of late season hurricanes in the beginning of November and Hurricane Lenny was as late as 16/17th 18th November.

These exceptions to the rule that hurricanes in the eastern Caribbean move from east to west, are very few and far between.

In 1800's Rodney arrived in Barbados at the end of October with his fleet looking for supplies only to discover that the island was in desperate straights, as a hurricane had started in Jamaica and gone across the Caribbean heading southeast. It passed over the top of St. Lucia, flattening that island and passing on directly over the top of Barbados.

Another odd one was in 1908, in <u>MARCH</u>. The hurricane started roughly 300 miles north east of St. Barts. It headed south passing just west of St. Barts, right over the top of St. Kitt's.

In 1954 in December 30th about 600 miles north east of Antigua hurricane Alice headed south east and passed over Nevis, north of Monserrat and finally turned south east and headed into the Lower Caribbean dissipating west of Grenada.

In early November 1984 hurricane Klaus started south of Puerto Rico heading east, passing over and doing extensive damage to the U.S.V.I., B.V.I. and Anguilla, St. Martins and St. Barts area before dissipating out in the Atlantic. Finally, in mid November 1999, hurricane Lenny started south of Jamaica and continued eastward doing extensive damage throughout the Caribbean.

Even though there was not a particularly huge quantity of boats in the southern Caribbean, since the hurricane was heading east, the dangers wherethe biggest seas were, was south east of the Caribbean rather than the normal routine of being north west.

Street, in *Li'l Iolaire*, was stuck in Bequia Harbour—but that's another story too long to recount here. He anchored in a thirty foot deep hole, with two lines off to the fuelling buoys, plus two anchors out. Periodically seas would break over a <u>twenty foot</u> deep shoal to the west of *Li'l Iolaire*.

As a result of these hurricanes, yachts have been flocking to Venezuela and Trinidad to be out of the hurricane area.

In 1992 Trinidad installed it's first commercial travel lift at Power Boats. Until that time there was really no hauling facilities for yachts as at Trinidad and Tobago Yachting Services Association was a bare 20 ton lift. Power Boats and then Peaks, were given tremendous impetus by Hurricane Hugo. Subsequent to which marine underwriters who had taken a serious loss, refused to insure boats north of $12^0\ 40$' north, causing boats to flood into Trinidad. Luckily has not been actually hit by any hurricanes, and so it has now become the hurricane refuge. I say "hurricane refuge" as Trinidad and Tob- ago Yachting Services Association estimate that in the height of the hurricane season, in 1999, there were 2500 boats in Trinidad. Were a hurricane or a tropical depression to come through, one hates to think of what could happen.

It should be noted that in 1892 a hurricane passed just north of Trinidad, and south of Tobago. In 1974 a tropical storm with 60-70 knots of wind passed over the southern end of Trinidad. In 1978 a tropical storm started just west of Trinidad at the eastern end of the peninsula du Paria. Another tropical storm passed over Trinidad in 1990 and again in 1993. Of course in those years there were so few yachts in Trinidad there was not much to be damaged. But a tropical storm today .....!

Finally if you are going to be in the Caribbean in hurricane season and doubt what I say, buy the NOAA Hurricane Book.

OVERALL VIEW

For an overall view of the entire Caribbean you should carefully read a copy of Street's Transatlantic Guide, study it's sections of Transatlantic Crossings and "getting there" from the States, leaving—the States, Europe and Panama, supplies, communications, touch-downs, wind weather and tides. This really is an essential companion to the other guides.

To find more about the islands and also some good advice, very carefully read the Foreword, Acknowledgements and the section on Charts.

1

Sailing Directions

The Lesser Antilles stretch east and south from Puerto Rico and St. Thomas in a great crescent. The entire sweep is best visualized by studying Imray-Iolaire Chart A, the only published chart that shows the Eastern Caribbean in a scale suitable for planning a cruise. Spread this chart before you, and, when making your plans, remember that the "northeast trades" are a misnomer—they vary continually, sometimes crawling all the way around to the north and, more often, especially in the late spring and summer, favoring the southeast to south quadrants.

A bit of advice for cruising the Lesser Antilles: Instead of making plans each morning after breakfast (thus getting a late start and arriving at the next anchorage at dusk or after dark—a dangerous thing to do), it is better to drag out the charts, the cruising guide, and the travel books the evening before. Study them well, and be sure to read the sailing directions for the area likely to be covered. Make your plans and then turn in, ready for the next day's adventures.

When arriving at a new island, as soon as you clear Customs and Immigration, head for the Tourist Office and pick up all the free material available on the area. Thus, you will have a map of the island (and perhaps the major town), in addition to lists of hotels, restaurants, car-rental agencies, and more. Since such information becomes dated very quickly, I feel it is unwise to include much of it in a cruising guide. It's always best to get up-to-the-minute advice from local sources. On some islands (such as St. Martin and Antigua), you can pick up a locally compiled marine directory that is published annually and thus is more up to date than any cruising guide can possibly be.

When working to windward (eastward) from the northern islands toward Antigua, be sure to remember that there is an average of one knot of foul current; thus, your speed to windward may be discouraging. Once you turn the corner at Antigua and head south—and similarly on your northbound courses from Martinique—remember that the current usually will be on the weather beam at approximately one knot, or often more. This will set you to leeward at a considerable rate.

If you are sailing at four knots, a one-knot current on the beam will set you to leeward roughly 15° in an hour's run; if you are sailing at five knots, the set will be 12°; at six knots, it will be 10°; at seven knots, it will be 8°.

It must be pointed out, however, that there are no hard-and-fast rules about currents in the Antilles. Changing tidal influences, varying wind strengths, and local topographical peculiarities all affect the movement of waters in the Eastern Caribbean. As a generalization, though, it is fair to say that the current runs to the west; consequently, when cruising in the Lesser Antilles, it is a good idea to stay to windward of the rhumb line between any two points. There are exceptions to this rule, but they are few and far between.

Figuring out currents in the Eastern Caribbean is a very complicated procedure. Even after all my years of cruising in the region, I feel I am doing fantastically well if I can honestly predict the short periods of easterly current 70 percent of the time. Being able to take advantage of a windward-going current can greatly minimize the amount of time spent slogging to windward, so it is worth trying to understand the patterns of currents and tides. (I recommend starting with the chapter on this subject in *Street's Transatlantic Crossing Guide and Introduction to the Caribbean.*)

When you reach the southern islands, remember that they are far enough apart that the next island is not always visible when you start off. Thus, you should lay off your rhumb-line course, set your actual course to allow for the current, then continually take back bearings on the island astern to make absolutely sure you are not set to leeward of the rhumb line. This is where a hand-bearing compass can earn its keep.

Proceeding East and South

The sailing directions in this chapter apply to passages made from island to island. Once you get close to an island, be sure to refer to the specific descriptions in the chapters that follow.

Most skippers bound for the Lesser Antilles from the north favor a landfall in St. Thomas. Invariably, a few every year are driven farther westward by southeast winds, so they must settle for San Juan and face the long haul eastward from there. However, if you are heading for the Virgin Islands from the Bahamas and have time to wait, there is a way to avoid the long, tedious beat through the Bahamas. First cross the Gulf Stream and wait in Grand Bahama. Then, when a northerly comes through, take off on the face of it through Northwest Providence Channel and Northeast Providence Channel. Since the islands are to the north of you, there will be smooth water despite plenty of wind, and you will fly onward. Then, when you leave Northeast Providence Channel, you will be broad-off. With luck, you will be blown *downwind* all the way to Puerto Rico.

Leaving San Juan Harbor, the only option is to sheet her flat and bull your way east against wind and current for the 60 miles or so to St. Thomas. Arrange your departure from San Juan so that you pass the northeast corner of Puerto Rico—where it is important that the sun be high—by 1100 hours. Work your way to the east, taking careful bearings. Put someone in the rigging to guide you into Vieques Sound through one of the breaks in the reefs that extend eastward from northeastern Puerto Rico. The reefs will afford a moderate degree of shelter. If you wish, you can ease sheets and stop at one of the many marinas on the coast of Puerto Rico. (For details, see *Street's Cruising Guide to the Eastern Caribbean: Puerto Rico and the Passage Islands.*) Instead of slogging to windward, you can cruise leisurely through the islands, visiting numerous secluded, uncrowded anchorages. The most important of these areas is the eastern end of Vieques. Here there are half a dozen pure, unspoiled harbors that are likely to remain this way for many years, as no roads lead to them. This is still a naval gunnery area, but the gunnery range is no longer used. Nonetheless, the navy is likely to keep control here for another century, so hoteliers will be unable to take over these beautiful bays. From Vieques, it is literally a short hop over to Brewers Bay in St. Thomas.

Boats headed for the Virgins from the Bahamas often make their landfall on the west coast of Puerto Rico, where there is a good harbor at Mayagüez. From here, the best route eastward, in my estimation, is along the south coast of Puerto Rico. This coast is somewhat sheltered from the full force of the trades (especially when blowing north of east); the swell is usually less, and there are plenty of good anchorages all along the route. As you work your way eastward, stay inshore on the Puerto Rican shelf and play the wind shifts for all they are worth. The shelf will act to reduce the westerly set of the current. At night, if the trades don't die out completely, they frequently shift to northerly, giving you a reach along the coast into early morning. As the land heats up after sunrise, the wind veers to the east. In the summer months, when the wind is east or southeast, it usually will die out at night and spring up from the east in the early morning, shifting gradually to the south as the day progresses. Keeping these variations in mind can save a lot of windward work. (For information on beating along the south coast of Puerto Rico, see *Street's Cruising Guide to the Eastern Caribbean: Puerto Rico and the Passage Islands*.

Generally speaking, five of the islands are good jumping-off spots for further cruising: St. Thomas, Antigua, Martinique, St. Lucia, and Grenada. They all provide air communication to the United States, harbors, shipyards where your boat can be minded in your absence, and stores and markets where you can resupply to continue your trip. St. Thomas is the starting point for most extended cruises of the Lesser Antilles, despite its being so far to leeward. Here are a few of the possible routes southward from there:

- St. Thomas through the Virgin Islands, island hopping to Antigua, 210 miles to windward, with possibilities of stopping and resting at various islands.
- St. Thomas to Martinique direct, 337 miles, course 143° magnetic; there is some possibility of laying the course.
- St. Thomas to Martinique via Necker Island Passage, course 152° magnetic.
- St. Thomas to St. Lucia direct, or from Virgin Gorda via Necker Island Passage; the same course as that to Martinique, except that the distance is somewhat greater.
- St. Thomas to Grenada direct, 423 miles, course 163° magnetic. The course can be laid once clear of St. Croix.
- St. Thomas to Grenada via Necker Island Passage, course 170° magnetic, about 400 miles. An easy reach from Necker down.

The Virgins stretch out to the eastward from St. Thomas, making a cruise through them a dead beat to windward. But this is not a difficult beat, since the islands are close together, and, even though the wind may blow hard, there will be nothing more to contend with than a large chop. The Virgins can easily provide a week to 10 days of pleasant cruising. (For sailing directions to help you thread your way through the U.S. and British Virgins, see chapter 1 in *Street's Cruising Guide to the Eastern Caribbean: The U.S. and British Virgin Islands.*)

ANEGADA PASSAGE

Once you leave the Virgins through Necker Island Passage or Round Rock Passage, there is little between you and Africa. The seas sweep across 3,000 miles of open ocean, and, as they enter Anegada Passage, they are influenced by the tide ebbing and flowing into the Caribbean. The islands on both sides of the passage disturb the natural flow of the waves, creating an area that is almost always rough and uncomfortable. When the trades really begin to pipe up, the passage is difficult for large boats and well nigh impossible for smaller ones.

In Anegada Passage, the wind generally is east and the current flows west to northwest at 1 to 1 1/2 knots—in other words, a dead slog to windward with a foul current all the way. There is some room for play in this passage, however, which I will try to explain with specific reference to the chart. The north equatorial current—which runs northwest as it passes Nevis, St. Christopher (St. Kitts), St. Eustatius (Statia), and Saba—swings toward the west between St. Croix and the other Virgin Islands. A strong eddy holds almost due north around the west end of St. Martin and Anguilla, then northwest along Horse Shoe Reef and the eastern shore of Anegada. Once it reaches the northern end of Anegada, it goes westward, with a strong back eddy looping eastward below the island on Virgin Bank. This eddy has been attested to by fishermen and pilots who have spotted large accumulations of sargasso weed between the westerly current and the easterly eddy, and by the surprising number of wrecks on the western reefs of Anegada.

A boat crossing Anegada Passage will be favored by the northerly current on its lee bow. Since this northerly tendency becomes less pronounced the farther off to the south you fall, you should stay well to the north. If you allow your course to sag off toward Saba, you will find the current right on your nose the rest of the way east to St. Martin. (As a general rule, if you cannot see Sombrero Light, you are too far off to the south.) For example, if the wind is well in the north, work your way eastward within the shelter of the Virgins before heading out through Necker Island Passage and standing across to St. Martin; however, if the wind is east or east-southeast, work your way much farther north before venturing out into the passage. Take advantage of the easterly eddy hooking around Anegada, and lay a northern course so that you pass close aboard the west end of Anegada. Stand far enough north to clear Anegada and Horse Shoe Reef in one tack. As you proceed southeastward on port tack, you should have an increasingly strong lee-bow current lifting you favorably. In short, my advice is to stay to the north—granting that there are exceptions to every rule. For instance, in the 1973 St. Thomas—St. Martin Race, one boat took a flyer from the rest of the fleet. He stood southeast to Saba Bank, then tacked, beating all his competitors by a country mile and confounding all the local sailing authorities.

The above description details the normal method used by many experienced sailors for crossing Anegada Passage. However, one longtime sailor who has had to cross Anegada Passage fairly frequently in recent years has studied the situation carefully and has evolved a slightly different method—one that has much to recommend it.

Dr. Robin Tattersall owns *Galatea,* a 36-foot Herreshoff Nereia ketch that, during 1977-78, pretty well cleaned house in the cruising division of the West Indies Yachting Association. (The only boat that seemed able to beat her was a Freedom 40.) Dr. Tattersall was based in Tortola and regularly went to Anguilla for a few days to perform surgery. Rather than fly over, he liked to sail across Anegada Passage. Thus, he has plenty of experience driving his boat to windward, and this stands him in good stead while racing.

His recommendation is to proceed to Eustatia Island, north of Virgin Gorda. This considerably shortens the distance across the passage—it being 75 miles on a rhumb-line course 115° magnetic from Eustatia Island to Road Bay, Anguilla, with possibilities of stops at Sombrero or Dog Island.

To Sombrero, the rhumb-line course is 090°, the distance 54 miles; to Dog Island, the course is 110°, the distance 62 miles. (You could also take off from the anchorage behind Necker Island.) The great advantage of taking off from either of these two points is that they both afford good daytime anchorages, good snorkeling, and excellent beaches. Here you can relax under the awning, have a good lunch and a snooze, and then depart early in the afternoon well fed and rested. Both islands have the advantage that they are accessible without your needing to slog to windward in the open ocean—as you would have to do if you left the Drake Channel farther west at Cooper or Ginger Island. You can beat up behind Virgin Gorda and enter Gorda Sound (if you draw six feet or less) through the Western Passage between Mosquito Island and Anguilla Point. You beat to windward across Gorda Sound in calm water, pass between Saba Rock and John O Point, sail on into Eustatia Sound, and then anchor behind Eustatia Island or continue north through the reef to Necker Island.

Dr. Tattersall advises leaving Eustatia or Necker about 1500 or 1600 hours. Once clear of Eustatia Sound or Necker Island (beware of the well-named Invisibles, half a mile east of Necker Island), stand to the north about four miles, keeping a careful check on your position in relation to Horse Shoe Reef. If the wind is in the north, Dr. Tattersall advises going back to port tack as soon as you can. Lay Dog Island, remembering that if you are able to lay 120° to 110°, a lee-bow current will be lifting you to windward. With any luck and a good boat, you should be off Dog Island at dawn. Drop the anchor, then enjoy a good breakfast, a swim, and a walk on the beach, after which you can continue to Anguilla, arriving in late afternoon.

In the spring and summer, however, when the wind is in the southerly quadrant (and provided the ground swell is not running), it is best to stand off on starboard tack once clear of Horse Shoe Reef. Aim for Sombrero— rhumb-line course 100°, distance 44 miles. The advantage of this course is that long before you lose the lights on the top of the hill on Virgin Gorda (given decent visibility), you will pick up the lights of Sombrero, where in normal weather it is calm enough to anchor. (If the ground swell is running, forget it.) In the lee of Sombrero, you can get the better part of a good night's sleep, then enjoy a good breakfast, a beach walk, and a swim prior to hoisting the anchor and continuing on to Anguilla or another island.

It should be noted that after all the discussion about the rough conditions in Anegada Passage, it is not always that way. In November 1977, *Iolaire* broad-reached across the passage from the Virgin Islands with the spinnaker before a light southwesterly. Similarly, many years ago, the late Bill Taylor, editor of *Yachting*, went south to sail with friends across Anegada Passage, about which he had heard horrendous tales all his life. He was most disappointed to have to motorsail across in light airs!

TO ANTIGUA

From Anguilla to St. Martin or St. Barthélemy (St. Barts) is only a day's sail, albeit upwind. A decision is required here. Sometimes it is a hard slog from St. Martin to Antigua (the wind usually swings from east-northeast to southeast just prior to Antigua Sailing Week, giving everyone a tough slog to windward). However, sometimes you can be lucky, and the wind will swing to northeast or east-northeast, which allows an eased-sheet reach from St. Barts to Antigua. This happened to us in 1990, when we were en route to Antigua. The wind swung around to the northeast, giving us a close reach. We made our first tack only when we entered Falmouth Harbour (12 hours from St. Barts to Falmouth—it happens only once in a while!).

If it looks like you will have heavy going to get to Antigua, you can ease the sheets for a pleasant reach down to the St. Eustatius (Statia)—St. Kitts—Nevis area. The latter route would require no more than a day. From Nevis to Antigua is an arduous 50 miles dead on the wind. Here the easy alternative is to stand southeast on port tack and sail 70 miles to Guadeloupe. This way, you can spend a few days cruising Guadeloupe and Iles des Saintes before heading north to Antigua by any of three ways: (1) close-hauled from Deshaies; (2) from Pointe-à-Pitre via the Rivière Salée; or (3) to English Harbour on a glorious broad reach from the eastern tip of the island, having worked your way to there in easy stages.

If you decide to sail from St. Barts direct to Antigua, stand southeastward on port tack hard on the wind. Stay north of the rhumb line between St. Barts and St. Johns, Antigua, since the current should be less and the water smoother within the partial lee created by Antigua and Barbuda. Do not sag south of the rhumb line from St. Martin to St. Barts to the southwest corner of Antigua. If you do, tack to the northeast to stay above the rhumb line.

SOUTH FROM ANTIGUA

With the wind well in the north, it is possible to pass to windward of Guadeloupe heading south from English Harbour. But this course is likely to produce either a long beat or a hard-on-the-wind port-tack fetch until you pass between Désirade and the eastern end of Guadeloupe. A better plan is to sail around the corner eastward from English Harbour to Green Island, spend a few pleasant hours snorkeling, having a huge continental lunch, and taking a nap, and then take off while the sun is still high enough for spotting the reefs. This should put you at the eastern end of Guadeloupe at dawn. Once around the corner, you'll find it easy to slide to Petite Terre, Marie-Galante, and Pointe-à-Pitre, the windward half of Guadeloupe that is seldom visited by yachtsmen.

If, however, you decide to pass to leeward of Guadeloupe, it usually is a fast, easy reach from English Harbour to Deshaies. But unless you plan your departure to reach Deshaies by noon, there is little or no chance of sailing through the lee of Guadeloupe without the aid of a motor, since the wind usually goes down with the sun, leaving you in the dark a few miles short of Basse Terre. And from Deshaies to the new marina south of Basse Terre, there is no good anchorage on the lee coast of Guadeloupe.

You should remember that there usually is no wind at dawn or dusk on the lee side of any high island. The wind picks up between 1000 and noon, then it dies between 1600 and 1700. During the night, in the lee of the islands, there probably will be a flat calm or a light offshore breeze, with occasional hard gusts as cold air falls down off the mountainside.

Nineteenth-century sailing directions recommend passing to leeward of the islands either seven leagues off (21 miles) or with a distance of two pistol shots. (British naval historian Dudley Pope states that a pistol-shot distance is 25 yards.) Fifty yards offshore is a little close, perhaps, but it does give the right idea.

The wind will hook around the ends of the islands—i.e., it will blow southeast at the southern end of an island and northeast at the northern end. Wind in the lee of an island frequently will alter without warning from east to west to produce instant tack: Hold your course and you are suddenly aback. For this reason, if your boat has a double-headsail rig, you should disconnect the staysail stay to allow quick tacking of the jib or genoa. Furthermore, if you switch up from working headsails to a bigger jib in the lee of an island, go with the number 2 or 3 genoa. The wind may be light, but hard squalls strong enough to shred a lightweight drifter can blast down through the valleys.

If you draw six feet or less, a third method of reaching Guadeloupe is to leave the English Harbour/Falmouth area at dawn and head south on a rhumb-line course of 175° magnetic (but allow for a set of 8° to 15°, depending on your speed, leeway, and the strength of the current). It's 40 miles to the northern entrance of Grand Cul-de-Sac Marin. Make sure you arrive at Passe à Colas by 1500, follow the marked channel (see chart in the Guadeloupe chapter), head south to Rivière Salée, pass through the river, and anchor just north of the bridge, which opens at 0530. Then you have only one mile to sail to Pointe-à-Pitre.

It is six miles from Passe à Colas to the anchorage off the bridge—an hour to one-and-a-half hours under sail and power—so leave Antigua at dawn! If you are going to arrive late at Passe à Colas, better anchor off Port Louis for the night. The next day, sail through Passe à Colas and spend the day exploring and enjoying the excellent diving in Grand Cul-de-Sac Marin. Then pass south through the river late in the afternoon, anchor for the night, and pass through the bridge at dawn.

SOUTH FROM GUADELOUPE

The normal first stop after Guadeloupe is Iles des Saintes, which can be a good, hard beat to windward from the lee side of Guadeloupe. To experience the least wind and the least sea, start early in the day, as the wind funnels between the Saintes and the southern end of Guadeloupe, building up during the day and dying off in the late afternoon.

From the Saintes, if the wind is in the north and you do not want to battle light airs or motorsail under the lee of Dominica, you would be well advised to stand north on starboard tack until you can tack to pass to windward of Dominica. Run down the east coast of Dominica, then ease off to leeward of Martinique and on to Fort de France. Passing to windward of Martinique is not worthwhile unless you are continuing straight down the chain to St. Vincent or Grenada, since there is only one port of entry—La Trinité—on the windward side of Martinique. La Trinité is not much of a harbor, and, in any case, has no facilities for yachts. From there around Presqu'île de la Caravelle is a hard beat against a short, steep sea and foul current. Better to head for the east coast of Martinique, to enter at Fort de France, and then to work your way around the south and east corners of the island in easy stages.

Proceeding North

MARTINIQUE TO DOMINICA OR GUADELOUPE

I prefer to head north from the east coast of Martinique after gunkholing around that interesting cruising ground. Take off from Tartane, clearing Presqu'île de la Caravelle, and lay a course for Scotts Head, Dominica, 45 miles away on a broad reach. If you wish to bypass Dominica, steer 010° magnetic for the light on Petite Terre southeast of Guadeloupe—a magnificent reach all the way.

If you decide to sail up the west coast of Martinique, don't start out before 1000, since there is no wind before then. With any luck, you will pick up a light breeze along the coast before clearing the lee of the island and setting out for Scotts Head. From Scotts Head to Roseau, it usually is flat calm—but not always. I once arrived in Roseau with rail down under headsails and storm trysail.

DOMINICA TO GUADELOUPE

From Roseau to Prince Rupert Bay is a picturesque daysail, leaving Roseau late in the morning. There should be enough wind after 1000 for a high-performance boat; a motorsailer probably would have to use the engine. It is a short distance from Portsmouth to Iles des Saintes—a passage that can be made easily in an afternoon. The entrance to the Saintes from the south is fairly straightforward.

North from the Saintes, your choice of route will be influenced by the amount of time on your hands. If you want to cross Guadeloupe via the Rivière Salée, the best plan is to leave the Saintes and sail up to Pointe-à-Pitre, arriving early enough to anchor and resupply from the excellent shops there. Continue on to anchor south of the bridge in order to pass through at dawn. (Detailed information on bridge opening hours appears in chapter 8.)

In the morning, it is six miles to the sea buoy at Passe à Colas, then a 40-mile rhumb-line run on course 355° magnetic (but allow 8° to 15° for current and leeway) to the English Harbour/Falmouth area. With luck, this should be an easy reach.) If you have more time in Guadeloupe, you can work your way along the south coast to Petit Havre or Saint François.

Otherwise, you can sail or motorsail up the lee coast of Guadeloupe to Anse à la Barque or Anse Deshaies, before continuing north to Antigua. On the way to Antigua, be sure to take repeated stern bearings, since the current is variable but in general will be on the weather bow as you head north. You also will be hard on the wind. Be sure to leave Deshaies in time to make English Harbour no later than 1600. Should fluky winds put you outside English Harbour at dusk, you will have great difficulty making your way into the anchorage. (And, as I have said so many times, do not enter strange harbors at night.)

From Petite Terre, it is a beautiful long, easy reach to English Harbour, distance 62 miles. But again, you must depart early enough to arrive at English Harbour in daylight, which may be almost impossible in a small boat unless you are flying a spinnaker.

ANTIGUA TO BARBUDA

If you want to visit this island from English Harbour, one plan is to beat around to Green Island and spend the night there or at Nonsuch Bay (an excellent anchorage when Green Island is glutted with charter boats). Leave early the next morning, timing your arrival in Barbuda, 30 miles away, for no later than 1400. You will need to do a tremendous amount of eyeball navigation while you are still well offshore from Barbuda, and this is best done when the sun is overhead.

Alternatively, you can sail westabout, visiting the excellent beaches on Antigua's west coast, and take off for Barbuda from Dickenson Bay, or continue on to the incomparable Parham and North Sound area, explore, buy supplies at the conveniently located Crabbs Marina, then jump off for Barbuda. (See chapter 6 for detailed sailing instructions for Antigua waters. Study them carefully the evening before you sail and then review them again in the morning.)

ANTIGUA WESTWARD

From Antigua, you are in a position to lay just about any island passage. You can set a course southward to Montserrat or slightly north of west to Nevis and on to St. Kitts, Statia, St. Barts, or St. Martin—all easy jumps from one island to the next. One word of warning, however, about night passages between the St. Barts—St. Martin—Anguilla area and Virgin Gorda. The current sets strongly to the northwest through here—at times as much as two knots. A number of yachts and commercial vessels bound from this area for Virgin Gorda or Round Rock Passage have received the surprises of their lives on Horse Shoe Reef. My advice to yachts making an overnight passage to the Virgins from St. Barts or St. Martin is to allow for a 10-mile northerly set. If you don't get the northerly set, there will be no problem. At dawn, you can head up to the Virgins. It may not be the fastest passage, but it will be the safest one—and, as the saying goes, it's better to be safe than sorry!

A light has been established on Pajaros Point, on the eastern end of Virgin Gorda—white flashing, once every 15 seconds, visible 16 miles from 294°

magnetic clockwise to 250° magnetic. It is obscured in the other sector by the high land of Virgin Gorda.

Be aware, however, that you cannot always rely on lights in the Eastern Caribbean. In November 1991, *Iolaire* was approaching the British Virgins direct from Venezuela, and we discovered that Ginger Island, Salt Island, and Pajaros Point lights were ALL OUT! When we went ashore and reported that the lights were out, the ensuing argument centered on whether they had been out for two, three, or four weeks! When one considers the amount of money that the British Virgin Islands government makes from the yachting trade, it seems entirely appropriate that they should at least keep the essential navigational lights functioning. The local power company is far more reliable than the marine department—there are very bright streetlights on the road that leads over the ridge to Virgin Gorda, and on a clear night they are visible 25 or more miles out to sea. (Again, despite what the RCC Lesser Antilles guide says, the lights in the Lesser Antilles—especially in the British and ex-British islands—are not reliable!)

Anegada and Horse Shoe Reef have nailed more than 400 vessels in the last couple of centuries, and in recent times they have nailed about three boats a year. It seems that despite a light on Anegada, the ship wreckers and salvors won't be unemployed. The current changes erratically from day to day, and there is no telling which way it will be running until you get out there. Therefore, in years gone by I preferred to leave Anguilla or St. Martin in the evening and lay a course midway between St. Croix and St. Thomas. Both of these islands usually would be visible by dawn. at which time I could alter course accordingly.

Nowadays, however, Pajaros Point (the easternmost point of Virgin Gorda) has a 16-mile light. The lights on the road leading over the hill from Gun Creek to Little Dix Bay are so high and bright that they usually are visible 25 to 30 miles away, as long as there is no rain squall to obscure them. Thus, when heading westward across Anegada Passage, I now set a course for Round Rock and allow for the current, figuring that if I am set too far north, I will see the lights of Virgin Gorda or Pajaros Point before I hit Horse Shoe Reef!

The loom of St. Croix can also be seen frequently, useful for rough bearings. The light on Salt Island is useless from this direction, as it is obscured by high land to the east and south of it. The Ginger Island light, flashing white every five seconds, is visible for 14 miles. Once you pick up that light (presuming it is in working order), you are set to swing into Sir Francis Drake Channel through any of the passages. The best one, in my opinion, is Round Rock Passage, which is wide and unencumbered by shoals. From there, it is a reach to Road Town, or a glorious smooth-water run, wing-and-wing, down through the Sir Francis Drake Channel, Pillsbury Sound, and on to St. John (Cruz Bay) or St. Thomas to enter. (Remember that it is much easier to enter in Cruz Bay than in St. Thomas.)

Another problem to be aware of is that if you head west from Anguilla or St. Martin, you usually will be dead before the wind. I have seen boats rolling and slatting endlessly, their jibs alternately filling and collapsing, their mains threatening to jibe, the sun directly overhead frying the crew's brains out. Don't do it this way. Instead, wing the jib on a whisker or spinnaker pole, guy the main boom forward, come down hard on the boom vang, and rig a cockpit awning that can be left up under sail. Then open a beer. Life will be a dream.

NOTES

2

Anguilla

(Imray-Iolaire Charts A, A-24, A-3)

Anguilla is a British colony 70 miles east of Virgin Gorda. It is low and flat, and thereby totally different from its towering neighbors, St. Martin/Sint Maarten, St. Barthélemy, and Saba. Long and narrow, the island takes its name from the Spanish word for "eel." Its highest elevation is 200 feet, which earns it very little rainfall. Nor does it have the mosquito- and fly-infested swamps that are found on the high, lush islands to the south.

Anguilla has even suffered such severe drought conditions that people almost starved to death in the late 1890s. In modern times, however, some bright geologist realized that wells could be drilled to obtain groundwater and free the islanders from their dependence on rainwater. We discovered this in 1992, when we saw fairly large water mains crisscrossing the island. Several pumping stations now supply Anguillans with a large quantity of piped water.

Many West Indian schooners have their homeports in Anguilla, where primary sources of income have long been shipping and salt. The salt from the island's salt ponds is shipped to the Grenadines for curing fish. The Anguillans enjoy an excellent reputation as sailors, making this one of the best islands in the Caribbean for finding competent native crew. The Anguillan schooners were the last of the northern island schooners to take down their topmasts and install engines.

As recently as the early 1960s, I can remember seeing a commercial cargo schooner coming into St. Thomas Harbor in the early morning light airs, flying the main topsail and the fisherman staysail. The boats were stopping at St. Thomas while en route from San Juan to Anguilla.

Anguillans have always been an independent lot. For decades they chafed under the government of

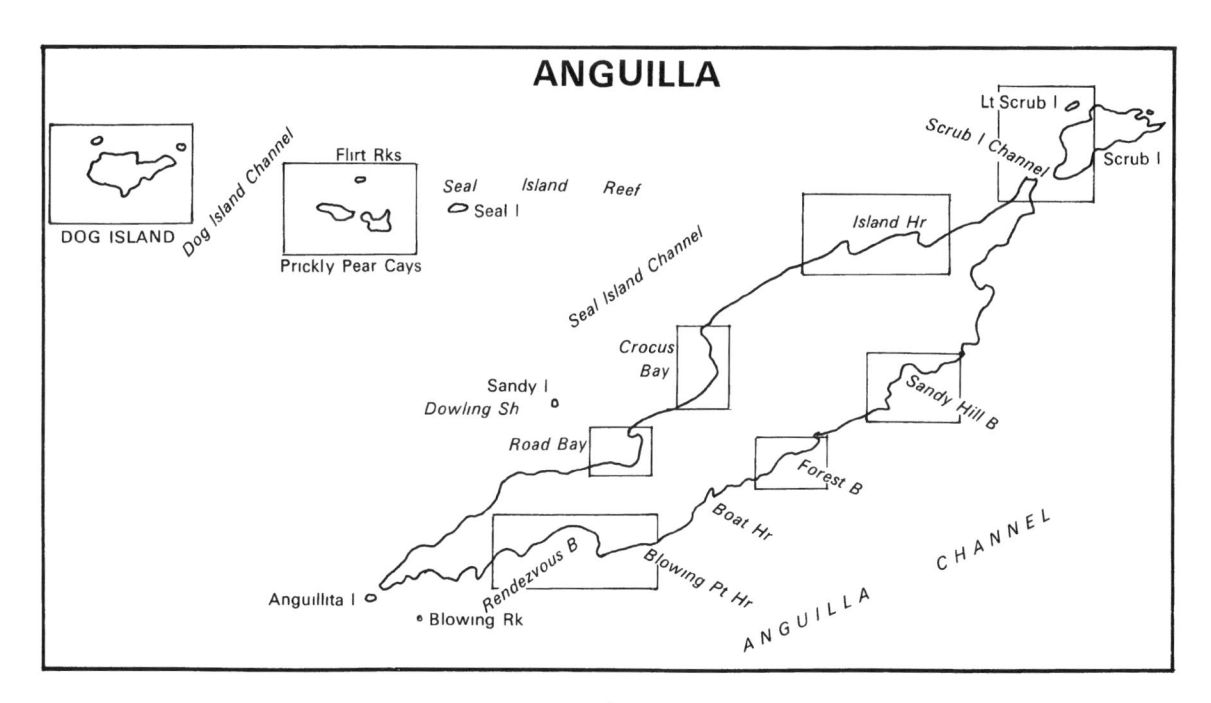

St. Kitts, which they finally chased off the island in 1969. The reverberations of this action spread throughout the world, and the insurgents were compared to Fidel Castro, the "villain" of the Caribbean. At tremendous expense, the British mounted an invasion of Anguilla, complete with warships, strike force, and parachutes. Most of the equipment was dropped from aircraft using highly sophisticated electronic gear. But the location of Anguilla had been mischarted by a couple of miles, and the expeditionary equipment fell into the sea. The British Foreign Office was not amused, and the affair dragged on far too long. A tremendous amount of money was wasted that could have been put to much better use in the construction of a saltwater distillation plant, in extending the airport runway, in building more docks, or in surveying the harbors.

Up to his dying day in 1978, Robert Bradshaw, the former premier of St. Kitts, claimed that Anguilla was still part of St. Kitts-Nevis, and that he was going to reassert his authority over the island. Evidently the British bribed him not to do so—they lent him the money to build an impressive jet strip in St. Kitts, an island that had absolutely no need for such a useless extravagance. Many people regard this as a prime example of the misguided British Foreign Office aid program in the Eastern Caribbean.

In his desire to assert his authority over Anguilla, Bradshaw was supported by other premiers of the British associated states. Almost all of the island governments are worried about the fragmentation of their nations by islands or groups of people wishing to break off on their own—a not-unwarranted fear given the nationalistic fervor rampant these days throughout the world.

Bradshaw was a colorful, controversial figure. Zane Mann's comments on him in his book *Fair Winds and Far Places* are short, brief, and pointed. For background on Bradshaw and the St. Kitts—Anguilla affair, I recommend *Under an English Heaven* by Donald E. Westlake, a book that should be read by everyone cruising the Caribbean.

For many years after the invasion of Anguilla, the police force was augmented by bobbies imported from London. The Anguillans are basically so law-abiding that the bobbies had little to do except go fishing, play cricket (a game the locals know well), and introduce the Anguillans to the finer points of soccer. Needless to say, the Londoners had a wonderful time. The Anguillans in turn enjoyed them, and the bobbies became such heroes that now in Anguilla, instead of the West Indian accent, you often will hear a Cockney accent that is so broad as to be incomprehensible to anyone but a Londoner.

The police force was run firmly and efficiently by a Major Roberts, who was originally from St. Kitts. He had spent many years in British Guiana—a tough training ground—and then served a short time in Grenada as police commissioner. He left Grenada rather suddenly, having had a difference of opinion (not an uncommon occurrence) with Premier E.M. Gairy.

Besides being firm and efficient, Major Roberts was blessed with common sense. On one of my visits to Anguilla, everyone was worried that an airplane bearing a huge quantity of paper and plastic cups was not going to arrive. I could not figure out the reason for shipping such a large quantity of these supplies until it was explained to me that a big three-day fête was about to begin and that the law of the island insisted that all drinks had to be served in paper or plastic cups—no bottles were allowed to cross the bar. Apparently in the old days at a big fête, there would always be a few big fights. Someone would hit someone else over the head with a bottle, considerable damage would be done, and police would have to arrest the combatants. The court would then have to try them for being drunk and disorderly, causing bodily harm, assault with a deadly weapon, etc. This kept the police busy, filled the jails, and tied up the courts.

So Major Roberts enacted the paper-cup law. The fêtes continue and drunks still get in arguments, but the fights now are settled with fists and usually result only in minor damage to the combatants. Even if the police have to be called in, it generally means only a night in the cooler, a fine, and release the next morning. Needless to say, this has considerably reduced the backlog in the courts.

Until recently, cars were left with the keys inside, and houses seldom were locked. When queried about this, a taxi driver replied, "Major Roberts is in charge, and no one wants to get up on the carpet before Major Roberts." Would that a few other islands in the Caribbean had as fair, tough, and efficient a police commissioner as Major Roberts.

The twentieth century has arrived in Anguilla, however, and the islands have been having a few more problems than Major Roberts and his force can handle. In the late 1980s, people began to realize, rightly or wrongly, that the island was ripe for development. Anguilla has no income tax, no corporate tax, and no inheritance tax, so money has poured in and been invested in numerous hotels, some exclusive private homes, and offshore banking enterprises. Also, day-trippers now come over from

St. Martin on fast ferries, and there are daysailing catamarans and visiting charter yachts.

Investment is booming here—but it is a very mixed blessing. Tax-free holidays are one thing, but one wonders how much of this money is just being laundered by the drug syndicates.

The problem of drug smuggling in Anguilla has raised its ugly head to the extent that a number of British policemen have been assigned to the Anguillan force to attempt to keep the situation from getting out of hand, as has happened in so many of the other islands. In most of the islands where the drug problem is out of control, the population is so small that everyone is related to everyone else. Who wants to arrest his brother, uncle, or first cousin? It's hard to say whether the addition of a few British policemen and a fancy patrol boat will really halt the drug smuggling. Perhaps it's time for the British to send out the super-secret Special Air Services (SAS) for some tropical maneuvers! The arrival of those rough-and-tough fellows would be guaranteed to scare the living daylights out of the few local dealers and convince them that the pickings are easier and better somewhere else.

One good reason to visit Anguilla is to watch the workboats race on the big holidays (usually the long weekends such as Easter Monday, Whitsun Monday, August Monday, and Boxing Day). Anguilla's small-boat racing is racing with a difference: The boats are local fishing sloops that are kept strictly for racing. Although they are operated in a fashion similar to the Saintes boats of Guadeloupe, they are quite different. Both designs have a hollow wineglass section amidships, but the flare of the topsides of the Saintes boats is much more pronounced than that of the Anguillan boats, which are slab-sided forward, making them much wetter when going to windward in a head sea. The rigs are similar, a leg-o'-mutton main and genoa jib. The sailing technique is the same for both types—pile everyone out on the weather rail, trim her flat, and have one small boy in the bilge bailing like mad.

The Anguillan boats are divided into three classes: class A, 26 feet 6 inches; class B, 22 feet; class C, 17 feet. As of April 1992, there were 17 boats in class A, 12 in class B, and 10 in class C. The only limitation is the length overall (LOA), so beam, draft, sail area, and construction technique are up for grabs, and the sky's the limit! The newest boats are so beautifully constructed that from 10 feet away you would swear that they were fiberglass—not plank-on-frame, epoxy-painted.

It would be most interesting to see what would happen if Anguilla's class B boats were raced against the boats from the French islands, which are about the same LOA but of a completely different design.

It is also worth noting that Anguillan racing is different from the racing in the French islands. In the latter, the boats are sponsored, but they only race for trophies. In Anguilla, some of the boats are sponsored but most are privately owned. (Apparently, owning a racing boat—or, even better, two—is more than a bit of a status symbol.) The Anguillan boats, however, race only for cash prizes. If the prize isn't big enough, only a few boats will compete. If there is a large "pot," everyone takes part! Cash-prize racing is a dubious blessing.

Anguillan racing rules stipulate that instead of starting on a line, the boats are set up on the beach facing dead downwind, fully rigged and fully crewed. At the gun, the boats are shoved from the beach and run dead downwind to a mark at the leeward end of Road Bay, where they often round in a tight bunch. After the beat home, the winner is the boat that picks a flag out of a dinghy moored off the beach, gets it ashore, and presents it to the race committee. With fierce competition and tough seamen—frequently well lubricated with good rum—a tight finish can produce plenty of excitement well worth watching.

So much for Anguilla's small-boat racing—don't miss an opportunity to see it.

Anguilla and the surrounding islands are known for their fine harbors and anchorages. A wind in the southeast favors the harbors on the north side of the island, and, conversely, a north wind favors the harbors on the south side. If a really big northwest ground swell makes up, though, many of the harbors become untenable, even on the south side of the island.

Anguilla and its offlying islands, being low and relatively unlighted, have brought many boats to grief. Particularly if you are coming from the north, Anguilla will be backed by the highlands of St. Martin in such a way as to make true distances difficult to judge.

In years gone by, it was alleged that the inhabitants of Anguilla supported themselves by being shipwreckers. This I can well believe, as in late 1985 or early 1986 they established a light on the eastern end of Anguilla, announced the existence of the light to no one, and installed it in such a position that it is a perfect booby trap for the unsuspecting yachtsman. We found out the hard way—we came within a hairbreadth of losing *Iolaire* on the first day of her eightieth-birthday transatlantic cruise!

We were heading north from St. Barthélemy, en route to Bermuda, passing east of St. Martin and

Anguilla. We picked up a light flashing once every 10 seconds and assumed it was on the eastern end of Scrub Island. (Hank Strauss of *Doki* points out that you assume nothing at sea—unless you see an aircraft carrier proceeding up the channel ahead of you, which should indicate there might be enough water for a yacht.) We set our course accordingly, to pass well to the east of the light.

I had just gone below to put my head down when my crew suddenly cried out, "The light's gone out, and I see land and breakers close aboard on the port bow!" I flew up on deck and we trimmed sheets, barely clearing the reefs off the eastern end of Scrub; then the light reappeared.

The light was on the end of Anguilla, marking the channel between Anguilla and Scrub—a mile to leeward of where we assumed the light would be located. It marked a channel that one thinks about using in daylight; not even a madman would attempt it at night.

When I contacted the British Admiralty, they knew nothing about this light, and only after they wrote the government of Anguilla did that government admit the existence of the light. Even then, they gave it a different light characteristic than we saw when we almost lost *Iolaire*.

The Admiralty continued to write letters to the Anguillan government, and so did I, to attempt to ascertain when the light was set up, who recommended its location, and who paid for it. Finally, in early October 1986, I received a letter from the harbormaster in Anguilla, who admitted that the light had been established in early 1984—but no one had been informed.

Then, in April 1987, when we were approaching Anguilla from the northwest, we spotted a quick-flashing white light on Dog Island. So I wrote to the harbormaster and asked for details and characteristics of that light. A few months later, I received a note saying that to the best of his knowledge, there was no quick-flashing light on Dog Island. Then he added that he had also discovered that the light on the eastern end of Anguilla had gone out, but no one seemed to know when enough money would be available to reestablish it. I would be willing to bet that he never informed the US Coast Guard or the British Admiralty about these changes!

In April 1992, when we were again in Anguilla, we were informed that the main leading light for the island had been out for at least 18 months! And so it goes—perhaps the Anguillans are getting back into the shipwrecking business that was so lucrative for their ancestors.

This saga should illustrate why I belabor the point that lights and buoys in the Eastern Caribbean should be regarded not as navigation aids but rather as booby traps to snag the unwary mariner and lead him ashore.

When approaching Anguilla from the southeast, there is no problem, since St. Barthélemy and St. Martin will be visible well before Anguilla, permitting the navigator to fix the position correctly. The same holds true out of the south and southwest.

The approach from the west and northwest, however, requires great care. Dog Island, eight miles northwest of Anguilla, is low-lying and surrounded by many hazardous reefs and shoals. Due east of Dog Island are Prickly Pear, Seal, and the Seal Island reefs—all of which would be impossible to spot at night. A light group flashing three every 20 seconds has been established at Road Point. This is a three-sector light, with two white sectors visible 10 miles; the red sector, covering the reef directly off Road Bay, is visible six miles away. The light is not visible from east-northeast (see Chart 1). The light at the western tip of Anguilla is visible for five miles.

Finally, don't even consider making a landfall at night from the north or northeast. I consider it unimaginable.

Passing from west to east around the southern end of Anguilla, I would not go between Anguillita Island and Anguilla. Although there is ample water, the wind and a very stiff current would be dead against you, making it a hard slog through a narrow passage. There is the additional hazard of a rock under three feet of water about 100 yards southwest of the tip of Anguilla. The submerged rock is about 50 yards northwest of the flat-topped rock shelf that bares about one foot at low water. Do not round up to head east until you are well to the west of the flat-topped rock shelf, or you will hit the submerged rock. In March 1984, we rounded up too soon and would have hit the rock dead center if it had not been for my ever-alert and eagle-eyed wife, Trich.

On the other hand, if you are coming from the east, running downwind, this passage should present no difficulty. Simply favor the Anguillita side of the channel and stand through.

North Coast of Anguilla

ROAD BAY

(Chart 1; II A-24, A-3)

Road Bay is well sheltered in all trade-wind weather. It is only exposed to the west wind, very uncommon in the Antilles. When a west wind does

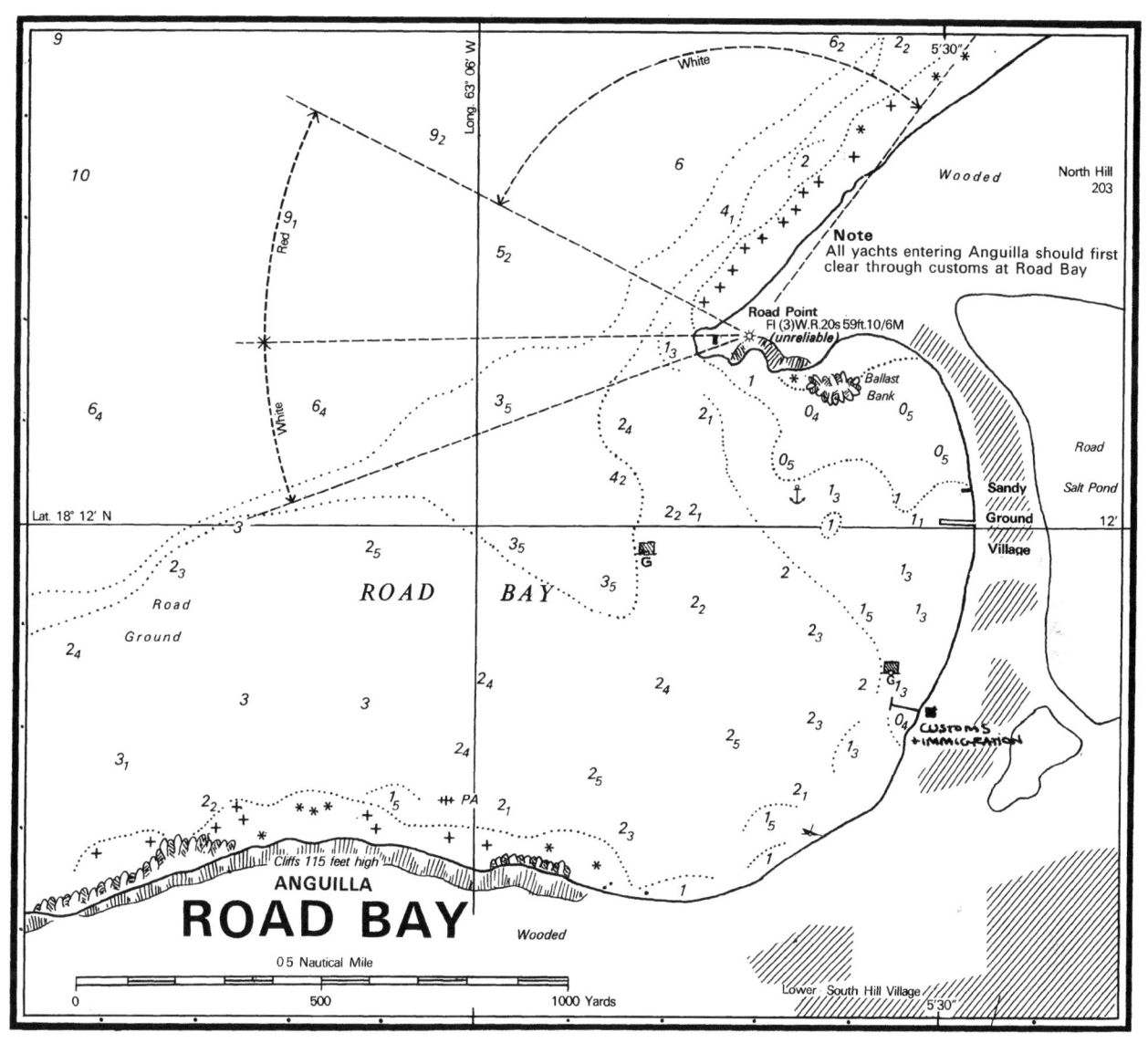

Chart 1 Road Bay   Depths in fathoms and feet

blow, it may be time to move anchorage to the east coast of St. Martin. Seal Island and its reefs afford the harbor some protection from the northerly ground swell.

Approaching Road Bay from the west, favor the Anguilla shore, since north-northwest of Road Bay are the twin dangers of Dowling Shoal and Sandy Island. Both are unmarked and unlighted, though easily seen by day. This is no place for a stranger at night.

For a number of years after Hurricane Klaus slammed through in late 1984, the harbor was littered with sunken freighters—some marked, some unmarked. Happily, all these hazards have now been moved (either by human hand or by God—i.e., Hurricane Hugo). I have been told by the harbor authorities that there are no longer any dangerous wrecks in Road Bay Harbour. Be sure to anchor clear of the buoyed channel that leads to the main commercial dock. There is ample depth in the main harbor, although for most yachts I would recommend the northeast corner to avoid the swell. Work your way in as close to shore as possible, anchor, and row ashore.

Land at the dinghy (north) dock, where you will find the Customs and Immigration office, which is open during normal working hours. You'll have a simple, cheerful entry, with no charge for visiting private yachts.

Charter yachts, however, are assessed a fee, and some people feel that in doing this, Anguilla is trying to kill the goose that laid the golden egg even before the goose has had a chance to lay it! Charter boats should check in St. Martin with other charter yachts, or the bareboat operations there, to see whether it is financially worth visiting Anguilla. (The fee tends to increase frequently, so there is no point in my specifying an amount here.)

When you go through entry formalities in Anguilla, they will hand you a map that shows where anchoring is prohibited. I urge that you assiduously respect their request for the use of specific anchorages. The main reason for the "no-go" areas is to protect the coral there. Too many yachts have tossed their anchors down onto the coral, and in a matter of minutes they have destroyed a century of coral construction work! The coral is then "dead," which ruins the sea for the reef fish as well as divers and snorkelers. Besides, the coral is very bad holding, and you are likely to drag. Perhaps the Anguillan authorities will establish special moorings—as has been done in Tortola in areas where yachtsmen are forbidden to anchor.

Most of the anchoring bans in Anguilla are understandable—except for Rendezvous Bay, where there is hardly any coral. The bay is big and beautiful, with a white-sand bottom—an ideal spot for anchoring. Perhaps the "no-go" label for this bay is related to the fact that one of the island's powerful politicians owns a hotel here. In addition, it may be true that in the past, visiting "yachtsmen" did not behave here like yachtsmen, but rather like "third-rate water people," and have given all yachtsmen a bad name. With luck, this situation will change, and yachtsmen will again be able to visit this wonderful bay.

Near the commercial dock is Tray's, a small supermarket that can supply the basic needs for a yachtsman, but it is no place for restocking. If you plan to buy eggs, be sure to take egg boxes to the store, as the local eggs—good and fresh—are sold individually and packed in plastic bags! The eggs are displayed in flat cardboard trays, but no matter how many eggs you buy, you cannot buy the tray. If you don't have a box, you may have to make a few quick omelets by the time you get back to your boat!

Lining the beach is a string of small bars and restaurants—too many to mention here. Stroll along, look over the menus, have a few beers, talk to proprietors and bartenders—then decide where you want to spend your time and money. There's a dive shop at the end of the beach.

At the north end of the beach is the fishermen's cooperative, where you might be able to buy block ice; otherwise, check with the local bars and restaurants to see who has the coldest bags of cube ice.

There are a number of small shops and boutiques along the beach and the road behind it. Some of them are located in nicely restored old West Indian buildings. The most attractive of all is the Gumbs House—the premier's house. This is not a government house, but rather a typical West Indian family dwelling. The first story is cut coral and the second story is wood, with balconies all around. The Gumbs family has been in the cargo schooner business for years, and the house has belonged to the family since its construction, probably in the middle of the nineteenth century.

Rental cars are available at reasonable rates. If you plan to stay on the island for more than a day, it is advisable to rent a car, as there are some well-stocked supermarkets beyond walking distance. Vista, an excellent supermarket, is located at the top of the hill by the traffic circle. There are two other good supermarkets in town, but none of the markets have good selections of fresh fruit and vegetables. It is best to buy those at the local produce market in The Valley. After you have run the requisite errands with the rental car, you can take time to explore the island.

West of Road Bay is a series of beaches backed by steep cliffs. These are within dinghy distance of the main harbor, and are secluded. With the wind in the southeast in calm summer weather, you can have a pleasant daytime anchorage off this shore. Under no circumstances should you use this area in the winter.

CROCUS BAY

(Chart 2; II A-24, A-3)

Crocus Bay once was one of Anguilla's main ports. It looks like it would be a rocky/rolly anchorage completely open to the ground swell, but the Prickly Pear and Seal Island reefs seem to break the worst of it. In past years, yachtsmen seldom visited this area, as it was the main fuel off-loading point for the island, and thus not very attractive. However, the oil storage tanks now have been moved to the south coast, so things are looking up. Roy's Place, an attractive English-style pub built here, serves draft British beer. Roy is an English ex—merchant seaman who has seen the world (including many islands) and decided to make Anguilla his home. He is always a font of information on the island. Food is available at reasonable prices, and you'll find good company and stories from all over the world.

When we visited Crocus Bay in 1992, it was amazingly calmer than Road Bay, and Roy assured us that it is seldom very rocky and rolly here. An

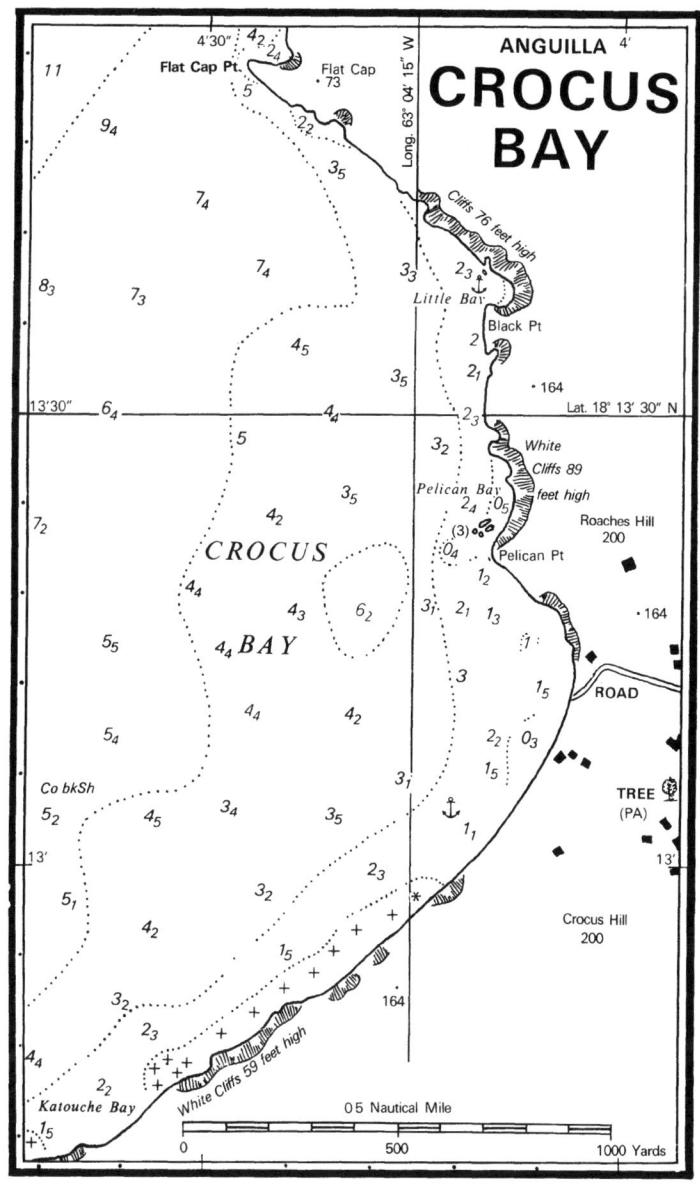

Chart 2 Crocus Bay   Depths in fathoms and feet

advantage of Crocus over Road Bay is that the taxi ride to The Valley is much shorter; a disadvantage is that you don't have as wide a selection of bars and restaurants.

On a cover of *Yachting* magazine some years ago was a photograph of Carleton Mitchell's trawler-yacht *Sans Terre*, anchored stern-to under the cliffs in an unnamed cove in Anguilla. This, of course, intrigued everyone, and many (myself included) looked vainly for Mitch's secret anchorage. Some time later, I visited him on board his boat in Antigua. Over drinks I offered to tell him of an anchorage he didn't know about (see Shoal Bay, below) in exchange for the secret of his anchorage. But, with a twinkle, Mitch refused the bait, explaining that if there really were still an anchorage in the Eastern Caribbean that I did not know of, he was happy to have some fun and let me continue searching.

Well, we had a drink on that, and it was not until the summer of 1978, sitting in Glandore Harbour, County Cork, Ireland, that I learned Mitch's secret. The charter yacht *Queen of Sheba* sailed into Glandore, and her owners, Mike and Jeannie Kuick, told me that after combing every inch of Anguilla, they had figured out that Mitch's anchorage was a cove under the cliffs a quarter of a mile south of Flat Cap Point (Chart 2). Apparently, at the same time that they were searching for this anchorage, Dr. Robin Tattersall was doing the same thing. He even had a copy of *Yachting* magazine to show to the Anguillans in hopes that that would help him identify the place. But even the locals couldn't figure out where the photograph had been taken. On his own, he finally reached the same conclusion as Mike and Jeannie.

They all report that it is an excellent anchorage, but with room for only one boat. You should bury an anchor in the sand on the beach and another anchor off the west, since the cliffs are so steep that the wind loops over the top and tends to drive a boat onshore. Furthermore, it is a tenable anchorage only when the normal trade winds are blowing and there is no ground swell.

North Coast East of Flat Cap Point

When the *Cruising Guide to the Lesser Antilles* was published in the fall of 1974, I made a standing bet that if anyone knew of an anchorage in the Lesser Antilles where a boat drawing six feet could be safely anchored, that was not mentioned in the book, I would pay for the evening's drinking. I have only been caught twice—only by Carleton Mitchell and once, amazingly enough, by the skipper of a 90-foot ketch: Hans Hoff of *Fandango*. He told me that the area east of Flat Cap Point, where the British and American charts show scattered coral heads and no soundings well offshore, is in fact an area of widely separated reefs with deep water in between.

One can stand in on starboard tack, keeping Shoal Point bearing approximately southeast and passing close aboard the windward reefs. Eyeballing it carefully, you can carry a full 12 feet, but it should be noted that southwest of this course depths range from nine feet down to seven feet. Alternatively, you can work your way eastward, pretty much paralleling the shore, eyeballing carefully to keep in deep water, watching for the offlying shoal mentioned above. The outer reefs serve as adequate protection, breaking most of the trade-wind sea and allowing you to anchor on white-sand bottom with good holding. But remember that you are anchoring in about 40 feet of water, so have plenty of line ready.

Furthermore, if you start to drag during the night, there is no hope of finding your way out of this spot, so it is essential to put down two heavy anchors. We found a good anchorage with Shoal Point bearing roughly due south magnetic. Be warned, however, that this whole part of Shoal Point is now covered with wall-to-wall hotels fronted by beach bars and snack bars.

An excellent beach stretching westward from Shoal Point and dropping off almost vertically to 30 feet of water provides supremely good snorkeling. There are plenty of small fish to look at, but nothing worth spearfishing—the outer reef probably provides excellent spearfishing.

SHOAL BAY

(Chart 3; II A-24, A-3)

Immediately east of Shoal Point, and practically up on the beach, the eyeball navigator can pick out a channel six feet deep (I advise using a sounding pole). This leads into Shoal Bay, with a pure white-sand bottom and depths of about six feet. It is completely clear of coral heads and is sheltered by the outer barrier reef. For the shoal-draft boat, this is a fantastic anchorage. As of March 1992, there still was little or no development along the shores of Shoal Bay—just miles of white-sand beach and no one anchored there. Warning, though: Shoal Bay is well named!

ISLAND HARBOUR

(Chart 3; II A-24, A-3)

This harbor appears to be completely exposed to the north. But because of the double row of reefs—referred to on the chart as Seven Stars Reef—it is well protected from the sea. Usually there is only a small chop in the harbor, and the wind sweeps in unobstructed by islands—to make it cool at all times of the year. Getting into Island Harbour is a problem, though, since I have never been able to discuss entrances to the harbor with any yachtsman who has entered, nor have I found a local Anguillan fishing skipper who knew the island well.

Apparently there is a gap in the reef bearing roughly 010° magnetic from Scilly Cay. And I have seen boats in the harbor drawing roughly five feet. So it must be possible to get in and out. *Einman's Guide to Anguilla, St. Martin, St. Barts, St. Kitts Area*, a newcomer in the cruising-guide field, has an excellent sketch chart of Island Harbour. However, having looked at Island Harbour from seaward, and talked to various people who knew the area, I feel that anyone entering Island Harbour without a local pilot is asking for trouble. That advice is reinforced by the fact that in April 1992, we were at the restau-

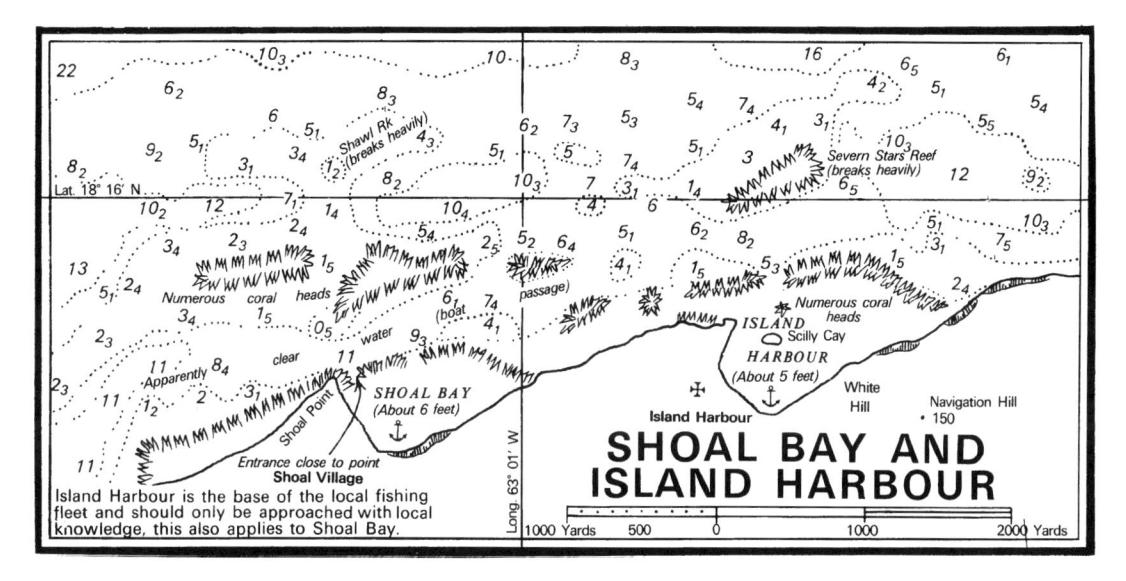

Chart 3 Shoal Bay and Island Harbour

Depths in fathoms and feet

rant overlooking the eastern end of the island and watched two or three local lobstermen threading their way cautiously through the reefs. This is definitely a small-boat harbor—maximum four-foot draft.

When you hire a local pilot in the Eastern Caribbean, it is essential to find one who really IS a pilot. There are a number of instances of boats hiring a "pilot" and then running hard aground. When the unfortunate mariner remembers to check the credentials of the "pilot," he discovers that the man is completely unqualified.

South Coast of Anguilla

COVE BAY

(Sketch Chart 4; A-24, A-3)

Shoal Bay and Maundays Bay, the two southernmost bays on the island, are not particularly good—exposed to the east and shallow. You would do better to proceed eastward to Cove Bay, where an anchorage can be had in the northeast corner of the bay in 1 1/2 fathoms. Keep your leadline working, since it is hard to judge the gradually shoaling depth of this bay, even though the water is crystal-clear. A lovely sand beach stretches for about three-fourths of a mile.

RENDEZVOUS BAY

(Sketch Chart 4; II A-24, A-3)

A beautiful, wide expanse, unencumbered by coral heads. The only danger is Shaddick Point, which extends much farther to the southwest than is shown on the chart. My favorite anchorage is in the northeast corner of the bay over a white-sand bottom. The only difficulty is a nonstop generator on shore that tends to interrupt the peace. Although anchoring has recently been prohibited here, it's possible that the ban will be rescinded by the time you arrive. Or perhaps they will install moorings, as has been done in the British Virgins and Bonaire. Inquire locally.

BLOWING POINT HARBOUR

(Sketch Chart 4; II A-24, A-3)

In the past, this was the major harbor for schooners loading and offloading cargo. The first time that I visited the harbor, *Endeavour*, a smuggler of great repute and undoubtedly the largest sloop ever built in the Lesser Antilles, lay here. She was built many years ago along the lines of a knockabout Gloucester fishing schooner, with overhanging bow, no bowsprit, no forefoot, low freeboard, fine rounded counter, and a carved wooden stern railing. She was sloop-rigged, with roughly an 80-foot boom—the largest and longest main boom I have ever seen. Moored in Blowing Point Harbour when I last saw her, she looked to be doing six knots just tied to her mooring buoy. She was said to be capable of 12 knots on a reach. Even allowing for gross exaggeration, she must have been very fast. But not fast enough to outrun the new Customs launches, which soon managed to put her out of business.

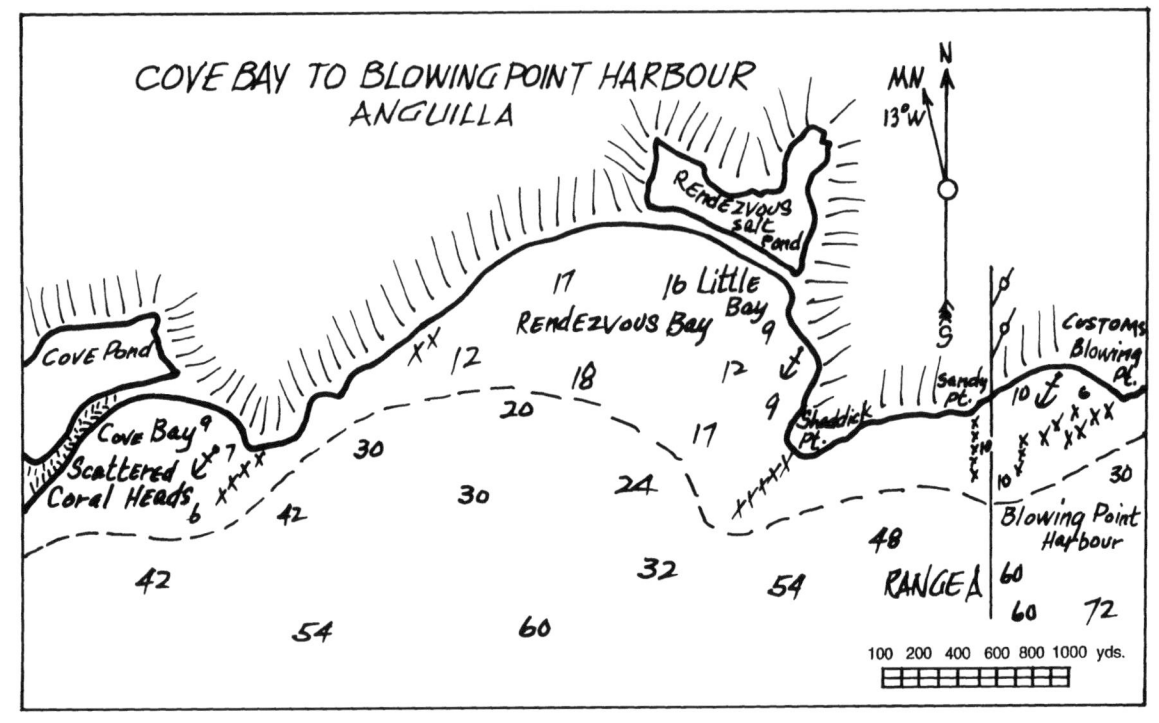

Sketch Chart 4 Cove Bay to Blowing Point Harbour

Depths in feet
Range A: Two white markers in line, 010° magnetic

Blowing Point Harbour is the homeport of the fast launches that connect St. Martin and Anguilla. In the old days, small boats chugged back and forth at six or seven knots, taking roughly an hour to do this run and delivering their passengers ashore wet, miserable, and seasick. Next came Hovercraft, which evidently were just too difficult and too expensive to maintain and did not stand the test of time. Then, a few years ago, a young Anguillan schoolteacher who was something of a boatbuilder (and who has turned out to be an excellent yacht designer) built two fast 40-foot launches with comfortable cabins, powered by two massive outboards. These vessels blast across the six-mile-wide channel in 15 minutes—that is an average speed of 24 knots, probably maximum of 30 or so knots. The launches are so fast that they guarantee you will not be seasick.

The boats are beautifully built by the WEST System epoxy method, and they appear to be superbly maintained. Since they are outboard-driven, they should not be plagued with the engine breakdowns that typically hamstring most high-speed ferry operations. With two ferries and four outboards, it is only a matter of an hour or so to switch to a spare motor when one begins to give trouble.

Development has mushroomed on St. Martin, and the interisland traffic has seen a corresponding expansion. The barrage of day-trippers to Anguilla has not just increased—it has boomed to the point where there is now a complete Customs and Immigration landing dock here. Ferries are constantly shuttling back and forth or are anchored out in Blowing Point Harbour. I strongly advise, therefore, that yachts NOT clear in this harbor. If you have to do so, send the skipper ashore to clear in the dinghy while the yacht circles the harbor. Do NOT attempt to anchor—there just is not enough room.

Entering Blowing Point Harbour is easy. From a distance, you can see all the power launches anchored there. Head for the western side. The range marks are no longer in place, but there is a 300-yard spit of coral that has been piled up by the current at Sandy Point. Keep the coral on the port side and there will be no problem—10 feet of water into the harbor, shoaling to six feet. Just don't plan to anchor.

BOAT (or LITTLE) HARBOUR

(II A-24, A-3)

This is too shoal- and reef-encumbered for the average yacht, but believe it or not, there is superb shelter. Having looked at it from the air and from the shore, I can state that there IS a channel leading into Boat Harbour (also known as Little Harbour). There is probably six or seven feet of water when you are inside, but the problem is how to get in. Further, once you are inside, there really is not much to do unless you like spending your money in very high-priced hotels—or you have a friend who owns one of the beautiful houses overlooking the harbor. The harbor has been completely developed, and there are now no secluded beaches.

FOREST BAY

(Sketch Chart 5; II A-24, A-3)

East of what is marked as Boat Harbour on the chart, Forest Bay formerly could be identified by a small Customs house and jetty. Today it can be identified by a small restaurant—The Customs House Restaurant, open only at night—and the fisherman's jetty, which they still use to land lobsters. If the wind is north of east, the harbor will be calm and clean. The reefs around the edges of the harbor provide good snorkeling.

Although this is the deepest harbor on the south coast of Anguilla, it is not very well protected and is difficult to enter. The reefs are not high enough to break the swell, which had tended to restrict its use to the larger Anguillan vessels. The channel is 10 feet deep on into the center of the harbor, but it is more tricky than it appears, and eyeball navigation is essential. Entrance is made from the southeast. Head in for the jetty on starboard tack until inside the reef, then bear off and anchor in the middle of the harbor. The private anchorage has room for only a few boats—the bottom shoals on both sides.

SANDY HILL BAY

(Sketch Chart 6; II A-24, A-3)

A first-rate anchorage well up the south coast of Anguilla. It can be spotted by the houses around the beach and by the small boats anchored in the western part of the harbor. This is not a port of entry. As you approach Sandy Hill Bay from the south, it may look as though there is not enough water all the way inside.

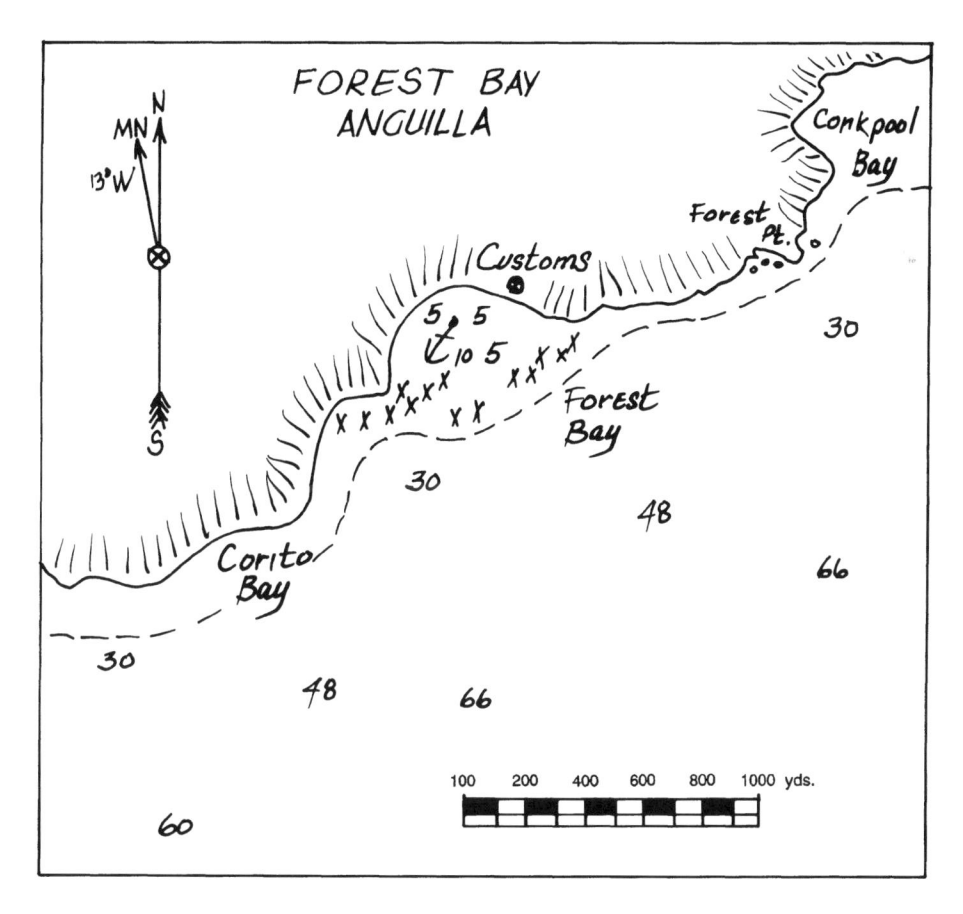

Sketch Chart 5   Forest Bay   Depths in feet

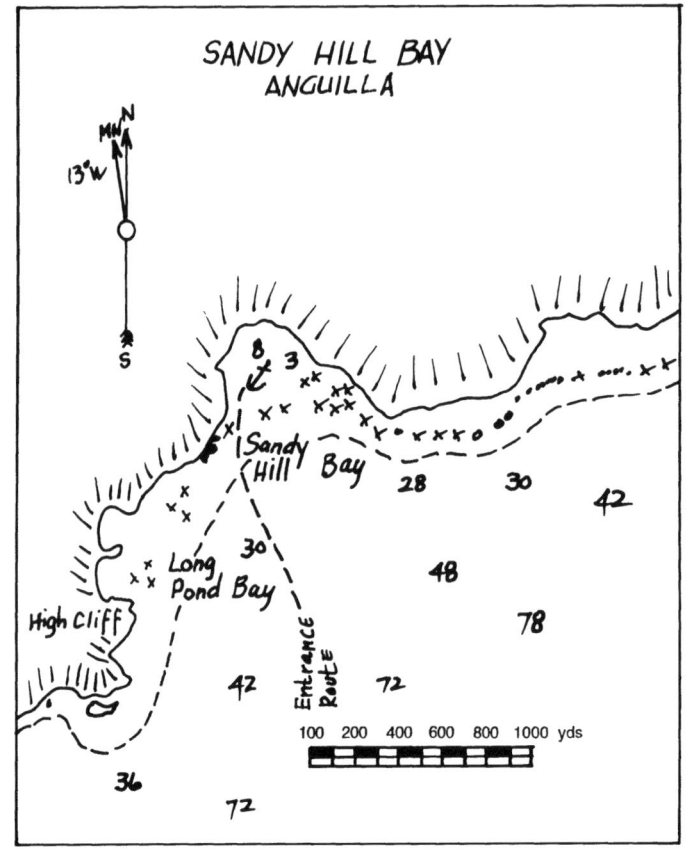

Sketch Chart 6   Sandy Hill Bay   Depths in feet

But as you will see from the chart, an anchorage can be reached within. Reefs extend from the eastern side of the harbor. West of these are three coral heads with about three feet of water over them. Pass to the east of the three coral heads and sail on into the bay, anchoring in about eight feet of water. The bay has a beautiful white-sand beach, which makes it a favorite picnic spot of the Anguillans.

In April 1992, my wife and I visited this bay via car, and we agreed that it is a beautiful harbor for swimming—it's understandable why it is so popular with Anguillans on weekends. There is also a considerable fleet of fishing boats, and one for sportfishermen—obviously a harbor for only a few yachts, so it is a good spot to get away from other yachts.

Caution: Some yachtsmen have warned me that this bay is very reef-encumbered and should be visited only by experienced eyeball navigators—and then only when the wind is north of east.

There are no harbors whatsoever on the south coast of Anguilla east of Sandy Hill Bay—only exposed bays and beaches. (See the discussion of lights on the east coast of Anguilla in the introduction to this chapter.)

Islands off the Coast of Anguilla

The islands off the coast of Anguilla provide opportunities for exploring, archaeology, wreck diving, beachcombing, and plain old lazing about. These areas are recommended for summer use, when the ground swell has subsided.

SCRUB ISLAND

(Sketch Chart 7; II A-24, A-3)
East of Anguilla, Scrub Island has a beautiful beach, which can be approached only during the summer months. The approach to the shore at Scrub Bay on the western side of the island is largely obstructed by coral and grass. However, in the middle of the bay, leading to the middle of the beach, there is a

narrow white-sand channel. Follow this channel toward the beach and anchor Bahamian style or bow-and-stern. The holding is good—no coral or grass to interfere with the proper set of your anchors.

On the eastern end of the island is Deadman's Bay, which is fully exposed and full of coral heads. I have flown over and seen campers inside, but there is no anchorage here, the only way of approaching it being by outboard-powered dinghy.

Jon Repke reported a few years ago, after flying over Scrub Island, that this once-deserted island was no longer deserted—an airstrip and a hotel had been built. However, a small hotel on an offshore island is always something of a gamble, and this one didn't make it, so the island is once again deserted—although it does have a crashed plane!

I have been reliably informed by the big Dutchman known universally as Willie that our Sketch

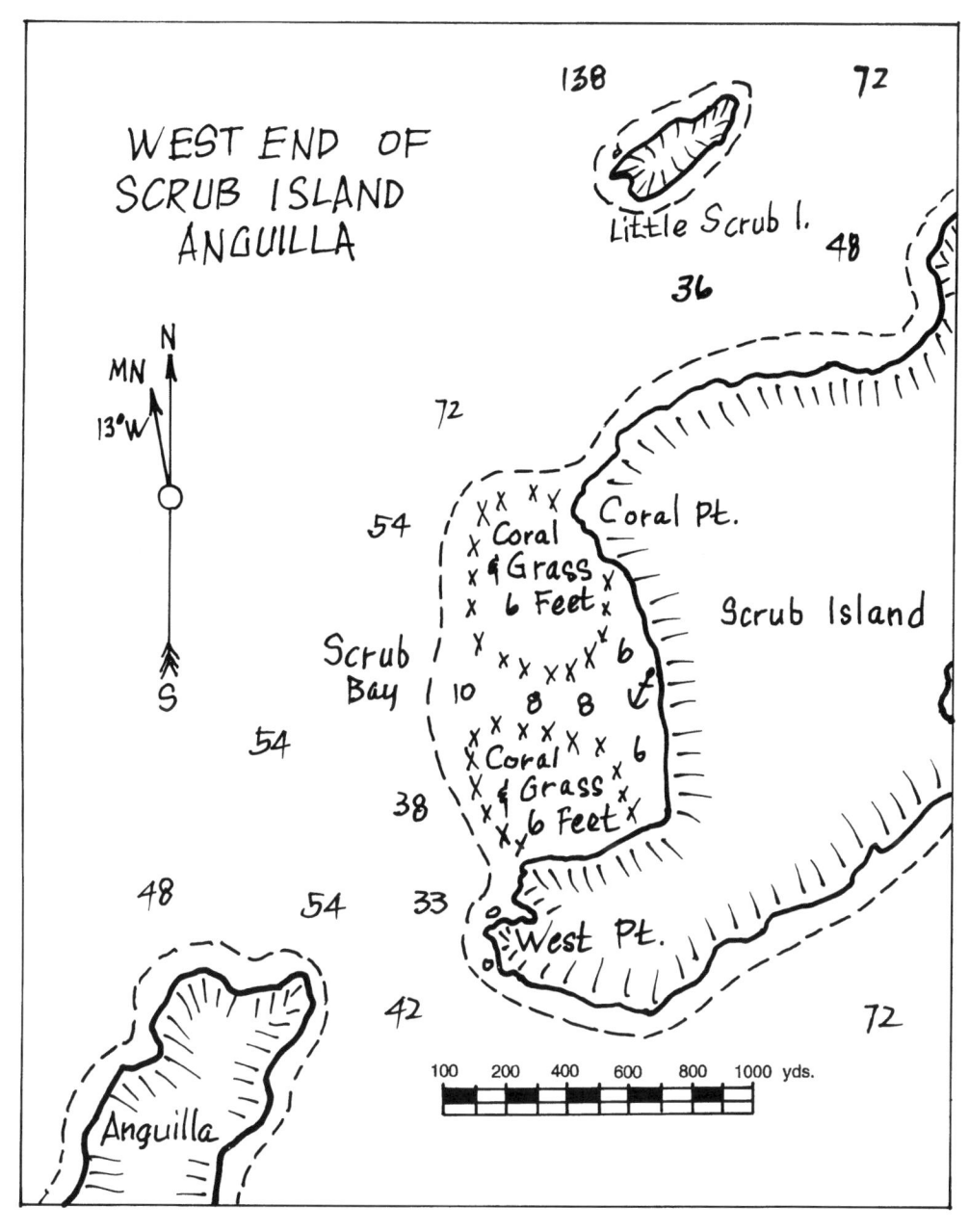

Sketch Chart 7 West End of Scrub Island Depths in feet
(According to Goran Karlssas of yacht *Akaia*, "The bottom is grass and sand, no coral, depth in the whole area 12 feet.")

Chart 7 is, in fact, correct—despite what other guides say about the holding here. You can anchor safely on the white-sand bottom in six to eight feet of water—provided, of course, that no ground swell is running. In any case, I would certainly moor bow-and-stem or on a Bahamian moor, as the ground swell can come up unannounced during the evening. Unfortunately this is all second hand information. Some people claim the information is not correct and others say it is correct. I can only say proceed with caution.

SANDY ISLAND

(II A-24, A-3)

Northwest of Road Bay, when it is not blowing too hard, there is a fine daytime anchorage along the shoal west of Sandy Island. Dowling Shoal to the northwest is a good area for swimming and snorkeling. For many years, this was one of those hard-to-find, idyllic, deserted tropical islands—a small sandspit under a few palm trees with a white-sand beach and crystal-clear water stretching all around.

The island is still idyllic, but it is no longer deserted, because a flood of day-trippers has resulted in a bar, beach chairs, and all the rest of the paraphernalia of "civilization." If you want to enjoy Sandy Island when it is peaceful and quiet, you have to arrive very early in the morning. I definitely advise against anchoring here overnight.

PRICKLY PEAR CAYS

(Chart 8; II A-24, A-3)

From the Prickly Pears eastward is a series of exposed reefs, small unnamed islands, and sandspits extending over a distance of seven miles. In settled weather, this is a fine area in which to anchor and swim. Only the Tobago Cays come near to rivaling them. Anchorages can be had almost anywhere behind the reef or in among the coral heads. (Even with the new BA chart 2047, don't go barging around without a careful lookout.) One of the most secluded anchorages lies northwest of the Salt Pond on Prickly Pear East (Chart 8). The everactive Dr. Tattersall has supplied information and sailing directions for getting into this snug but tricky spot. (He warned that I might have trouble getting *Iolaire* all the way in.)

According to the doctor, the best approach is from the southwest, sailing between Prickly Pear West

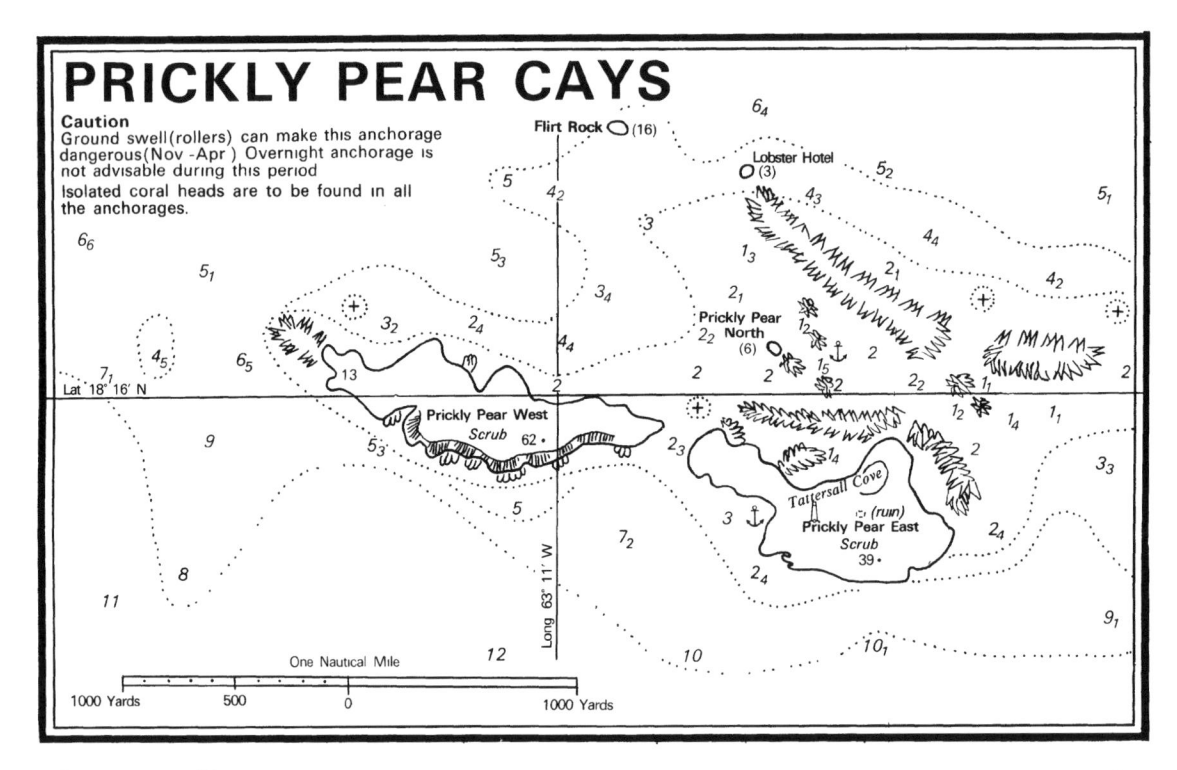

Chart 8 Prickly Pear Cays   Depths in fathoms and feet

and Prickly Pear East. There is 15 feet of water through the pass, shoaling to 12 feet north of it. (The BA chart is slightly inaccurate, since there are rocks north of the northernmost point of Prickly Pear East.) Sail northeast beyond Prickly Pear North, then tack south and head in toward a slightly rocky point shown on the first lump of the western end of Prickly Pear North on the British chart. When close in to that point, turn southeast and pass between the northern reef and the shore. Eight feet can be taken through this pass. Anchor between the inner and outer reefs. There's good shelter and calm-weather snorkeling directly from the boat—no need to moor the dinghy. Dr. Tattersall refers to this as the "outer anchorage."

If you are not very confident of eyeball navigation, the doctor advises anchoring in the bay in the southwest corner of the island. This is an excellent spot with good swimming and snorkeling. And you can walk across the island and inspect the north-side anchorage before trying to enter there.

The reefs northeast of Prickly Pear East give a large degree of shelter to everything south of Flirt Rock. A good, though rolly, anchorage can be had southwest of Prickly Pear North—white sand and good holding.

In periods of settled weather, it is possible to anchor out among the coral heads to the east of Prickly Pear East. The reef extends all the way to Seal Island. Dave Ferneding of *Whisper* reports that scuba divers can have a field day exploring the underwater caverns in Flirt Rock. (Both Dave and Chris Bowman of *Water Pearl of Bequia* have been extremely helpful in passing on to me the results of their explorations.)

Since the reefs are five miles away from Anguilla, they are not completely fished out, and there is a fairly good chance of obtaining fish and an occasional lobster.

For some reason, there is a landing strip on Prickly Pear West, but I have never seen it used.

Prickly Pear Cays is an extremely interesting area, but you need to be a good eyeball navigator and use common sense and extreme care when in this area.

As of April 1992, you were not allowed to anchor north of the Prickly Pear Cays because of all the coral, but I prefer to include all of the above information about the area in hopes that permanent moorings eventually will be established north of the Prickly Pears. Then, yachts will be able to go in, pick up a mooring, and snorkel or dive there without having to make a long dinghy or ferry trip.

The bight on the south side of Prickly Pear East is the usual anchorage now, and it should be good for anyone who wants to spend the night in the Prickly Pear Cays. During the day, catamarans loaded with day-trippers arrive, so a beach bar has been set up ashore for snacks and drinks. Come midafternoon, however, everyone departs, so yachtsmen who spend the night can be guaranteed peace and quiet. Plus there is always the quiet time in the morning before the day-tripping horde arrives.

SEAL ISLAND/SEAL ISLAND REEF

(II A, A-24)

From the air, it looks as though there are numerous anchorages in and around Seal Island, and especially Seal Island Reef. If the wind is in the north and the ground swell is not running, there appears to be a good anchorage due south of Seal Island. If the wind is in the east or south of east, this would not be a good anchorage, since the wind would be blowing parallel to shore or onshore. In the summer, when the wind is well around to the south, an anchorage probably can be found on the north side of Seal Island. In almost all conditions, the brave and skillful can tuck themselves right behind the two south-jutting fingers at the eastern end of Seal Island Reef and anchor within swimming distance of the snorkeling area. I certainly hope the Anguillan government will establish moorings in this area and thus open it up to divers, as a dinghy trip of seven miles takes most of the fun out of diving!

DOG ISLAND

(Sketch Chart 9; II A, A-24)

There are three anchorages along the west coast of Dog Island, and, even though the charts do not show it, there is ample water for yachts of normal draft to sail between Dog Island and West and Mid Cays.

Spring Bay, on the northwest corner of the island, has a sandy beach that is beautiful to look at but is hazardous for swimming, since it is all coral and loose rock from the water's edge down. This beach also boasts a prodigious crop of natural sponges. An old landing strip on the island is no longer used.

South of Spring Bay lies Baileys Cove—strictly a dinghy landing spot. The dinghy must be anchored bow-and-stern to keep it off the rocks. The snorkeling is superb, and I imagine the fishing is quite good.

If you continue sailing southeast, you will arrive at what I will categorically declare to be the finest beach in the Lesser Antilles—Great Bay. As long as the ground swell is not running and the wind is not

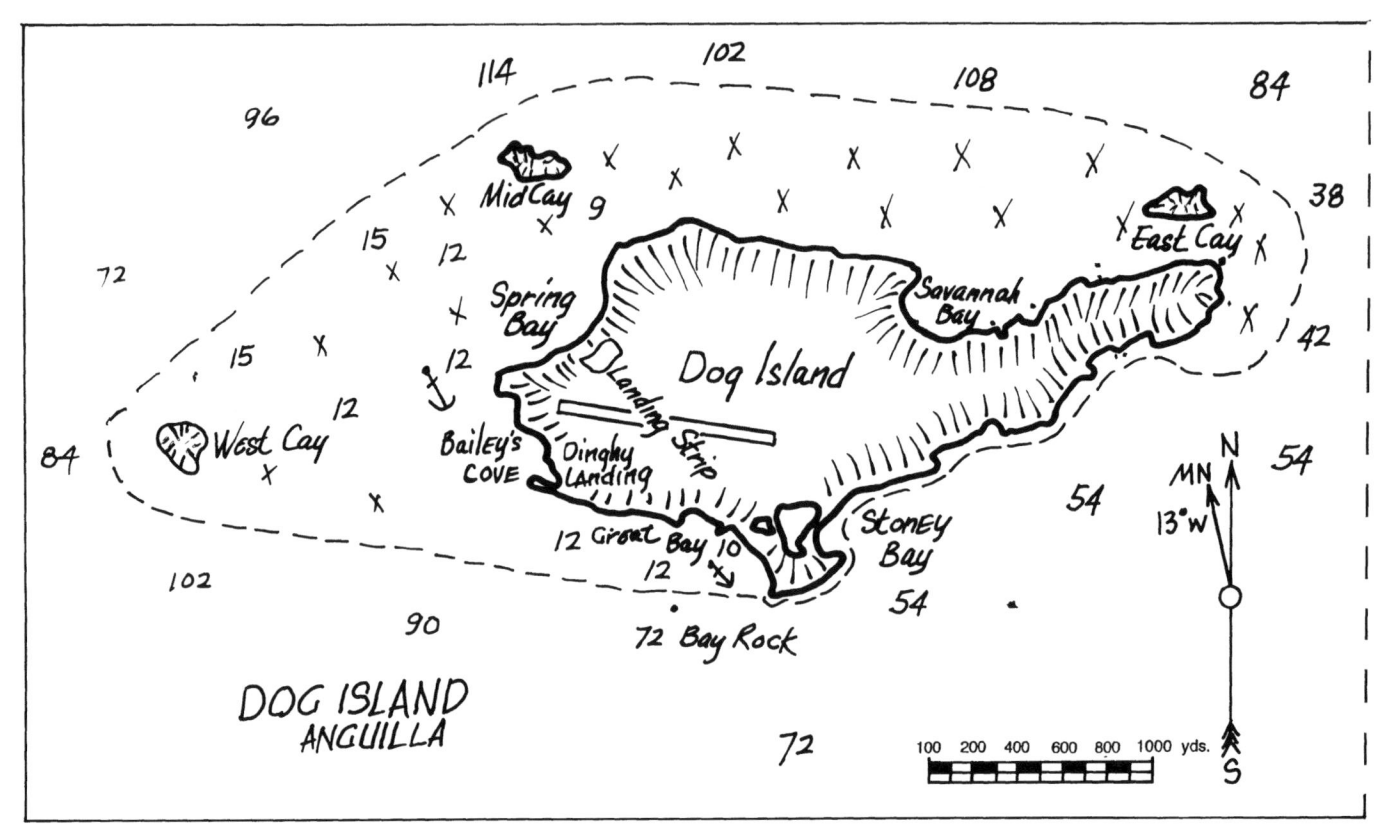

Sketch Chart 9   Dog Island   Depths in feet

in the east, a good anchorage can be had in the southeast corner of this paradise. When entering, be careful to avoid Bay Rock, which just barely breaks and could easily do real damage. The beach is about 500 yards long and divided into halves by a four-foot-high stone wall. (Two particularly short couples can skinny-dip on each side in complete privacy.) At the western end of the beach, the sea has hollowed out a bowl in the rocks into which it sluices from time to time, creating a clear, warm, saltwater bath. If you moor in Spring Bay, you can reach the beach by walking over the ridge southeast of the end of the runway and around the salt pond. Head south, pass the western edge of the salt pond, and—voilà—the perfect beach.

One interesting feature of Dog Island, as with many of the other islands in this area, is the stone walls—four feet high and two feet thick—that cross the island in a straight line from the northern shore to the southern shore. Like New Englanders, Anguillans had to remove the rocks from their fields before they could farm—hence these walls. I must say they were excellent stonemasons, since these dry stone walls are about the best I have seen in the Antilles.

There are wonderful cruising opportunities throughout this area. In settled weather, one could easily spend from 10 days to two weeks exploring the coast of Anguilla and its offlying islands. But yachtsmen are well advised to do so quickly—before the hoteliers and tourists move in for keeps.

3

St. Martin

(Imray-Iolaire Charts A, A-24, A-3)

Years ago, when I first arrived in the Lesser Antilles, the small, high, and sparsely populated island of St. Martin was enjoying the beginnings of a tourist boom. It was nice. The positive aspects of what we call civilization (electricity, frozen meat, ice, and a few hotels) had arrived without the curses of neon lights, traffic jams, and insolent taxi drivers. Air communication with St. Thomas, Antigua, and San Juan was meager. Since that first visit, however, the airport has expanded, and now direct air service exists from Europe, the United States, and South America. Americans have flocked to the island to escape high taxes and pollution. St. Martin is booming with hotels—from the huge casino type to little guest houses—as well as countless "timeshares." The influx of tourists and hotels has completely taken over the economy of the island—to the point where it is difficult to find any sign of the original small, sleepy villages of Philipsburg on the Dutch side (Sint Maarten) or Marigot on the French side.

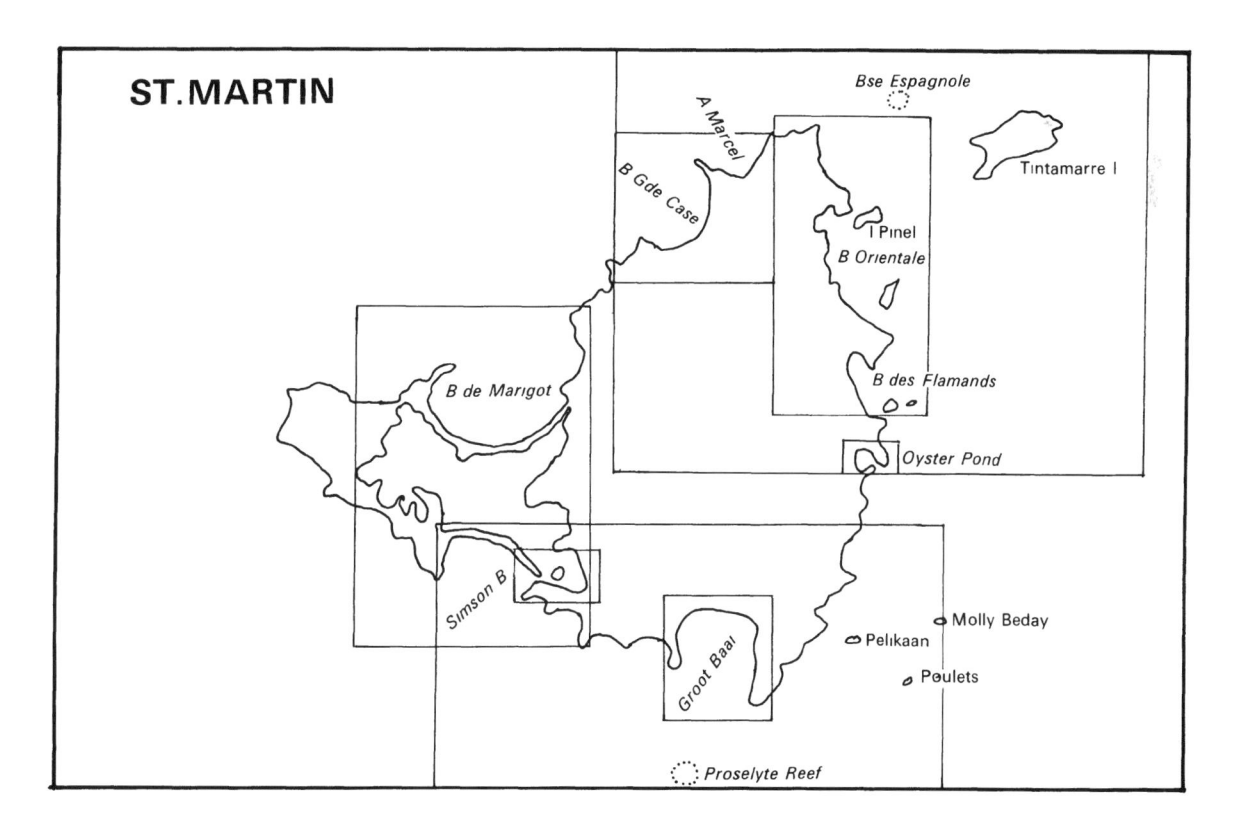

The foundations of this curious two-country situation were laid in 1648, when squabbling French and Dutch settlers agreed to divide the island between them. The Dutch took 21 square miles in the south and the French took 16 square miles in the north. Although the treaty is now into its fourth century, it is still in force. The island can be discussed as a single entity, however, inasmuch as no one seems to pay much attention to the border.

Until about 10 years ago, St. Martin/Sint Maarten had remained a quiet little island in the process of developing gradually. Then the development began in earnest. As I see it, the developers of St. Martin examined the development of St. Thomas and decided to adopt and compound all of the errors that had been made on that island! The crime situation has been getting out of hand and now unfortunately it has spilled over onto the yachting scene. In one night in Simpson lagoon, nine yachts were robbed. The person who told us about it, woke up to find an intruder onboard. The owner was hit across the face by an iron bar and woke up in the hospital two weeks later. Luckily he survived and is still sailing

The Dutch side developed faster, becoming a veritable "concrete jungle" that sprouted an inordinate amount of incredibly ugly architecture. The French side developed slowly until the enactment of defiscalization laws—which allowed French individuals and corporations to take their tax money and invest it in islands (or a charter boat) in the French West Indies, in return for a 100 percent tax rebate. The money had to remain invested in the organization or vessel for five years, after which the business could be sold. All proceeds of the sale would be tax-free. Who could resist? Toward the end of the 1980s, the scheme made St. Martin take off like a rocket. Hotels and apartments went up at a ridiculous rate, and the building continues! How will the facilities now under construction ever be filled? One important note, however: The architecture on the French side is infinitely superior to that on the Dutch side.

Another reason the French side has been developing more rapidly is that it is a "département" of France, and any French citizen (and, in fact, any citizen of a European Community country) can come to that side of the island and work or set up a business without obtaining a permit. The Dutch side is part of the Netherlands Antilles—a state that is semi-independent from Holland—so a Dutch citizen coming to Sint Maarten needs to obtain a permit in order to work, establish a business, or buy land. One upshot of all this is that many EC citizens live on the French side, where they have no immigration problems, and have jobs on the Dutch side! They find that it is pretty much impossible for the Dutch immigration officials to catch up with them.

The Dutch side of the island has become a veritable yachting mecca. Bobby, of Bobby's Marina in Philipsburg, is constantly expanding his facilities. He has, for example, replaced a 70-ton Travelift with a 100-ton one. The yard is supported by a stainless-steel welding and fabrication shop, a sail loft (Shore Sails), an electronics shop, and a bareboat charter operation. Plus there are shops, restaurants, laundry facilities, and showers. The Dockside Management office here serves as a communications center for a large number of private and charter yachts, as well as itinerant yachtsmen. (The office also organizes refueling of gas bottles—if you leave them off before 1015, you may get them back the same day.) From the office you can send faxes, make telephone calls, and send and collect mail. Needless to say, there is a charge for all this. It may not be cheap, but it certainly is efficient, and it sure beats struggling with the commercial phone system. There are card-phones on both sides of the island, but it's always a major hassle to buy the cards! On the Dutch side, you can get them at the post office and the front desks of many of the hotels. On the French side, however, where most of the phones are card-phones, the cards are supposedly available at the post office. But it can be a real pain in the neck to stand in a post office queue for an hour and then find, when you get to the counter, that they are sold out! (In years past, telephone calls from the French side to the Dutch side were routed via Guadeloupe, Paris, and Rotterdam! It was almost cheaper to rent a car and drive to the Dutch side than it was to make the phone call!)

(All is not lost on the French side, however, as the Bar de la Mer in Marigot not only has a VHF you can use but also has a coin-operated telephone. In Grand Case, the girl who runs the first "lolo" north of the gap, usually has phone cards. If she does not, a fellow at the Superette (small supermarket) at the north end of town (west side of the street) not only has cards but also has in his head the dialing codes for most countries. He'll be glad to rattle them off for you! A good "come-on" for customers.)

There are now also special phones marked "USA Direct"—from which you can make long-distance calls using an AT&T credit card. I was able to call Ireland, England, and Grenada from one of these phones. Ma Bell is wonderful!

Across the road from Bobby's Marina is Robbie Ferron's Budget Marine, which is an Imray-Iolaire chart agent. He also stocks books, including Street guides. Budget Marine is well named, as the prices are very competitive, and when he doesn't have an item in stock, he will do his best to obtain it for you in short order. I would rate Budget as the number-one marine-hardware store in the entire Caribbean.

The marine supply store at Bobby's is a division of Island Water World, whose main store is at Grand Etang de Simsonbaai (contact them on VHF channel 74). Among other items, they stock books and Imray-Iolaire charts. Next to Bobby's Marina is Chesterfield's Marina, with a popular open-air restaurant. Water, electricity, and fuel are available. You will also find NIS—Nautical Instrument Services—which carries charts, guides, marine supplies, and groceries all in one store.

Both Chesterfield's and Bobby's are always talking about expansion of their breakwaters, but it doesn't always happen. The charts were accurate as of April 1992, but there may be changes by the time you arrive. Just proceed with caution and remember that bulwark breakwater extensions in the Caribbean seldom are lighted while they are under construction—another very good reason for not entering strange harbors at night!

When it comes to outboard parts and repair, every type of outboard known seems to have an agent in St. Martin. It's a matter of picking up the annual, free-of-charge *St. Martin Marine Guide* (available at all the marine stores) and looking up the name of the agent for your type of outboard.

On the French side of the island, yachting has not developed at anywhere near the pace that it has on the Dutch side. Team I in Marigot is the major marine supply store on the French side. They stock Imray-Iolaire charts and Street guides and have a fair amount of marine supplies. Fishermen will be happy to know that the store is loaded with fishing gear. The store hours are a little unpredictable, but across the street is a very attractive little park, so just sit in the shade there and read while you wait for the chandlery to open. Or go across from the park to the open-air restaurant, where you can buy a good breakfast, a light lunch, or dinner.

St. Martin is the catamaran center of the Caribbean. In the 1960s, Peter Spronk arrived in the islands from South Africa and built his first catamaran, *Blue Crane,* in Grenada (where Spice Island Boatyard is now located). Then he and his wife, Myrna, moved to St. Martin, where they set up the Lanseair Catamaran Center and built dozens of fast, low, light, and good-looking catamarans. They really established passenger-carrying catamarans in the Caribbean, but when they began having problems with the Dutch government regarding work permits, they shut down the operation and emigrated to the east coast of England—a real loss for St. Martin. Dougie Brooks, Peter's brother-in-law, worked with him for many years and now builds Spronk-style cats in St. Kitts. The boats are slightly different—a development of the cats that Peter built originally.

The high point of yachting activity in St. Martin is now the Heineken Regatta, which was started by Robbie Ferron when a few of the boys wanted to get together for some informal racing. It has become one of the major regattas in the Caribbean and is generously sponsored by Heineken, KLM, the French and Dutch governments, and numerous business organizations. One of the most attractive aspects of the regatta is that the sponsors provide a considerable amount of money, which makes entry fees very low. And the "freebies" (unlike at Antigua Sailing Week) are plentiful. One of the best of these is the *free* launch service that runs until about 2 or 3 in the morning.

In 1992, the sponsors brought in a great number of yachting writers, as well as the famous British photographer Beken of Cowes—all expenses paid. (Antigua Sailing Week organizers, please note!)

The Heineken Regatta is also distinctive in that monohulls and multihulls race on the same course. (Remember that this is the Caribbean catamaran capital.) Watching one of the big cats zooming along at 20 or 25 knots is certainly awe-inspiring. The three-day regatta begins around the first week in March (the dates are different each year), and it is worthwhile keeping an eye on your calendar if you expect to be in the area at the time. Consider entering and racing, or anchor your boat and offer to crew. Or just "spectate." (The Heineken Regatta and Lulu's St. Barts Regatta are held within a couple of weeks of each other—just enough time to recover from one before the other starts!)

Food shopping is excellent in St. Martin. On the Dutch side, within walking distance of the marinas, is a Chinese supermarket. A bus ride out of town takes you to two or three wholesale supermarkets. On the French side, there are a number of small supermarkets in downtown Marigot, but on the outskirts is a mega-shopping store, the Food Center—a truly magnificent French emporium. The shopping generally is less expensive on the Dutch side, but if you want the quality of French meats and cheeses, then head for this Marigot mega-market.

On Wednesday and Saturday, there is an open-air market on the Marigot waterfront. Fruits and vegetables are brought in direct from Dominica.

Chesterfield's is the base for daysailing catamarans that sail to St. Barthélemy every day—a speedy, exhilarating ride. The trips are very popular with tourists, as well as with yachtsmen who just want to go out for a daysail on a fast cat.

The gas-bottle situation in St. Martin is none too

good. On the French side, camping gas bottles can be exchanged, but it is impossible to have propane bottles filled (according to locals, who should know). You have to take them over to Philipsburg, and since the bus drivers won't allow them on the buses, you have to conceal them inside a sail bag.

If you were on the Dutch side in past years, you could take the bottles directly to the gas plant and have them filled while you waited. Now you need to take them to Vance James early in the morning, and then retrieve them later in the afternoon. Or leave the bottles at Dockside Management no later than 1015, which is much easier. With luck, you will be able to pick up the filled bottles by 1715, or at worst the next day.

The ice situation in Philipsburg is easy. Go ashore to either Bobby's or Chesterfield's for either cube or block ice. If you are in Marigot, cube ice is everywhere, and block ice sometimes is available at the Customs dock. Or, if you really need block ice, take the bus to the Food Center and do all your shopping. Then take a taxi to the block-ice plant—which is on the Marigot-Philipsburg road about 200 yards south of the Food Center—and bring back food and ice in a single taxi trip.

In Philipsburg, showers are available at Chesterfield's and Bobby's; in Marigot, at Port la Royale Marina. If you drop off laundry at Bobby's or Chesterfield's, it will be done for you. In Marigot, east of Port la Royale, you can do your own laundry or have it done for you.

Entering St. Martin is relatively simple. On the French side, go ashore at the head of the ferry dock in Marigot and look for the Customs and Immigration sign. In April 1992, the charge for entry and clearance was US$10. Entering on the Dutch side is only a bit more complicated. Head into the main square by the post office in Philipsburg, then turn north and go two blocks to Holland Road. Look for the brand-new police station, where they handle Immigration procedures. After you finish there, walk about 100 feet to the west to the tax office, where you will pay the harbor dues—which are all of US$2.00! On both sides of the island, only the skipper needs to go ashore to clear; the rest of the crew can go ashore and have a good time.

Throughout the Caribbean, the drug situation is becoming more and more serious. In some areas, drug smuggling is a major problem and is rapidly getting out of control. In other areas—Anguilla and St. Martin, for example—a real attempt has been made to curb the trade. Because everyone is related to everyone else on these small islands, extreme measures have been undertaken. The French side has gendarmes imported from France and the Dutch side has special police sent from the Netherlands, as well as a new patrol boat. The boat, however, is a mixed blessing, as sometimes the crew just does not use common sense. For example, yachts have been called on channel 12 and asked to identify themselves. If there is no response (perhaps because the yacht is listening in on channel 16 or 68), the patrol-boat crew has reached the conclusion that it is a "suspicious vessel." They have proceeded to escort the unfortunate yacht to the dock and rifle the vessel for drugs. Therefore, I advise all yachts approaching St. Martin to announce on channel 12 that they are arriving, and also specify where they are bound. If you have not done this and you spot the patrol boat, switch immediately to channel 12 and identify yourself. Ask whether they have any specific requirements that should be met.

Be aware that dinghy-stealing is fairly common in St. Martin. Dinghies often disappear on Wednesday and Saturday nights, which just happens to be when the schooners and sloops are heading back to Dominica. So be forewarned!

St. Martin lies 72 miles southeast by east of Virgin Gorda by way of Necker Island Passage, and it is the usual landfall for boats proceeding eastward from the Virgin Islands. St. Martin is sufficiently high and well lighted that it can be spotted at night from a safe distance. However, do not approach the island from the north or northwest at night, since St. Martin, rising over the lowland of Anguilla, is apt to make you misjudge your distance off the latter island. Should this happen, you will be on the reefs before you realize your mistake. In fact, Anguilla is four miles away from St. Martin, but this distance is not apparent at night.

Boats approaching from the south must watch out for Proselyte Reef (Man-of-War Reef). With only 2 1/4 fathoms over it, in rough weather it sometimes breaks and is the single danger on the southerly approach. The ranges to clear this reef are given in Chart 10.

Boats rounding the western end of St. Martin must take care, since Pointe Basse Terre is continually extending to the westward. At night, give this point a berth of at least 1 1/4 miles. During daylight, do not approach the point closer than one mile without putting a lookout in the rigging. Numerous boats have grounded on this point, and many have been lost.

Regarding radio communications, VHF channel 16 supposedly is the contact channel, but different businesses in St. Martin operate on different fre-

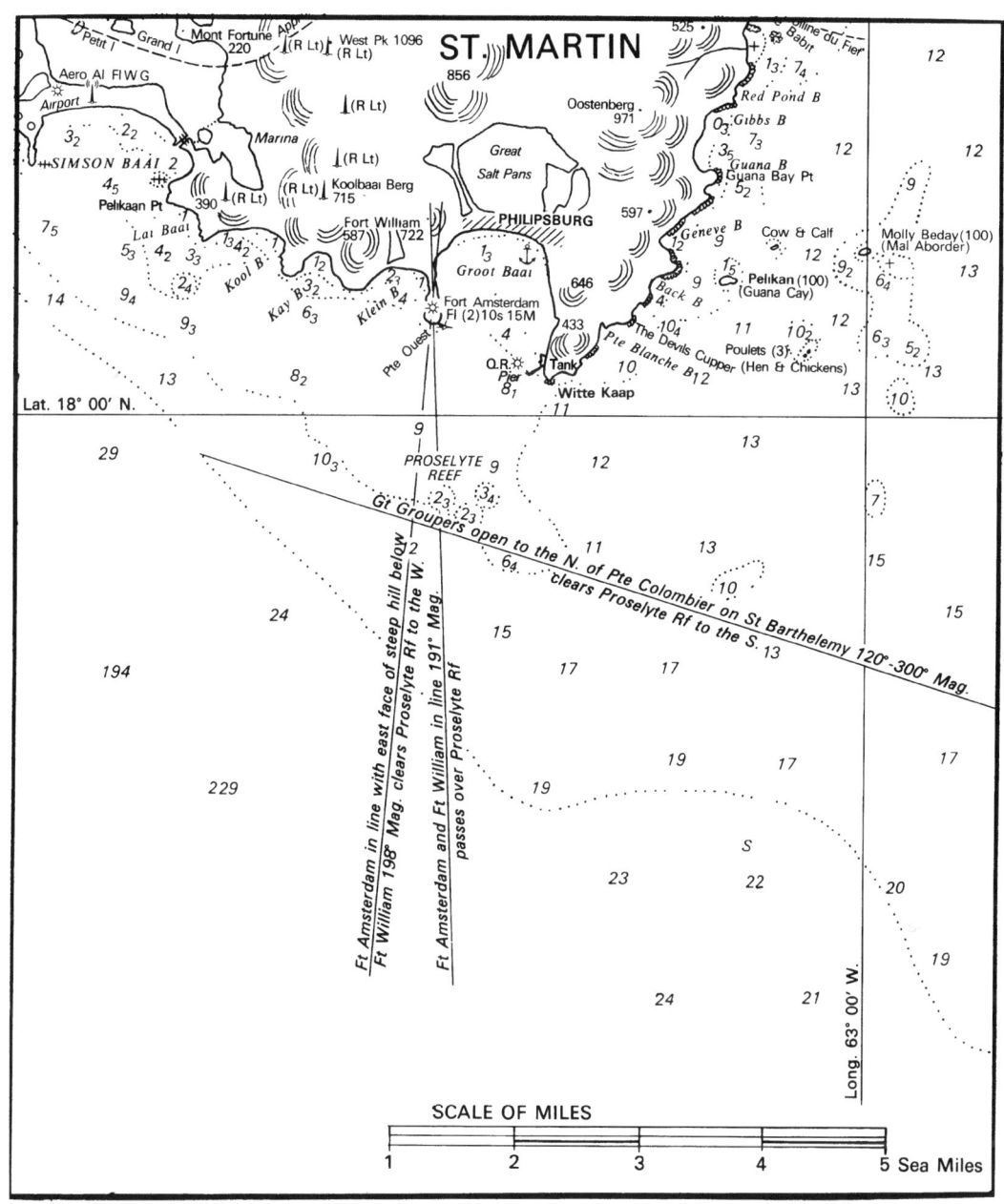

Chart 10 Ranges for Proselyte Reef   Depths in fathoms and feet

quencies. Sunsail Yachts uses channel 72, Bobby's Marina uses 16, Island Water World uses 74. Other yachts stand by on 68, but the harbormaster and the police launch use channel 12.

If you are having trouble contacting someone, you can try channels 16 and 68 and also ask any yacht for the channel of the people you are trying to contact.

PHILIPSBURG

(Chart 11; II A-2, A-24, A-3)

This is a good harbor in most weather, but it is open to the south. When the wind is south of east, it is wise to go to Marigot on the French side. Also, a big ground swell from the north is apt to make Philipsburg uncomfortable. Sometimes this swell even sweeps all the way around the island and enters Philipsburg from the south! Should this happen, set two anchors, so your boat will lie facing south despite the wind. A single anchor could break out in

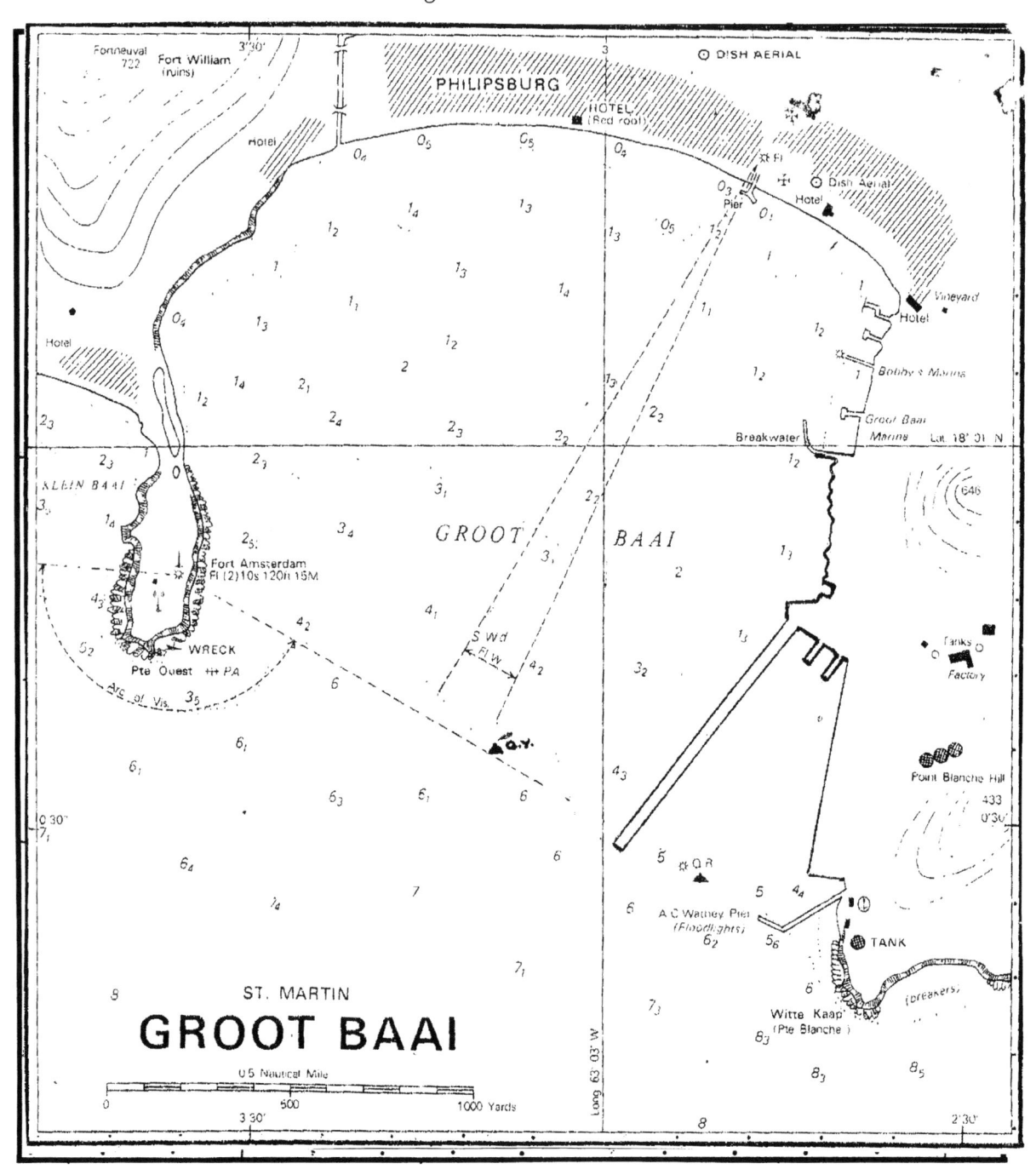

Chart 11   Groot Baai and Philipsburg   Depths in fathoms and feet
Note: It is forbidden to pass between the buoy off the A.C. Wathey Pier and the pier itself.

a heavy swell, and your vessel would be ashore before you could do anything. For the most part, though, the harbor is breezy and cool, with only a slight swell in normal trade-wind weather.

When approaching Philipsburg from the south at night, be aware that the Klein Baai Hotel and the development around it have many more lights than Philipsburg. Be absolutely sure you are heading for Philipsburg and not Klein Baai. A number of yachts have made this mistake and ended up high and dry on the beach. Place the fl(2)10s light of Fort Amsterdam on your *port side* and all should be well.

(You should be able to see the lights of the steamer pier on Witte Kaap from eight to 10 miles off.)

When approaching Philipsburg—Groot Baai stay well clear of the new Cruise Ship pier. if buoys are placed to the southwest of this pier stay outside the buoys. Anchoring is not permitted in the area leading up to the launch pier at the head of the harbour. Also the anchoring area in Groot Baai is rather restricted as the launches from the cruise ships go back and forth across the bay and cause you to rock and roll very uncomfortably.

Groot Baai has always had a problems with the bottom shoaling drastically as a result of hurricanes and periods of heavy ground swells. Also, the building of a new dock will probably change the currents in the harbour and move the sand around. Thus, any boats with draft of more than seven feet should proceed with extreme caution in Groot Bay—as the depths shown on this or any other chart may not be correct.

Bobby's Marine is usually so crowded there is not enough room for visiting yachts. You will have to check first. At Bobby's Marina one can find a hauling facility of 60 ton travelift, also Island Water World Marine Supply Store; Dockside mail pickup, fax and phone plus USA direct phones. There is also a restaurant and commissary.

When anchoring in Groot Baai you are anchoring in sand, holding is good but avoid the patches of grass.

SIMSON BAAI
(Chart 12, Sketch Chart 13; II A-2, A-24, A-3)

West of Philipsburg, the only other anchorage on the coast is Simson Baai, which is behind Pelikaan Point. This is satisfactory in normal weather, as a breakwater has been built extending Pelikaan Point out to the south, thus eliminating most of the surge that develops when the wind is in the southeast. The wreck of the barge that was a navigational hazard years ago has now been broken up by subsequent hurricanes, so a normal yacht (i.e., one drawing no more than 10 feet) can sail over it. This has become a good snorkeling site. Simson Baai is a popular spot to anchor to wait for the swing bridge to open into Grand Etang de Simsonbaai (see below), but it is not wise to land your dinghy on the beach—better to take the dinghy up into the lagoon and tie it up to one of the many docks there.

The major hazard in this area comes in the form of tourists screaming around the harbor on jetskis. And they really *are* a hazard. A catamaran was nailed—literally—when jetskis were buried in one of its hulls, causing serious damage to the boat and equally serious damage to the jetskier!

Also see NOTES at the end of this chapter on page 44.

GRAND ETANG DE SIMSONBAAI
(Chart 12, Sketch Chart 13; II A-2, A-24, A-3)
See updates on Page 43.

A swing bridge gives access to Grand Etang de Simsonbaai. As was demonstrated during Hurricane Klaus in 1984, this was thought to be a superb hurricane hole. Although there are not enough hills around to break the wind entirely, the lagoon is completely land-locked, and no sea can build up. Even if a boat did drag ashore, it would come up on sand and can be pulled off easily.

In 1984 there were probably only forty or fifty boats in Simson Lagoon—but in the late 1980s and early 1990s the yachting population of the eastern Caribbean expanded exponentially!!! In 1995 when hurricane Louis and then Marilyn swept over St. Martin there were over 1000 boats in Simson Lagoon—resulting a disaster about 900 sunk or blown up on the beach—subsequent hurricanes have also wrought heavy damage in Simson Lagoon. Read *Reflections on Hugo* and re-read the Prologue on page 8.

There are two major problems with Grand Etang de Simsonbaai, though: getting in, and getting around once in there.

The first is getting in. Two bridges block the way—one from Simson Baai on the Dutch side to the south, the other from Bale de Marigot on the French side to the north.

The Dutch have built a new bridge, but the official opening times tend to change, so it's best to check the schedule when you arrive in St. Martin. In April 2000, the hours were 0600 to 1100 and 1600 to 1800.

The people who control the bridge on the Dutch side of the lagoon are not noted for their efficiency. When Hurricane Klaus came through unexpectedly, the bridge was opened to allow boats into the lagoon, but then the bridge was closed and the bridgetender disappeared to "parts unknown"! As the hurricane approached, St. Martin was continually broadcasting: "Does anyone please know the whereabouts of Mr. Brown? If they do, would they please get him to return to the bridge, as there are boats wanting to come through!" Mr. Brown was gone for the rest of the day—he never returned until after the hurricane had swept through!

Recently there was another horror story. After two boats had passed through, the bridgetender, for reasons best known to himself, decided to close the bridge. But a third boat had already entered the channel (more boats were astern, lining up to pass out). The unfortunate third boat backed down as hard as possible, but the current was so strong that the boat was swept into the bridge and jammed against it crosswise. In the chaos of trying to extricate the vessel from its predicament, the poor owner died of a heart attack.

The horizontal clearance on the bridge appears to be narrow, but it is used by catamarans, whose skippers claim the width between the piers is about 35 feet maximum. Half tid depth in January 2000 12 feet. But it must be remembered that the Caribbean can be 18inchest to 24 inches lower in May, June and July.

The whole situation on the French side of the lagoon is in a state of flux. The channel has been dredged to 12 feet, but unfortunately it shoals up

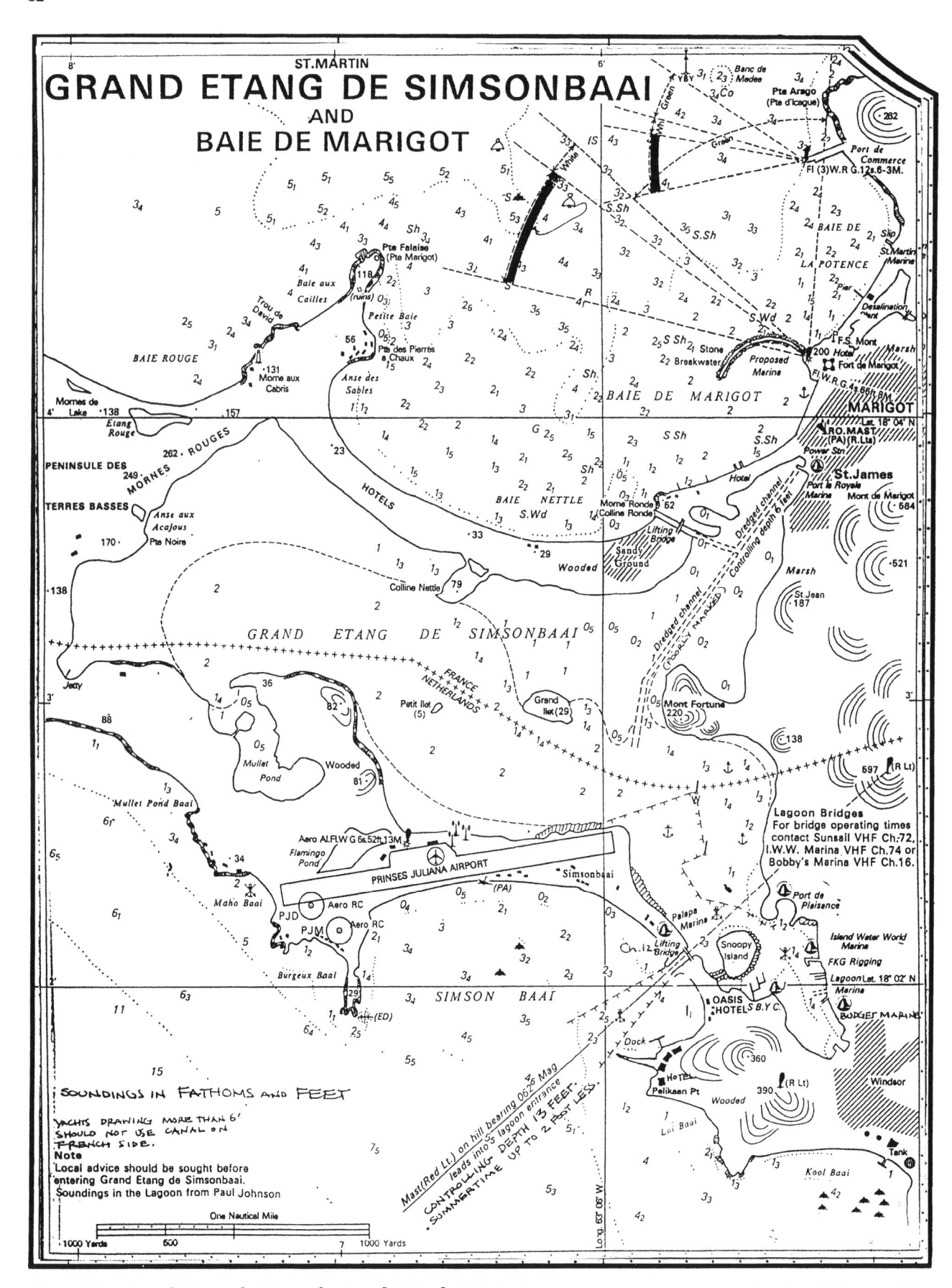

Chart 12 Grand Etang de Simsonbaai and Baie de Marigot   Depths in fathoms and feet

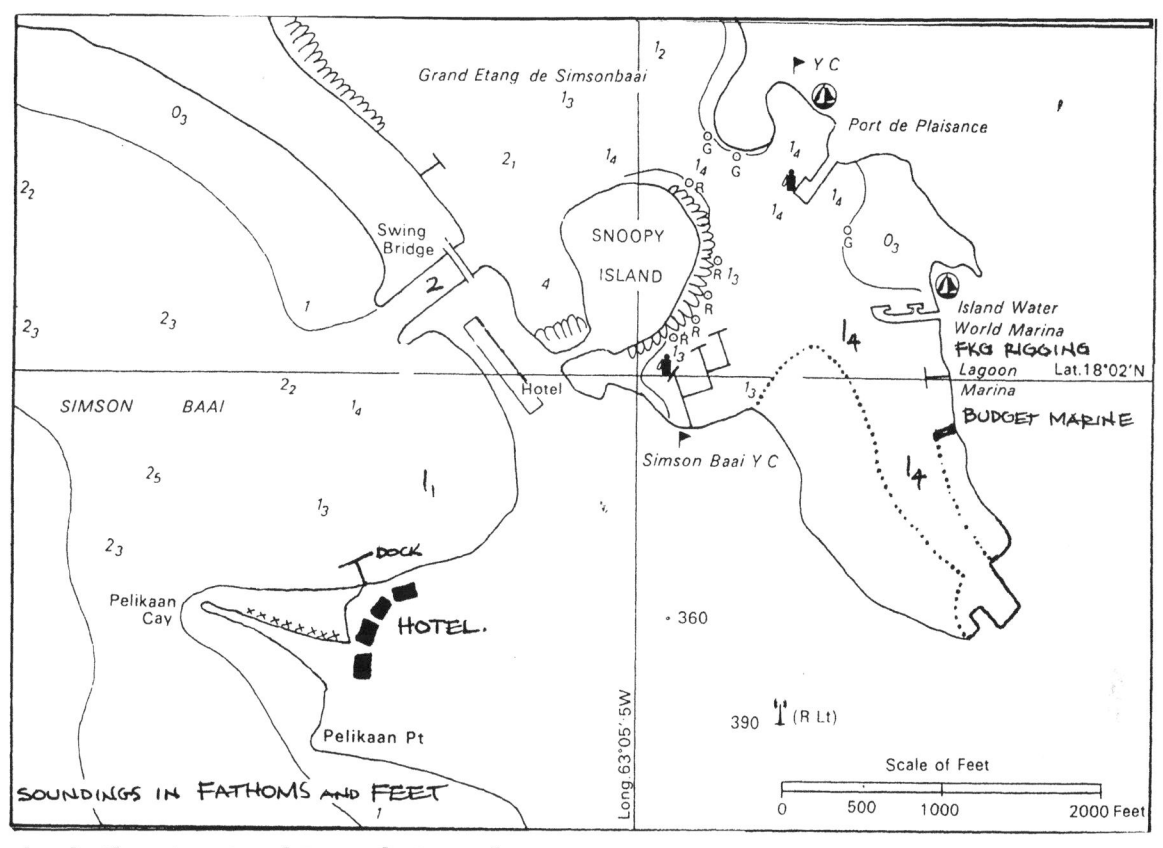

Sketch Chart 13 Grand Etang de Simsonbaai   Depths in fathoms and feet

outside the channel, which is silting. Boats drawing more than 6 feet should not use this channel as there is no room for them once they get inside the channel.

The shoals change drastically in Baie de Marigot because of the ground swell. In the summer of 1991, Dale Mitchell (mate on *Iolaire* during the winter of 1991-92) took boats drawing 11 feet in and out of the French side of the lagoon by lining up the tower on Morne aux Cabris with the channel—a course of 123°. He put the tower on his stern and the channel on the bow. However, in May 1992, when we sounded this range with a leadline, we found only seven feet of water. We did discover that by approaching Morne Ronde on a bearing of about 220° magnetic, staying about 50 yards off Morne Ronde and eyeballing it until the channel lines up, eight and half (possibly nine) feet can be squeezed in. I suggest, however, that any boat drawing more than seven feet should sound out the approaches to this channel. This bridge is too narrow for catamarans.

The French side is open as 0600, 1100, 1600 and 1800. On weekends and holidays, there is no 1600 opening. As with the Dutch side, however, it's best to confirm the schedule when you reach St. Martin.

A channel was dredged from the French side to the Dutch side, controlling depth 9-ft. and was bouyed in 1992. But, no one maintained it. Now the channel has filled in; 6-ft. is the most that can use the channel, and even then it is only with local knowledge.

Sketch Charts 12 and 13 show the approximate extent of the dredging. I say approximate as dredging continues, but also where dredged it frequently silts in.

Check the local marine directory for the latest information on Marina's, hauling facilities, and marine supplies. It is an ever changing scene.

The two big marine supply stores, Budge and Island Water World are both accessible by dinghy. As is the major rigging supplier, FKG Rigging.

Island W. W. always seems to have a wooden boat up on the hard undergoing refit/rebuild. I suspect that

Paul Marshall has a soft spot in his heart for old wooden boats.

You will find that if you are based at the marinas on the Dutch side of the lagoon, you are a long way from places to buy food. A few restaurants are available, however, including some on the water that are accessible via dinghy.

On the French side of the lagoon, at the Port la Royale Marina, you are right smack in the center of Marigot, where all day-to-day needs are within walking distance—but marine supplies and repair facilities are minimal. Also, it can be very difficult to find space alongside at the Port la Royale Marina—we can only hope that this situation will be improved by the time you arrive.

Regarding dredging on the French side of the lagoon, a lot has been done around the entrance channel, where the depth has pretty much flattened out to about eight feet. The dredge is slowly moving in a southerly direction, but I understand that it is working not so much to deepen the harbor as to collect sand for the island's many construction projects. One can only hope that the need for sand to develop St. Martin eventually will result in a channel dredged from the French to the Dutch side of Grand Etang de Simsonbaai. At present, the only vessels that can pass from the French to the Dutch side of the lagoon are those drawing less than five feet!

Development has been planned for years on the French side of the lagoon, but I will believe that when I see it.

A new bridge is in the works at the French entrance to the lagoon. The present bridge is only one-way and very narrow, so it creates an awful traffic bottleneck. Skippers always have to worry about hooking the rigging on the bridge if it is not fully open. The long-range plan is to build a causeway across Grand Etang de Simsonbaai to bring auto traffic across the western end of St. Martin and onto the Marigot road without routing it through the town of Marigot—which already suffers from traffic gridlock at certain times of day.

The second problem with Grand Etang de Simsonbaai is getting around in it once you are there. To start with, the area has been only partially sounded—the depths on the harbor chart were provided by Paul Johnson of the gaff-rigged ketch *Venus*. His soundings don't cover the whole lagoon, but at least they show some parts where you can go safely. Robbie Ferron urges caution for a four-foot shoal spot. He says that skippers come through the bridge, see a gap in the anchored boats, take it for a channel, and run hard aground.

Furthermore, the channel from the French bridge—allegedly dredged to seven feet all the way to Port la Royale Marina—was still unmarked last time we checked.

The final drawback to getting around is the matter discussed above—the absence of a channel running from one side of the lagoon to the other. I am told that only 150 yards of dredging would do it, and this would prove of vital importance in storms, when one of the two entrances might not be navigable. Why don't the French and Dutch governments get together and do what's necessary to make the lagoon the perfect hurricane hole for the northern end of the Caribbean? In fact, it seems to me that just a little more effort could turn St. Martin into a major focal point for yachting in general.

One promising step in that direction is the Port la Royale Marina, which might be compared to Marina du Bas-du-Fort in Guadeloupe. Of course, until a cross-lagoon channel is dredged, you can get to this marina only from the French side—via the bridge from Baie de Marigot.

See update at the end of this chapter regarding entrance via Marigot and channel through Simson Bay.

BAIE DE MARIGOT

(Chart 12; II A-2, A-24, A-3)

See updates in the NOTES at the end of this chapter on Page 43.

The French port and town of Marigot is an open roadstead, and at one time boats had to anchor quite far offshore. However, the sleepy little town of Marigot is no more—it has become a thriving French metropolis. Luckily, the architecture is mostly traditional West Indian style, and buildings have been restored. The inner 200-yard area of Marigot Harbor has now been filled and bulkheaded with riprap—i.e., huge, sharp rocks. In the northeast corner, a long dinghy dock has been built over the riprap. It looks perfect, but is not. Be sure to carry a stern anchor, as your dinghy can go under the dock at low tide and be trapped.

Because of the filling and bulkheading, the currents evidently have changed and scoured out the bottom. The older charts are wrong; the entire harbor northeast of a line drawn northwest from Morne Ronde is a full two fathoms deep. This is a mixed blessing. You are now tempted to anchor as close to the bulkhead as possible to shorten your dinghy ride to shore. Normally, the trade winds blowing from southeast to northeast would be blowing you offshore, away from the bulkhead. However, don't be tempted, as you can end up with a very dangerous situation— such as what happened to *Iolaire* in April 1993.

We sailed in and anchored about 0900, wind dead out of the south, blowing 15 to 20 knots. We used two anchors, set them well, and went ashore to do errands. Luckily, my secretary, Sophie Munro, was on board, and my mate, Dale Mitchell, and his girlfriend, Caroline Schmidt, arrived back on board about 1700. It was raining and the wind was light. Suddenly the wind switched from a light southerly to 40 to 45 knots directly out of the north. This, of course, waltzed us around 180 degrees on our anchors. The anchors broke out and *Iolaire* started dragging toward the bulkheading and riprap. (Remember that there is now deep water right up to shore.) There was no time to row out another anchor. Dale, Sophie, and Caroline, with consummate seamanship, hoisted the main, backed the mizzen, rolled out the staysail, jettisoned one anchor, and cut the other. Once again, *Iolaire* was saved by a sharp knife!

They sailed off into the squall and then reanchored at the outer edge of the fleet. This episode is a fine illustration of the reason for carrying numerous anchors and plenty of spare line. The crew had no problem digging out two extra anchors and plenty of line.

Of course, this circumstance was unusual. Normally, from December to May, squalls in the Eastern Caribbean do not come up against the wind (although they certainly do so in the Chesapeake and along the East Coast of the United States, especially in Long Island Sound). It is almost unknown in the Caribbean at that time of year.

I must admit that the 1993 season had the craziest Caribbean weather in nearly 40 years. We arrived in Antigua to discover that it had hailed in St. Johns for the first time ever (the locals maintained it was raining ice cubes!). And a water spout passed south of Antigua and over to Nevis and almost totally destroyed the local hospital!

If *Iolaire* had dragged ashore before the bulkheading was done, it would not have been too serious, as she would have run aground on sand and could have been towed off by a powerboat. But had she blown up on the riprap, she certainly would have suffered major damage—if indeed she had not been sunk.

Three boats (with engines!) anchored near *Iolaire* ended up on the riprap, but, luckily, fast-thinking powerboat crews got lines on them and towed them free before there was serious damage.

Lesson learned: Don't anchor on the inner edge of the fleet at Marigot in order to shorten your dinghy ride ashore. Moor out in the middle or at the edge of the fleet, so that if anything happens, you will have plenty of room to drag, reset anchors, set anchors, drop anchors, set sail, or what-have-you.

As mentioned previously, the ground swell moves things around rather drastically in the harbor, and the western side becomes quite shoal. To get the best anchorage, keep the leadline going as the bottom gradually shoals, then anchor at a depth suitable for your draft. The farther in you go, the more comfortable you will be. The seas do not tend to swing around in the eastern end of the harbor. Take special care in the western end, however, as the ground swell and shoaling is potentially dangerous. Even in less than extreme conditions, the swells hump up and break. If the harbor is very crowded—which tends to occur rather often during the winter—many boats anchor north of the fort in Baie de la Potence. When anchoring, just be sure there is enough water under you and enough swinging room.

The fort and the Roman Catholic church are worth visiting. Shopping is very luxurious and restaurants are too numerous to list. One popular spot for yachties is Bar de la Mer, where you can use the VHF set behind the bar to call your boat and have the dinghy sent ashore. Upstairs is a pool table—something to keep the crew distracted.

In addition to the supermarkets that are within walking distance of the waterfront, there is an excellent bakery across the street from City Hall. Nothing like fresh French bread baked early in the morning to take back to the boat for a relaxing brunch! Out on the road leading to Baie Grand Case is the megasupermarket mentioned in the introduction to this chapter. Once you stock up there, it will be a taxi ride back to the dock—unless you are very young and very energetic.

As of April 1993, water was available only at Port la Royale Marina (where you can also buy ice).

Getting from Marigot to Philipsburg (or the reverse) is dead simple—easier, cheaper, and quicker than making a telephone call! There is an excellent bus service that charges $1.50—but choose your time to avoid the island's monumental traffic jams. If you are planning to catch a morning bus, make sure to take it before 0730, or wait until later. In the afternoon, make sure you have hopped on the bus by 1530; after 1600, you probably will be sentenced to a two-hour trip! There are just too many cars on St. Martin, and total gridlock is not uncommon in the morning and evening rush hours.

One final reminder about Baie de Marigot: As a result of Hurricanes Klaus (1984) and Hugo (1989), plus serious ground swells in October and December 1991, the shoals in the harbor have continued moving around, so proceed with the utmost caution!

East of Baie de Marigot, there are almost no all-weather anchorages. But if the ground swell is not running, a pleasant anchorage can be found in Baie Grand Case or Baie de Friars.

BAIE DE FRIARS

(II A-2, A-24, A-3)

Anchor in the northeast corner here if there is no ground swell. I have only visited this bay by car, but it appears to be a good anchorage and has an excellent beach with a good restaurant. It was all very peaceful when we were here—and only one boat was anchored off the beach. Finding an uncrowded anchorage in St. Martin is a real boon. Although the beach and restaurant probably make this a popular place during the day, you are guaranteed some solitude in the evening—and you won't have to listen to someone else's generator!

BAIE GRAND CASE

(Sketch Chart 14; II A-2, A-24, A-3)

Baie Grand Case provides about one mile of white-sand beach with the village of Grand Case stretching either side of the dock.

There are probably more restaurants per square foot in this tiny place than anywhere else in the Eastern Caribbean. In 1984, we counted 21 in less than half a mile; in 1993, there must have been more than 50 in the same area. They vary from reasonable to outrageously expensive, and some are in beautifully restored Antillean houses. Everyone seems to agree that the barbecued chicken and spareribs served at the little dock restaurants offer good value for money. If you go to one of these open-air restaurants (locally known as "lolos"), you can give your boat's cook a day off but not go broke in the process!

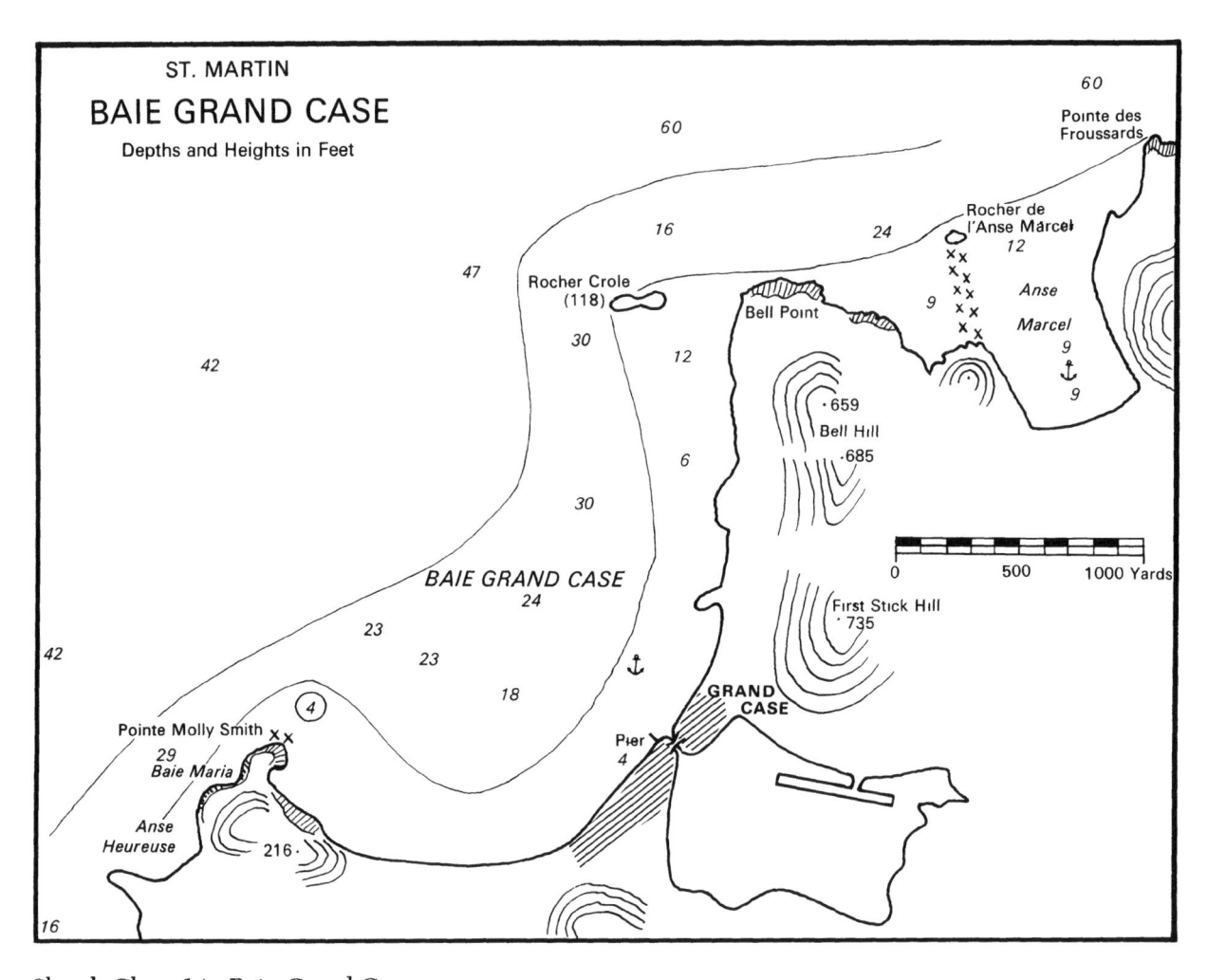

Sketch Chart 14 Baie Grand Case

Shopping is fairly good here. At the eastern end of town is Lawrence's supermarket, with mainly canned and frozen goods. (He also sells phone cards!) At the western end of town, and of interest to the yachtsman, is Tony's, which opens at 0730 and usually stays open until 2100.

At Grand Case, you'll see on the beach the French equivalent of the Anguilla racing sloops—but all are of one size, comparable to the medium-size Anguillan sloop, about 22 feet overall. They race out of Grand Case, but on big regatta days in Anguilla, they frequently tow the fleet over there and race against the Anguillan boats.

Even more interesting are the models of these St. Martin boats—about three feet long, radio-controlled. The models have only been around for about two years, but 20 or so have been built. It seems that a boatbuilder got to drinking one night with a sailor who owned a shop that sold radio-controlled airplanes. The sailor insisted he could, by adapting standard components, create a radio-controlled outfit that would not only steer a boat but also trim the main and jib. What's more, he insisted that it would be able to retrim the genoa jib on each tack.

The boatbuilder said, "Fine. I'll build two models and make the spars, rigging, and sails. You supply the radio-controlled outfit. We'll have two boats to race in solid comfort: We can sit at the end of the pier, drink beer, race our boats, and stay dry." So the plank-on-frame models were built, the radio controls were installed, and they had a fine old time racing the boats around triangular courses in Grand Case.

People began to come to watch the racing, and many became interested; a class was launched, and now 20 or so owner/skippers sit on the dock, drink beer, and race their little models.

This is a far cry from the little boats raced in Bequia from time immemorial. The kids there designed and built their boats, rigged them, and trimmed them so beautifully that they could sail on a straight course on any point of sailing. When racing them on a windward leg, the kids would swim along behind them. Every time they wanted to tack, they would give the stern a whack to get the boat pointed off on the new course.

The electronic age has affected model-boat racing in St. Martin; I wonder whether it will spread to the other islands, such as Puerto Rico, where the boys build fantastic models in Salinas, on the south coast.

There is really no problem entering Baie Grand Case. Just stay well clear of the southernmost point on the harbor. Give it a minimum clearance of 250 yards, as the shoals extend well off this point. There is a deep-water pass and then a nobby—coral head—with about four feet of water over it. (The Imray-Iolaire chart shows it correctly.) The two gendarmes, M. Seulin and his assistant, took us out in their launch to the coral head so that I could double-check our bearings. The US and British Admiralty charts show this rock considerably farther northeast of the point than it is, and they also show a deep-water passage between the rock and the point. If you round the southernmost point of the bay and try to pass inside the rock, you probably will hit it. Stay well north of the point and the rock. The RCC Lesser Antilles Pilot, the DMA, and many other guides have this rock mis-plotted. Use Imray-Iolaire Chart A-24 and this volume for the correct location.

We found a good though windy anchorage due north of the town pier in three fathoms with a white-sand bottom and good holding.

ANSE MARCEL

(Chart 15; II A-2, A-24, A-3)

Anse Marcel, northeast of Baie Grand Case, provides a good anchorage as long as the ground swell is not running and the wind is not too far to the north. Eyeball navigation is essential.

Once a deserted cove, Anse Marcel now boasts a large new resort, including a marina dredged out of the salt pond behind the hotel. The development, Port Lonvilliers, is very interesting, and the architecture is superb. Even if you cannot find dock space here, it is well worth anchoring, taking the dinghy in, and visiting the shops and restaurants—which vary from reasonable to extremely expensive.

Partly as a result of the French defiscalization laws described earlier in this chapter, there are dozens of yachts—perhaps even a hundred—in the Port Lonvilliers marina. Supposedly they are for charter, but none of them ever seem to go out! They all look as though they have come straight from the box!

When these boats start coming up for sale after the five-year "investment period," it will be interesting to observe the effect on the secondhand-boat market. Of course, some surveyors maintain that the vessels are so badly constructed that they won't last more than five years anyway!

The Port Lonvilliers marina is the home of Swan charter yachts, and expansion continues, with the goal of doubling the present capacity. When that happens, The Moorings plans to move its St. Martin

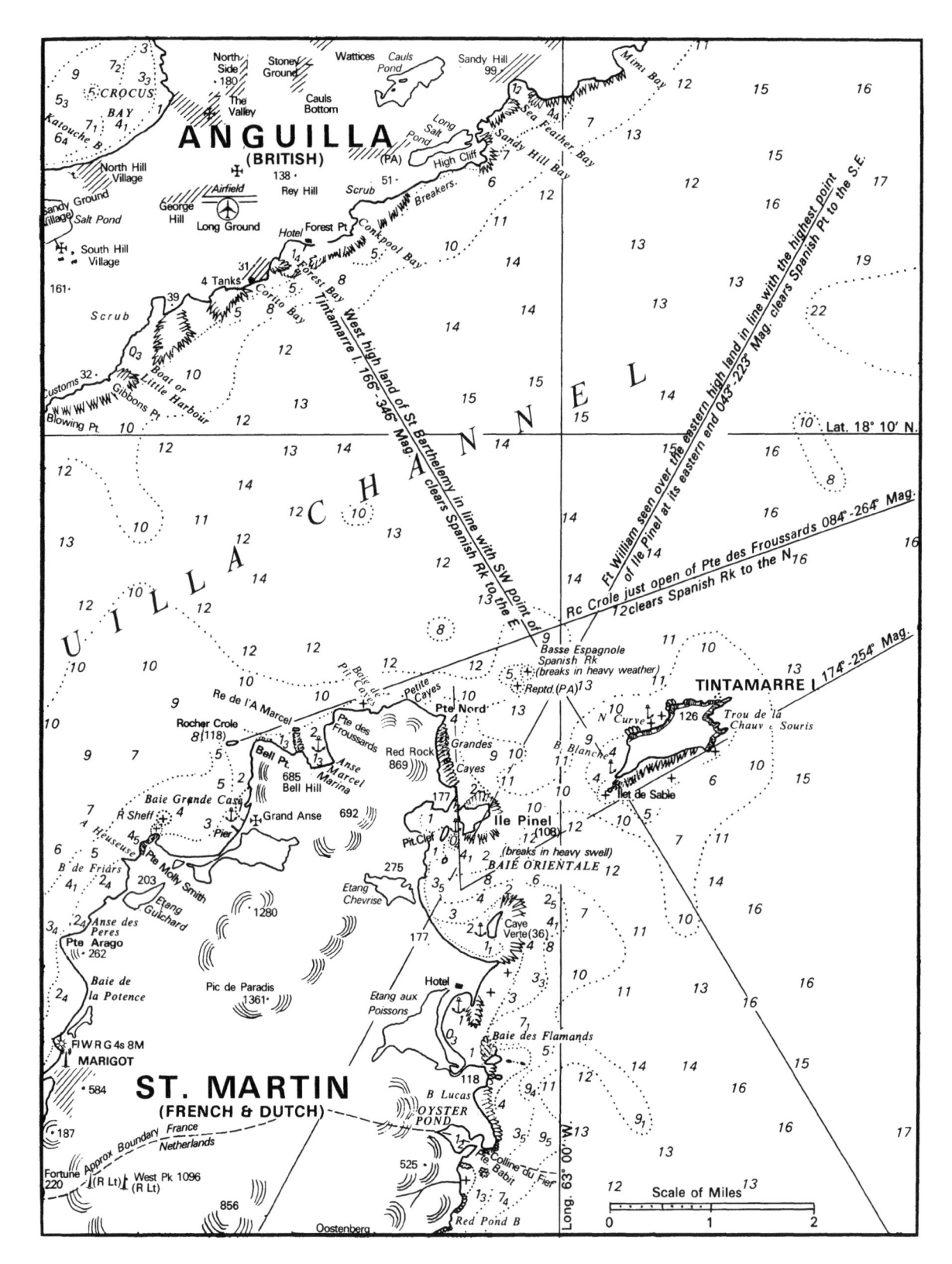

Chart 15 Northeast Coast of St. Martin: Baie Grand Case to Oyster Pond   Depths in fathoms and feet

Note: Bahamas Yachting Services (BYS) urges yachts to favor the Caye Verte side of the entrance when entering. Sunsail Yachts has positioned a day marker at the north end of Caye Verte and has buoyed the four-foot shoal in the entrance to the cove behind Ile Pinel.

base here from Oyster Pond, where it is very difficult for boats to get in and out.

The channel leading from Anse Marcel into the marina is a one-way channel, so call the marina on channel 16 before you head in—otherwise, you may encounter a boat trying to go out, and you will need to perform a long backing exercise.

East Coast of St. Martin

In my first cruising guide in 1966, I discouraged exploration of the east coast of St. Martin, pointing out that it is a dead lee shore open to the Atlantic. Then, when I became tired of visiting the same anchorages and of being surrounded by charter yachts, I tried some exploring in *Iolaire*. Adding the knowledge gained from my own forays to that gleaned from other adventurous yachtsmen, I have concluded that the east coast of St. Martin has at least four perfectly acceptable anchorages—Ile Pinel, Caye Verte, Baie des Flamands, and Oyster Pond.

When proceeding through Anguilla Channel, the navigator should have no problems, since there is deep water close to shore on both islands. If you are heading south between Tintamarre and St. Martin, however, beware of Basse Espagnole (Spanish Rock), a hazard that breaks only in heavy weather and is difficult to spot under normal conditions. (See Chart 15 and Imray-Iolaire Chart A-24 for ranges to avoid this rock.) After much investigation, it was discovered that Spanish Rock is in effect two rocks a few hundred yards apart; the second rock is southwest of the charted rock. Therefore, pass *east* of Spanish Rock. (This information is courtesy of Malcolm Maidwell of the catamaran *El Tigre*.)

When sailing through Anguilla Channel in the region of Tintamarre, do not close Rocher Crole with St. Martin. If you intend to beat south through the passage between Tintamarre and St. Martin, stand well to the eastward in Anguilla Channel and tack when you are far enough to windward to lay the line of bearing between Tintamarre and the high land of St. Barthélemy.

When there is no ground swell running, you can find a pleasant anchorage in calm conditions under the lee of Tintamarre. You can anchor on a clear bottom in four fathoms of water off the white-sand beach on the western shore. The snorkeling is exciting off the north and south coasts of this interesting island. During World War II and for a few years afterward, Tintamarre was used as an airfield, so you might find bits and pieces of old aircraft lying around. Since no one seems to know what was going on at the airport at that time, the speculation potential is unlimited.

ILE PINEL

(Chart 15, Sketch Chart 16; II A-2, A-24, A-3)

There is an excellent anchorage due west of this little island. In fact, it's so pleasant that charter skippers hesitate to take their charter parties into this anchorage at the beginning of a cruise because it is such a tough act to follow. It is surrounded by land, and there is no possibility of disturbance in any weather; nor can a ground swell get into the anchorage.

Some other guides mention entering through the northeastern channel between Ile Pinel and the mainland of St. Martin. I know that my old friend Mike Kuick of *Queen of Sheba* has done it in a boat drawing seven feet, but after having looked at that channel a half-dozen times, I would *never* try it. Therefore, I am providing no directions for entering that way.

Many boats coming in by the southern entrance have passed too close to Ile Pinel, crossing the 12-foot shoal where the sea tends to crest and break in heavy weather. This can cause the boat to broach, or capsize the dinghy, or knock the dinghy against the stern of the boat. Then, once past the breaking seas, some of these hapless skippers have turned into the anchorage and bounced off the five-foot rock. All this sounds rather horrendous, but if you carefully follow the directions presented here, you will have no problem getting into this wonderful anchorage.

Although the anchorage is likely to be crowded with day-trippers, it will be peaceful in the mornings and evenings.

Coming from north or south, hold your course until the southwestern tip of Ile Tintamarre bears 074° magnetic. Then immediately bear off and run in on a course of 254° magnetic, with a back bearing of 074° on Tintamarre. This course will take you into Baie Orientale in eight fathoms of water with no chance of breaking seas.

(According to Doyle's guide, you can pick up a radio tower as an entrance range, but Martin Challis, check-out man at Sunsail Yachts, who has been sailing in the area for 10 years, points out that he has great difficulty picking up the radio tower—and in fact he usually cannot pick it up. Thus, he feels it is a very poor leading mark to use on your approach.)

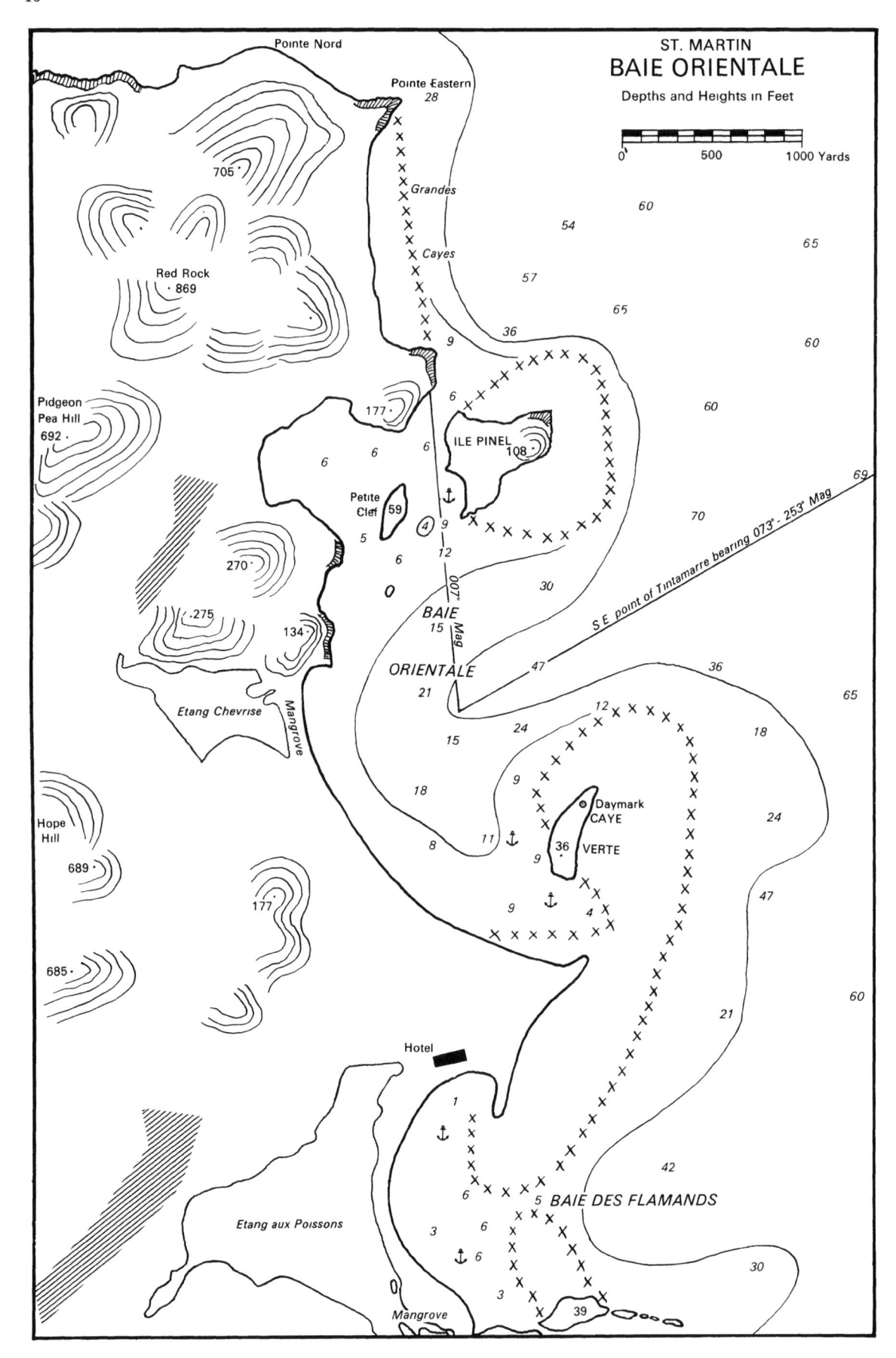

Sketch Chart 16 Baie Orientale, Ile Pinel, Caye Verte, and Baie des Flamands

Continue on the course of 254° magnetic until you see light between Ile Pinel and St. Martin. As soon as the gap appears, come right to 008° magnetic and follow this course accurately until the south end of Ile Pinel bears 101° magnetic. Then bear off or head up as you wish (or as you might have to do to avoid boats in this sometimes-crowded anchorage), and place your anchor. Just choose the depth suitable to your draft.

When leaving the Ile Pinel anchorage, stand south toward Caye Verte, where there is deep water quite close to shore. When you have almost reached Caye Verte, tack and stand to the north—this should easily keep you in the deep water clear of the breakers. However, it is still wise to exercise caution. Should the bottom be registering anything under 40 feet, tack back to the south and stay in deep water—out of the short, steep swells. (This advice, too, comes from Martin Challis of Sunsail.)

There has been talk of development at the head of this harbor since 1973, but not much has happened.

One problem with this anchorage is that the natural beauty ashore may be destroyed by the trash left by those who have preceded you. The old-time Caribbean yachtsmen always buried, burned, or took away their garbage. Many modern "yachtsmen," alas, do not.

CAYE VERTE

(Sketch Chart 16; II A-2, A-24, A-3)

A superb anchorage and excellent shelter can be found behind Caye Verte. If you are coming from the south, sail north until the southwestern corner of Ile Tintamarre bears 074° magnetic, then bear off on a course of 254° magnetic. Run on in, jibing over when Caye Verte is slight aft of abeam; sail south and anchor under Caye Verte. You can anchor south of Caye Verte, but beware, as the swell pours over the reef and makes a rocky and rolly anchorage.

Apparently there is a nude beach on Caye Verte, and evidently some sailors, in their eagerness to visit it, have taken a shortcut across the gap between the island and the mainland to the south. All, needless to say, have resulted in disastrous groundings, and many have ended up as total losses. *Do not try it.* Do not bear off and head to 074° unless you have absolutely checked your back bearing of 254° magnetic on the western end of Tintamarre. This is very important.

Once you are anchored behind Caye Verte, you will find not only a "dress optional" beach but also numerous beach bars and restaurants, sailboarding schools, and other beach activities.

BAIE DES FLAMANDS

(Sketch Chart 16; II A-2, A-24, A-3)

Baie des Flamands provides splendid shelter to anyone brave enough to enter. Visiting yachtsmen definitely should not try to enter this bay unless they are accompanied by a local who knows the bay and has entered it previously by boat. Even if I were on familiar terms with this area, I would be leery of the onshore breakers at the entrance to this harbor. There is no possible range, since the land behind the harbor is low and flat. Behind Lime Reef, at the head of the bay, you will find excellent protection—provided you have a shoal-draft auxiliary (drawing no more than four to five feet) that can slip through the narrow break in the reefs. Once in, you can run down behind the reef and anchor at the north end of the bay. It can be done. We spotted a centerboarder inside the harbor at the north end of the bay, but we also figured she must have been a local boat familiar with the area.

OYSTER POND

(Chart 17; II A-2, A-24, A-3)

This is an excellent sheltered harbor—once you are inside. Both entrance and exit have been rather treacherous for years, and they should be attempted only by the adventurous. (Paul Johnson—who sailed in and out of Oyster Pond regularly in the gaff-rigged ketch *Venus*—has been generous over the years with information on conditions here.)

Sailing instructions for getting in and out of this harbor were published in the last edition of this book, but now they probably would be indecipherable, as certain "conspicuous white houses" are no longer so conspicuous because of all the construction that has been going on in this area!

This is another harbor that "took off" when the French defiscalization law went into effect. When the law was enacted, bareboat companies were desperately looking for harbors in French territory where they could set up businesses, and several realized they could use Oyster Pond. So Sunsail Yachts (ex—Stevens Yachts), Sun Yachts and The Moorings moved in and are practically shoehorning boats into Captain Oliver's Marina on the French (northern) side of Oyster Pond, while the Dutch (southern) side of the harbor is empty. It is interesting to note that on the old Moorings charts, Oyster Pond is marked in red as a "no-go" danger area! (The Moorings is planning a move to Anse Marcel when facilities there are expanded, but seeing is believing.)

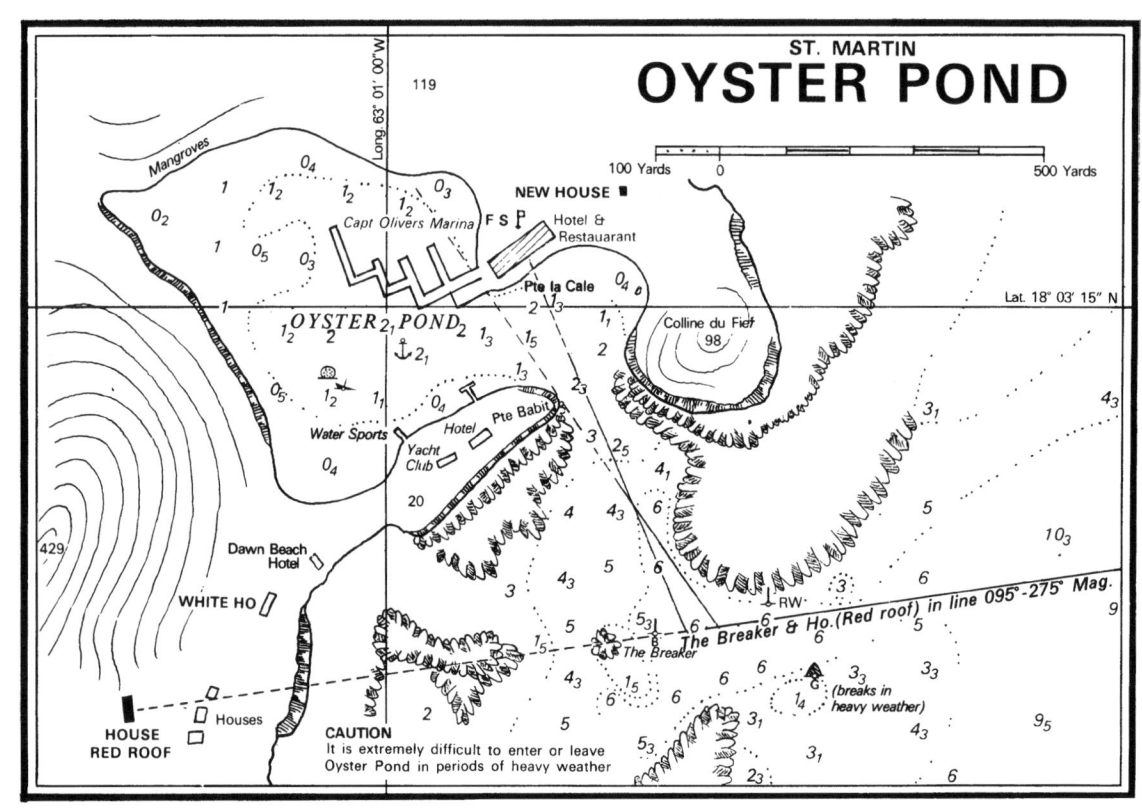

Chart 17 Oyster Pond   Depths in fathoms and feet

When approaching Oyster Pond from the north, stay east of a line of bearing of 015° on Molly Beday—for the same reasons given above. The entrance range is 275° magnetic. Place the orange triangular mark (on a post in the sea) under the distinctive T-shaped red roof on the hill above the beach). Run in on this line of bearing, keeping the diamond shape and the two buoys close aboard (15 to 20 feet) to starboard until the flagpole at Captain Oliver's bears 350° magnetic. Come right to this course and then run on in. Favor the starboard side of the channel, because if anything goes wrong, the seas will be pushing you off and putting you into deeper water, whereas if you run aground on the port side of the channel, then each wave will bounce you into progressively shallower water.

Admittedly, entrance is much easier now that Captain Oliver's Marina has buoyed the entrance (and maintains the buoys). Even so, I would not enter Oyster Pond unless conditions were ideal. The bareboat companies have to send out a chase boat to lead their boats in safely, and they usually put a pilot aboard when the boats are departing. Under power, in normal conditions, the entrance is not too difficult, but once the wind begins to blow, it becomes very hard (no—damned near impossible) to enter Oyster Pond. And once in, it can become all but impossible to leave.

In the winter of 1975, Joel Byerly of *Etoile de Mer* entered Oyster Pond, spent a number of days weatherbound in there, then finally had to leave anyway. As he motored out with *Etoile*—a heavily built trawler-type yacht with plenty of power—she actually stuck her nose so far under the waves that only the pilothouse was above water. I advise checking the weather conditions very carefully before playing around with Oyster Pond.

Even though there is complete shelter once inside the harbor, the docks are likely to be loaded with bareboats. And the anchorage space is restricted because of the number of boats moored here. The harbor has an excellent bar and restaurant, but this is all pretty much for bareboats, and it is not a harbor that most cruising yachtsmen would choose to visit.

Roland Bennet, assistant manager of Sunsail Yachts, has provided new sailing directions for entering Oyster Pond.

It must be remembered, first of all, that there is nothing but open ocean between the east coast of St. Martin and the west coast of Africa, 2,200 miles away. During periods of heavy weather, a large ocean swell can build up to such a point that the seas will begin to find the bottom and hump up in any depth less than 40 feet. They can frequently break on the windward side of St. Martin (and other Caribbean islands) in 20 to 25 feet of water.

When approaching Oyster Pond from the south, stay east of a line of bearing of 030° magnetic on the south end of Ile Tintamarre. Keep on this course until you reach the entrance range to Oyster Pond. If you do not do this, you might land yourself in shoal (20 to 30 feet) water south of Oyster Pond, where the seas will hump up and give you an uncomfortable or dangerous ride.

No yacht should enter Oyster Pond without checking first with either Sunsail Yachts (VHF channel 72) or The Moorings to ascertain whether or not conditions are suitable for entering.

GRAND ETANG DE SIMSONBAAI
(Chart 12, Sketch Chart 13; II A-2, A-24, A-3)

Anchorage in Simson's Bay is a bit rocky and rolly. The holding is extremely poor—exactly why I cannot figure out. But, we had a tremendous amount of trouble dragging with *Li'l Iolaire* in December 1999 and again in January 2000.

When entering through the bridge call on the VHF The Bridge Channel 12 or Island Waterworld Channel 74 for opening times. Channel depth as of January 2000 at half tide was 12-feet. The bridge width is 39-feet. There is a strong reversing current running through this channel. Once inside Simson Lagoon there are numerous marinas catering to every size yacht. There is no use in my listing the marinas here as by the time you read this they will have already expanded. Proceed with caution as Simson's Lagoon has not been acurately surveyed. If you do run aground it will only be bad if you are going fast. Proceed slowly, then if you run aground you can back off.

Customs and Immigration are in the building on the western side of the bridge entrance. It is best to clear before entering Simson's Lagoon as among other things, when you enter you can pick up the St. Martin's Marine Trade Directory. From this you can ascertain the up to date situation on the marinas and make your decision as to which marina suits you, or if you should anchor out. A quick glance through the Marine Directory will reveal that anything a yacht needs can be catered for in St. Martins.

Budget and Island Waterworld are major marine chandleries. What they don't have they can order. FKJ Rigging is renowned up and down the Caribbean as the top riggers in the Caribbean. They also have a machine shop and a hauling facility.

There are a number of sail makers in St. Martins, also awning makers, upholsterers, electronic specialists etc.

Hauling facilities are limited to the size of the travel lifts at Island Waterworld, FKJ and Bobby's Marina. Check upon arrival as both organisations are regularly updating their equipment—i.e. increasing the capacity of their travel lifts. For smaller boats, 30 tons and under—there are a number of hauling facilities.

Poor communications—all one can say is that the phone system in St. Martin's is the worst and most expensive in the whole Caribbean. If you can find a U.S.A. direct phone, they usually work. Otherwise in the Simson's Bay area the best thing to do is to go to MailBox, which has phones, fax, email services plus photocopying and secretarial service—you name it they have it.

Basic food supplies and many restaurants can be found on the road to the airport west of the bridge

BAIE DE MARIGOT
(Chart 12: II A-2, A-24, A-3)

This harbour has been vastly improved as in late 1998 they built a 1200 foot breakwater. This gives shelter to the eastern side of the harbour. A marina is proposed but as of January 2000, nothing has happened. Something may happen in the future. The bridge at Marigot—for information call Sun Yachts on Channel 72, yachts drawing more than 6 feet should not use this entrance. The approach moves around so much that anything more than 7 feet has extreme difficulty finding their way into the entrance to the channel for the bridge. Anything more than 6feet should not use this as once inside the northern end of Marigot Bay it is so restricted with live aboard boats that any boat drawing any more than 6feet ends up anchoring right in the middle of the channel. Not a good situation. Further, the channel leading from the north end of Marigot Bay to the southern end which was dredged in 1992 has shoaled up such that it is difficult to get 6 feet through this channel. The channel is very poorly marked. Groundings are pretty much inevitable for someone who does not know the area.

Port de Royale Marina is so crowded with bare boats and local boats that the chances of getting a slip are minimal. In Marigot for phone, fax, email The Marine Times provides these services. The Marine Times is found inside the harbour on the south of the break-water.

SIMSON BAAI

(Chart 12, Sketch Chart 13; 11 A-2, A-24, A-3)

When approaching Philipsburg—Groot Baai stay well clear of the new Cruise Ship pier. if buoys are placed to the southwest of this pier stay outside the buoys. Anchoring is not permitted in the area leading up to the launch pier at the head of the harbour. Also the anchoring area in Groot Baai is rather restricted as the launches from the cruise ships go back and forth across the bay and cause you to rock and roll very uncomfortably. Groot Baai has always had a problems with the bottom shoaling drastically as a result of hurricanes and periods of heavy ground swells. Also, the building of a new dock will probably change the currents in the harbour and move the sand around. Thus, any boats with draft of more than seven feet should proceed with extreme caution in Groot Bay—as the depths shown on this or any other chart may not be correct.

Bobby's Marine is usually so crowded there is not enough room for visiting yachts. You will have to check first. At Bobby's Marina one can find a hauling facility of 60 ton travelift, also Island Water World Marine Supply Store; Dockside mail pickup, fax and phone plus USA direct phones. There is also a restaurant and commissary.

When anchoring in Groot Baai you are anchoring in sand, holding is good but avoid the patches of grass.

4

St. Barthélemy (St. Barts)

(Imray-Iolaire Charts A, A-24, A-3)

Universally known as St. Barts, this island is one of the favorites of the Caribbean, since it is the "freest" free port in the whole area. This has been the case since 1784, when France ceded the port to Sweden in exchange for trading rights in Stockholm. At that time an agreement was made to the effect that St. Barthélemy would forever remain a free port, thus guaranteeing the French a harbor in which they could unload the loot from their privateers. Later, St. Barts developed into a port for smuggling goods into the British islands, which in fact it still is today.

The Swedish colony proved so unsuccessful that by the middle of the nineteenth century most of the Swedes had left; Sweden gave the island back to France in 1877. The only Swedish name left on the island seems to be Marius Stackelbough. While a large portion of the island's population have blue eyes and fair hair, this coloring probably stems from the Norman French who arrived in the 1880s.

The economy of St. Barts is based largely on trade, both legal and illegal. In 1960, Hurricane Donna destroyed most of the working sloops and schooners that were owned and sailed by locals. Although most of the boats were uninsured, that storm did not financially devastate their owners—nor did it put an end to the St. Barts trading fleet. In traditional thrifty French fashion, the skippers slit open the mattresses where they had been stowing their profits over the years, went to Guadeloupe, and, with the help of the French government, bought motor vessels. Just the same, it was another body blow to working sailboats.

An example of the frugality of the St. Barts Frenchmen and the prosperity of the islanders is

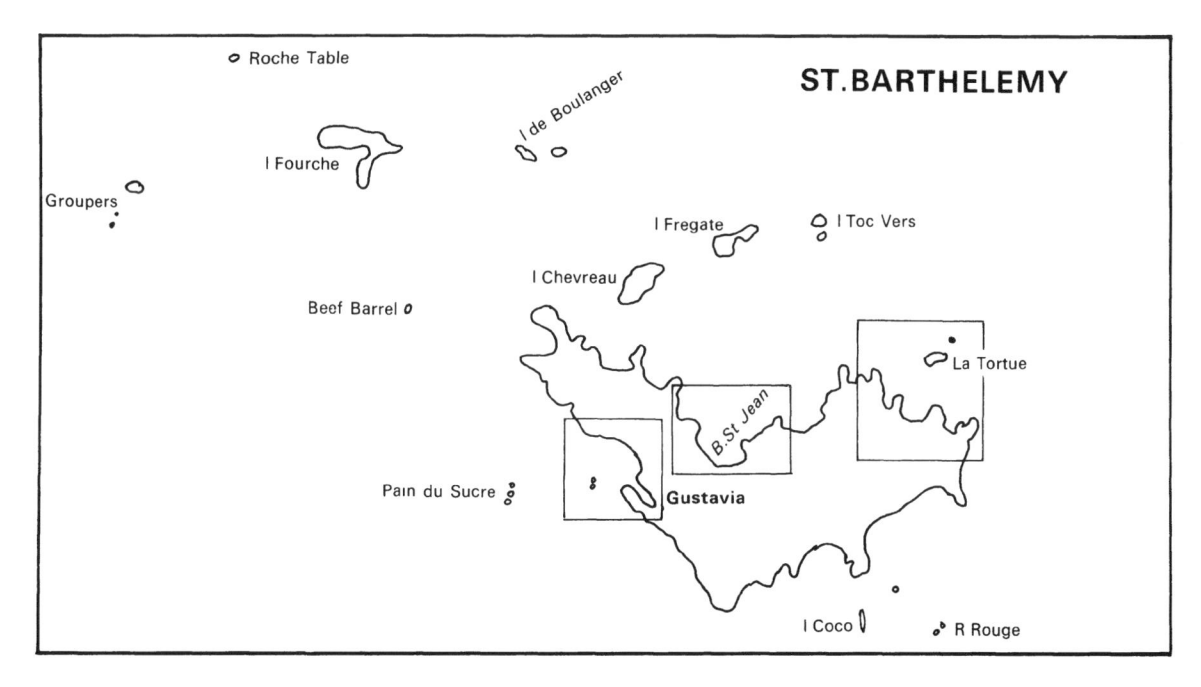

45

reported in the excellent little book *Clean Sweet Wind*—the story of the Eastern Caribbean boatbuilding and schooner trade.

It seems that when the French went from the old franc to the new franc and called in all the old money, government representatives flew to St. Barts with what they considered was an adequate supply of the new currency. They ran out of money in 15 minutes and had to make two more trips to Guadeloupe before they paid off the 2,000 men, women, and children in St. Barts. The total amount exchanged was US$2.5 million—an average of US$1,250 to each citizen in the island. In today's money, that probably would have been about $18,000 per person.

In years gone by, local schooners had an ingenious law-beating gimmick. Although it was illegal to import cattle into French islands from non-French islands, St. Barts, being a free port, did not have to abide by such regulations. The St. Barts schooners would sail to Tortola or St. Croix and buy several head of cattle, sail to St. Barts, sell them to a "brother," buy them back, reload, and sail off to Martinique or Guadeloupe with documents that proved the cattle had been bought in a free port acceptable to the French. Later, these entrepreneurs did not even unload the cattle. They simply bought and sold them while the vessel remained at anchor.

Today, liquor, cigarettes, and perfume are the main items of sale. The French don't waste their own energy smuggling. Instead, they sell to others who want to smuggle. In 1973, Mount Gay Eclipse Barbados rum sold for US$1.50 a bottle (ex-bond) in Barbados and in most other British islands. In the free port of Gustavia, St. Barthélemy, the same rum sold for US$6 *a case*—sometimes less. Small island sloops sail 400 miles from Grenada to St. Barts, pick up a cargo of Barbados rum, and sail the 400 miles back to smuggle the rum into Grenada. Thus, the rum travels 800 miles to be smuggled into an island that is only 90 miles from where it was made!

A number of other good buys could be unearthed on St. Barts in past years. There were, for example, wonderful old copper kerosene running lights that had internal chimneys and didn't blow out. Tremendous quantities of marine supplies were available in the back of the Alma store. You would have had trouble locating some of their stock anywhere else in the world. All this has now changed, as St. Barts has entered the twentieth century—especially twentieth-century France. The emphasis now is on everything being utterly chic, upmarket, and very expensive.

The owners of the Alma store, the Magras family, run a vast business enterprise. Monsieur Magras wanders among the three stores run by his sons while managing to keep a watchful eye on his myriad other enterprises. Years ago, money was kept in an old shoebox in the Magras office. If you went in to cash some checks, Magras would open a drawer where there would be tens of thousands of dollars in various currencies. When too much money accumulated—which happened occasionally—it was stuffed into a brown paper shopping bag and handed to the mate of one of the schooners heading for St. Thomas for deposit there. Now St. Barts has a bank, and the procedures are a little less free-wheeling.

Lulu Magras, the youngest member of the Magras clan, ran one of the Alma stores. He was a go-getter who developed an especially good stock of marine supplies and was extremely efficient at obtaining whatever anyone needed. He always stocked the Street guides. He also carried the original 1965 *Cruising Guide to the Lesser Antilles*—which was also known as the "Cursing Guide to the Lesser Ant-Hills" (i.e., CRASH! There's another ant-hill old Street didn't tell us about!). Lulu was also one of the first people to jump on the bandwagon in the development of the Imray-Iolaire charts.

Unfortunately for yachtsmen, Lulu discovered that there are a lot more tourists than yachtsmen in St. Barts. Thus, instead of having an excellent marine hardware store, he has an excellent boutique with a secondary line of marine hardware and fishing equipment. (The best selection of marine supplies is now available from Lulu's cousin in his store, The Ship Chandler.)

Lulu is the organizer of the annual St. Barts Regatta, which is without a doubt one of the great "fun" regattas of the Eastern Caribbean; well more than a hundred boats show up. The rating rules are a little mysterious, but Lulu and the other French organizers urge people to remember that racing should be fun and not taken too seriously. Protests are definitely discouraged. Everyone has a good time and everyone receives a prize of some sort. The parties are memorable!

If you are in St. Barts during February, it is well worth inquiring about the regatta. If you don't join in the racing, join in the fun!

Also, be sure to visit Lulu's to meet the man himself. He is a font of information about the yachting scene and the island itself, but watch out! He probably will sell you something from his boutique that you don't need at a price that you can't afford! He is such a compelling character, and his wife Jenny is so charming, that it doesn't even "hurt" when they relieve you of your money!

On my latest trip I found that Alma, now run by Raymond Magras, Lulu's older brother, has moved out of town. It is the island's main construction supply business, and still worth a visit. Take your dinghy down to the commercial dock in Anse du Public and walk a couple of hundred yards up the road to the warehouse and store. The store contains a veritable treasure-trove of tools, batteries, plumbing fittings, plastic ball-cock valves, and the like.

St. Barts has changed so much that now there are three building supply stores in the same area, so you can find just about anything imaginable in the way of building and plumbing supplies.

In past years, the provisioning in St. Barts was meager, and you could barely get enough to carry you through to the next island. This, however, has changed completely. The AMC Supermarket has progressed from a small shop that mostly carried liquor to a superb emporium complete with a delicatessen stocking the best cheeses. It also has a fine butcher shop, one of the best in the Eastern Caribbean. The AMC is now an excellent place to shop, but be sure to cross the threshold with a couple of bucketloads of cash! St. Barts is a very pleasant place to stock your boat—if you can afford it.

Years back, a Frenchman who had decided he had too much of cold weather in France moved to St. Barts and opened a fantastic modern bakery (next door to the post office). He made so much money that he sold out and retired, but luckily the operation continues in the time-honored fashion. It opens at about five in the morning, and you'll need to go early. Best idea is to have one member of the crew run in before breakfast and purchase hot croissants. If he is fast, he can get back to the boat while they are still hot. With café au lait, you can enjoy a true continental breakfast.

Baking has become such a competitive business in St. Barts that another bakery has opened up just across the street. Much to my amazement, I also discovered (via Marius Stackelbough, owner of Le Sélect bar) that at the head of the road leading to the hill from Lulu's marine store is the traditional West Indian bakery. It is still running, producing bread that has quite astonishing qualities: On the first day it is excellent; on the second day you can break it up and put it in soup; on the third day it is as hard as wood; and on the fourth day you can drill a hole in it, put a handle on the end, and use it as a caulking mallet!

Everyone loves French bread, but it is not suitable for an American's beloved sandwiches. Cut the loaf vertically and you get a lot of tiny sandwiches; cut it lengthwise and it is too thick to get in your mouth. Hearing complaints to this effect, the baker at the original French bakery came up with a fantastic solution: the "Big Boy," a loaf of bread about two feet long and six inches in diameter. Ask for it at the bakery, and be prepared to make wonderful Dagwood sandwiches.

Gustavia itself is well worth some exploring. Many of its buildings date back to the days of the Swedish occupation, and the massive stone architecture is quite different from the typical West Indian houses. The town is essentially French. The houses belonging to the wealthy people present a stern and forbidding exterior, but in back there usually is a beautiful, cool, walled-in garden where the family entertains.

There has been an enormous amount of new construction in and around Gustavia. Happily, almost all of it is in the traditional West Indian style—or a close approximation thereof. This gives the whole town a very attractive appearance. The only eyesores are the previously mentioned AMC Supermarket and the Presque Isle Hotel, both of which were built in the early 1960s in a style I refer to as "West Indian Modern"—which is singularly unattractive. I have often said that an architecture degree just gives some people a license to charge an exorbitant amount of money for a very bad design.

You can walk to Fort Karl, southwest of town, take in an exquisite view, and then go down to the beach that was created when the harbor was dredged. (Although the natives claim no success spearfishing there, the last time we fished the beach, one of our party caught a 40-pound grouper!) If all of this walking has made you thirsty, stop by Marius Stackelbough's bar, Le Sélect, at the head of the dock, to pick up news and enjoy a spot of booze. It's also the best place to meet all the locals. Marius, the last Swede on St. Barts, is very much a local celebrity. He has literally been entertained royally—by the King of Sweden—and he is a confidant of everyone who comes to St. Barts, from poor sailors to internationally known celebrities (among them Jimmy Buffett). Marius is one of the best informed residents on island lore, and what he does not know about St. Barts is not worth knowing.

Pay a visit to the fishing village in Anse du Corossol via taxi or dinghy. It is totally isolated from the rest of St. Barts. Formerly, the village had no road. And even though there is one now, most of the villagers still travel to and fro by small boat.

The completion of a wharf in 1960 removed one of the most interesting spectacles in St. Barts. In earlier days, ships had to anchor off the outer harbor and lighter their cargo ashore. The lighters were propelled by two oars—one rowed in the usual way over the side, the other used over the stern as a sculling oar. Why they didn't go around in a circle beats me. The loading and unloading of cattle was a particularly good show—as long as you were not a loyal member of the ASPCA.

Although the landing strip has received a coat of tarmac, it can still give a strong man a weak heart. It is rightly regarded as the most dangerous airstrip in the islands, with a record of many crashes to ensure this status.

In the early 1950s, the St. Barts boys were considered the best West Indians to hire for yacht crews. Their English was abominable, but they were skilled divers and good small-boat sailors, quick to learn, honest, hard-working, and fearless. There was the added bonus of their cooking prowess. After a few days out, a St. Barts crew would be heard to mutter, "Yes, I am not a cook but I make something in the kitchen for you." In no time at all, marvelous aromas would emanate from the galley, and from then on the smart charter skipper would surrender the galley to the man who insisted he was not a cook.

Many such islanders crewed on charter yachts and then moved on to high-wage jobs aboard large, lush, American yachts. With the true frugality of French West Indians, they spent virtually nothing. After 15 or 20 years, they took their substantial nest egg back to St. Barts, where they invested in small guest houses, restaurants, and shops.

Nowadays, however, most of the men on St. Barts are doing so well that they no longer need to ship out as crew.

For many years, despite the expansion of small enterprises on the island, St. Barts itself did not change drastically. Little development money for St. Barts came from outside the island, and that was the way the islanders wanted to keep it. Their honesty was legendary. You could leave your car unlocked with groceries, liquor, camera, and gold watch on the dashboard.

Alas, things have changed now. The island has become extremely popular with visiting sailors, who are not all as honest as they might be. And, St. Barts being part of France, it has been flooded with European French who flock to the island and set up businesses, buy property, and build houses. This has created such a labor shortage that labor is imported from Guadeloupe and Martinique. The crime rate in St. Barts is still extremely low, but there definitely is crime—some of it quite sophisticated. A friend of mine had a safe broken into, and the job was so professional that he did not realize he had been robbed until a couple of days later.

Back in the 1960s and 1970s, the gendarmerie of St. Barts consisted of a sergeant, a corporal, and a private. Now there are roughly 15 of them. Things are so civilized that they even give breathalyzer tests. (Luckily, they had not started that practice the night we went to Jimmy Buffett's pre-Mardi Gras party. If any of us had breathed into a breathalyzer, it probably would have exploded.)

The language of St. Barts has come full-circle. In the 1950s and early 1960s, relatively few people spoke English. But more and more yachts visited the island, and more and more locals went to St. Thomas to work on the yachts. By the mid-1980s, a progressively larger number of people were speaking English. Then came the invasion from metropolitan France. The French insisted on French being spoken, and they even went so far as to chastise the St. Barts shopkeepers for speaking English to American tourists! They were barking up the wrong tree, however, because St. Barts shopkeepers know that if they can make some money they will learn to speak any language—even Swahili if it's needed!

One encouraging aspect about the development of St. Barts is that most of the buildings erected during the 1980s blend in extremely well with the existing style. A sad matter is that nobody has seen fit to rebuild a beautiful old building, on the starboard hand coming into the harbor, that has only four walls standing. Some people claim it was an opera house in the heyday of St. Barts, but I think it was more likely a government office or Customs House. The roofless old Customs House has been magnificently restored to be the St. Barts Museum and Library. It is very definitely worth a visit. Allow yourself an afternoon as it is certainly a three to four hour museum.

St. Barts is part of the *département* of Guadeloupe. A *département* is a sort of state, the same as a province in France, which means St. Barts has its representative in the French legislature in Paris. This can be a mixed blessing, since it brings with it the inevitable bureaucracy. But I must say that the situation in St. Barts for incoming yachtsmen is excellent. Entry is dead simple; go to the Port Captain's office on the dock and everything is taken care of with speed, charm, and efficiency. For a while, the office was run by a collection of ex-gendarmes, but now it is run by three St. Barts citizens who will lean over backward to accommodate any true yachtsman.

There is about 300 yards of bulkheaded waterfront for yachts. Water is available there, as are showers, which are kept immaculately clean. As far as I can see, they are hosed down four times a day.

Needless to say, there are fees for mooring in the harbor, plus a surcharge if you are moored stern-to the dock. The rates are subject to periodic increases, but they have been quite reasonable each time I have been there. NOTE: Do not moor stern-to at the south end of the dock (i.e., the old commercial dock). It is pretty much reserved for the passenger-carrying catamarans that ply between St. Barts and St. Martin. During working hours, call on channel 16 to find out where you should moor. After hours, if you want to dock stern-to, find an empty place and then check with the harbormaster first thing in the morning. One word of warning, however: If you are moored in St. Barts Harbor and a northwest ground swell starts coming in, or the wind goes around to the north, a godawful surge can build up, making it impossible or dangerous to moor stern-to. The surge came in one time when we were there. *Iolaire* was about 10 feet off the dock, where we imagined she was secure. but then an extra-powerful surge came in and damaged *Iolaire's* tail feathers (*Iolaire* means "eagle" in Old Celtic), requiring a medium-size repair job on the taffrail.

Ice is available on St. Barts in a print shop, of all places! It's located behind the Presque Isle Hotel on the west side of the harbor. Sometimes you can find block ice in the first green building on the east side of the harbor, but not very often.

As mentioned earlier, the principal marine supply store in St. Barts is The Ship Chandler, which also stocks Imray-Iolaire charts. Even though this operation does a good job, it is nowhere near as interesting, picturesque, and amusing to the yachtsman as Lulu's always has been. Incidentally, Lulu's brother, Charles, was the brains behind the development of racing boats in St. Barts.

We noticed, while in Iles des Saintes (off Guadeloupe), a bunch of racing boats that had been built of wood using natural crooks in the traditional way. They had heart-shaped transoms and high, flaring bows forward. Curious about the design, we asked what was going on. It seems that back in France, the traditional style of boatbuilding is once again being encouraged—to make sure the art will not be lost. The financial backing for this traditional boatbuilding has filtered across the Atlantic to the French Antilles, and the result is a tremendous revival in the racing of Saintes-type fishing boats.

They certainly are an interesting class. As of 1992, there were 11 in the Saintes, 23 in Guadeloupe, and 10 in St. Barts. (The St. Barts fleet is expected to increase considerably.) The racing rules are interesting: 5.65 meters is the hull length from tip of bowsprit to stern; 6 meters is maximum. The beam is unlimited, but there has to be a full keel with an attached rudder. Six crew provide stability, but now built-in lead ballast is being allowed. (It will be interesting to see which is faster—lead keels or live ballast!) Rig height is limited to 8.5 meters, with the boom a maximum of 5 meters in length. The jibstay must be attached to the mast 5 feet below the masthead. (Only French Antilleans would switch from meters to feet in their racing rules!)

In Anguilla, the boats race strictly for big cash prizes. In St. Barts, many of the boats are sponsored, but it is strictly no-cash, as the regatta usually is sponsored by a hotel or beach bar. These patrons provide sandwiches and a bottle of champagne for each winner, three small plaques, and a lot of beer! Evidently everyone has a good time.

In St. Barts, you must know how to row and sail before you can leave school. The school system runs sailing classes in Optimists and 420s, rowing classes in Alden (or similar) ocean shells.

If you are approaching St. Barts from the south, leave Pointe Nègre to Starboard, Les Saintes to port. At night, it is best to leave both Pointe Nègre and Les Saintes to starboard. Enter the port by staying in the white sector of the light (see below). There are no dangers along this part of the coast, and there is ample water between Les Saintes and the mainland. You can tell the maximum depth by the color of the water. When Fort Oscar is abeam, start rounding up and flattening sheets, stand into the harbor on starboard tack, make one or two tacks, and you will be in the anchorage. It is steep-to close to shore. If you make passage outside the Saintes, watch out for the shoals that extend north of them.

Coming from the west and the northwest in daylight, there are no dangers for a yacht. Everything is visible above water and steep-to. Northwest of the island, at night, Roche Table is dangerous—despite being only 147 feet high, it is hard to spot.

The details of the light at Fort Gustave are shown on Imray-Iolaire Chart A-24. This light is group flashing, three colors: red, white, and green. It is confusing in that, at the extreme of visibility when you cross from one sector to another, the light disappears. The white sector of the light is visible 10 miles, the green seven miles, and the red six miles. It is green from northwest to north, and from south to southwest. The light is white and red for the rest of the west half of the compass. The red sector covers the area that is encompassed by Gros Ilets and Pain du Sucre. This means that if you are in the white sectors of this light, you are in good water and not in danger. Remember, this light is obscured by high hills northwest by north clockwise around to south southwest. Do not approach St. Barts from directions where the light is obscured. Since there are few recognizable lights on shore on a dark night, you could be on the beach before you realized it was there.

During the day, pass close aboard the rocks off the western end of Anse de Colombier. Hug the coast, staying 100 yards off, since it is steep-to all the way. The old Sailing Directions warn that "the vessel must be at all times kept under command as the flaws coming from the highland may catch the vessel aback." Being caught aback was a great danger for an old square-rigger, which had considerable difficulty maneuvering in restricted waters. But these same "flaws" are a plus for the modern yacht. Tack on every header, take advantage of the lifts, and you will really make good to windward with considerable time saved.

If you should be forced offshore, beware of La Baleine, an awash rock 300 yards west of Gros Ilets.

GUSTAVIA

(Chart 18; II A-24, A-3)

Gustavia is becoming more and more crowded as each year goes by. Do not try to anchor at the southern end of the harbor. It is taken up completely by resident yachts moored bow-and-stern. There are a

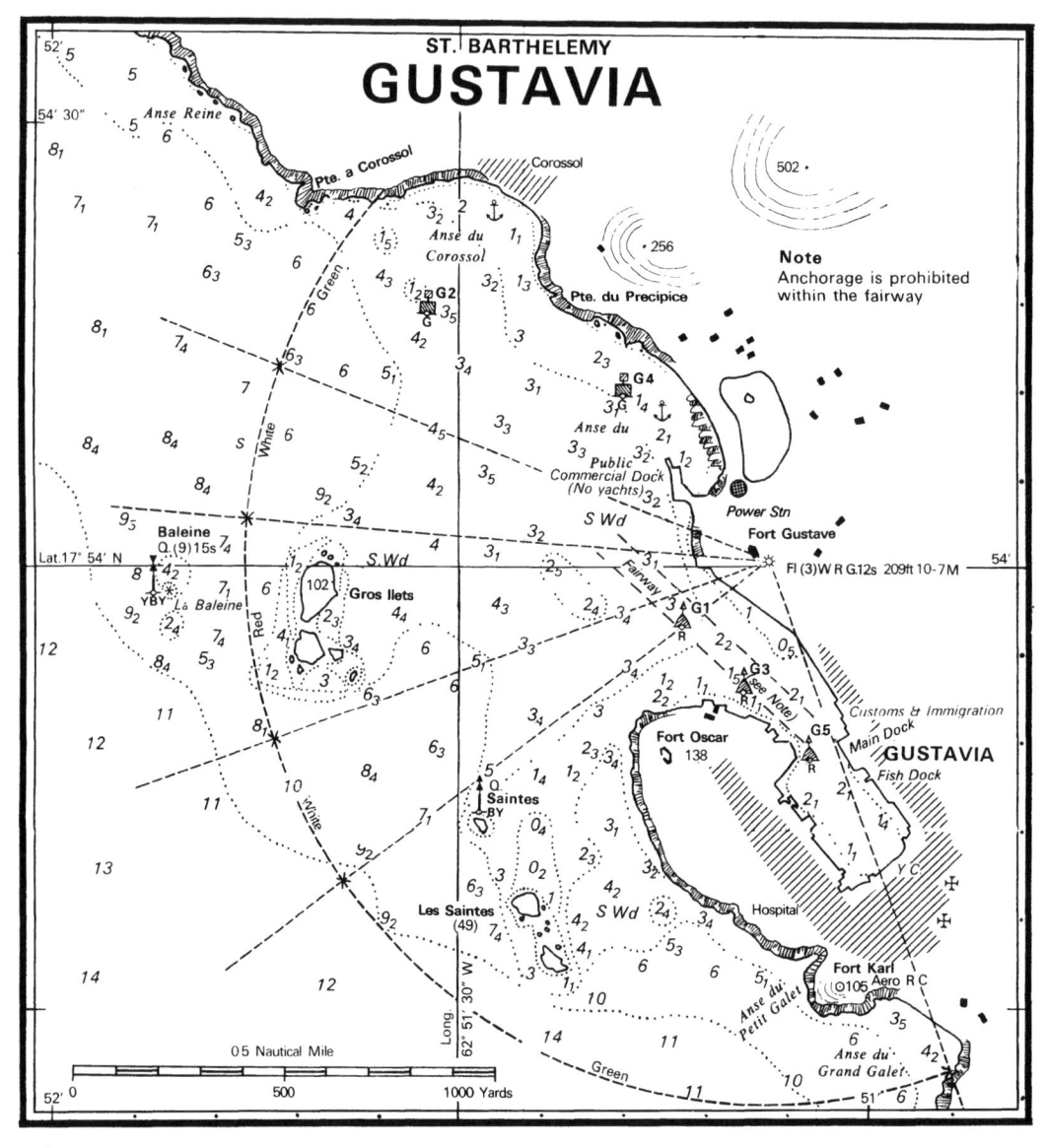

Chart 18 Gustavia   Depths in fathoms and feet

couple of options. You can anchor stern-to the wa- terfront, as mentioned earlier, or you can anchor out—but just make sure you are out of the fairway, as large ships come into the commercial dock at Anse du Public. Anchoring out can cause problems, though, because one group of yachts will throw out an anchor and let the wind and the tide determine their direction, another group will be anchored bow-and-stern; and a third group may be on a Bahamian moor. The result is mass confusion when the wind dies down at night. When anchoring in St. Barts, do your best to anchor well clear of other boats and keep your fenders out. When boats start swinging against you at two in the morning, try to hold your temper and keep your sense of humor!

The marine supply situation in St. Barts. is now excellent. Le Ship run by Sully Magras, is a really good marine chandlery. What he doesn't have he can probably obtain and between Sully Magras and his No. 1 assistant Jean Francois they will be able to tell you where any work can be carried out—sails repaired, machine work done, outboards repaired. St. Bart's is so small they do not put out a Marine Directory, but a visit to Le Ship chandlers on the east side of the harbor will answer all your questions.

As of April 2000 additional stem-to anchorage was being established on the west side of the harbor by the old Customs House.

This building has been beautifully restored and is now an excellent museum—worth a four hour visit.

ANSE DU PUBLIC
(Chart 18; II A-24, A-3)

This is another excellent anchorage, and much cleaner than the town anchorage. It is isolated enough to allow an early-morning skinny dip, yet only a short dinghy ride from town. But you have to put up with the racket from a power plant that runs all night. A new pier has been built in the southeast corner. Be sure to stay well clear of the pier to allow maneuver- ing room for the ships; if you don't, the harbormaster will come out and demand that you move

ANSE DU COROSSOL
(Chart 18; II A-24, A-3)

This is an attractive anchorage and an alternative to the dirty harbor of Gustavia. The bay has a white-sand beach, a small fishing village, and a single restaurant right on the beach that is owned by an ex-yachting crew who worked for me on *Iolaire* 37 years ago!

ANSE DE COLOMBIER
(II A-24, A-3)

The north shore of St. Barts provides two good anchorages. Anse de Colombier on the northwest tip of the island is satisfactory as far as shelter is concerned, but the holding ground is poor (mixed sand and grass), so be sure that your anchor is well set. This anchorage is only practical in normal tradewind weather. If the ground swell makes up from the north, move around to Gustavia. The cove is easily recognized by the large house built above the beach by one of the Rockefellers. Everything is steep-to, and you should find no problems in approaching. It is legal to land there, where you will find an appealing sand beach. Under French law, everything from 14 feet back of the high-water mark to the shore is public property. To remind Mr. Rockefeller of this fact, the local French have pic-

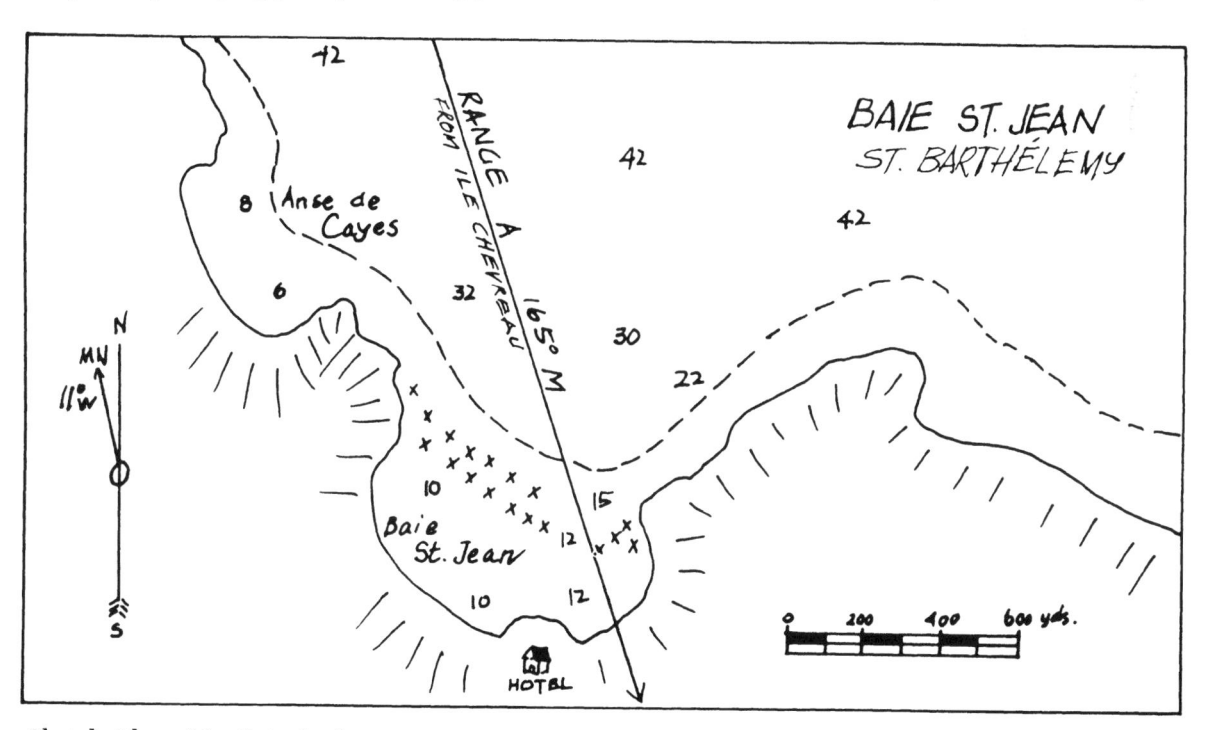

Sketch Chart 19   Baie St. Jean

Depths in feet

nics on his beach on the big French holidays. This being the game, I doubt that he could object if visiting yachtsmen did the same.

BAIE ST. JEAN

(Sketch Chart 19; II A-24, A-3)

This is easy to spot because of the Eden Rock Hotel, owned by René de Haenen, who settled on St. Barts during World War II and has been there almost ever since. For many years, René had the only hotel on the island, had the only aircraft, served as mayor, and at other times served as the elected representative to the French legislature. You will not find this harbor on the standard chart, but Sketch Chart 19 provides an idea of the approach. Put your stern on Ile Chevreau and steer a course of 165° magnetic, aiming for the middle of the beach; white-painted coconut trees are no more. Do not be confused by the buoy that marks the reef on the western side of the harbor, since the buoy may or may not be in the correct position. Do not enter unless the sun is high, because you must use eyeball navigation.

Yachts are not allowed to anchor off Baie St. Jean. It is strictly for sailboarding, snorkeling, and swimming. How rigidly this rule is enforced, I am not quite sure.

ANSE DE MARIGOT

(Sketch Chart 20; II A-24, A-3)

Both the US and British Admiralty charts are incorrect on this area, so beware of them. Anse de Grand Cul-de-Sac and Anse de Petit Cul-de-Sac are, as the names suggest, entirely obstructed by reefs. Only a small dinghy can make it over the reefs and into these bays. Similarly, passage only for the shoalest-draft boats can be found between La Tortue and the St. Barts mainland. You *can* get into Anse de

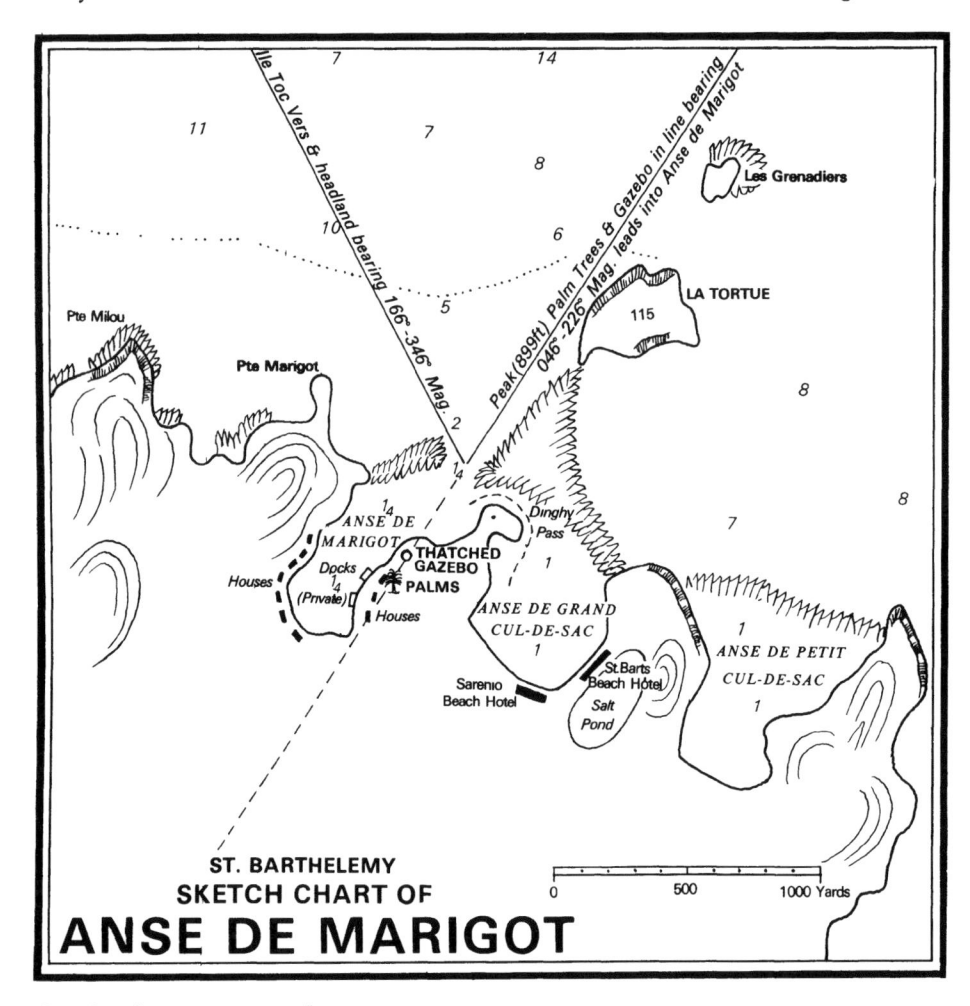

Sketch Chart 20 Anse de Marigot   Depths in fathoms and feet

Marigot, though. Sail east until you line up Ile Toc Vers (see Imray-Iolaire Chart A-24) and the headland on a bearing of 164° magnetic. Run in on this bearing, keeping a sharp eye out for the reef that will appear close aboard to starboard. Sail until the 899-foot peak (the highest on St. Barts) lines up with the palm trees and the gazebo (a thatch-roofed open bar) on the beach at a bearing of 215°. Swing right onto this course and run on into the harbor. Once past the reefs, all is clear; the eastern side of the harbor is deeper.

This is a harbor that few yachts use; you'll find a nice beach at the end of the harbor, a small bar, and a phone.

During the summer, with the wind in the east, the harbor will be calm and the water clear; in the winter, with the wind northeast, it will be a bit rolly, so you'll have to anchor bow-and-stern to be really comfortable. The bottom may be a bit murky then, but your chances are good of having the place to yourself.

ANSE DE SALINE

(II A-24, A-3)

If the wind is in the east and not blowing to hard, Anse de Saline is a lovely daytime anchorage, well tucked up in the northeast corner. You will find a white-sand beach and no roads, and you'll probably have the place to yourself.

Tuck right up in the northeast corner. This is becoming increasingly popular, as it is a "dress-optional" beach. If you want to spend the night here, anchor with two anchors (bow facing into the swell) or on a Bahamian moor. The wind probably will die out and you don't want to wake up during the night and find your boat waltzing around a single anchor.

ANSE DU GOUVERNEUR

In Anse du Gouverneur is a tiny anchorage that is not even noted on Imray-Iolaire Chart A-24. It's a little cove west of Anse de Saline. Use it only if the wind is in the north or northeast. If the swell is running into the cove, anchor bow-and-stern facing into the swell. Before you land the dinghy, have someone swim in and check. People have been seriously injured by dinghies capsizing on them in surf. This happened to four sailors landing on Green Cay in the British Virgins. They were rescued by the VISA-R launch and all landed in the hospital! Surf can be dangerous.

This is only a calm-weather daytime anchorage. I would be extremely leery of spending the night here.

North of St. Barts are numerous islands that are reputed to provide splendid spearfishing and diving for the adventurous. Most of these islands have no landing, however, so yachts need to heave-to off the island while divers go in by dinghy.

ILE FOURCHE

(II A-24, A-3)

This island provides one decent anchorage, and only one. Ile Fourche ("Fork Island") is referred to as though it were five islands because, when seen from a distance, its five peaks look like separate islets. It is shaped like the thumb and index finger of the right hand: thumb faces south and index finger faces west. In the northeast corner is an excellent anchorage with three fathoms of water. Be careful of the exposed rock off the southern tip (the thumb) and the submerged reef off the western end of the island. This exquisite anchorage has a beach and some lovely views, but the island has no bushes, trees, or water. It would be a good place to abandon a mutinous crew, as they probably wouldn't survive.

Ile Fourche is known for having the largest and most hazardous cacti in the world. Not only do their spines penetrate "go-aheads" (flip-flops are also called go-aheads; have you ever tried going backward in them?), but I have also heard claims that they even go through Topsiders. So if you want to go ashore, you'd better be wearing army boots! You might prefer to stay on the boat and enjoy the snorkeling in solitude. Even if boats come in, you can be sure they will depart quite soon.

NOTES

5

Saba, St. Eustatius (Statia), St. Christopher (St. Kitts), and Nevis

(Imray-Iolaire Charts A, A-25, A-3)

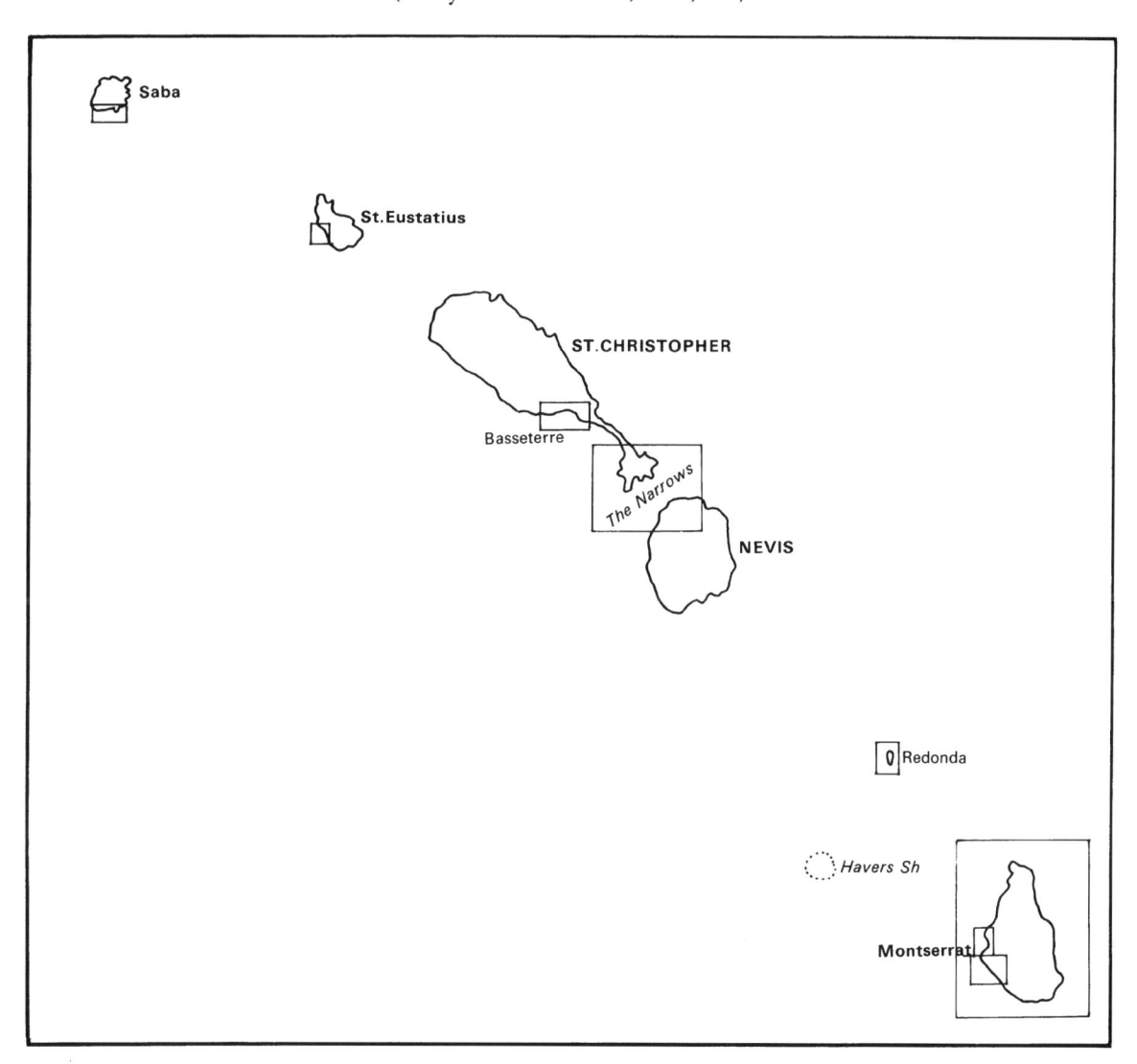

Saba

Eighty-four miles southeast of Necker Island Passage and 23 miles southwest of St. Martin lies Saba, a pinnacle of rock rising 2,854 feet out of the sea. It is a most frustrating island to sail to because it is visible for 40 miles on a clear day. You can spot it by dawn, and it can still be tantalizingly out of reach by nightfall. And in the old days, it was often too rough to land after you got there. No harbor existed, nor was there any hope of building one, and there were only the barest traces of a boat landing. Nor was there much in the way of arable land. It's a wonder that the Dutch chose to settle on Saba at all, what with so many more attractive and accessible islands nearby. No history book I have read has come up with a satisfactory answer to this puzzling question.

Even more amazing than its original settlement is why someone should fight over it. From 1635 (when Pierre d'Esnanbuc claimed the island for France and started a settlement) until 1815 (when the Dutch were finally, permanently given the island), it had changed hands more than a dozen times. Why anyone would want to fight over this certainly baffles my mind.

Today, however, the situation is a bit different. A harbor has been built (or, rather, a large dock that provides shelter), a narrow road winds up the hillside, and an airport is precariously perched on the northeast corner of the island. What has not changed is the fact that once you get there, you will find it to be an exceptionally interesting place, totally unlike any other West Indian island. Its two towns make one think immediately of Holland. Their houses are neatly painted, often trimmed with "gingerbread," and surrounded by beautifully tended gardens. Women sit in the doorways making lace, for which they are justly famous. (The ones not making lace are likely to be inside at the stove, busily stirring huge pots of Saba Spice, a local brew that goes down easily but packs a bit of a punch if consumed in quantity.) Because there is so little agriculture, Saba's men turned to the sea, being rigorously trained for it in the island's sturdy surfboats. For hundreds of years, Sabans have held an enviable reputation as the best sailors in the West Indies. Today there are master mariners all over the world who began their careers in Saba. But now the surfboats are a thing of the past. I wonder what will become of the members of the new generation once the skills of launching, maneuvering, and landing these craft are absorbed by motor. Probably more and more of them will go to work in the oil refineries in Aruba and Curaçao, and eventually the Saban tradition of consummate seamanship will be lost.

The island is high and steep-to, and although it has substantial rainfall (the peak of Mount Scenery usually is hidden in a cloud), the climate is healthful. There are no lowlands to breed mosquitoes and the various fevers and illnesses found on other islands. For this reason, the Sabans are a hardy sort and seem to live forever. Maybe the settlers knew what they were doing after all.

The island's main town—inside an extinct volcano—is called The Bottom. To get there, you must first go up over the rim of the volcano. This used to mean a laborious climb up steps cut into the rock. But in the early 1950s, the Sabans succeeded in building a road, so the climb no longer is necessary from Fort Baai. In 1960, in the appropriately named area of Hells Gate, they also carved out a small airstrip for single-engine planes. Since this so-called airfield is strictly for the brave, it didn't open the floodgates to tourists. It is cut through a saddle in the hill, and mountains rise sharply on both sides. At each end of the runway is a sheer drop into the ocean, 1,100 feet below. No place for engine failure and a good place for heart failure.

Saba is seldom visited by yachts, although local officials are working hard to change this. Much of the time it is too rough to anchor, although on occasion it can be as smooth as a millpond. Even in the latter instance, however, care is essential, since the sea can build up very quickly. There are two anchorages: South Side Landing (Fort Baai, Chart 21) on the southwest corner and Ladder Landing (Ladder Baai) on the west coast. At Fort Baai you will find the Customs House, a road, taxis, and a dock constructed about 1972. The small freight-carrying steamer that connects Saba to the outside world lies alongside this dock when it calls, and its passengers get ashore over a gangway—rather than, as before, by leaping from the deck of a surfboat. The dock is about 100 yards long, with sufficient depth for the largest yachts. Yachts are allowed to stay alongside the wharf, but they may be requested to move if a freighter is due—the dock is, after all, primarily for commercial vessels. If you do tie up, be prepared to use plenty of fenders, since the small local sloops and schooners are likely to raft up outboard of you if you have a relatively large craft.

Normally, lying alongside the dock is comparatively calm, but you should use a breasting-out anchor rigged to hold you off the dock. In the winter months, when the ground swell can build up rather

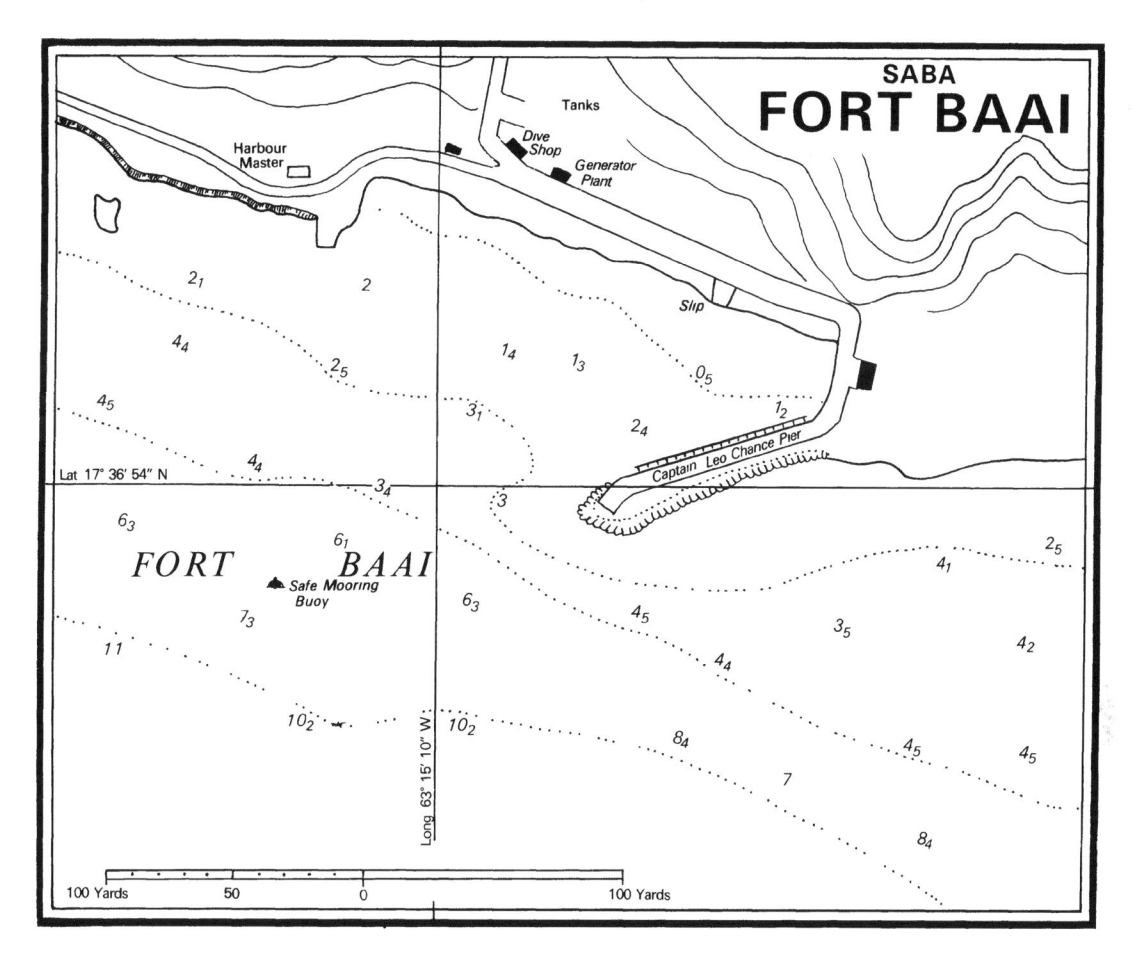

Chart 21 Fort Baai, Saba   Depths in fathoms and feet

rapidly, enough crew should be left on the boat so that, if necessary, the boat can be moved.

If a freighter is at the dock, the best place to lie is alongside the freighter. The freighter goes back and forth with the surge and you will move back and forth with the freighter. This procedure will require fewer springlines than you'd need if lying alongside the dock. Further, the surge builds up at a narrow angle at the head of the dock, so try to tie up as far out on the dock as possible. If the surge is too great to lie at the dock but the wind is not too strong, you can put down an anchor and run a line to the mooring buoy set out to the west of the pier; then go ashore to the dock in the dinghy. If wind and weather conditions do not permit this, lie off the dock and then try anchoring off Ladder Landing. If the surge has been caused by heavy trade winds, Ladder Landing is likely to be calm and comfortable. But if the surge has been caused by the northwest ground swell swinging around behind Saba, *do not*

go to Ladder Landing, since the anchorage would be untenable and a dinghy landing impossible.

A dinghy dock has recently been built at Fort Baai, opposite the harbormaster's office, and mooring buoys are being set out—white for local dive boats, yellow for visiting dive boats, and orange for visiting yachts.

If you decide to move around to Ladder Landing, keep in mind its chief disadvantage: There is no road. You must ascend steps ("The Ladder), follow a path to the nearest road, and then try to flag down a taxi or car. Good luck. And even in calm weather, you should leave someone aboard at this anchorage, too. If the ground swell begins to roll in, you will want to get offshore in a hurry. When the swell gets worked up, it has to be seen to be believed. Once when we were *becalmed* off Saba, we estimated that the surf was sending solid water some 150 feet up the cliffs!

Anchoring is difficult in Saba, as the bottom drops off so steeply. If the anchor hooks on something, it probably is too deep to pull it up. During the winter of 1991–92, the skipper and mate of a mega-yacht were lost when their anchor was fouled in 120 feet of water—they could not break free even with their engines. The skipper and mate decided to dive down to try to free the anchor, and that's the last anyone ever heard of them.

My advice is to anchor in Saba only in fine weather, for starters, and use a Bruce or a plow anchor. Shackle the anchor chain onto the lifting ring at the head of the anchor, then lash the chain to the head of the anchor with four or five turns of 1/4-inch nylon. The strength of 1/4-inch nylon is about 300 pounds, so four turns equals 1,200 pounds, which is sufficient to hold an anchor chain in line with the head of the anchor; all will be well. When the time comes to leave, if the anchor is fouled, with enough strain put on the anchor line pulling at right angles to the stock, the nylon lashing will break. Then the anchor will be attached to the chain by its lifting eye and should come free, allowing you to retrieve both anchor and anchor line.

Despite all these caveats and hair-raising descriptions, Saba is supremely worthwhile if the weather is good. Some yachtsmen have enjoyed it so much that they have remained for days, with the crew staying aboard in shifts. My own feeling is that a visit to Saba, even with its built-in difficulties, is an experience you have only once in a lifetime.

Once ashore in Saba, find yourself a taxi driver and tour the island. (Local taxi drivers have a habit of "adopting" visitors and will keep in touch with you for the duration of your stay.) There are only about a thousand people living in Saba's four little villages—The Bottom, Windward Side, Hells Gate, and St. Johns. The houses all look like something out of a storybook: white gables, gingerbread carvings, red roofs, lovely little gardens. The single road—which meanders across the island—is very narrow, but it is well surfaced and has an amazing history. Years ago, Dutch engineers insisted that it was impossible to build roads on Saba—but they failed to realize how industrious and clever the Sabans are. Under the leadership of Mr. Hassell, they carved roads by hand out of solid rock, then paved them. The Dutch government finally admitted that roads could be built on the island, somehow got a bulldozer ashore, aided in the road construction, and eventually built the airport.

There are a couple of small hotels and a number of guest houses with wonderful names. Ask your taxi driver to arrange for lunch, then take your tour, come back for lunch, and return to the boat. If you are starting late in the day, have him (or her) arrange for dinner.

Diving has become very popular in Saba, and several diving operations are based on the island. They are all working together to preserve the environment and are doing an excellent job. Coral is fragile, and when damaged, it takes centuries to regenerate. Thus, there are dive sites all around the island where anchoring is forbidden. I am told on very good authority that the diving firms would not object to your picking up one of their dive-site buoys and mooring to it. Needless to say, this should apply only to moderate-size boats—the dive boats are only 35 to 40 feet. As in Bonaire, all spearfishing has been outlawed. The local fishermen do not take very many fish, so divers get to enjoy their sport surrounded by multitudes of fish that are just a step away from being tame.

Another indication of the seriousness of Saba's dive firms is the existence of one of the few operating decompression chambers in the Eastern Caribbean. The only others I know of are the chamber in St. Thomas and the US Navy chamber at Roosevelt Roads on the east coast of Puerto Rico.

Saba is connected to St. Martin by ALM Netherlands Antilles Airlines, the West Indian division of KLM.

South of Saba lies Saba Bank, an area where it is impossible not to catch a boatload of fish in a few hours. (Don't eat barracuda caught here, however; they are likely to be poisonous.) The area is shoal—you can almost always see bottom—but it is deep enough that only the largest steamers are likely to run aground. Nonetheless, DO NOT BEAT TO WINDWARD ACROSS IT. When coming from the Virgin Islands, under no circumstances allow yourself to sag down onto the bank. Tack to the north if necessary. The current runs strongly to the west across Saba Bank (despite what various sailing directions and pilots say), and its shoal water causes the seas to become short and steep, sometimes even square—six feet high and six feet between crests. Even a powerboat driving into this head sea can get into difficulty. I know of one that broke every bottle of beer in its locker. The crew thought they had sprung a leak—until they discovered that they had lost 20 cases of beer into the bilge. Despite the extra distance, discretion is essential. When heading east, alter course to travel around Saba Bank.

Oil companies did some drilling on Saba Bank, and although the oil rigs themselves were very well lighted, their offlying buoys definitely were not. In 1977, en route to Antigua Sailing Week, we came within an ace of losing *Iolaire*. We were beating to windward rail down with a whole-sail breeze on a clear night with no moon—position estimated to be at least a mile off the well-lighted oil rig. To windward of us we noticed a large oceangoing tug lying-to with lights ablaze, but we thought nothing of it. Our running light, a three-way masthead light, was on and easily visible to the deck watch on the tug—if he were awake. All was apparently well, until I almost died of heart failure. There, passing by about 15 feet to leeward, was a large, unlighted steel buoy probably eight feet in diameter and standing 15 to 18 feet high. I then gave the helm to someone else, ran up to the bow pulpit, and sat there watching carefully with night glasses. Over the next 15 or 20 minutes, we spotted two more unlighted buoys. A collision with one of them would easily have sunk *Iolaire,* despite the fact that she is a heavily constructed cruising boat. I hate to think what would have happened if a modern, light-displacement boat would have collided with one of these massive navigational hazards.

That drilling rig has disappeared from Saba Bank, and I hope it will never be back. But if you see a Texas tower anywhere in the Caribbean, give it a very wide berth and watch out for offlying, unlighted buoys.

St. Eustatius (Statia), St. Christopher (St. Kitts), and Nevis

These three islands lie on the eastern side of the Anegada Passage about 30 miles south of the Anguilla—St. Martin—St. Barts group. They are all essentially mountain peaks with their heads in the clouds and no real harbors on their shores. Statia, a Dutch island, is sparsely settled and has a subsistence economy. St. Kitts is an independent nation, heavily populated, and grows a great deal of sugar. Nevis, politically part of St. Kitts, is a relatively populous island whose people grow a variety of crops on small holdings. Historically, the three have had their day in the sun. Now in eclipse, they are trying to find something new to bolster their economies.

None of these islands is large enough to block the trade winds effectively, so the climate is sunny year round. The rainy season brings showers and squalls rather than the all-day torrents that inundate the high islands to the south. Tides are only about one foot and there are no particularly narrow passages to block the flow of water, so the currents are minimal.

Statia has little to offer in the way of food—nothing more than the basic staples. Getting on and off the island is strictly a dinghy trip. No hauling or repair facilities exist on Statia or Nevis, but Dougie Brooks in St. Kitts has a big catamaran building and repair facility. (He's the brother-in-law of Peter Spronk, who established catamarans in St. Martin.) Dougie can haul any multihull of 14 tons or less, and he has plenty of experience in both boatbuilding and repair.

St. Kitts is a good place to provision. There is plenty of canned food available, as well as good meat. The ice here is the cheapest in the Caribbean, if not the world. In the past, there was little fresh produce, but over the years the sugar-based economy has diversified, and the municipal market now offers a wide variety of fresh fruit and vegetables at a reasonable cost. Fuel and water can be taken on board (with great difficulty) at the main commercial dock in St. Kitts.

Nevis has an excellent fresh-produce outlet at the head of its dock. At the Nevis fish factory, ice is made in five-gallon pails. It is not cheap, but it sure beats ice cubes! Water can be obtained, but with great difficulty, and only if you are really stuck.

Nevis and Statia have small airstrips, while St. Kitts has an international jetport dating from the early 1980s. This reputedly is because the late St. Kitts premier, Robert Bradshaw, was told he could have an international jetport if he would renounce all claims to Anguilla.

St. Eustatius (Statia)

Historically, Statia has the distinction of being the first place that accorded a salute to the American flag in foreign waters; in 1775, the Dutch governor fired a salute to the flag flown by the American privateer *Andrea Doria.* It was a free, neutral port where privateers and pirates could unload and auction off their booty. Then, in 1781, Rodney captured the island, seized the goods, condemned them, and auctioned off goods, ships, and sundries as prizes of war. He burned what he could not auction off and spent the rest of his life involved in lawsuits brought by the merchants of St. Kitts.

Every historian knows the above, but the sequel is both interesting and amusing. The British stationed a garrison on Statia to reinforce Fort Oranje. Governor Cockburn stated that with 1,000 men (which he had), he could defend Statia against 8,000 with no trouble. However, someone forgot to tell the French about this, and they recaptured Statia on the morning of 15 November 1781—with fewer than 1,000 men! A small French fleet sailed by the island and hove-to on the northwest coast off Jenkins Bay.

There, with great difficulty, they landed through the surf. I say "with great difficulty" because contemporary newspaper reports, which can be seen in the Statia Museum, tell of boats being capsized and many men being drowned. However, by dark the survivors had managed to get ashore, where they fought their way upward through brush, making a three-mile march throughout the night. They arrived at Fort Oranje just at dawn as the British troops were lining up for morning parade. Governor Cockburn was going down to take the morning salute when the French, aided by a regiment from the Irish Brigade, attacked the town, grabbed the governor, and stormed into the fort.

The British troops retreated to the inner keep and started cranking up the drawbridge. With some well-directed fire, the French drove off the drawbridge crew, poured into the fort, and captured it lock, stock, and barrel. The following day, they sailed over to St. Martin and recaptured that island. A contemporary account of the battle appears in the Statia Museum, which is well worth visiting.

From that time until recently, Statia has been practically a ghost island. Nothing but an open beach with a ruined jetty greeted visitors where at one time they would have seen hundreds of sailboats anchored in the roadstead and innumerable warehouses on shore and on docks for unloading. Statia's one anchorage southwest of town is sheltered from the normal trade winds. An uncomfortable swell almost always comes in, however, so the anchorage is predictably rough. The swell makes landing on the beach an experience best avoided.

A big, long pier finally was built, but that was badly damaged during Hurricane Hugo in 1989. Although the surface may look all right, the underside has reinforcement rods dangling out of it like old spaghetti! In any case, this 1,000-foot-high dock is too tall to be of any use to yachtsmen. There is a smaller dock for dinghies, but be sure to carry a stern anchor to hold the boat off. Once ashore, go to the main dock and look for the harbormaster. Do the entry formalities and then head to town. Everyone is very friendly; stick out your thumb and you are likely to get a lift quickly. In town, go to the police station for Immigration procedures.

In 1996 the pier was built which although it does not give enough shelter for yachts, it does provide a basin where a dinghy can be landed and tied off with a stern anchor in all but the worst weather.

There are a couple of nice, old churches to explore in town; Fort Oranje has been completely restored and offers a magnificent view. The Statia Museum is open seven days a week (but only in the morning on weekends).

Ask around for Ditrick Gibbs, an ex-seaman who builds wonderful plank-on-frame models of traditional West Indian schooners. They are wonderful, as they are scale models fashioned by a true boatbuilder in the style of the old vessels. The frames are natural crooks of white cedar, the planking is pine. His shop is only 100 yards from the museum. If you have any leather goods that need repair, take them along, because Gibbs also is a trained cobbler.

The tourist office can provide a helpful list of bars, restaurants, hotels, and guest houses. When we were in Statia in March 1992, there were two hotels close together on the waterfront. The restored Old Gin House is a bar, restaurant, and guest house with more than a bit of "olde worlde" charm. In contrast, next door is the Golden Mirror Hotel—a new hostelry whose architecture I would classify as "West Indian modern." In the upper part of town is the Talk of the Town—a hotel, bar, and restaurant. Entertainment in Statia is interesting: It only happens late on Saturday nights! The best plan is to sleep until 10 p.m. on Saturday and then get up for dinner and dancing, as the parties start at 11 p.m. and go on until dawn.

There is a very helpful dive operation on Statia —Statia Dive Shop. Contact them on channel 16. They will arrange dives as well as package deals in which they book you into a hotel and arrange for diving every day (sometimes twice a day).

This is a very active bunkering station, as it is used not only for offloading cargo from giant tankers into smaller tankers but also for bunkering small freighters of all sizes and shapes. When we were there in March 1992, six ships were standing by for fuel. Reportedly this operation has produced as many as 120 jobs for islanders, but it most definitely is a mixed blessing for Statia, as the oil gets all over everything. After one night anchored off the island, our waterline and topsides were so covered with heavy globs of tanker fuel that we scrubbed for six hours to remove it. Who knows how long it will take to get the oil off our anchor line. A chat with local divers revealed that this was not a one-time occurrence—apparently it happens about twice a month. The fishing boat that was moored astern of us was tide-rode for a few hours and swinging up into us. With the mizzen and the large awning up, we were wind-rode. It was two days after full moon and the tide had overcome the equatorial current. (See *Street's Transatlantic Crossing Guide and Introduction to the Caribbean,* chapter 6, for a description of Caribbean tides.) Thus, the oil was carried up into the anchorage. This probably happens only on spring tides (i.e., a couple of days after full moon and new moon), so my advice is to visit Statia only on neap tides.

Oranjestad (Chart 22) is built atop the cliff looking down into the roadstead, and it is hard to see. The ruins of the warehouses stand at the foot of the cliffs, and a road leads up to the town. Northwest of town lies an old battery, and numerous fine beaches run along the north side of the island. Since the days of the drilling on Saba Bank, the major development in Statia has been the construction of a huge oil tank farm on the western end of the island. The VLCCs come to Statia from the Far and Middle East and pump their cargo into storage for the smaller tankers that take the oil on to the United States. They can do this despite the exposed anchorage at Statia, because what is a rough sea to us is only a mild chop to the tankers.

Possibly the biggest event in Statia since Rodney captured the town in 1781 was the Bicentennial celebration on July 4, 1976, when 17 yachts took part in a sail-by to commemorate American Independence Day.

St. Christopher (St. Kitts)

Mount Misery, the main peak on St. Kitts, is 3,792 feet high and usually hidden in the clouds. The island slopes gently from there into the sea. This fertile, well-watered lowland is covered with sugar cane, a remnant of what once was the island's sole economy. St. Kitts estate owners made little attempt to diversify into other crops or to introduce new industry. In recent years, this attitude has somewhat changed, and, especially high up in the hills, open tracts of pastureland and plowed fields reflect new agricultural diversity.

As we sailed up the coast in March 1992, we were suitably impressed by the wide array of crops

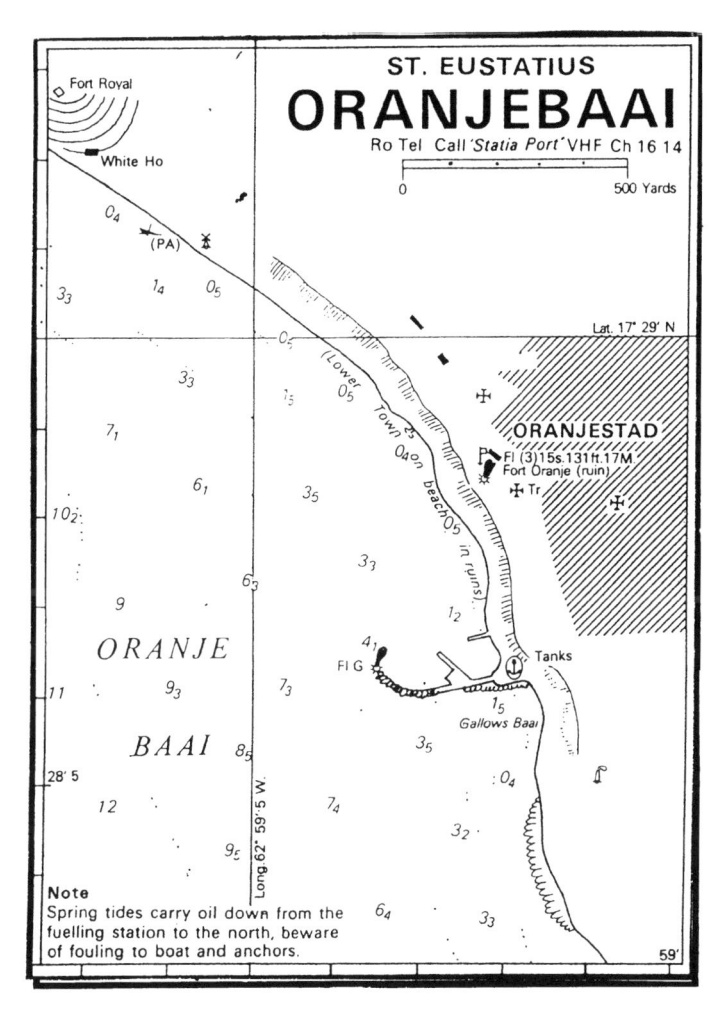

Chart 22 Oranjebaai and Oranjestad, St. Eustatius

Depths in fathoms and feet

planted in the upper fields of the old sugar plantations. We could see large groves of citrus and palm trees, and the fields were plowed and planted with provision crops. This diversification is reflected both in the economy and in the amount and variety of foodstuffs stocked in the markets.

St. Kitts was the last refuge of sailing lighters in the Antilles. With no steamer dock, all cargo had to be off-loaded into lighters and sailed into small docks. The open lighters were 35 to 45 feet long, with 15 feet of beam, and crudely rigged. Some had a single leg-o'-mutton sail with a mast raked well forward and the boom peaked up to a 45-degree angle. Larger lighters were sloop-rigged, with overlapping jib, short mast, and longer boom peaked up to clear the cargo. The lighters no longer off-load cargo, but as of 1992 two of them still operated between St. Kitts and Nevis.

St. Kitts was for many years ruled by Robert Bradshaw, one of the most controversial politicians in the Lesser Antilles. Among other things, he made life very difficult for visiting yachtsmen. Since 1978, however, when Mr. Bradshaw departed for the next world, that situation has improved.

Nonetheless, even after his death, he is surrounded by controversy—primarily because of his beautiful canary-yellow Rolls-Royce! The country was broke—the sugar holdings had been taken over by the government and the estate owners have not been recompensed yet! Despite this, he was still able to buy himself the Rolls, which probably is worth a fortune and still sits in Bradshaw's garage. The family and the government continue to argue about whether the car belongs to Bradshaw's heirs or to the government of St. Kitts.

The paranoia that developed as a result of the Bradshaw regime is still evident in some ways in St. Kitts. For example, when you clear out of Nevis, you are officially allowed to go only to Basseterre, and then you must beat to windward and visit the beautiful anchorages on the southwest coast of St. Kitts. Luckily, this ruling does not seem to be heavily enforced today!

It should be noted that even though the crime rate in St. Kitts is very low, the police are armed. This, I presume, is a legacy from Bradshaw, who was continually on the alert for assassination or a potential revolution.

An extremely interesting book that gives this background information on St. Kitts is Donald E. Westlake's *Under an English Heaven*. It is must reading for anyone sailing the islands.

St. Kitts is well worth a visit and a tour. The highlight is Brimstone Hill, one of the most magnificently preserved old forts in the Eastern Caribbean. For many years, this fortress was described as the Gibraltar of the Caribbean. As you wander around on the ramparts, you can visualize the furious battles between French and English for possession of the fort. Alec Waugh, in his highly recommended book *A Family of Islands*, points out that in the first great fight between the French and the English over Brimstone Hill (which the French finally won), the fort was actually nothing more than earthworks. The English defenders were further hampered by the fact that the planters were so furious at the British navy for having seized Statia (through which they had been trading illegally with the colonies for years) that they refused to supply the slaves to move the cannons up to the top of the hill. As a result, much of the siege was conducted by French troops using British cannons, powder, and shot that they found sitting at the bottom of the hill when they arrived.

Reportedly, Brimstone Hill has a large cannon with a wonderful inscription:

> Ram me well and load me tight,
> I'll send a ball to Statia's height.

That would have been one hell of a cannon! Unfortunately, I have not been able to find this wonderful weapon among those on Brimstone Hill—but it is still a good motto.

If you are the least bit interested in old forts and the like, don't miss this superbly restored site.

The French did capture the British forces on Brimstone Hill. The brilliant and tough defense put up by British generals Shirley and Frazer (whose names recur constantly in Eastern Caribbean military history) so impressed the French that they were allowed to surrender with the honors of war, i.e., to keep their regimental flag and sidearms. Generals Shirley and Frazer were sent back to Antigua—where they immediately started taking on the French again.

Meanwhile, a more important historical event had occurred at sea. The French fleet had been anchored off Basseterre, but the British fleet under Hood outmaneuvered the French, under de Grasse, and lured them offshore, where they fought an indecisive battle. Hood gained the advantage, though, and got back to Basseterre, forcing de Grasse to go to Martinique to lick his wounds before proceeding to Havana to join the Spanish fleet. This delay was crucial in the history of the Caribbean. Had the French and Spanish fleets joined up, they might have swept everyone before them in the West Indies and perhaps up to North America. As it was, another British fleet under Rodney arrived in Barbados in time to team up with Hood and descend on de Grasse near a group of islands called the Saintes when he left Martinique. The combined British fleet soundly whipped de Grasse at the Battle of the Saintes, which many historians regard as one of the pivotal naval engagements of the late eighteenth century. But, as naval expert Albert Thayer Mahan has pointed out, it all hinged on Hood's expert outmaneuvering of de Grasse off Basseterre.

St. Kitts is known as Little England (as is Barbados), and, except for a brief interlude, has been British since the seventeenth century. Many estates were in the same families for 300 years until they were done in by a combination of falling sugar prices and the Bradshaw government.

One of my most pleasant outings in recent years was in St. Kitts. My wife Trich and I picked up a car, did shopping in town, bought ice—the cheapest in the Caribbean and probably in the whole world at US 85 cents for a full hundredweight (112 pounds of good ice)—hauled that to the boat, and then drove around the entire island.

St. Kitts is especially interesting because outside of Basseterre, little construction has taken place in the last 20 years. It almost looks like time has stood still—except for the fact that the little steam engines that used to pull the sugar carts on the narrow-gauge railway have now been replaced with diesel engines.

We stopped and inspected numerous churches and other old buildings, had lunch at Rawlins Plantation, and then drove down the east coast up to Brimstone Hill and back to the boat. A wonderful day trip! At Rawlins Plantation, we had a splendid West Indian buffet, plus we were given much information about the island and local sailing conditions by Philip Walwyn, who at the time operated the plantation in the winters and spent the summers doing numerous transatlantic catamaran passages. Then, for a number of years, he had a successful career racing Six-Meters, including one built by Dougie Brooks in St. Kitts. Now he sails on a rather esoteric 30-foot boat with a pivoting rig like those on model yachts. The end of the main boom carries the tack of the headsail and pivots out to windward. This arrangement works well on models—but on a full-size yacht? No one has yet been able to make it work for a full-size yacht, but perhaps Philip will succeed! He has also installed a pivoting keel à la *Procyon*. This, however, is not a new idea—L. Francis Herreshoff proposed it during World War II, and it was his "dream sailing machine."

Philip no longer runs the hotel, but he still owns the old plantation house, which has been in the family since the mid-eighteenth century, when a Walwyn married a Rawlins and thus acquired the estate.

As each year goes by, more and more of the old estates are being bought up and converted to guest houses, restaurants, and hotels—really wonderful establishments. Even if you cannot afford to stay at one of them, it is well worth going to the bar, buying a drink, and admiring the grounds.

When you arrive in St. Kitts, stop in at the Tourist Office and pick up a copy of the *St. Kitts Traveller*, which lists all the island's hotels, restaurants, guest houses, and restored estates.

When the Bradshaw government took over the sugar industry in the early 1970s and brought it to its knees, many of the old island families left, and the St. Kitts Club (reportedly the oldest men's club in the Western Hemisphere) fell on hard times. They finally closed their doors, but luckily this fine specimen of Georgian architecture now is operated as a restaurant—although we were informed in 1992 that the food left something to be desired. By the time you read this, however, it probably will be under new ownership, or the cook will have been changed. In any case, it's certainly worthwhile going by just to see the handsome building.

Another favorite restaurant used to be The Palms, overlooking the main square of St. Kitts, but unfortunately it has closed down. Before its incarnation as The Palms, it was known as Shorties, well beloved by Carleton Mitchell, Alec Waugh, and others—and famous for the fact that one flat price covered bed, board, and booze—all you could eat and all you could drink. If the walls of The Palms/Shorties could talk, I am sure they could write a wonderful story of the Caribbean with a fantastic cast of famous people.

Fortunately, the Ballahoo restaurant and bar has opened on the northeast corner of the main square known locally as "The Circus." (Where the name came from is beyond me! It is a circle ringed by palm trees with a beautiful seventeenth-century clock tower in the center.) The Ballahoo's upstairs balcony overlooks the square and is an excellent spot for a midmorning coffee. You can relax and watch the people in The Circus, admire the surrounding buildings, and rendezvous with crew members who have been wandering around Basseterre.

The wonderful old ice factory in St. Kitts is gone, but ice is still produced in St. Kitts at the lowest prices anywhere (EC$4.00—approximately US$1.50—for a 40-pound block.) At the sugar factory, you can buy these large blocks of ice, but they are available only early in the morning. The best plan is to anchor at the deepwater port, clear, and then rent a car about three or four o'clock in the afternoon. That way, you will have a car for going out for dinner, and in the morning (about 0600) you can send one of the crew to the sugar factory to pick up the ice—you probably will be able to buy only one or two blocks at the most.

One way' to get around this limitation, of course, is to send two people (both drivers) for the ice. One person hops out ¼ mile down the road from the sugar factory and waits; the driver goes to buy all the ice they will sell him (or her). Then he goes back down the road and switches places with the person waiting. The second person then goes and repeats the first one's actions! I doubt very much if, at 0600, the iceman will recognize the same car returning!

After the ice is stowed, have an early breakfast, pile in the car, and drive off toward Brimstone Hill. En route, stop off at the Texagas bottling plant on the waterfront on the way into town. They will fill your gas bottles while you wait.

Arrive at Brimstone Hill at about 0900. Even though they officially open at 0930, they will sell you a ticket and let you go on up. You can spend half an hour wandering around the fort and you will have the place completely to yourselves. When the shop and the exhibits open, you will be well ahead of the huge influx of tourists that come streaming in from the cruise ships between 1000 and noon.

After your tour of the fort and its exhibits and shops, drive clockwise around the island. Stop for a long lunch, then drop off the car and return to the boat. Pick up the anchor and make a fast run down to White House or Ballast Bay.

If you are approaching St. Kitts from the west, tack up to the lee of the island as soon as you can. If you are approaching from the north (from St. Barts, St. Martin, or Anguilla), round the northwestern side of St. Kitts half a mile off, and then work down the shore. The flaws in the wind will probably drive you offshore, so you will need to make frequent tacks back close in. You will find plenty of water along the whole coast, smooth water close to shore, and spasmodic strong puffs of wind that come off the mountain. These vary as much as four points, so be careful of being caught aback.

However, if you are approaching St. Kitts and Nevis from the east, be sure to check carefully the ranges on Chart 24 or Imray-Iolaire Chart A-25. The shoals east of The Narrows are definitely hazards for the average yacht, and seas will break over them in heavy weather. (See more about this tricky area in the discussion of The Narrows.)

BASSETERRE BAY

(Chart 23; II A, A-25)

Basseterre is the main town and port of entry for St. Kitts. Sail east of town to the new main steamer dock and anchor as close in behind the dock as you can, of course leaving room for the cruise ships. Set bow and stern anchors, facing the boat southwest into the swell so that she will hobbyhorse rather than roll your guts out. I will not say this is a perfect anchorage, but it certainly is much better than it was before the steamer dock was built.

Once anchored, go ashore and find a taxi into town to clear Customs and Immigration in the main port office. If it happens to be Thursday afternoon, and the office is closed, go to the police station, where they will stamp your passports; you can return to Customs the following morning.

The one problem with anchoring behind the dock is that there is no decent place to tie up your dinghy. The low part of the dock, which looks like the logical spot, is NOT—that's where the ferry comes in! Any dinghy left there will either be crushed by the launch or perhaps untied by a dock worker and retied God-knows-where to bash itself to pieces on rocks.

Make sure you have a good dinghy anchor. Then unload on the north landing, drop the dinghy anchor, and tie up somewhere off the north part of the jetty. It is hard to get into and out of the dinghy there, so assign the most athletic crew member to that job!

According to the St. Kitts tourist brochure, the Turtle Bay Inn, a very attractive restaurant overlooking the water in Basseterre, also has a marina. In March 1992, however, this was NOT TRUE. There was a small dock, a bit of a breakwater, but no stretch of the imagination could call it a marina. Possibly there will be a proper one by the time you read this, but check before you make plans. there is now a marina with Customs and Immigration in town.
See updates in the NOTES at the end of this chapter on page 71.

SOUTH FRIGATE BAY

(II A-25, A-3)

Frigate Bay, southeast of Basseterre, is not the world's greatest anchorage, but it certainly is a worthwhile lunch stop, and perhaps an overnighter in the right conditions. The beach is excellent, as it should be, given the rocky and rolly anchorage. The wreck of a freighter in the middle of the bay used to

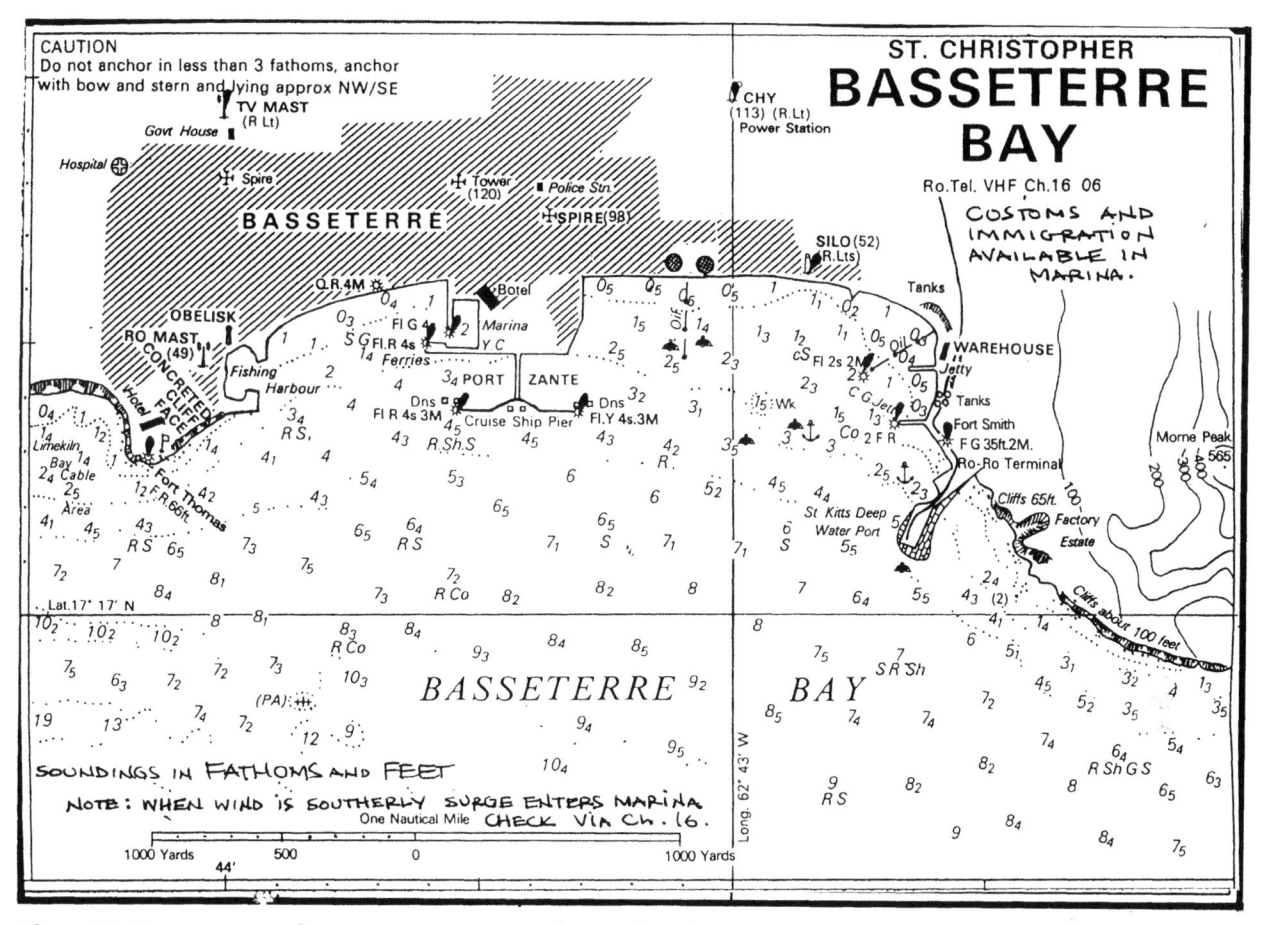

Chart 23 Basseterre and Basseterre Bay, St. Christopher (St. Kitts)   Depths in fathoms and feet

be clearly visible, but Hurricanes Klaus (1984) and Hugo (1989) bashed the wreck down to the point that it has 20 feet of water above it, so it no longer is a navigational hazard. The wreck provides excellent diving for both amateur snorkelers and experienced scuba divers. Ashore, not visible from the sea, is the Four Seasons Hotel, which I am told is very well run, has excellent meals, a very nice beach bar, and a fine golf course.

If, at the end of the day, you decide that the anchorage is too rolly, it is only a short sail down the coast to other anchorages.

Continue farther south along the coast of the larger bay and you will gaze on a splendid selection of white-sand beaches. You can come right up to the steep shore and use either a Bahamian moor or set bow-and-stern anchors and lie in the axis of the swell. During the winter, Frigate Bay and the anchorages immediately to the south are apt to be rough, but in the summer they are calm and smooth. The beaches are deserted for miles. There used to be no road access from Basseterre to the peninsula, but now a beautiful highway goes down to the beaches on the southern end of St. Kitts. However, the small beaches on the west side of the peninsula are accessible only by dirt tracks—perfect for adventurous explorers! So if solitude is what you want, you will be ecstatic. Also, White House Bay, with the single beach just northeast of Guana Point, often is an excellent, calm anchorage. Stand in toward shore and anchor at a reasonable depth.

WHITE HOUSE BAY

(Chart 24; II A-25, A-3)

The first really good anchorage south of South Frigate Bay is White House Bay, easily identified by an old, ruined house on shore, a sunken trawler in the southeast corner of the bay, and a small dock in rather poor condition. White-sand bottom, good holding (anchor at a depth suitable for your boat), good snorkeling on both sides of the bay. Dougie Brooks, the catamaran builder, informs me that the

St. Kitts Yacht Club plans to build a small clubhouse at White House Bay. A developer has obtained all the necessary government permits, and Customs and Immigration also will open an office. (That certainly will be a huge boon.) Don't hold your breath on this one, but if it comes to pass, it will be a great plus for visiting yachtsmen.

BALLAST BAY

(Chart 24; II A-25, A-3)

Unnamed on the British and American charts, Ballast Bay is the bay west of the Great Salt Pond at the southern end of St. Kitts. Despite the fact that both the British and American charts show deep water right up to the beach, there is an extremely good anchorage in 1 1/2 to two fathoms of water on the shelf—which extends a good 200 yards out from shore. No road reaches this area, which has a beautiful, deserted beach and good diving on the reefs.

When entering, be careful of the rocks extending from the north end of the bay (Guana Point).

SHITTEN BAY

(Chart 24; II A-25, A-3)

The temptation to make a bad joke about the name of this place is waived in deference to the quality of the anchorage, which is calm and offers good shelling. The small bay with its shingle beach lies just north of Nags Head.

MAJORS BAY

(Chart 24; II A-25, A-3)

If the ground swell is rolling in along the whole coast, as it might be in winter, sail around Nags Head and up into the northern end of Majors Bay. Unless the wind gets well around to the south, you should be comfortable here. Nevis, only 2 1/2 miles away, shelters this anchorage all year, and it is not horrible even when the wind in the south. This is an exceptional place to lie, because it is completely deserted and has white-sand bottom and beaches. Be aware, however, that the white-sand bottom is in *PATCHES*—some areas are covered with grass and seaweed. Make sure you set your anchor in a patch of white sand and ascertain that it is secure. Then take a second anchor and set it in another white-sand patch. A Bahamian moor is advisable here, as the wind tends to waltz around at night.

Majors Bay makes a wonderful place to start exploring St. Kitts. Old, abandoned ruins of a fort can be found on the ridge extending northward from Nags Head. You might also try snorkeling off both points at the end of the bay, since the area abounds in lobsters.

In March 1992, this was still a beautiful, deserted bay, but the highway has arrived—along with a water line and a huge generator. Obviously, "development" is on the way. What shape it will take, my crystal ball will not reveal!

BANANA BAY/COCKLESHELL BAY

(Chart 24; II A-25, A-3)

East of Majors Bay are Banana Bay and Cockleshell Bay. The anchorage is in the northeast corner, with Scotch Bonnet bearing southeast. Here, the wind whistles over the hill, and you are likely to waltz around your anchor. The holding ground is none too reliable, and a Bahamian moor is essential. Make very sure that your anchor is well set. I have heard stories of people who have tried to anchor here 10 or 12 times, and, unable to get the flukes to grab, have gone elsewhere. We have anchored here three times in *Iolaire* without much difficulty. I guess it just proves that—despite what some tests say to the contrary—the world's best all-around anchor is still the Herreshoff.

The Cockleshell and Banana Beach hotels that used to be here were leveled by Hurricane Hugo in 1989 and have not been rebuilt.

MOSQUITO BAY

(Chart 24; II A-25, A-3)

This definitely is NOT an anchorage, but there is a very nice beach bar/restaurant, Turtle Beach, which is open from 1000 to 1800 for drinks, lunch, and light snacks. Turtle Beach (contact on channel 16) also serves as a base for diving, good snorkeling, sailboarding, canoeing, etc. If you contact them from any of the bays on the southern end of St. Kitts, they will send a car gratis to pick up the crew so you can enjoy Mosquito Bay. On Sunday nights, Turtle Beach reputedly has a very good buffet.

SAND BANK BAY

(Chart 24; II A-25, A-3)

On the southeast coast of St. Kitts, this can be entered in the summer months if the wind is in the southeast. It is dangerous and shoal, however, and boats drawing more than six feet should not attempt it. Avoid this harbor in winter, because if the ground

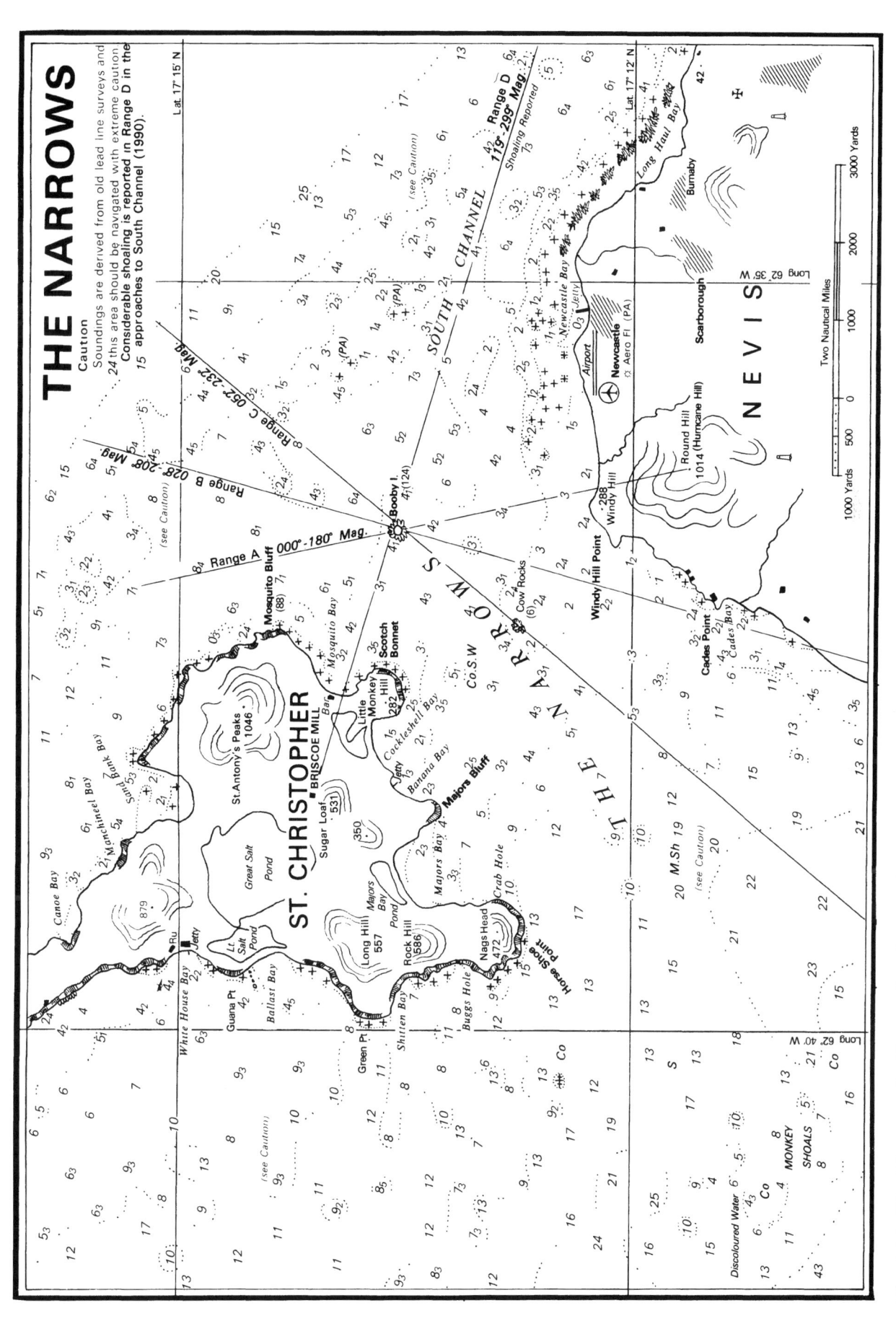

Chart 24 The Narrows, St. Christopher (St. Kitts) and Nevis

swell builds up, you can easily be trapped inside the bay and will be unable to leave. There is no road access—which, of course, means that you will be all by yourself here. The diving around the edges of the reef is rewarding.

DIEPPE BAY

(II A-25, A-3)

Also called the Punch Bowl, in the northeast corner of St. Kitts, this probably was used in past years as a loading point for sugar when there were no adequate roads. Dieppe Bay is strictly a small-boat harbor for fishing boats that can be hauled out of the water once they are inside the reef; it is not a yacht harbor of any kind.

THE NARROWS

(Chart 24; II A-25, A-3)

The passage between St. Kitts and Nevis, referred to as The Narrows, is filled with reefs and shoals, some of whose depths are less, I'm quite sure, than those shown on the charts. Because the ranges are not easy to identify, this passage should be navigated in midday and with extreme care. In heavy weather, the entire shoal area east of The Narrows will be solid breakers. Even in calm weather, you can easily run aground trying to cross the shoal. Carefully read the directions for the ranges, choose the appropriate range, and *stay on that range until you are well past the shoals.*

If you are approaching The Narrows from the north, it is possible to pass west of all the shoals. Steer for the eastern extremity of Mosquito Bluff, and, while still well offshore, bring Booby Island in line with Hurricane Hill (Nevis). Run down this range (Range A). Then head for Booby Island until Mosquito Bluff is abeam. Ease sheets and run down the south coast of St. Kitts, or proceed to Nevis, leaving Cow Rocks to port.

If you are approaching The Narrows from the northeast, keep well off the shore of St. Kitts until the west side of Booby Island lines up with the church at Lowland Point (Range B). Or, if you cannot bring the Lowland church into view, get a bearing on the west coast of Booby Island and the westernmost point of Nevis. Go west of this bearing by the width of Booby Island, and you will avoid the shoals to the east. To be sure that you avoid the shoal water, do not stray east of this range. If you are going to Basseterre, head directly for Nags Head; if

---

RANGES IN THE NARROWS

A. Booby Island in line with summit of Hurricane Hill, 000°–180° magnetic. Leads west of the shoals, northeast of Mosquito Bluff.

B. Booby Island in line with Lowland church, 028°–208° magnetic. Leads into deep water between the two shoals; best approach from the northeast, as it keeps you in deepest water.

C. Booby Island in line with Cow Rocks, 052°–232° magnetic. Easy to pick up, but leads across shoal that can be lumpy in heavy weather.

D. North end of Booby Island in line with Briscoe Mill, 119°–299° magnetic. Warning: Shoaling reported; this range should not be used by boats drawing more than 10 feet. The shoaling probably is a result of the October 1974 earthquake.

---

you are continuing to Nevis, leave Cow Rocks 200 yards off the port hand and run down the coast.

Should you be coming from the east, stand to the north until Booby Island is in line with Cow Rocks. Then run down this range (Range C), leaving both Booby Island and Cow Rocks to port. Once you have Cow Rocks abeam, you are clear of danger.

The approach from the southeast is the most difficult, since Range D is hard to spot. Briscoe Mill is not shown on the US chart, but it is in the valley northeast of Sugar Loaf on St. Kitts, and it is visible over the beaches of Mosquito Bay. Once you have Hurricane Hill (Nevis) abeam, you have passed all dangers.

When using Range D, stay absolutely on it. If you stray the least bit north of the range, you will run over a 13-foot spot that shoals rapidly to nine feet. Even when you are on the range, the controlling depth evidently is about 14 feet. Two different yachts reported this to me after Agents Week in 1990. The first boat was sailing down the range when the skipper noticed the bottom coming up on his fathometer. It stopped at 14 feet, which nearly gave the man a heart attack, as his board was down and drawing 13 feet. He reported this to one of his friends, who sailed the same range a few days later and discovered the same situation. Both men are very competent skippers, and I am absolutely sure they were on the range.

The only explanation I can suggest is that on 8 October 1974, an earthquake (7.4 on the Richter scale) shook up the islands of Nevis, St. Kitts, and

Antigua. The epicenter was somewhere between Antigua and St. Kitts, and it must have caused a change in the bottom of South Channel. Thus, boats drawing more than 10 feet should not use this channel.

Beating to windward through The Narrows is not easy, particularly during the winter, when the trades are boisterous and the shoals are breaking. Do not pass between Cow Rocks and Nevis unless you have a shoal-draft boat. The best passage is north of Cow Rocks, favoring the St. Kitts shore. From Mosquito Bay, tack to the south, if necessary taking a few extra tacks to get to weather of Booby Island, tacking to the north when Booby Island lines up with the Lowland Point church (Range B).

If you can lay this range, fine, but if not, bear off to Range A, 353°–173° magnetic, Booby Island on east face of Hurricane Hill (Range E), to pass to leeward of the shoal (which may crest and break in heavy weather).

Nevis

Although Nevis and St. Kitts are separated only by The Narrows, the two islands are very different. In keeping with this fact is the old rule of thumb concerning St. Kitts—Nevis anchorages: If the anchorage at Basseterre is bad, it will be good at Charlestown, and vice versa. When heading from Basseterre to Nevis, there are no dangers. Monkey Shoals have four fathoms over them, and that should be enough for anyone. The anchorage at Nevis is off Charlestown. If you approach it from the north, you will find no dangers; from the south, be sure to give a wide berth to Fort Charles, at the south end of town, since the shoal extends half a mile offshore. Because of the low land, one tends to get too close inshore and can easily bounce off the bottom. The anchorage is due west of the dock. Expect three fathoms and a sand bottom that means good holding.

Give Dogwood Point on the southwestern corner of the island a wide berth, as the shoals extend farther offshore than the Admiralty chart shows. This shoal inflicted serious damage on the big schooner *Te Vega* and the 90-foot ketch *Harbinger*, and it has caused the total loss of three or four local schooners.

The contrast between St. Kitts and Nevis can be seen immediately. St. Kitts is a bustling, populous island with the vast majority of arable land owned by the government, which took over all the sugar estates in the early 1970s. Nevis is the land of the small farmer who grows a bit of everything, has no money, yet is much more pleasant to deal with than his St. Kitts cousin.

A trip to Nevis is not complete if you do not hire a car. Swing by the Tourist Office in Charlestown, pick up a brochure, and do a tour of the island.

Charlestown is architecturally interesting. Most of its buildings are built of heavy, cut-coral blocks and date back to the eighteenth century, when Nevis was a great sugar island and health resort.

In the 1970s, the large plantation houses stood almost totally abandoned on the island's hillsides, their vast palm groves unworked. Squatters took over the land and developed small holdings. Now, happily, almost all of these large estate houses have been bought and restored into magnificent hotels and guest houses. Even if you do not stay at one of these establishments, drive up and take a look at them; stop in to have a drink at the bar. It is a pleasant way to admire the impressive restoration that has taken place.

In years past, Nevis was considered a prime Caribbean health resort, and a spa was built here by the Hot Sulphur Springs Hotel to offer heated baths ostensibly with medicinal properties. However, the hotel fell into "disrepair" (as they say in the West Indies), and it was finally abandoned. Now the government of Nevis has taken it over and is restoring it, and hot sulfur baths are once more available.

Visitors with a historical bent will appreciate the fact that Nevis is the birthplace of Alexander Hamilton, who spent the first nine years of his life here. The house is long gone, and other buildings have been built on its foundations, but the museum in Charlestown is given over to the interesting history of Nevis and the Hamilton connection. Also in the museum (which is within walking distance of the main dock at the north end of town) is a nice model of the local sailing lighters. These 45-foot sail-powered craft had a 45-foot mast, a 45-foot boom (!), and a 17-foot beam. In the past, all the cargo for St. Kitts and Nevis was offloaded from boats anchored off Basseterre into small lighters that would sail into St. Kitts. The larger, 45-foot lighters would sail over to Nevis. Amazingly, two of these lighters are still around. We saw one of them anchored off Charlestown in March 1992. My first mate, Dale, was incredulous when I told him the boom had been *shortened*—they must be going to high-aspect ratio! The boom was only 30 feet long, not the standard 45 feet!

Nevis is also noted as the home of the wife of Admiral Horatio Nelson. Nelson not only obtained a wife here but a wealthy one at that, and the widow

Nesbit funded his subsequent naval career. In the Caribbean, he was particularly unpopular, as he was assigned to enforce the Navigation Acts, which forbade trading with the American colonies. All cargo from New England had to be shipped first to England and *then* down to the Caribbean (a six-month voyage that could otherwise have been made in two weeks!). Nelson seized large quantities of trade goods, and incensed planters tried to sue him. Local sentiment in Antigua was so strong against him that he convinced the courts that any jury there would be biased against him and thus he could not receive a fair trial. He persuaded the judges to move the trial to Nevis, where he was acquitted of all charges!

The lawyer who defended Nelson happened to be Mrs. Nesbit's father—who gained the acquittal and lost a daughter. Nelson, on the other hand, gained both a wife AND a fortune!

Another of Nevis's interesting features is its churches. The island seems to have more churches per square mile than anywhere else I have been in the Eastern Caribbean. Most are old stone buildings beautifully constructed in the late nineteenth and early twentieth centuries. Some of the churchyard gravestone inscriptions are particularly elaborate and intriguing.

Nevis has plenty of nice, small shops and boutiques—no "high-fashion wear," but attractive items nonetheless. The pace here seems rather like all of the islands used to be years ago.

Grocery stores are adequate, but this certainly is no place to stock up. Restaurants are too numerous to list, but the Tourist Office can help with suggestions. I must say that The Courtyard is appealing— alfresco meals (including evening buffets) at decent prices. Most important, when I wandered in there for a noontime beer and decided to stay for a snack, I could see that most of the clients were Nevis folk, not tourists looking for gimmicks.

We found ice down on the fishermen's quay—in five-gallon pails. It wasn't exactly cheap, but it won't break the bank. At least it WAS available! Filling gas bottles in Nevis is a "sometime" situation. It can be done, because we called Nevis Gases in March 1992 and were told that they could fill the bottle, but they didn't have the gas that day and didn't expect it until the following day. We then called Delta, and they reported that they could fill our tanks only when they were filling their own. When would that be? They were not sure. In the end, we carted the bottle back to St. Kitts with us and had it filled there.

In the 1970s, Nevis had a very good ice plant that sold cheap ice, but it broke down and has never been replaced. I think it was another one of those deals with the Bradshaw administration—since the plant was not on St. Kitts, the money available was used for some other project on St. Kitts. As another example of this sort of thing, St. Kitts received money from Great Britain to build a dock in Anguilla. Bradshaw, however, disliked the Anguillans, so he built the dock in St. Kitts and called it The Anguilla Dock! No wonder the Anguillans revolted (see chapter 2)!

The Customs office is right at the head of the dock. Immigration is 200 yards down the road at the police station. After hours, wait for the next day.

If you are anchored off Charlestown and want to relax on the beach, my advice is to tie up the dinghy to the dock in town, walk northward up the road out of town (stopping off to look at the museum), and continue on to Pinney's Beach Hotel. Quench your thirst there and then drop down through the hotel to the breakwater. Here you will find a path leading north right to the beach. You can stay there for some privacy or walk farther to a beach bar and restaurant.

If you are looking for something fancy, continue on to the Four Seasons Hotel. (I'm afraid it really is TOO fancy for my taste!) You probably will see a large number of boats anchored off the hotel, where the anchorage sometimes is better than off town. However, there's a hitch: You cannot take your dinghy into the hotel dock, or offload goods, or even carry passengers to and from the dock! Supposedly, the reason for this is that Customs officials fear that people will smuggle drugs ashore in their dinghies via the hotel! Such gross illogic! What drug smuggler would want to be so obvious as to use a hotel dock?

The ban on use of the hotel dock may lead you to opt for landing a dinghy on the beach, but my advice is, "Don't!" One time, I sat in the beach bar at the south end of the beach for about half an hour and watched the swell. That day—a calm one—it certainly was too dangerous to land a dinghy. For five or 10 minutes at a time, there would be just small waves lapping on the beach—no problem—but then one or two huge waves would roll in, definitely enough to capsize a dinghy. Even if you do get ashore there, it is a long walk into town. If you are going to the Four Seasons for an expensive dinner, you are likely to arrive soaking wet!

The hotel, by the way, supposedly is staffed by highly trained hoteliers, but I had an encounter there that led me to believe otherwise. When I asked a staff member if they had the ESPN Channel—so we could see some of the America's Cup elimination races—the man replied that they had both European and American ESPN. When I asked him if he knew the evening's schedule, he said he didn't know it and had no way of finding out! If I were a guest at that hotel, paying $400 or $500 a day, I would be rather indignant to discover there was no way of finding out the ESPN schedule!

I have been told that if the anchorage off Charlestown is too rocky and rolly, another option is to go north along the coast to Cades Point, where there is a small but highly recommended bar and restaurant. They have a very helpful staff who will run you into town for errands and also arrange tours of the island. Before Hurricane Hugo, they had a dinghy dock, but all the dinghy docks were destroyed by the storm, and none have been rebuilt.

Supposedly, marinas were slated to be built near old Fort Charles and in Newcastle Bay, but as of 2000, neither one had been started. In any case, I cannot imagine a marina being built in Newcastle unless someone wants to spend massive amounts of money.

Nevis is something of a backwater but well worth visiting. It is semiconnected to the outside world via small planes that fly on a very erratic schedule to and from Antigua.

Nothing much has changed at Nevis other than they have built a deep water dock at Lowlands Point. Unfortunately shortly after the dock was built hurricane Lenny came along and pretty much demolished it. It now has to be rebuilt. It was stated when the dock was built that Customs & Immigration would move from town down to the dock. However, subsequent to this announcement a friend was in Nevis and Customs & Immigration.

informed him in no uncertain terms that they were not moving out of town and down to the new dock. as to what the situation will be when you arrive, is problematical. Hopefully you will be able to anchor in the normal place off town and clear Customs & Immigration and not have to proceed two miles down the coast to Lowlands Point

BASSETERRE BAY
(Chart 23; II A. A-25)

There is a vast improvement for the yachtsman as they built a cruise ship dock in Basseterre and on the western side of the cruise ship dock they built a marina. Now yachts can berth in the marina, go ashore and clear with Customs & Immigration right there at the marina.

However, care must be exerted here as if the wind goes south east or south a surge can build up in Basseterre Bay and pour into the basin making it almost like a washing machine—making it all but impossible to stay in your berth. For that reason it is best when approaching Basseterre and before entering the marina to call the Marina Office on Channel 16 and ascertain the conditions inside the basin. If the wind goes around to the south east or south and begins to blow, get out in a hurry and proceed down towards Frigate Bay or White House Bay and hope to find shelter there.

The marina is definitely not a hurricane hole. Each hurricane that has gone by St. Kitts has demolished the marina and the lower part of town. But each time it has been rebuilt.

6

Antigua and Barbuda

(Imray-Iolaire Charts A, A-26, A-27, A-271, A-3)

Antigua

Antigua lies well to the east of the St. Kitts group and due north of Guadeloupe. It is relatively low, with its highest benchmark at 1,300 feet. Though it suffers from an almost perpetual drought, the dependable trades make it relatively cool and ventilated.

The island's innumerable hotels now luxuriate in air-conditioned comfort, but for many years they were hard-pressed even to keep themselves supplied with fresh water. The improved situation has come as a result of a dam-building campaign begun on the island a few years back. Water comes from a number of small ponds and also from the Potswork Reservoir, a dammed-up pond that is now a mile long by half a mile wide—the largest single body of fresh water in the Lesser Antilles. However, severe droughts can still drastically limit the supply of water, as occurred in 1984 and twice since then—the most recent instance being 1992.

Even though the water system has been expanded, the demand has increased out of all proportion to the supply. A new desalination plant has been built on the Crabbs Peninsula, but it does not provide enough water, as the piping system throughout the island is inadequate to take all the desalinated water that is produced. Allegedly, 50 percent of the fresh water generated is pumped back into the sea because there is no way to get it through the pipes! It looks as though someone didn't do the necessary homework! In any case, the plant is a boon to those who own water trucks, as there is always a long string of these vehicles—all day, everyday—lining up to pick up water for delivery around the island.

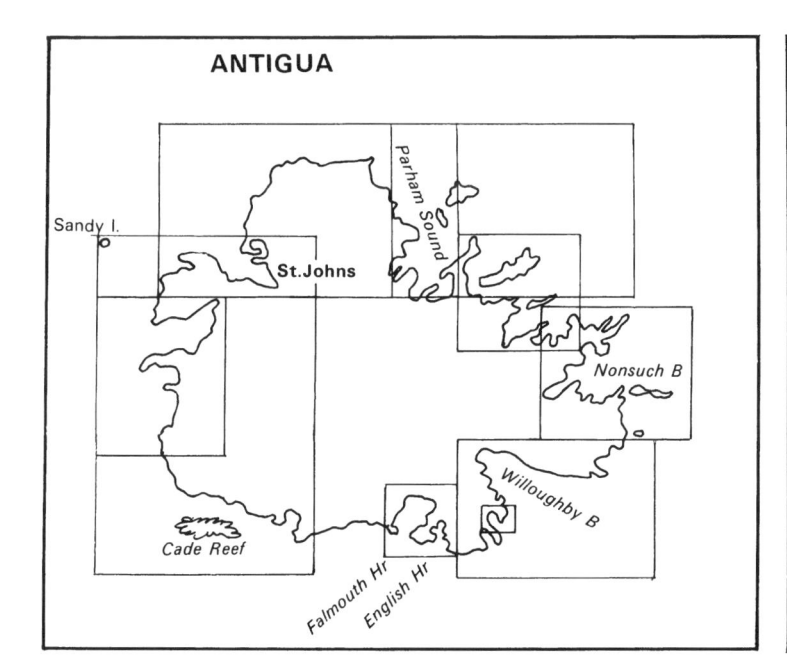

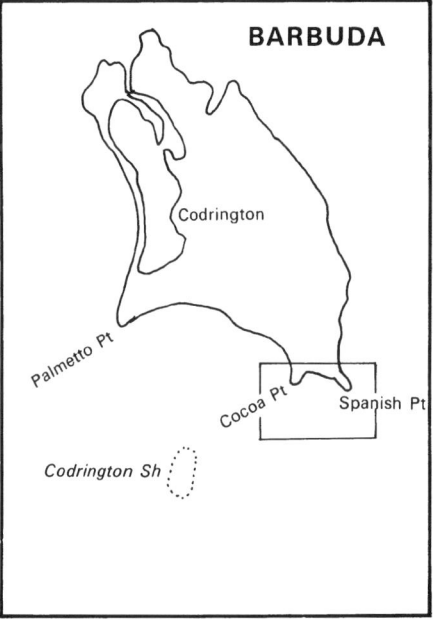

A certain amount of progress has been made with the water situation in that all new construction must have guttered roofs and adequate cisterns. If this law had been enacted 40 years ago, it might not have eliminated the current problem, but it certainly would have minimized it.

In March 1992, it was very frustrating not to be able to get water in Falmouth. Frequently it was impossible to take a shower or even flush toilets, as the water was turned off for days at a time. Yet every time a rain squall passed overhead, hundreds of gallons of water came gushing out of the downspouts from the gutters on the roof of the Antigua Yacht Club. It all went into the sea instead of into cisterns!

One place that has done a wonderful job of utilizing all the water God provides is Jolly Harbour, which has the best water-planning scheme I have seen anywhere in the Caribbean. (More about this later.)

During the 1992 drought, a local radio announcer pointed out, "What Antigua needs is brain, not rain!"—the ability to use the rain God gave them, even though the water given to Antigua by God is extremely inadequate.

The "brain" situation also holds true in the agricultural sector. The sugar industry in Antigua closed down completely in the early 1980s. The sugar-cane fields lay fallow and are now covered with grass. Vast areas of these fields have been taken over by the government—with no apparent plans for using them. In St. Croix, it has been proven that beef and dairy cattle can be bred in the tropics—they have even developed their own special breed of cows. One only has to drive around to compare the fat herds of cattle in St. Croix with the scrawny beasts that live on the other islands. The Caribbean islands need some creative brains in the agricultural arena.

With its extensive open areas, Antiguans could certainly take a cue from Texas agricultural history. They could let the cattle run loose, sort them out every spring, and brand them. Antigua could become the cattle kingdom of the Caribbean. It could produce fresh milk for the island and have a large meat-exporting business as well. Needless to say, the grazing areas would have to be fenced to contain the cattle. At the moment, Antigua law stipulates that cattle must be chained. If a cow gets loose and you hit it and damage your car, you are not held responsible for the cow. In fact, the cow's owner is responsible for the damage to your car! This is a far cry from most areas, where a collision with a cow or bull is likely to cost you a fortune—primarily because the owner always maintains that the victim was the prize of his herd!

Antigua was first settled for the British by Sir Thomas Warner, and, with the exception of a brief French occupation in 1666–67, has remained British ever since. In the early eighteenth century, when the British realized Antigua's strategic importance and the superb shelter afforded by English Harbour, they proceeded to fortify the hills above the harbor and built a dockyard for naval supply and repair. But with the introduction of large, steam-powered ships in the nineteenth century, English Harbour went into a decline from which it did not recover until recent years.

There is regular and frequent air service between Antigua and all parts of the world, which makes the island an excellent place to rendezvous with crew members. It also makes Antigua a transshipment point for airline passengers, baggage, and freight to other parts of the Eastern Caribbean. If you lose any of the three, Antigua is the place to start looking. (If lost baggage does not turn up there, however, the next place to look, believe it or not, is the Middle East. It seems that the airline abbreviation for Antigua is ANU. Somewhere in the Middle East there is an airport labeled AKU. All too often, a busy ticket attendant grabs an AKU baggage tag when reaching for ANU. Result? No clothes for your cruise.)

Because so many yachtsmen use Antigua as a starting or ending point of a cruise, far too many of them equate Antigua with English Harbour, a long taxi ride to the airport, and maybe a visit to St. Johns, the capital. (Despite the massive restoration going on in one corner of St. Johns, I still think it is one of the least attractive towns in this part of the Caribbean.)

Actually, Antigua and Barbuda—the latter belongs to the former—are wonderful islands for cruising, with countless coves, reefs, and inlets. You can easily cruise for two full weeks without getting more than 60 miles from English Harbour and without anchoring in the same place twice. If you start from English Harbour, you can visit the Parham/North Sound area and resupply at English Harbour. If your cruise takes in Barbuda, your longest haul in the 25 miles separating the two is usually an easy beam reach.

Or you can start your cruise at Crabbs Marina, cruise to Barbuda, then back down to Nonsuch Bay, resupply in English Harbour, then work your way back to Crabbs—a perfect 10-day-to-two-week cruise that saves you from entering or clearing customs anywhere!

What if you want to go to any of the other islands or island groups instead? The sail to St. Barts is a glorious 90-mile broad reach, but it is a hard slog back. St. Kitts—Nevis is 40 miles dead downwind on a sleighride; the beat back to Antigua from Nevis or St. Kitts may be one of the longest 40 miles you have ever done.

English Harbor to Deshaies, Guadeloupe, usually is a great reach with the wind a little aft of abeam; all too often, in the winter, it is dead to windward back to English Harbor. Or if the wind is well to the north, you end up on the west coast of Antigua, where you anchor and then slog your way back to English Harbor or Crabbs Marina the following day. You will encounter none of these problems if you just stay in Antigua and Barbuda.

The sailing itself is varied and exhilarating. The eastern side of Antigua has great Atlantic rollers crashing on shore. Beating to windward is an exciting experience and a good test of spirit and rig. The lee side has that ideal combination of steady winds and no sea. It is the thrill of a lifetime to hold a booming reach along the lee shore of Antigua, rail down through the smooth, crystal-clear water, while the magnified underwater terrain races past below.

One of the great advantages of the coves and anchorages through the Antigua—Barbuda area is that many have no hotels on their shores because they are almost completely inaccessible by land. Furthermore, these coves are largely neglected by the charter boats, which usually head off south to Guadeloupe and other areas. In short, if I were to start a two-week cruise from Antigua, I wouldn't go anywhere else except Barbuda.

I strongly recommend NOT using the British Admiralty or DMA charts, as they contain too many errors and are not up-to-date enough. I advise using Imray-Iolaire Charts A-27 and A-271 for Antigua, as they contain numerous ranges, as well as navigational warnings, that do not appear on either the British or American charts. Imray-Iolaire is also trying to keep up with the installation of lights and buoys in Antigua.

The point is that Antigua has plenty of reefs, as well as a buoyage and light system that leaves much to be desired. The problem is not that no money is being spent; it's that the money is, in my opinion, not being spent wisely. Lights are placed where they are not needed; buoys are also misplaced, have the wrong color, and are poorly maintained. What is needed is an overall plan for navigational aids for the island that would maximize use of the funds that are available. As a result of this situation, I have compiled an up-to-date list of the major navigational hazards, which are described below.

Navigational Warnings

1. Shirley Heights. As of May 1993, Shirley Heights light had been out for about four years. When it is operative, the light is only visible at 12 miles maximum and from 108° magnetic clockwise to 278° magnetic. It is obscured from 278° magnetic to 108° magnetic. Thus, you can run up on the east coast of Antigua while looking for the light, or you could clip the end of Cade Reef while working up the south coast. If the light had red sectors for these areas, the mariner would know exactly when he was heading into danger.

2. English Harbor. At considerable expense, a new range was established in English Harbor bearing 068° magnetic red isophase. This is twice cursed. First, it brings you in on an approach that seldom can be sailed; you must douse sail and then power in on a range where the sea will be on your beam. If the engine fails, you will be up on Snapper Point before you can anchor or reset your sails. Second, when large yachts are anchored in Freeman Bay, the forward light of the range frequently is obscured. (This range was established in opposition to the sentiments of all yachtsmen and mariners who use English Harbor.) SEE ALSO THE NOTES FOR UPDATES AT THE END OF THIS CHAPTER ON PAGE 120

I strongly advise everyone to use Range A (Sketch Chart 25): beach house and hotel in line 039° magnetic—basically the range that has been used for the last 300 years.

3. Falmouth. The Falmouth range is correct. If you insist on coming into Antigua at night—and I strongly advise against it—you should use the Falmouth range, carry on into the harbor stay directly on the range, and anchor once inside the harbor. I should report that as of December 1992, the range lights of Falmouth Harbor could only be described as unreliable! In daylight, however, you can become very confused, as buoy "2" is a starboard-hand buoy leading up the range toward the Catamaran Club and Marina. Yet many yachts will want to turn eastward to head for the Antigua Yacht Club jetty. Since buoy "2" is a starboard-hand mark, they are likely to leave that to starboard, come around to head due east, and make a screeching stop on a five-foot shoal. Correctly, buoy "2" should be a midchannel mark showing a channel division to starboard and port. (See Sketch Chart 25.) SEE ALSO THE NOTES FOR UPDATES AT THE END OF THIS CHAPTER ON PAGE 120.

4. Cade Reef. Hurricane Hugo in 1989 moved things around so much that it piled dead

coral into a ridge as much as six feet high, caus- ing the submerged Cade Reef to become what amounts to Cade Island! However, even though it breaks water, the hazard still nails boats, as it is unmarked, and far too many yachts coming up from Guadeloupe are set farther to leeward than they realize. They spot the lights of the Curtain Bluff Hotel and mistake them for the lights of English Harbor. Heading for the lights, they pile up on Cade Reef. This happens with an alarming degree of regularity. Despite what the RCC Lesser Antilles guide may say, DO NOT attempt to enter English Harbor at night, as you could easily come to grief on Cade Reef and end up supporting one (or both!) of the local salvage services. (More about those later.)

Many other yachts pile up on the western end of the reef. They leave English Harbor in the afternoon, run westward outside of Cade Reef, turn northwest toward St. Barts, and hit the end of the reef. Finally, boats approaching the English Harbor/Falmouth area come around the southwest corner of Antigua and see the waves breaking on the outer reef. So they decide to go up inside Cade Reef in calm water. Provided that the light is good, this is an excellent way to work eastward—by short-tacking between the reef and the "mainland." It can, however, be a booby trap. I say this because the western entrance to Goat Head Channel is like the mouth of an alligator and will quickly snap up any passing yachts.

What is referred to as Cade Reef is, in fact, two reefs. The outer one is Cade Reef, which always breaks; the inner one, Middle Reef, NEVER breaks. The channel between them is the aforementioned "mouth" of the alligator—into which yachts sail much too often. If you do find yourself between the inner and outer reefs, the best maneuver is to turn around and go out the way you came in. I have ended up there three times. The third time, the light was perfect and I had a good crew on board, so we managed to thread our way through the eastern gap between Middle Reef and Cade Reef. We could not turn west and go back out, as it was about 1600, and the sun was in the west. This gave us good light for going east, but not west. Even though we managed to do it, however, I would never want to do it again!

5. Boggy Peak. At 1,450 feet elevation, this light should be a beautiful landmark for approaching Antigua. However, it is frequently out.

6. Sandy Island. This light, allegedly with 13-mile visibility, also should be an excellent landmark for approaching Antigua. Yet not only is it frequently out, but its realistic range is six to nine miles—not the 13 miles shown in the government light list. The only reliable light seems to be on the Lighthouse Radio tower behind the Jolly Beach Hotel near the shores of Morris Bay. The Light and Tower have long since disappeared in the various hurricanes and will not be re-established.

7. Diamond Channel. The miniature Texas tower on Diamond Bank was lighted at one time. It was an excellent mark when approaching Antigua from the north. However, for reasons best known to the Antiguan government, this light has been discontinued. The miniature Texas Tower similarly has disappeared in the hurricanes.

8. Parham Harbor. The channel leading into this harbor is buoyed RED/LEFT/RETURNING. Why? The buoys are gone (April 2000). Will they ever be replaced??

To sum up this catalogue of navigational problems:

- Do not negotiate the region of Cade Reef or the northeast coast of Antigua except in good light.

- Do not approach Horse Shoe Reef after 1500.

- If you are foolish enough to approach English Harbor from the south at night, bear off and head for Falmouth; you have a better chance of staying out of trouble.

- If you approach from the west at night, the lights of Boggy Peak, and Light- house Radio tower should guide you into Mor- ris Bay; with luck, two of these three lights will be on. Plot your way carefully into Morris Bay, anchor in suitable depth, and wait until dawn to sail into English Harbor.

- The range into the main harbor of St. Johns exists but is hard to spot.

- The Warrington Bank buoys are large and unlighted and the fueling pier and its attendant buoys are poorly illuminated—another bunch of booby traps to snare the unwary. Bishop Shoal buoy went adrift in late 1985 and was not replaced until 1992!

- The leading lights to Falmouth Harbor are unreliable. So much for any guide that advises entering English Harbor at night.

I have urged the Antiguan government to collect the information and advice offered by all the mariners who cruise here and come up with an overall plan for buoys, ranges (transits), and lights for Antigua and its waters. There has been no response.

So far, we have been lucky; many boats have run aground, but no lives have been lost. How long will Antigua's good luck continue?

Incidentally, electronic navigation has cost the underwriters of Lloyd's about a million dollars as a result of three separate electronically controlled groundings in the area around Antigua. The navigators spent their time staring at their SatNav and GPS instruments and did not have the sense to check with their eyes, radar, or fathometers. This occurred because Antigua "ain't where it oughta be." In the Eastern Caribbean, electronic navigation is a lot more accurate than the charts. Almost all of the islands are anywhere from tenths of a mile to half a mile out of their apparent positions. In the case of Antigua, it appears to be a mile and a half out of place. (In the Pacific, however, the situation is infinitely worse—some islands appear to be as much as six miles out of their charted positions.)

All Imray-Iolaire charts of the Eastern Caribbean have been redone to WGS84. On most charts your GPS position may be plotted directly on the chart. On a few of them there are off sets which must be calculated in to give your correct GPS position.

In the older Imray-Iolaire charts this off set was given in latitude and longitude. Now all the Imray-Iolaire charts have that off set expressed not only in longitude and latitude but also in bearing and distance. In very few cases is the off set more than two to three hundred yards. When you are that close to an island, you should be using your eyes rather than your GPS.

Approaching Antigua

When approaching from due south (departing from the northern entrance of Grand Cul-de-Sac Marin or Deshaies, in Guadeloupe), remember to allow for the current set. The current will be on the weather beam about one knot. If you are doing four knots, you have to allow for 15°; if you are doing six knots, allow for 10°; if your speed is seven knots, allow for 8°. Plus, of course, there is the leeway of your boat, which on some cruising designs may easily be 10°! Check to see how much you drift. You should stay on a rhumb-line course. Lay your course for English Harbor.

Coming from the west and southwest, take care to avoid the shoals along the western side of the island and the exposed reefs south of Johnson Point. It is best to get inside Cade and Middle reefs if proceeding east to English Harbor. That way, you will be sailing over calm water as far as Curtain Bluff. ONCE INSIDE THE REEF, KEEP IN MIND THAT THE OUTER REEF (CADE) WILL BE BREAKING WATER, WHILE THE INNER REEF (MIDDLE) WILL NOT BE BREAKING, AND CAN ONLY BE SPOTTED BY THE COLOR OF THE WATER. DO NOT CONFUSE THE TWO REEFS.

If you are coming from the west, avoid the shoals west of the southwestern part of Antigua by passing outboard of Five Islands. Then put Sandy Island on the northeast side of the highest of the Five Islands (Range E, Sketch Chart 25), continuing south until you have cleared the reefs off Johnson Point.

When approaching from the north or northwest, put a crew member on the upper spreaders. The coast is lined with reefs that are notoriously difficult to spot, and I advise against trying to pick your way through unless you are very familiar with the area.

For an approach from the northwest, pass westward of Diamond Bank. Use the range of Mt. Thomas and signal station in line of 186° magnetic - see Chart 32. If you are coming from the north, use Diamond Channel on a range with Boggy Peak and Great Sister in line 010° magnetic; or enter to windward of Diamond Bank. As previously noted the Texas Tower is now gone.

The northeast coast is low and featureless, and while there are several radio towers in the vicinity of the airport, they are not marked on the chart with enough accuracy to fix a position. When coming in from the east, always approach Antigua from the southeast, as the northeast coast is without doubt the most dangerous area in the entire Eastern Caribbean. As soon as you get into about seven fathoms of water, be very cautious. Long Island is low and hard to spot, and the reefs north of Bird Islet Reef can give you a scare (see Chart 31 and the discussion later in this chapter for detailed sailing directions). From the northeastern corner of Antigua at Indian Town Point to the southern coast, there are no offlying dangers, and it is an easy matter to lay a course south along the east coast to English Harbour.

Approaching English Harbour/Falmouth Harbour

If you are making a landfall on Antigua from the southeast (after a transatlantic crossing, for example), you probably will pick up the lights of Désirade first. You should then aim for English Harbour. Once Antigua becomes clearly visible, head for Shirley Heights, a flat-topped hill with ruined fortifications on the eastern side of the harbor. When shore details come into view, post a lookout for the Pillars of Hercules (see Chart 26), a clearly distinguishable rock formation that looks like the entrance to a Greek temple in the cliffs forming the eastern side of the harbor entrance. Do not approach at night,

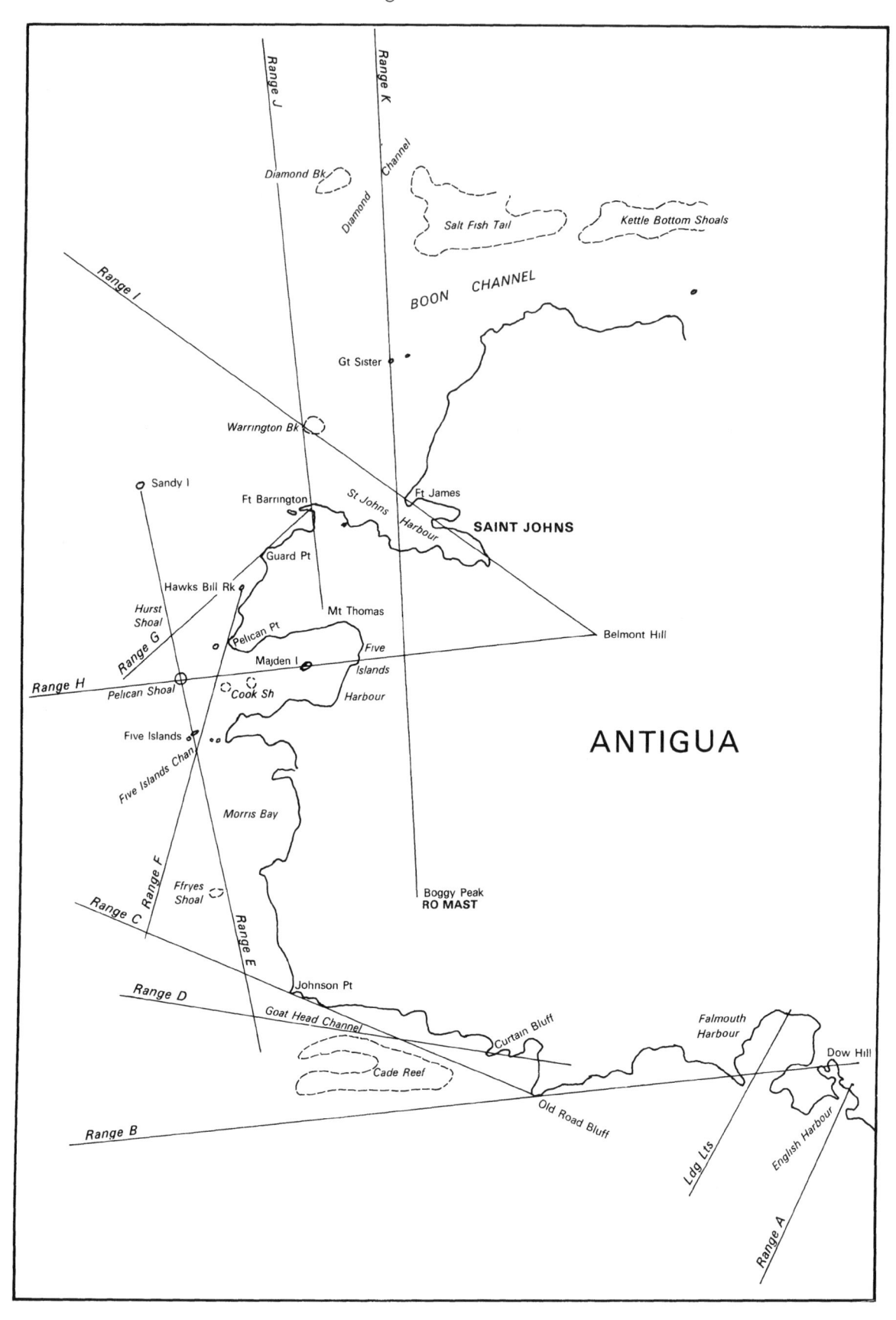

Sketch Chart 25   Ranges for Antigua

since it is possible to mistake the lights of the Curtain Bluff Hotel on Morris Bay to the west for those of The Inn in Freeman Bay, English Harbour. By day the approach is not difficult. Once you spot the Pillars of Hercules, head directly for them until you are close to shore, bearing off to clear the reef off Charlotte Point. The beach house at Freeman Point placed in line with the Inn (the large white hotel higher on the hill) leads clear of all dangers. Barclay Point is steep-to.

If headed for Falmouth Harbour from the south (or even English Harbour), look for Monks Hill (location of Great George Fort), the flat-topped mountain that is di- rectly behind Falmouth. Being flat-topped and higher, it is easier to spot than Shirley Heights. Keep this slightly off the lee bow and you will be fine. As a result of hurricane Filly there is a deep gouge in Monks hill which is easily visible 10 miles off. Put that on the bow and it will lead you into Falmouth harbour. Needless to say, do not approach from the west at night because of the previously mentioned danger of Cade Reef. On arriving in daylight, if you are good at reef piloting, the best thing to do is sail inside the reef in calm water. Tack into Old Road Bay and then tack up the shore from Old Road Bluff to Falmouth or English Harbour. Take very short tacks, as this technique will keep you out of current and sea. See also the NOTES for updates on page 120.

Approaching at night. Despite what appears in the RCC Lesser Antilles guide, I strongly advise against approaching Antigua at night. Experienced yachtsmen in the Caribbean maintain that the light and buoyage system in the ex-British islands is set up so that harbor pilots, ship wreckers, and salvage men will never starve to death! Dr. Nick Fuller, who has run his salvage business since about 1987 as a sideline to his medical practice, backs me up. He maintains that 80 percent of his work is as a result of vessels navigating in and around Antigua at night. He feels that if people used common sense and stood off until dawn, he would not even be in the salvage business. John Bentley, who has been doing salvage for about 15 years, also agrees. Dr. Fuller (telephone: 809-463-3010) is based on the north side of the island; his vessel is *Nicol*. John Bentley (telephone: 809-460-1154) is at Turtle Rock (shore station) on the south side of the island, and aboard *Sea Pony*; both maintain a 24-hour watch, seven days a week, on channel 16. They will arrive posthaste and try to provide help immediately. Both feel that the RCC guide will provide them with plenty of salvage business over the years unless yachtsmen learn not to accept the RCC's contention that all navigation lights are reliable in the ex-British islands.

Remember that these men are in the local salvage business and are not supported by the government as a rescue service. Thus, they will offer to help you on the basis of the standard Lloyd's open form—"no cure", no pay. There is no "cure" unless the boat is delivered afloat to a safe anchorage, or, if not floatable, the boat is hauled ashore. If you are in trouble and they arrive, don't argue. Agree immediately. They will not attempt to assist any vessel whose skipper tries to negotiate a price at the time of the salvage.

One major problem is that mariners have many misconceptions about salvage and salvage charges. Whether you accept the towline from the salvage vessel or you send over your own makes NO difference whatsoever in the final bill. After a salvage operation is completed, the salvor and the underwriter (or, if the boat is not insured, the owner) sit down and negotiate a mutually agreeable figure based on a percentage of the SALVED WORTH of the vessel. In other words, the vessel may have been worth US$500,000 when it grounded, but its salved worth could be only US$200,000 after it has been salvaged because of the damage done during the grounding. The salvor earns a percentage of the salved worth, NOT a percentage of the value of the vessel before the grounding. The percentage earned by the salvor is based on several factors: how dangerous a position the stranded vessel was in when the salvage vessel arrived on the scene; how skillful the salvage vessel was in effecting the operation and minimizing additional damage; and how dangerous the conditions were for the salvor's vessel and his crew.

The lights at Mamora Bay, the St. James's Club, are visible for 20 miles out to sea and make a good leading mark. As they come abeam, heave-to and wait for dawn before entering English or Falmouth Harbour.

Do not be confused by the new flashing (every second) red light on the Radio Tower on Dow Hill—This lines up with range to enter English Harbour but must be kept broad on starboard bow when approaching Antigua from the east.

The south shore of Antigua is emblazoned with the lights of many hotels, which serve as beacons of a sort. If you reach the south coast at night, though, stand off until dawn—All too many boats have mistaken the lights of the hotels in Rendevous Bay and Curtain Bluff for English Harbour and Falmouth—and thus sailed hard aground on Cade Reef!!!

ENGLISH HARBOUR

(Chart 26; II A, A-27)

English Harbour, on Antigua's south coast, is all but landlocked, and it provides an almost ideal haven—just as it did in Admiral Nelson's time. The wind sweeps across the island through the low valleys, making the harbor cool most of the year.

English Harbour was once the main anchorage for the British West Indian Squadron, until it was abandoned in 1899. Watching the old square-riggers entering the dockyard must have been an awesome

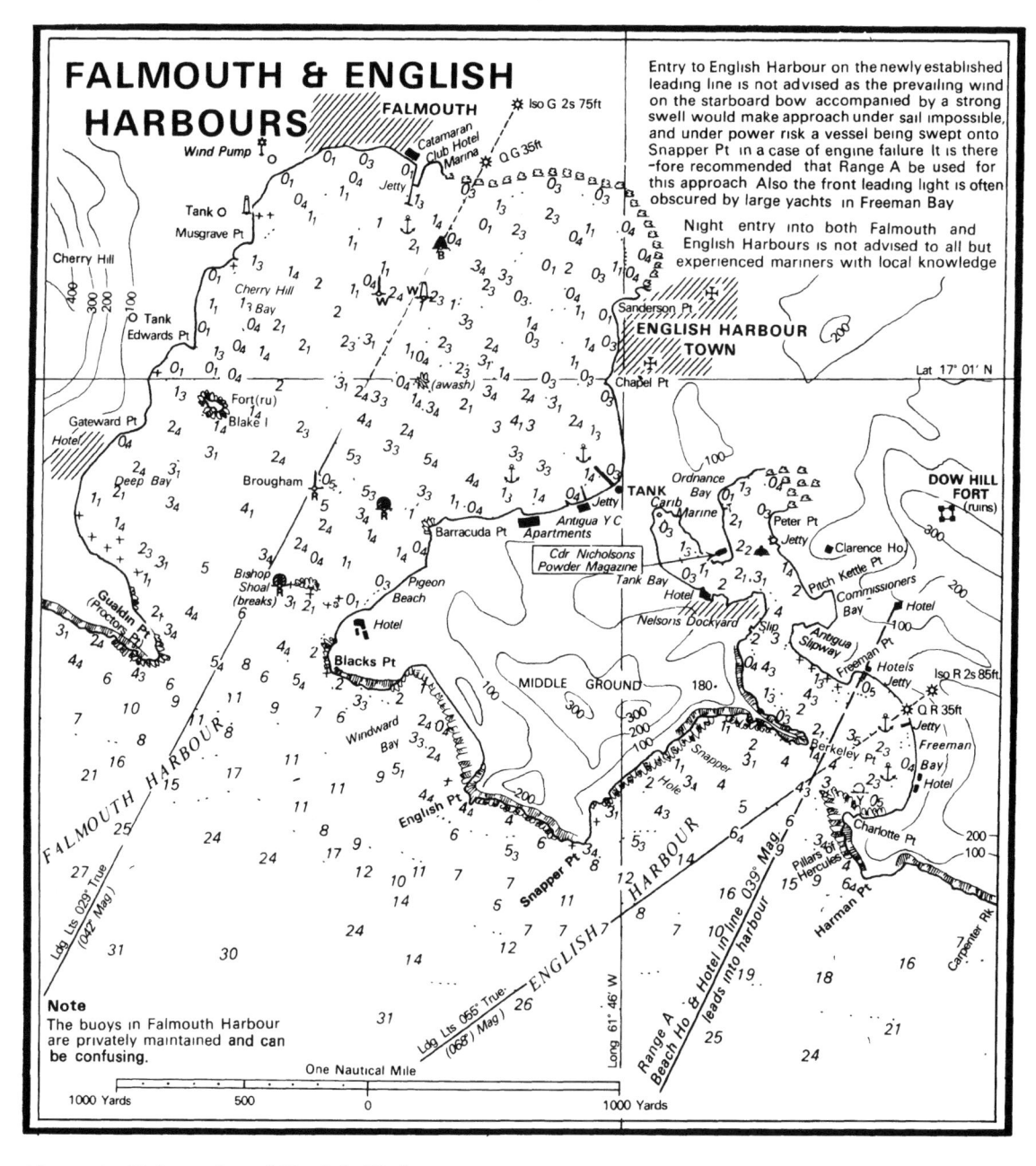

Chart 26   Falmouth and English Harbours   Depths in fathoms and feet

sight. A nineteenth-century edition of *Sailing Directions* gives some idea of the laborious measures involved: "Intending to enter the harbor with the prevailing wind at east, stand boldly in under the heights, a little to windward of Fort Charlotte Bluff. Keep the ship under full plain sail, trimmed by the wind, hug the lee shore, giving the bluff a berth of one cable length, and having rounded the buoy close aboard to starboard, keep the leading mark on until the dockyard staff is on with the end of Fort Barclay, then luff close up, take in the course, and if you have a strong way, you will probably shoot around the point to Fort Barclay, before the wind from the highlands comes off from the northern shore. If the ship loses way and becomes unmanageable before this, you must anchor immediately; if you succeed in shooting in, be prepared to wear short around, and when in the center of the channel, clew up, as you will most probably have sufficient way to carry you to the anchorage off the dockyard." WHEW! What a task!

Nowadays, once you are past Charlotte Point, you can round up and anchor in Freeman Bay or continue sailing on into English Harbour. If there is space, moor stern-to in English Harbour or tie up to the Antigua Slipway docks and then hoist your "Q" flag. The skipper should go ashore alone to Customs, which is on the ground floor of the eastern end of the Officers' Quarters in English Harbour. Mr. Blake, who has been here for many years, will help with entry procedures.

Regarding mooring stern-to in English Harbour, avoid the north side, as Limey's Bar has parties one or two nights a week with speakers stacked six-high. The sound will deafen you and make your boat uninhabitable. The concept of "noise pollution" is sadly nonexistent in the West Indies. SEE ALSO NOTES FOR UPDATES ON PAGE 120 AT THE END OF THIS CHAPTER.

You may anchor anywhere in the inner harbor, or drop an anchor and back down stern-to on the quay; but be sure to use a heavy anchor and plenty of scope, as the bottom in English Harbour is very soft mud and the holding is none too good.

When you get ready to leave, if you have hooked onto the old hurricane chain, or a big abandoned anchor, or any of the other junk that litters the bottom, contact John Bentley aboard *Sea Pony* on VHF channel 16; he is an experienced diver who has reduced the clearing of fouled anchors in English Harbour to a fine art and a nice little business. Another possible contact is Tony Fincham at Antigua Divers.

English Harbour became a premier yachting center because of the vision of the late Commander V.E.B. Nicholson (RN Ret.), who arrived here on *Mollyhawk*, a 72-foot staysail schooner. He, his wife, and two sons had sailed across the Atlantic en route to New Zealand to seek a new life, as they felt that Europe—and Ireland especially—was recovering too slowly from the ravages of World War II. In the winter of 1949, they anchored in English Harbour and discovered a totally derelict dockyard: Everything had completely collapsed except the Officers' Quarters, which had been restored by a Canadian insurance company in the mid-1930s and were unoccupied in 1949.

Commander Nicholson met some people from the Mill Reef Club who wanted to go sailing, and he then discovered that people were willing to pay him to do what he did for pleasure. He certainly knew a good thing when he saw it, and he proceeded to do a few charters on *Mollyhawk*. Next he contacted friends who owned boats that could be purchased cheaply or were sitting idle. Thus began the Nicholson charter fleet.

The commander moved into an abandoned paymaster's office (rent free, since the roof was collapsing), and, with some interested Americans, Europeans, and Canadians, put together the Friends of English Harbour in 1951.

With almost no money, they commenced the restoration of the old dockyard where Nelson once walked, and in the more than four decades since then, it has become the most important yachting center in the Eastern Caribbean. In the process, they turned the English Harbour/Freeman Bay area into the wealthiest part of Antigua, thanks to the money spent by the resident and visiting yachtsmen.

First the Nicholsons refurbished the old Officers' Quarters to provide accommodations for sons Desmond and Rodney, who had married and were raising families. Then the Friends took a long-term lease on The Admiral's Inn, which had no roof. The government probably laughed all the way to the bank about this crazy Irishman and his friends taking a lease on four empty walls. But The Admiral's Inn (known locally as "Adds") opened in 1960 with a terrific party—which I well remember because I helped Desmond hang the door on the head for opening night. We had taken the door off *Mollyhawk* on temporary loan—it was still there 32 years later. The Admiral's Inn has been going strong all that time.

A superintendent of the dockyard was appointed, and the Friends of English Harbour began collecting dock fees. The Nicholsons started Carib Marine and sold marine supplies out of the old paymaster's office. Rodney established a primitive radio communications office and the commander set up a charter organization that lured clients to the Caribbean from Europe and North America.

Commander Nicholson was a typically charming West Cork Irishman who could talk the wallpaper right off the wall! His Irish charm persuaded the government of Antigua to lease derelict buildings to him for "peppercorn" rent. With enviable skill and a whole lot of guts, he then talked American and English businessmen into backing him for the rebuilding project. The following story reveals a lot about this memorable character.

In the 1950s and 1960s, the Nicholson charter fleet was run on the basis of the phrase, "I owe my soul to the company store." The skippers were given cash advances and were allowed to charge against income. When the winter chartering season was over, there was a late-spring final accounting. Typically, skippers found that even after they had worked hard chartering all winter, the costs of maintenance, brokerage fees, commission, boat storage, and wages ate up all the profits—and often there was no money left over. I can well remember skippers arriving in English Harbour swearing that they could not wait to get hold of V.E.B. Nicholson and beat him to a bloody pulp! In each case, they would storm into the office—only to meet a smiling commander who would say, soothingly, "Wouldn't it be preferable to discuss this over a drink at The Admiral's Inn?" So off the two would go—the commander with his irrepressible good humor and the charter skipper with smoke coming out of his ears! After a few beers, and usually a lunch as well, the commander had calmed the irate skipper and they would depart The Admiral's Inn arm in arm, bosom buddies again!

It must be remembered that in the 1960s, English Harbour was the poorest part of Antigua. Nowadays, even though many of the businesses are owned by expatriates, many others are owned by long-time Falmouth and English Harbour families. If nothing else, they frequently are the landlords of the "expat" businesses, so they now can sit back, relax, collect the rent, and laugh all the way to the bank! If it were not for V.E.B. Nicholson, English Harbour and Antigua's yachting industry would not be what it is today. His are shoes that will never again be filled.

Eventually the need for a boatyard became evident, and Antigua Slipway was established in 1969. Progress there was very slow until the arrival of David Simmons, who decided that the buildings were nice, as were the shops and the marine store, but the slipway was essential. He wanted to start slipping boats immediately, so he set up a slipway using Egyptian skidding. It was crude and labor-intensive, but at least it worked. He hauled boats of up to about 50 feet until 1974, when the proper railway was installed.

Over the next 10 years, David developed what was undoubtedly the best boatyard east of Miami. He trained a crew of shipwrights to work on wooden yachts, and they restored *Vanda*, a 1907 teak ketch. Then they carried out a complete restoration on the 103-foot gaff-rigged ketch *Cariad*—built in 1897! *Vagrant*, an 88-foot Herreshoff schooner built in 1911, was completely restored for Peter de Savary.

The yard also repairs fiberglass boats and has an excellent chandlery to back up the operation. It boasts an incredible stock of marine gear for boats 40 feet and over. For many years, the engine-repair service left a little to be desired—primarily because David basically did not like engines—but now that he has retired, the engine and machine shops have improved.

David is a tough act to follow. His management skill was the major reason that Antigua Slipway has been so successful. At the age of 14, the English education system decided that David was not a student, and they threw him out on his ear. He apprenticed himself to a good boatbuilding yard and then spent a lifetime in the business. He is the only person in the Eastern Caribbean who can make that claim. Everyone else who is operating marinas or yacht yards in the region has made money elsewhere and decided to have some fun playing in the yachting game. As a result, there is a tremendous amount of inefficiency in the islands, and many businesses have come and gone. Antigua Slipway, however, is still running and running well, although the absence of David and his charming wife, Maggie (who for many years ran the marine store), is sadly noted by the old-timers.

When it comes to woodworking, everyone's first thought is Antigua Slipway, but there are *three* small, independent shops that are good. They cannot haul your boat, but they can sell wood, do woodworking jobs in their shops and install them, or work directly on your boat.

The older of these shops is Chippy's, run by Jerry Bardoe. (I knew him for 10 years before I found out his real name!) The shops are Winkie Woodwork, and now Knothole. Call for Chippy, Winkie Woodwork, and Knothole on channel 68, and they will appear! In addition, there are numerous well-trained shipwrights living on their own boats in Antigua. Just spread the word you are looking for a "chippy" and they will pop out of the woodwork.

Yacht facilities in English Harbour and Falmouth are increasing all the time, and the marine-supply situation is excellent at the moment. In addition to Antigua Slipway (basically geared for boats over 40 feet), the Chandlery (on the eastern side of Falmouth Harbour near Pumps and Power) is new and expanding. Further, Carib Marine, formerly stuck in the corner of the Carib Marine food store, now has a separate facility on the south side of Falmouth Harbour at Temo Sports. Finally, even though it is not in English Harbour, I should mention Budget Marine, which has opened up in Jolly Harbour and is expanding rapidly. (If Budget Marine in Philipsburg on St. Martin is not the best marine-supply store in the Caribbean, I would be hard put to name a better one.)

You can take gas bottles to Pumps and Power early in the morning and pick them up filled the following day.

Seagull Services—Pumps and Power—in Falmouth has an excellent machine shop; they offer steel, stainless, and aluminum welding; engine and electronics repair; and sales and repair of inflatables. The firm also is a licensed check-out facility for most of the best-known life-raft manufacturers. There are also excellent electronics repair firms. Signal Locker is run by Cap Green, who has been doing repairs in Antigua for more years than he'd care to admit! He has developed a good staff of Antiguans who do not only electronic and electrical repairs but also superb refrigeration repairs. I cannot speak too highly of them. The other two firms are new: Marionics is run by Arougoo Adams at Seagull Services while Trevor Odlum, who started his career working for Cap Green, is now considered the local B&G expert.

Latest news in the electronics department is that John Eyers, who for many years was in partnership with Cap Green, has returned to Antigua with his wife, Ann. They moved to England in 1982 so their daughter could attend school there. Now that she is on her own, they have returned to Antigua and have joined up with Trevor Odlum in Cay Electronics, the major electronics and refrigeration firm that also has major operations in Tortola and Newport, Rhode Island. Having bases in these three locations should mean that they can obtain parts from the United States almost instantly. However, everyone always promises the sky and doesn't always produce it. When our portable radio needed parts, Cay Electronics claimed that they could have it repaired for me in Tortola and it would be waiting for me in Antigua. Three weeks later, when we reached Antigua, still no radio. They lent me a hand-held radio until they repaired mine! Cay Electronics is on the north side of the road from English Harbour to Falmouth, halfway between Cogs Cross School and the Catamaran Club. Best way to contact them is via VHF channel 68.

All of this entrepreneurial activity is good for yachtsmen, as nothing is better than healthy competition to keep businesses on their toes.

Inside the dockyard, in the building just north of the sail loft, are Tony Fincham's Antigua Divers and Julian Guildersleeve's WaterMaker Services. Julian has spent a lifetime skippering large yachts and re-commissioning boats that have been laid up for eons. He is one of the most competent people in and around English Harbour—I can recommend him highly as a watermaker installer, diesel mechanic, sailor, and adviser on all things maritime. In the same shop is Tend-Aloft Rigging, run by Bruce Nodine. They can do rigging of all sizes and shapes, and their machine shop is equipped to tool bits and pieces so that everything fits.

Two companies—Outfitters and Antigua Slipway—offer rapid-delivery services for supplies shipped into Antigua. They guarantee 24-hour delivery from Miami; it takes slightly longer from elsewhere in the world. Dale Weston, who runs Outfitters, has built a massive business in importing yacht and other supplies into Antigua. He has even established Outfitters International, with offices in England, the Mediterranean, Australia, and New Zealand. Thus, it hardly matters where your equipment originates—they have agents who can dispatch it rapidly to Antigua (or anywhere else in the world). If you are anywhere in the Caribbean, you are probably wise to contact Dale Weston and get him to order what you need and ship it to you.

When it comes to sail repair, there are two choices. Antigua Sails has an office at the eastern end of the lower floor of the Officers' Quarters. The office is run by Rena Knight, assisted by her partner, Graham Knight (no relation). Rena's first career was as a nurse (she is an excellent one), so if one of your crew members needs emergency repairs and you are having trouble finding a doctor, contact Rena to help you out. Beware, though—she has the bedside manner of an irate rhinoceros, so seek her out only if someone really is sick or badly damaged! She is infinitely more charming if you go in to have your sails repaired or an awning made. She also operates a clearinghouse for skippers and owners looking for crew, and for crew looking for jobs. Graham has gained such renown as an awning maker that during the summers he measures up boats in the Mediterranean, makes up the awnings in Antigua, then ships them to the Med. In some cases, the boats even sail transatlantic to have the awnings fitted! Antigua Sails may not be cheap, but their work certainly is superb. As with anything in life, you get what you pay for.

Just inside the dockyard gate is A&F Sails, run by Adolphus and Franklin, who began their careers working for Rena and Graham. They then set up on their own and have done very well. Which sailmaker should you use? If you have an emergency and need a sail in a hurry, it's a matter of finding out which one has time to do the job. Both firms are good and both have done work for me on *Iolaire*. In every instance, I have been extremely happy with the quality of the work from both sailmakers.

Jenny Eason's boutique within the dockyard has women's fashions, and the women along the roadside outside the dockyard have all sorts of inexpensive, cool frocks. If you are looking for jewelry, visit the excellent little gold shop in St. Johns run by Hans Schmidt, a Dutchman and an OWIH (Old

West Indies Hand) who has been in Antigua so long that even the locals consider him Antiguan; he often can be found around the dockyard.

Regarding food, fresh fruit and vegetables usually are available from the market women in the dockyard or along the roadside. Otherwise, go to Malone's fruit and vegetable shop on the west side of the road from the dockyard. For more extensive food shopping, go to Carib Marine at the head of the harbor. There is even a dinghy dock where you can tie up your dinghy while you shop. The food there is not cheap, but you'll find quantity and quality. They operate a catering service for charter boats, and you can go in and drool over the exotic items that the charter cooks are rustling up for their guests—food that I, for one, cannot afford! Carib Marine also stocks some marine equipment, Imray-Iolaire charts, and Street guides. You can make arrangements for them to deliver your purchases to your boat, which is especially convenient if you are based in Falmouth and have no car. You can also buy food at Bailey's Supermarket in Falmouth, 300 yards east of the Catamaran Club.

For heavy-duty shopping, most people go to St. Johns to Bryson's and Drew's supermarkets (only 100 yards apart). If you have a car, you can drive out to the new Food City supermarket, which is highly regarded by the locals for quality, quantity, and prices. When we were there in May 1992, I thought that the store was large and excellent, but there were obvious gaps in their stock. No doubt these gaps will be filled in the next year or so. Once you have obtained your supplies in the supermarkets, you can buy fresh fruit and vegetables either along the street outside the post office or at the local market. Antigua's local market has improved dramatically over the years. Go very early, and you will find an amazing amount of good-quality produce at reasonable prices.

As far as restaurants are concerned, there are so many in and around the English Harbour area that anything I might suggest is sure to be out-of-date by the time you read this. The best idea is to ask fellow yachties which restaurants they prefer.

For buying and selling yachts, there is Nicholson Yacht Sales (in the old paymaster's office), run by Joel Byerly, another OWIH. He has been in the islands for more than three decades, and he is an excellent raconteur. Every morning at 0900, he gives the weather forecast after the broadcast from V.E. Bird Airport. (Don't ask me what I think about weather reports!) Joel also provides local information and announces birthdays and other events. His broadcasts are not audible over at Barbuda or on Antigua's north coast, so Harmony Hall rebroadcasts the report after Joel signs off. They will also relay messages to English Harbour from the north side of Antigua and Barbuda.

As for laundry, I have had it done by Mrs. Malone for nearly 30 years, so, needless to say, I recommend her highly. If you ask her to wash, dry, and fold your laundry, it will look just fine, and the price is reasonable. If you want it ironed, the price goes way up. Put a tag on the bag reading, "Wash and dry only. No ironing." Outside the dockyard, on the Falmouth road, is Sam and Dave's laundry, which is fast, cheerful, and efficient. They work overtime when necessary, even laboring on "Labor Day" (first Monday in May) to get everyone's laundry done after Antigua Sailing Week.

Mail is something of a problem. Letters can be sent to the English Harbour post office, but it always seems to be the wrong time of day when I try to collect my mail there. It's better to have Nicholson's receive and hold your mail, although you will need to make prior arrangements with them.

Transportation to and from English Harbour has improved immeasurably since the old days. Buses leave very regularly from outside the dockyard; the ride is an adventure, since the drivers seem to have an ongoing contest to see who can drive to town fastest and who can cram the most passengers in at once—especially returning from town in the late afternoon. The price is right, however, and the experience is amusing. Check to see when the last bus leaves town for the dockyard in the afternoon. There are also plenty of taxis now, but some drivers are a lot nicer than others—ask around. We use Nevil Bailey and his wife, Dorris. (Nevil's younger brother, Oliver, quit the taxi business to put his savings into the interisland freight business; he is now successfully running a small freighter.) Other taxi drivers who have served yachtsmen for many years are J&B and Ivor's Taxi. Contact all taxis on channel 68.

The radio situation in English Harbour finally is improving. I could compile a whole book on the subject of radio communication in the islands during the 1950s and 1960s. It would make very amusing reading! Nicholson's maintains radio standby on SSB 8294 during working hours (i.e., 0900 to 1200 and 1300 to 1600 Monday through Friday; 0900 to noon Saturday). They also stand by on VHF channel 68.

Regarding VHF, note that it is very important never to use channel 16 except in a dire emergency. Always use channel 68 as your contact channel and then switch. As of May 1992, the frequencies in English Harbour and Antigua in general have been assigned as follows: Contact channel is 68; switch to channel 5 through 7, or 69 through 78.

Telephone communications out of English Harbour have improved dramatically, but they still are a long way from being perfect. At the entrance to English Harbour is a battery of card phones—the cards are available at the Copper and Lumber Store. With the aid of a card (and provided the phones are working), you can call anywhere in the world. At the entrance to English Harbour is a phone exchange from where you can make a call and then pay for it—but the exchange has rather peculiar working hours (posted on the door). Periodically, the card phones seem to go on the fritz—they always seem to be nonoperational during Antigua Sailing Week and Nicholson's Agents Week. You can't make a phone call unless you use a boat phone—efficient but expensive! It's an interminable mystery to me why the card phones miraculously begin to work again shortly after Agents Week and Sailing Week. As each year goes by, more and more people are buying fax machines, so if you need to send or receive a fax, just make inquiries locally.

Here's the situation as of June 1993 vis-à-vis showers. Showers are in the English Harbour dockyard and are available every day from 0600 to 1800—if, of course, the water is on! (In March 1992, there were drought conditions—and thus no showers.) In June 1993, I was caught in the following ridiculous situation. I was covered in filth as I had just pulled the engine out of my son's 28-foot sloop *Capadena*. I was dead tired, walked the half mile from Falmouth to the English Harbour showers, and arrived at 1740 to discover the showers were closed despite the sign that said they were open from 6 a.m. to 6 p.m. Assuming there are no problems when you need them, the shower fee is EC$4.00. Two girls sit at the entrance to collect the fees, but I am sure the amount taken in could not possibly cover the two girls' wages and leave any profit. It seems ludicrous! Why, oh why can't they follow the example of the other Eastern Caribbean marinas (including Antigua's own Jolly Harbour Marina) that have installed coin- or token-operated showers? Everyone who has taken this step has transformed a frustrating, money-losing setup into a profitable business. The showers are available from Dick Morris, REMS Inc., Pasea Estate, Roadtown, Tortola, BVI. Telephone: 809-464-2694.

When one is cruising in the tropics, one should be able to put one's feet up at 1700, have a sundowner, and then wander ashore and get a shower. In the English Harbour/Falmouth area, this is impossible—if you are not in the showers by 1800, you will be dirty until the next day. In fact, sometimes you can rush to arrive at the showers by 1750—only to find that the girls have closed up 10 minutes early or the water is not operating. This is particularly aggravating if you are lying in Falmouth and have just walked all the way from there to English Harbour. The shower situation has improved in English Harbour under the auspices of the Park Department.

They are clean, with plenty of pressure and cost $2.oo per shower. I am sure with the cost of collecting the $2.oo the showers are losing money. Why, oh, why don't they go to coin operated machines. The opening and closing hours of the showers are still erratic.

Some things never change. In the shower area, there are sinks for washing clothes—but no plugs for the sinks! In the 20 years that the sinks have been there, I have yet to see any plugs, so bring your own. Some bright spark could make a killing selling sink plugs here. Perhaps Tend-Aloft Rigging should have a sideline of selling plugs to yachtsmen. There are washing lines available, but I do not recommend using them. Too many stories have filtered back about people leaving damp clothes on the lines to dry for a few hours and returning to find some or even most of their garments "missing." From the types of things stolen, it is painfully obvious that the thieves are not, in fact, the island's inhabitants, but rather our "fellow" yachties with light fingers.

The trash situation in and around English Harbour has changed markedly. Whereas formerly there were open rubbish tips spoiling the landscape and breeding rats, now there are closed metal containers that keep the situation under control—at least until Sailing Week. Then, obviously, there is a temporary overflow. The one problem staring everyone in the face is that the fittings on the municipal garbage trucks do not match up with the trash containers provided by the Park Department in English Harbour. The dockyard park department has its own truck of rather ancient vintage, and everyone is holding his or her collective breath because if the truck goes "belly up," a disaster is likely to ensue inside the dockyard. It would take a few months for the authorities to once again get on top of the interminable garbage problem.

The dockage situation in Antigua is rather interesting. In the 1970s and early 1980s, the stern-to dockage in English Harbour was jam-packed full. It was run pretty much on a "first come, first served' basis—you found yourself a spot and wedged yourself in. That was another advantage of *Iolaire*—she has only a 10-foot beam. No matter how crowded it was, friends would always yell out, "Don't worry, Squeeky. We can always squeeze *Iolaire* in!" It was OK for narrow boats, but no go for beamy ones. In those days, that was the only dockage in Antigua. The dock situation in Antigua is that now if anything there are more docks than can possibly be filled up. There is dockage in English Harbour at Antigua Slipway, plus stern to in Nelson's Backyard. Falm- outh Harbour has three separate marinas; Antigua Yacht Club Marina, Falmouth Harbour Marina and the Catamaran Club. Even for Nicholson's Agents Week when the place was inundated with boats, there was still dockage space available Now there are plenty of other options: Antigua Slipway, Antigua Yacht Club Marina, the Catamaran Club (where the dock was extended 100 feet in the summer of 1992), plus the Jolly Harbour Marina, which opened in the spring of 1992 and provides another 150 slips. Antigua now seems to have an excess of slips for cruising yachtsmen, and there never is a problem with dockage in the English Harbour/Falmouth area. Even during the height of 2000 Antigua Week, when there were 238 entrants and probably a further 150 boats that arrived to be part of "the scene," dockage space was available stern-to at English Harbour.

Ice has been another perennial problem in English Harbour. Years ago, the only place to get ice was at the US naval base on the other side of the island. (Those were the days when my English yachting friends would sit around pontificating that ice is not necessary in the tropics, and then they would pour rum drinks and scarf up all the ice that they could cadge from visiting American boats.) In the 1980s, another ice plant supplied ice erratically to yachts in English Harbour, but during Antigua Sailing Week there is almost never enough to go around. In 1984, for some unimaginable reason, the ice plant was dismantled and rebuilt during Sailing Week. That year, I think gold was easier to find—and cheaper—than ice. Now, happily, ice machines are all over the island. You have to make do with cube ice, which doesn't last and is expensive. But at least you don't have to race on warm beer!

Only cube ice is available in Antigua. Supposedly the story goes, the block plant broke down and there is only one ice plant on the island of Antigua. They suddenly discovered that they made more money by not selling block ice as the cube ice disappeared so fast. So the block plant has never been repaired. The only way to find block ice is to find a friendly soul that has a deep freeze and who freezes ice in plastic buckets.

Customs and Immigration at English Harbour should be dead simple—but it isn't always so. As mentioned at the beginning of this section, you just go into the Port Authority offices at the eastern end of the ground floor of the old Officers' Quarters and everything is right there: Customs, Immigration, and the Port Authority. Certainly Mr. Blake, the Customs officer who has been there for years, could not be more helpful, friendly and courteous. However, the same CANNOT be said for the Immigration officers. At one point, they were only allowing yachtsmen to clear for 30 days; after that, you had to take the entire crew via an expensive taxi to the main police station in the center of the island, waste many hours, and pay EC$150 per crew member. Then you would have to take another expensive taxi back to your boat. After a number of veteran yachtsmen raised cain about this situation and pointed out to the government that this policy was driving yachts away from Antigua and thus costing Antigua money, yachts and crew were granted 90 days. But it seems that the Immigration officers have decided to have the last laugh, as it is now mandatory for crew members to be physically present to sign off before flying out of Antigua. Therefore, if one of the crew flies out early, he has to go in person to sign off accompanied by the skipper. At times—after Antigua Sailing Week, for example—it can be a real bore when literally hundreds of people who sailed in are flying out. Signing off my wife and 12-year-old son (my wife has been going in and out of the island for some 25 years) took us an hour and a half! The upshot of all this was that my wife became so irate and frustrated by the whole procedure that she vowed she would never come to Antigua again—and she would recommend that none of her friends ever come to Antigua. This appalling situation will no doubt change in time, but who can say when?

When will Customs and Immigration officers ever realize that ON EVERY ISLAND THEY ARE TWO OF THE MOST IMPORTANT PEOPLE THAT A TOURIST OR YACHTSMAN WILL EVER MEET? THEY ARE THE FIRST ONES YOU MEET WHEN YOU ARRIVE AND THE LAST ONES WHEN YOU DEPART. AND THEY SET THE TONE FOR THE WHOLE ISLAND. If you have a hard time at Customs or Immigration upon arrival, no matter how wonderful the island is, no matter how wonderful the people are, you still have a bad taste in your mouth. Customs and Immigration should of course be firm. They should make sure that everyone obeys the law and no one "pulls a fast one," but they can be firm and still be cheerful and polite. Some definitely are neither cheerful nor polite, but fortunately, some are, such as the previously mentioned Mr. Blake. In 1999-2000 the Immigration officer in Antigua at the dockyard became very friendly and helpful. Let us hope that this change of heart continues. As before, Mr. Blake continues to hold forth with charm and efficiency.

Antigua Sailing Week

Twice a year, there are huge assemblages of yachts in the English Harbour/Falmouth area. Large charter yachts, plus a number of megayachts, congregate in December for Nicholson's Agents Week and in April or May for Antigua Sailing Week. The charter brokers claim proudly that these are the greatest gatherings of charter yachts run by the most competent skippers and mates in the world. Ostensibly that is true, but they also are the most irresponsible and inconsiderate mariners in the world! Their behavior on the water has resulted in at least one serious accident each year. The accidents over the years are too numerous to mention. Suffice it to say that it's a miracle there has been only one fatality. Watching this scene brings to mind the theory of spare parts explained to me by Jon Repke of Power Products. He feels that there should be an equal number of horses' heads and horses' asses in the world, but, as he has noted, the Caribbean marine sector has many more horses' asses than horses' heads!

People continually talk of the dangers at sea and the chances of being "done in" while at sea. The eternal great fears are mainly of fire, or being run down by a merchant ship on autopilot (nobody on the bridge, or, if there is someone, he's may be back in the chart room looking at pay records). Hitting a waterlogged but still floating container also rates high on the list of the mariner's fears, as is being caught in a force 12 hurricane. However, despite all these common fears, there are many who would argue that the greatest danger to life and limb facing the seaman in the Eastern Caribbean today is not found at sea but rather riding in a dinghy in the Falmouth/English Harbour area during Agents or Sailing Week! A substantial number of people feel this way because, day and night, both harbors are being crisscrossed constantly by high-speed launches bent on reaching their destinations in record time. (Or perhaps they are deluding themselves that they actually are impressing onlookers!) High-speed launches, Boston whalers, semi-rigids, and inflatables with tons of power scream across the harbor doing anything up to 30 knots—despite the fact that there has been a 5 mph speed limit (posted but unenforced) for at least 20 years! In an article in *Caribbean Boating* (which, incidentally, seems to have fallen on deaf ears), I pointed out that a dinghy traveling at four knots takes five minutes 20 seconds to go from the farthest reaches of Freeman Bay to the dinghy dock at English Harbour. At 20 knots, it takes one minute 30 seconds, and it's the same from the farthest reaches of Falmouth Harbour to the yacht club dock. When one considers the additional time necessary for the passengers to get in and out of the dinghy and onto the dock, the time difference is almost nonexistent. It's the difference between an unsafe speed in 7 1/2 minutes and a safer, slower 11 minutes. It is just not true for these speed demons to protest that they are saving time! Most of us came to the Caribbean to avoid the hurly-burly rush of the big city. Here, however, we are still plagued by certain maniacs with their "need for speed" as they screech back and forth in their launches. They make as much noise as several demented banshees and create wakes that all but capsize dinghies. They are a major safety hazard.

During Agents Week, Joel Byerly gets on the radio and pleads with mariners to respect the speed limits, but to no avail. For years I have been suggesting a simple solution to the problem: Station policemen at the English Harbour and Antigua Yacht Club Marina dinghy docks, where they could keep an eye on the speed of the launches. Anyone obviously speeding would have a summons slapped straight on them (with a copy given to Customs and Immigration). The summons would demand that they appear in court for trial, and they would be fined if convicted. Since the police would not be able to prove excessive speed, the culprit probably could beat the rap if he had a good lawyer, but at least the process would be a nuisance. He would be bound to go to his hearing via an expensive taxi or a cheap, slow bus, and then he would have to bide his time until his case came up in a hot, stuffy courtroom. After that, I am sure he would not be so eager to repeat his offense. If he never showed up in court, Customs and Immigration could refuse the offender clearance until he had proven that he had attended the court hearing. The speeding in English Harbour/Falmouth has to be stopped now!

Amazingly, despite all the accidents, no one was killed until December 1992, when a jetskier charging around the harbor (what was a jetskier doing in the harbor?) capsized and fell in front of a high-speed launch. That was the end of the jetskier.

And that brings me to Antigua Sailing Week itself—without doubt the finest racing in the Eastern Caribbean, probably in the Western Hemisphere, and maybe in the world! Weather conditions are superb, the race courses are varied, the race committee is of international caliber. Competition is of the highest quality, the protests are handled ably by first-rate juries, and all in all it is a fantastic event that I would not miss for the world. But it is expensive, and it is getting more so each year.

First of all, by 1993 the entry fee had risen to US$250. Then there is the launch fee of US$1.00 per trip per person. Since 1983, yachts have not been required to carry dinghies on deck, so the launches are more overloaded than ever—and often are operated by drivers who seem to be high on something other than the fun of it all. On *Iolaire* in 1984, I kept careful count of what we spent on launches each day; despite the fact that we used our dinghy as much as possible, I figure that the crew altogether spent about US$200 on launch fees—and that figure would be much higher now. Ali Baba and his 40 thieves were pikers compared to some of the bumboat drivers we encountered during the 1993 Sailing Week! Then you have to figure in the docking fees, the cruising permit, Customs and Immigration fees, plus exit fees if your crew flies out. It all adds up.

Furthermore, although Antigua Sailing Week is held the last week in April or sometimes the first week in May—which elsewhere in the Caribbean is the low season—rates in most Antigua hotels during Sailing Week are higher than at the height of the season. In addition, drinks at most bars are 20 percent more than usual, because 20 percent goes to the Antigua Hotel Association to help defray the costs of publicity, printing of the brochure, and other Sailing Week activities. So, if you go to Sailing Week, you had better carry a bucket full of money—and make it a big bucket, or maybe even two or three buckets.

The amount of money that Antigua as a whole (and the Antigua Hotel Association in particular) receives from the money generated by Agents Week and Antigua Sailing Week is massive. In December 1992, the *Providence* (Rhode Island) *Journal* reported that the University of Rhode Island did a study of the money generated by yachting for the state of Rhode Island, and in particular the amount generated by the start of the Newport-to-Bermuda Race. Because many boats were doing fairly major refits prior to the race, they calculated that starting the race in Newport brought in a total of US$6 million, with $1.4 million of it spent in the final four days preceding the start. Bermuda officials figured that the end of the race brought in about US$1.3 million.

When you consider that both Agents Week and Antigua Sailing Week are outside the normal hotel season, and that many more yachts are attracted to Antigua by these two events than are attracted to Newport or Bermuda by their race, it means that these two events probably generate annually US$4 to $5 million worth of business for Antigua. The hotel association should be doing handstands for yachtsmen in gratitude for the business, and it should be handing out all sorts of "freebies." But nothing could be further from the truth. Drinks are more expensive during Sailing Week than they are during the height of the season; yacht entry fees are climbing steadily; and, most galling of all, the yacht club, which does an enormous amount of "gut labor" for Sailing Week, has never been allowed to see the balance sheet—apparently a military secret reserved for members of the hotel association. The Antigua Yacht Club should be receiving enough money from the hotel association to maintain the club facilities in style for the entire year!

When all is said and done, Antigua—with a population of under 100,000—probably collects more money from yachts and yachting than any other place in the world, yet the government, the hotel association, and local businessmen do little or nothing to help yachtsmen.

In the early years of Antigua Sailing Week, hotel owners laid out the red carpets to attract yachtsmen. Today they just hold out their hands to relieve yachtsmen of their money. Yet all of us still come, as this is the best racing in the Caribbean, if not in the world.

Expensive or not, Antigua Sailing Week certainly will always appeal to cruising yachts. The committee has made a very concerted effort over the years to encourage the cruising divisions: cruising, cruising/racing, and bareboat; these comprised more than half of the 230-plus entries in 1993. This is because many members of the sailing committee either race or have raced in the cruising divisions, and they know what makes for good racing in these classes—including, among other things, courses that aim at providing one-third windward work and two-thirds off the wind. Splitting all these boats into the correct divisions is a difficult and unenviable job. The members of the committee know the boats well, plus they exhibit the wisdom of Solomon and the guts of a lion! And when skippers complain, they have enough common sense to remain anonymous!

Formerly, the divisions were racing, cruising, cruising/racing, and traditional. The traditional class has died out completely, but it is not dead. It has surfaced in another form: The Classic Yacht Regatta is held the week before Antigua Sailing Week. Established in 1987, it is very well run and growing each year. In 1993, there were 38 entrants. Boats varied from classics more than a century old to modern classics 15 or 20 years old.

Anyone interested in classic boats should not miss this four-day, fun-filled regatta. On the first day there's a parade of sail, plus dinghy races of various types. Then come three days of racing, but it's not particularly hard racing, as classic boats really don't want to beat their brains out slamming to windward. The courses are laid out to provide plenty of reaching and running, and little beating to windward. A prize ceremony wraps it all up. The regatta is sponsored by Baron von Rothschild's CSR Rum and by Wayfarer Marine, the Camden, Maine, yard renowned for its splendid work on classic yachts. Local businesses contribute so many prizes that almost every boat that enters receives a prize of some sort. IYRU racing rules prevail, but the race committee does not want to hear protests. Ratings are a bit by guess and by golly, but since no one takes the racing extremely seriously, there are few problems. It's all very much like Antigua Sailing Week was in its early days. If you are interested in the Classic Yacht Regatta (which is a wonderful gathering of the old-timers), write to Joel Byerly, Nicholson Yacht Charters, English Harbour, Antigua.

The BVI and Rolex Regattas have changed radically over the years in that more and more boats are going into the cruising or the cruising/racing division rather than the flat-out racing. Rolex, at one point, tried extending its three-day Easter Regatta to a five-day event, but, as my old Texas friend would say, "That dog wouldn't hunt!" It wasn't a success. Whereas the BVI and Rolex Regattas have pretty much stagnated, Antigua Sailing Week seems to go from strength to strength.

I think there are several reasons for these different outcomes. First of all, both the Rolex and the BVI Regattas use the PHRF (Performance Handicap Rating Formula) for racing. This is fine for standard "factory" boats, but a good sailor with a one-off boat usually is hammered so badly by the PHRF that there is little point in competing. Plus, the PHRF is very mixed up in local politics (some of the members of the rating committees are actually racing themselves), and many feel that some of the ratings are way out of line. For Antigua Sailing Week, even if you do not agree with the CYA rule, at least you know exactly where you stand and whether or not you have a chance in the regatta. If it's a case of "no chance" because of your rating, you then have the option of saying, "The heck with it; I'll enter anyway," or not entering. Further, the most interesting point about Antigua Sailing Week is that no matter how small or slow your boat, there is still plenty of excitement on the water. The slower boats usually start first and the larger boats then sail on through them. What could be more exciting than sailing along in your 35-footer and seeing 90-foot and 100-foot boats storming right by you?

By contrast, if you are on a small or slow boat in the cruising division of the Rolex or BVI Regatta, the only time you see any action is right at the start for about 10 minutes. After that, it is a case of being "tail-end Charlie," racing only against the clock with absolutely no excitement. If you don't have a fast, competitive boat, Antigua Sailing Week is the only place to be!

Although Antigua Sailing Week is organized and financed by the Antigua Hotel Association, the day-to-day operation of the week, the setting of the courses and marks, the organizing of the committees, and the gut labor for the week is all done free of charge by the members of the Antigua Yacht Club. They do a magnificent job on a purely volunteer basis. The yacht club people (and others) refer to the restaurant on the ground floor of their building as the Antigua Yacht Club, even though any Tom, Dick, or Harry (whether or not he is a yachtsman, a gentleman, a golfer, or a bum) is served there. The real Antigua Yacht Club comprises the private bar, lounge, reading room, and sun deck on the second story of the building, where only club members are allowed.

It has been said that an Englishman's home is his castle, but his club is the one place where he can pull up the drawbridge behind him and be safe from his wife, creditors, and anyone who is not a member of his club. Not only has the Antigua Yacht Club drawn up the drawbridge, but it also has stationed archers on the battlements and populated the moat with sharks and alligators to make sure its members are safe from the members of other clubs. The regulations for the use of the upstairs are the most restrictive of any yacht club in the world. (The only other comparably restrictive club that I know of is the Guadeloupe Yacht Club.) The upstairs is off limits to everyone except members and their invited guests; a member must accompany a guest, and guests may use the facilities only three times in one calendar year.

There are NO RECIPROCAL PRIVILEGES with any other yacht club, nor are two-week guest cards or temporary memberships available. Antigua Yacht Club maintains that since it is at a yachting crossroads, the club would be inundated if it allowed reciprocal privileges or issued guest cards. Nuts! If they merely restricted access to the upstairs facilities to AYC members and members of accredited yacht clubs who could present a membership card, they would not be inundated and would be in line with other yacht clubs in the world. Guest privileges and two-week guest cards should be issued to these bona fide yachtsmen, with a limit of two a year. If a visiting yachtsman is staying for an extended period in Antigua and wishes to avail himself of their hospitality and bar, he should be allowed to take out a month's membership in the club. In my own case, the rules are very relaxed, but I feel that all legitimate yachtsmen who can prove they are members of another yacht club should be treated the same way I am treated. (Incidentally, during the 1992 America's Cup Series, the AYC rules were relaxed, and the club's hospitality was very generous.)

Despite the restrictive AYC regulations, and probably despite the out-of-sight expenses, Antigua Sailing Week seems destined to remain the "happening" of the Eastern Caribbean for all us cruising sailors—sort of like the gathering of the clans at the Highland Games. The racing and the parties are great, and it's a last chance to get together with friends before everyone heads out at the end of the season. We all plan to keep on being there!

HAPPILY AND POSSIBLY AS A RESULT OF WHAT I STATED IN MY 1993 EDITION OF THIS GUIDE, THE SITUATION AT ANTIGUA YACHT CLUB HAS CHANGED DRAMATICALLY. If you are a member of a recognised yacht club, introduce yourself to the manager and guest privileges will be arranged if you are only there for a short time. If you are there for a few months, a monthly membership for a reasonable fee can be purchased—a wonderful change from the old days. Further, Antigua Yacht Club is doing a wonderful job of training the youth of Antigua. They have a fleet of Optimist prams for training the smallest of the children who once they become competent as Optimist sailors, then progress on to Lasers. The younger generation of local Antiguan sailors has really developed to the point that hot sailors like Hans Palmers and Jeff Pudock have a tough fight to get themselves up to the middle of the fleet. Jeff reports that these kids "are just too damn good."

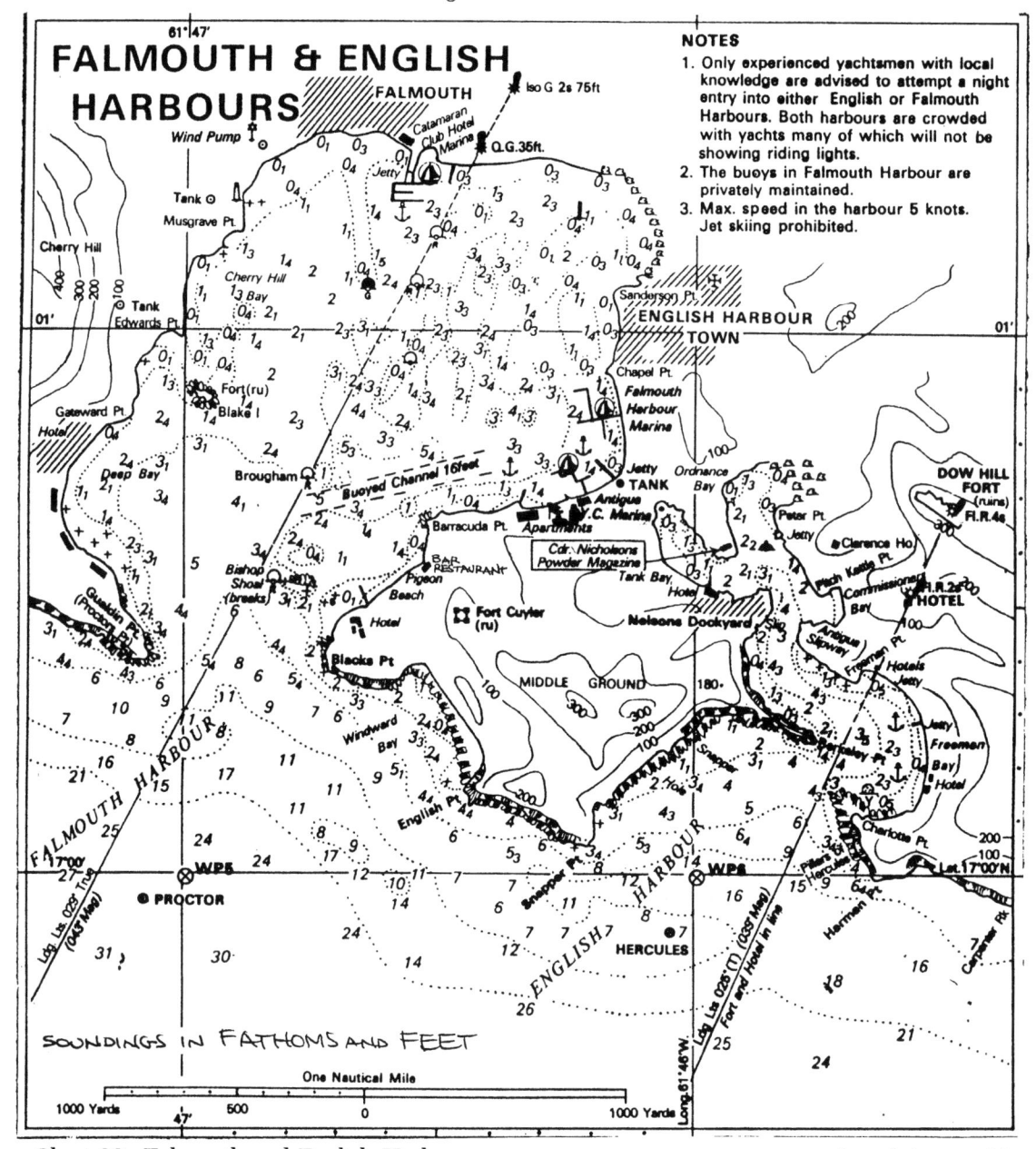

Chart 26 Falmouth and English Harbours   Depths in fathoms and feet

FALMOUTH HARBOUR

(Chart 26; II A, A-27)

This major harbor just west of English Harbour is also sheltered in all kinds of weather. When beating up the south coast of Antigua, the entrance to Falmouth Harbour is a great sight, as you can stop there and eliminate another half hour of beating on to English Harbour. (It is legal to anchor in Falmouth and have the skipper walk over to English Harbour to clear with Customs and Immigration.)

There is ample water if you proceed carefully.

Enter in midchannel and check the buoys very carefully on Chart 26 and on the Imray-Iolaire charts, because buoyage is extremely confusing and unreliable. The buoy to the west of Bishop Shoal obviously should be left to starboard; the second buoy you encounter is on the five-foot spot and should also be left to starboard—if you are proceeding on the range. You can spot this range east of the Catamaran Club Hotel; after lining up a bearing of 042° magnetic (erratically illuminated at night by two green isophase lights), stay right on the range, leaving

Bishop shoal and Broughan. However, if you're headed for the anchorage off the Antigua Yacht Club in the southeastern corner of Falmouth Harbour, you must leave Broughan to *port,* as it is actually a channel-division buoy. If you leave it to starboard and then turn east, you will come to a sudden stop on the five-foot shoal.

There are various white Antigua Yacht Club racing marks that do not indicate shoals. If you stick to the range, 15 feet can be carried to the Catamaran Club Hotel jetty on the north side of the harbor, where Hugh Bailey has built a beautiful new, small marina that has ice, water, electricity, and fuel. The latter can be ordered in bulk duty free via Outfitters.

Incidentally, Hugh Bailey got his start as a boy working for Commander Bruno Brown (Royal Navy, retired) as crew, then mate, then skipper of various charter boats. He then opened a small hotel, bought a freighter, and now has the small marina, which is popular with the old-time charter boats such as *Gitana IV, America, Puritan,* and the three-masted schooner *Jessica.* Yachting has helped him and he's doing well by the yachtsmen—the story of many English Harbour folk.

Many yachts anchor in the southeast corner of Falmouth Harbour, since it puts them within easy dinghy distance of the new fueling jetty, and of Sam and Dave's laundry and the various restaurants along the road from English Harbour village to the dockyard. (It is also within dinghy distance of the Antigua Yacht Club marina dinghy landing dock.) Carlos Falcon has now opened Antigua Yacht Marina, with electricity, fax, and phone facilities. Diesel fuel is easy to get in Falmouth as the Catamaran Club, Falmouth Harbour Marina and Antigua Yacht Club marina all sell diesel. But no one sells gasoline for outboards. It is a case of taking a taxi over to Antigua Slipway or running your dinghy around to Antigua Slipway and purchasing gas or call the very friendly and efficient water taxi—M & M. He will pick up your gas cans take them to English harbour, fill them and return them for a very reasonable fee.

The yacht club and yacht club marina have four showers for members and crews of boats renting space at the dock. The Port Authority had showers, but, for reasons best known to itself, closed them down a few years ago. If any of these three operations would install coin- or token-operated showers—as I have recommended so many times—they would be laughing all the way to the bank. During Antigua Sailing Week and the Classic Yacht Regatta, the yacht-club shower doors frequently are left open—or boat crews in the marina let their friends in. It is sort of open house. Since people turn the showers on and let them run, God knows how much water is wasted.

There are NO trash-disposal facilities at the Antigua Yacht Club; the garbage tips are up by the Port Authority dock—the ONLY place where trash should be left. The Port Authority dock can also be used for loading fuel or water.

It is only a short walk from the southeast anchorage over to English Harbour. Marine supplies are available in Falmouth Harbour at the chandler at the head of Port Authority dock or in Antigua Slipway outlet at the Antigua Yacht Club marina or the Catamaran Club.

For more than 200 years, people have talked about digging a channel from Tank Bay, in the northwestern corner of English Harbour, to the southeastern corner of Falmouth Harbour. Especially nowadays, this would serve two good purposes: First, it would allow small boats to pass between the two harbors, and thus make Falmouth a more attractive anchorage than it is now and relieve the congestion in English Harbour; second, it would allow stagnant water to circulate from the inner reaches of English Harbour to Falmouth Harbour and on out to sea. As I say, this idea has been around for two centuries, and plans have even been drawn for it, but so far nothing has happened. Things move slowly in the West Indies!

The opening of a channel between English Harbour and Falmouth harbour almost happened in the middle 1980's as the Canadian Government offered to finance the digging of a channel. However, the whole thing died on the vine with the grandios plans of Nelsons Dockyard. Instead of investigating the cost of digging a ditch between English Harbour, Tank Bay and Falmouth Harbour and making it only big enough for outboards, with a fixed bridge for the road a grandios plan was drawn up for a channel deep enough for boats drawing five to six feet to go through with a lifting bridge to clear their masts. The whole plan was so vast that the Canadians backed off immediately. It is alleged that the amount of money spent on the engineering to draw up the design was enough to have dug a ditch big enough for the outboard dinghies and a fixed bridge.

The plan is now as dead as a Dodo bird and so much construction has happened in the area that it would be impossible to open up between English Harbour and Falmouth Harbour.

INDIAN CREEK

(Chart 28; II A, A-27)

A small, sheltered, and deserted cove one mile east of English Harbour. There is a dangerous rock at the entrance that can be spotted by the breaking sea. Inside there is plenty of water, but limited space. This is a good hurricane hole—if you can get there first. The snorkeling is excellent on the eastern point of the cove.

The wind bounces off the lee cliffs here, making it difficult to sail out unless you have a boat that sails and tacks well.

MAMORA BAY

(Sketch Chart 27, Chart 28; II A, A-27)

This bay is excellent shelter, with a white-sand bottom, but it definitely is not deserted. It is home to the St. James's Club, formed a number of years ago by Peter de Savary, the British 12-meter syndicate head. De Savary has since sold out, but the St. James's Club is still an exclusive, upmarket hotel that offers all sorts of goodies to its guests—Texas quarterhorses water skiing, diving, etc.—at an all-inclusive price. There usually are one or two megayachts moored stern-to the dock, plus a couple of ultra-plush charter yachts. Visiting yachts can anchor in the harbor, tie up to the dock, and make arrangements to use the facilities for a fee. Call the club on channel 68 to confirm the fee situation. The harbor is reputed to be able to

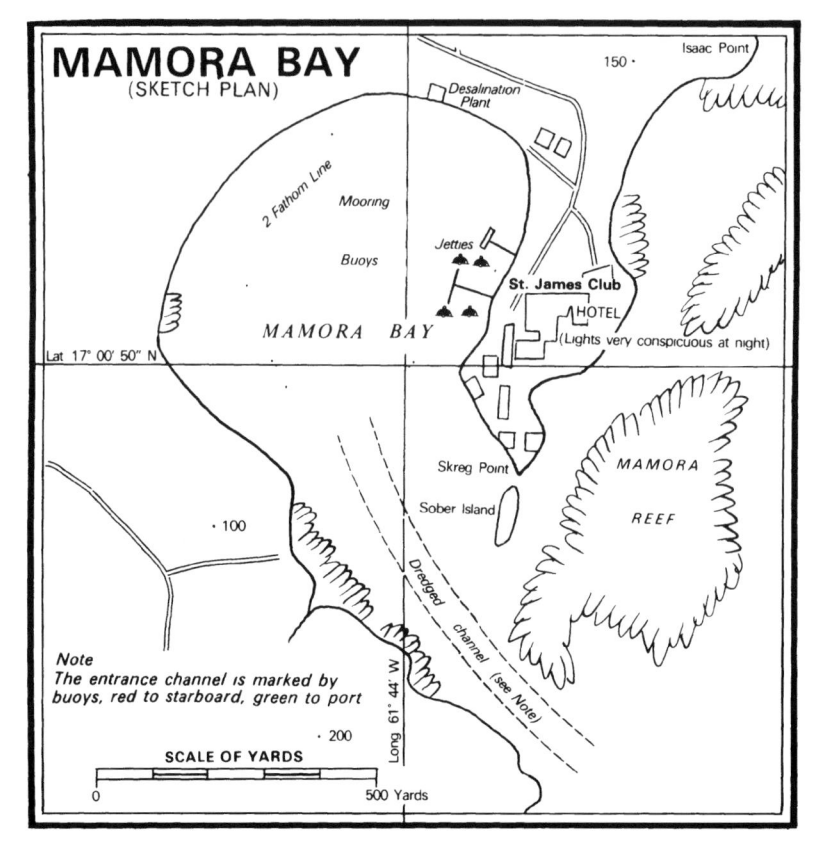

Sketch Chart 27   Mamora Bay   Depths in fathoms and feet

carry at least 12 feet, although it is subject to shoaling. In May 1992, the channel's outer buoys were very small and hard to spot—and so rusty that it was impossible to tell which was red and which was green! Favor the west side of the harbor while entering until you pick up the buoys; then follow them to stay in the deepest water. To be absolutely certain of the depth, contact the harbormaster at the St. James's Club.

WILLOUGHBY BAY

(Chart 28; II A, A-27)

Willoughby Bay is a wonderful anchorage largely ignored by yachtsmen. I cannot understand why, because it offers good shelter and good diving. You will be completely by yourself unless Joel Byerly decides to go there to hide away from everyone.

The best approach is to line up Christian Point with the white school at Bethesda, bearing 322° magnetic. Running in on this bearing, you will easily spot the reefs on the starboard hand; keep them close aboard and do not try to pass through the break between the first and second reefs. Once past the second reef, round up to starboard and tuck yourself right in behind the reef, where there's complete shelter and plenty of wind, but no surge coming across the top of the reef. Or sail roughly due north and work your way closer inshore. If you're really skillful, you can work your way into Barnakoo Bay right off Lynch Point—but don't try it unless the light is good and conditions are perfect.

Why beat to windward all the way up to Nonsuch Bay when Willoughby Bay is so close to the English/Falmouth Harbour area and is virtually deserted? At most, you may find one or two boats here.

GREEN ISLAND

(Chart 29; II A, A-27)

Between Willoughby Bay and Green Island, none of the bays are viable except for a hell-bent surfboarder. Green Island is very attractive and has two small anchorages on its southern coast. The larger and better of the two is Rickett Harbour, which has room for three or four yachts. Protected from normal trade-wind weather, it is exposed only to a summer southeast wind and swell. If Rickett Harbour is crowded, try the small cove east of it, called Ten-

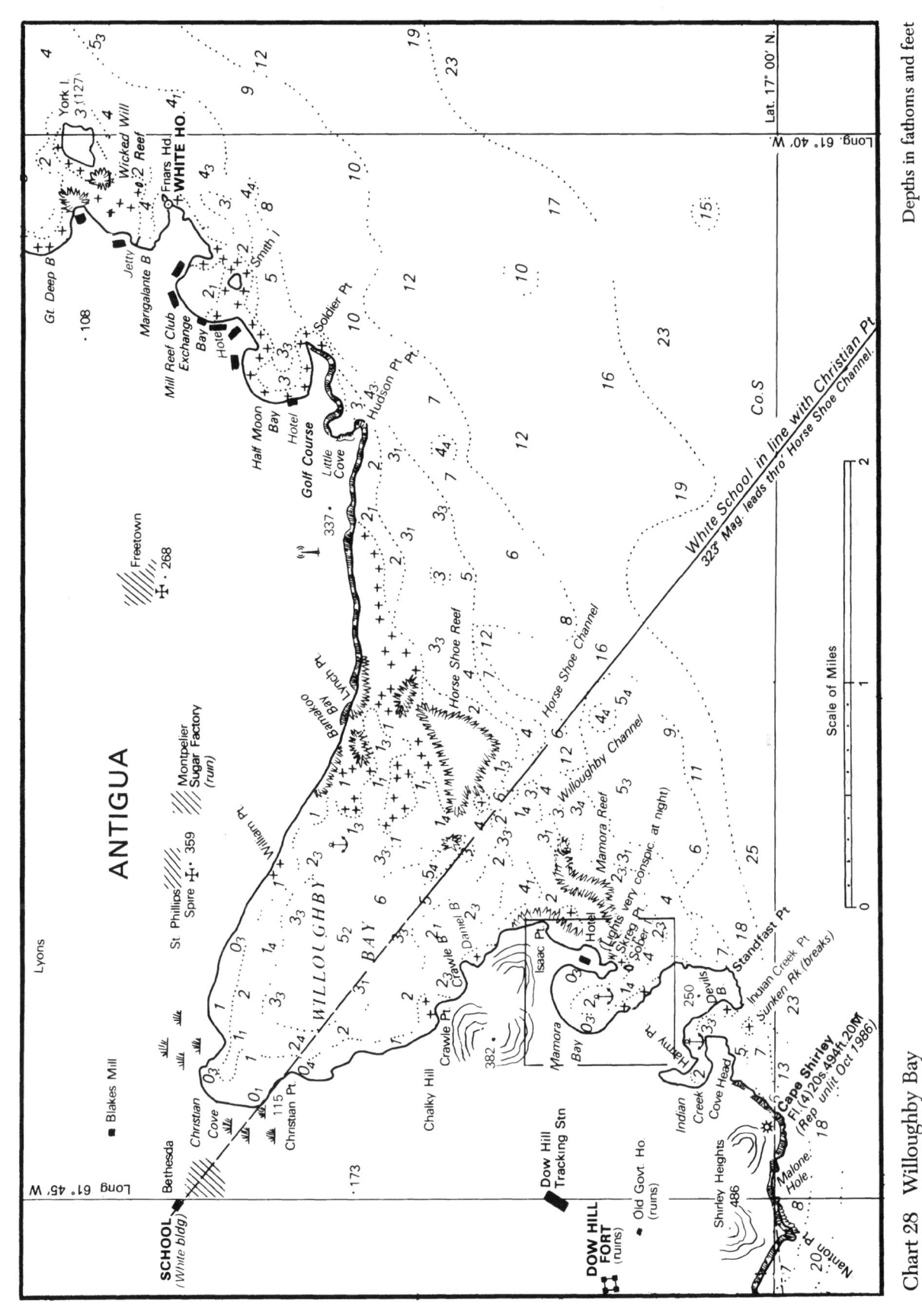

Chart 28 Willoughby Bay

pound Bay on the American chart and unnamed on the British chart. There is room for only one boat here—total seclusion.

The entrances to both harbors call for careful eyeball procedures in good light. Feel your way in, being careful to avoid the reef east of Rickett Harbour, which extends farther south than the chart indicates. All dangers will be clearly visible in good light.

It should be noted that Green Island is privately owned by the Mill Reef Club. They are not overly friendly to visitors on the island and become downright unfriendly when they arrive at one of their beaches for a picnic and discover people rebuilding boats or strewing trash around. Further, remember when sailing to windward of Antigua—such as to and from Green Island—that you should not throw trash (even biodegradable) overboard, because it blows right back onto the beautiful beaches on the eastern side of the island.

NONSUCH BAY

(Chart 29; II A, A-27)

A large, unprotected bay with innumerable anchorages. It is the ideal spot for dinghy sailing, swimming, and snorkeling. Nonsuch Bay has a lot more water in the various nooks and crannies than is shown on the chart, but the water is muddy in the coves, making eyeball navigation difficult. For example, an uncharted rock has been discovered northwest of Hughes Point. (It is shown on Chart 29 in this book and the new Imray-Iolaire Chart 27, but not on old Imray-Iolaire charts or on BA or DMA charts.) So proceed cautiously, using leadline, fathometer, or sounding pole—or send the dinghy ahead.

The northernmost bay—Ledeatt Cove/Gaynais Bay ("Clover Leaf" in Chris Doyle's guide)—is actually four separate coves on the east, north, and west. There is ample water in the entrances to all the coves, but they all shoal at their heads. Feel your way in and anchor in a suitable depth.

After visiting this area in May 1992, I feel that the eastern and western arms of the cove (or, rather, series of coves) are excellent hurricane holes. When hurricanes appear in Antigua, everyone tends to hunker down in the mangroves in English Harbour. Few skippers think of clearing out of English Harbour and heading eastward into Nonsuch Bay. But before you decide to go looking for a hurricane hole, be sure to reread "Reflections on Hugo," in the Foreword to this book.

The western side of the cove is the site of the New Emerald Cove resort, with an upscale housing development and a beach club. Roads have been built and some construction has been done, but as of mid-1992, it was not enough to disturb the yachtsman in search of some peace and quiet. It may be a bit of a euphemism to refer to these bulldozed tracks as roads, however, and it is not wise to try exploring ashore here unless you are on foot or have a four-wheel-drive vehicle. If moored at the head of Ledeatt Cove on the northern arm (on the western side of the cove), you can fight your way ashore through the bush and eventually come to a track (not a road, but it's passable with a four-wheel-drive vehicle) that leads up to the main road. Following the main road eastward for a mile, you'll come to the Long Bay Resort, with cottages, beach bar, restaurant, and so on. A mile to the west along the main road is Willikies, a moderate-size Antiguan village where you can buy basic supplies.

If you really want to be off by yourself and your boat draws six feet or less, and you are an experienced eyeball navigator, work your way northeast around Flat Point and find a suitable anchorage. Fanny's Cove has no beach and is surrounded by mangroves, but anchor to windward of Fanny's Cove. Put your bow anchor in shallow water and your stern anchor in deeper water to make sure that you don't swing around if the current does strange things in the night or the wind dies down. You will have a breezy, cool anchorage with few neighbors and good diving right under the bow of the boat.

A really good reef pilot with six feet or less of draft can continue north to Tonnies Cove, where it is certain no one else will turn up. The reef forms an excellent breakwater and the wind sweeping across the reef keeps everything cool. There is no habitation ashore.

If the light is good, you might try anchoring among the reefs downwind of Rat Island. Then you can explore the reefs directly from the boat without having to launch the dinghy. South of Little Bird Island is another secluded anchorage with a white-sand bottom that makes good holding—and the reef to windward breaks the swell. This is a breezy, cool anchorage with good diving under the bowsprit.

In years gone by, West Beach was a perfect anchorage—very secluded, with a white-sand beach, a reef to windward to keep the sea down, and a good, strong breeze to keep the bugs at bay. More and more bareboats now come to the island, however, and even at the quietest time of year, there may be half a dozen boats anchored off West Beach. During the busy chartering season, the anchorage can become unbearably congested.

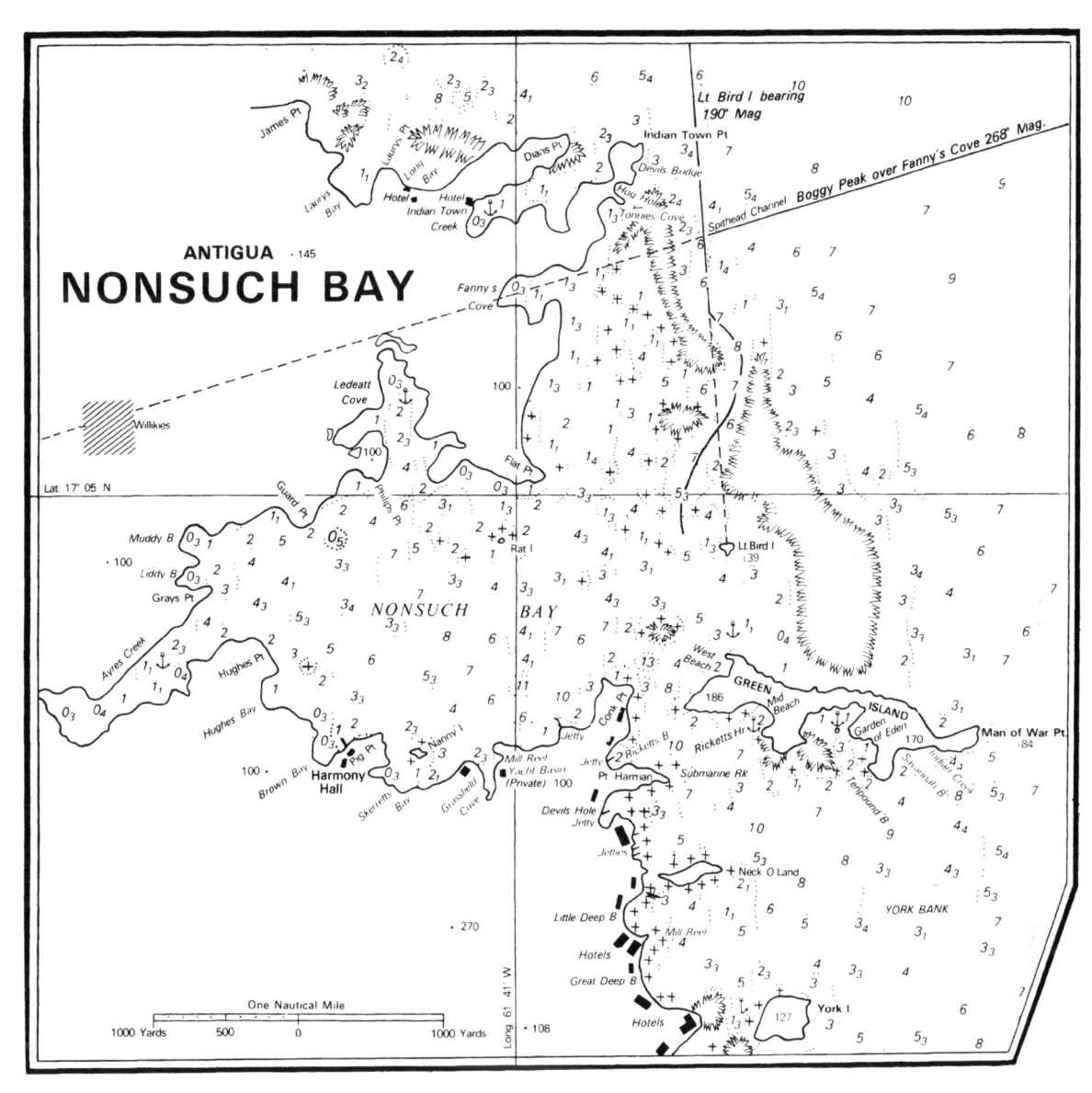

Chart 29 Nonsuch Bay   Depths in fathoms and feet

SPITHEAD CHANNEL, RANGES FROM THE NORTH

A. 268° magnetic on Boggy Peak, with distinctive round-topped hill, and Fanny's Cove in transit.
B. When Indian Town Point bears 340° magnetic, be prepared to jibe over to enter channel.
C. Little Bird Island, 183° magnetic, leads into channel.
D. Reef north of Conk Point slightly open to east of Conk Point, 210° magnetic, leads into Nonsuch Bay, but avoid isolated coral heads.

WARNING! IF APPROACHING SPITHEAD CHANNEL FROM THE NORTH, READ SAILING DIRECTIONS ON PAGE 97 CAREFULLY *BEFORE* ENTERING THE CHANNEL. IF LEAVING HEADING NORTH THROUGH THE CHANNEL, READ PAGE 96.

All is not lost, however. Just sail north—westward from West Beach—and as close to the reef as your draft will allow. Anchor bow-and-stern, or use a Bahamian moor, in case the wind dies out or the current changes. You still will be within dinghy distance of the beautiful West Beach.

Do not be tempted to anchor in the cove in the southeast corner of Nonsuch Bay—the land is all owned by the Mill Reef Club, a private establishment for the very wealthy. They most definitely do not like visitors—especially visiting sailors who may or may not be yachtsmen.

Harmony Hall sugar tower—with a shingle roof on the hill above Brown Bay—not only is a good landmark but also serves other purposes. As previously mentioned, they rebroadcast Joel Byerly's 9 o'clock weather report immediately after he has signed off. They also serve as a message and relay center between yachts in the English/Falmouth Harbour area and yachts in the Parham/North Sound area and Barbuda.

Harmony Hall is quite an establishment—a bar and restaurant, an art gallery and a boutique, plus beautiful gardens. Reservations are not necessary for lunch, but if you provide 24-hour notice, they can prepare a fantastic dinner. Eight people (combine two boat crews) can then have sundown cocktails on the terrace and enjoy a delicious meal. The view from Harmony Hall over Nonsuch Bay is superb. Even if you are not planning to have lunch or dinner here, take the dinghy over to the dock, walk up the hill, and have a drink at the bar while you take in the view. But watch out! It may be an expensive drink if some of the crew become too enthused over the boutique or the art gallery.

In May 1993, Harmony Hall was being run by experienced sailors Alan and Kristy Dunkerly and their daughter, Caroline. Alan worked for many years in Australia building topnotch Solings and Etchells 22s. When he became tired of playing the boatbuilding "game," they started wandering, ending up in Antigua. Now he races his boat *Winter* in the cruising division during Antigua Sailing Week. Needless to say, he is a font of information on sailing in and around Antigua.

A WORD OF CAUTION regarding Nonsuch Bay: The entrance and exit are best made to the west and south of Green Island. The northern entrance—Spithead Channel—is strictly for the brave and the experienced! A number of boats have grounded hard and become stuck on the coral reefs on the windward side of Spithead Channel, and many others (yours truly included) have bounced off the coral heads on the eastern side of the channel on the way in. Plus, I have had two bad scares sailing out of Spithead Channel.

WARNING: Read the following carefully before entering or leaving Spithead Channel.

The southern entrance to Nonsuch Bay via York Island is easy. Pass about 200 yards to windward of York Island, then head for Submarine Rock, bearing approximately 345° magnetic from York Island. Pass 50 yards to windward of Submarine Rock to clear all dangers. Once you reach Submarine Rock, you may head up into Rickett Harbour or bear off and run through the channel between Green Island and Conk Point into Nonsuch Bay. If you are heading up around the end of Green Island to West Beach and the area behind the reefs, give the western tip of Green Island a 100-to-150-yard berth, to avoid the shoals extending out from the island. The eyeball navigator can nip in tightly around the shoal, as it drops off suddenly into deep water.

When leaving Nonsuch Bay, if you are heading north to Barbuda or going up the eastern coast of Antigua and swinging around into the Parham/North Sound area, you may be strongly tempted to depart via Spithead Channel. This is an acceptable option if the conditions are exactly right. The light must be good, it should not be blowing too hard, and the wind must be east, NOT northeast. If it is blowing hard when you leave Spithead Channel, remember that the water shoals from six fathoms to four and then three fathoms off Indian Town Point. There is nothing between you and Africa. In periods of heavy weather, the sea will be breaking well out to windward of Indian Town Point. Further, the wind has to be in the east because there is no room to tack in Spithead Channel—you must be able to lay the course. Anyone sailing out this way is well advised to motorsail or keep the engine running until clear of the point.

Twice when we were sailing out in the engineless *Iolaire*, I thought we were laying the course very easily and then discovered we were being headed—with no space to tack! It was a case of fighting every inch to windward until we cleared Indian Town Point and finally were able to breathe a sigh of relief.

When heading north through the channel, the beginning is well east of north. The course is 030° magnetic, but steer 040° magnetic to allow for leeway. Then, as you reach the reef that extends south from Indian Town Point, bear off to a course of approximately north.

The east side of the deepwater channel is a real

booby trap. The British and American charts are wrong. Yes, you'll find two fathoms of water, but there are coral heads sticking up a full fathom from the bottom, which means you basically have only one fathom of water! So, if you are to windward of the channel, it is easy to crunch into a coral head. Not only does this destroy the coral, it certainly doesn't do your boat any good.

Since you are beating to windward with the natural leeway of the boat—plus the facts that the sea is setting you to leeward, you might get headed, and there is no room to tack—favor the windward side of the channel. Put the crew's best reef pilot on the bow—or, better, on the spreaders. It will be rough at the northern end of Spithead Channel, as the depth is only three fathoms. The seas will begin to hump up, but as you pass north of Indian Town Point, the water becomes deeper and the seas will lengthen.

If you must approach Nonsuch Bay/Spithead Channel from the north and you are close inshore, pick up Indian Town Point (the hotel and beach bars in Long Bay are distinctive landmarks). Pass 100 yards eastward of the point, then head eastward until Little Bird Island bears 183° magnetic. Hold this course and eyeball your way south through the channel, which, from deck level, looks like a solid line of reef. However, if someone is STANDING on the bow pulpit, or, better, on the lower spreaders, the channel will be evident.

If approaching from well offshore, the northeast coast of Antigua is low and featureless. Indian Town Point is difficult to spot when approaching from offshore. Pick up the radio mast of Boggy Peak and bring it to a bearing of 268° magnetic. A distinctive round-topped hill will appear under Boggy Peak. Stay on this range (transit), which lines up with Fanny's Cove. As you approach shore and Indian Town Point comes to bear 340° magnetic, be prepared to alter course and bear off when Little Bird Island bears 190° magnetic.

Running in on the bearing of 268° magnetic on Boggy Peak, be very careful; use eyeball navigation on your final approach. This bearing leads very close to the northern end of the eastern reef of Spithead Channel. If in doubt, alter course to starboard toward Indian Town Point. When Little Bird Island bears 190°, jibe over and run into Spithead Channel, bringing Little Bird Island to bear 183° magnetic.

Once in the channel, eyeball your way southward. At this point, you will need to break the normal rule of sailing through a channel—"Always stick to the windward side, because if you run aground, the wind and sea will be pushing you off into deeper water." John Bentley, who has salvaged a number of boats that have run aground in this channel, points out that this is the one exception to the rule; you should hug the LEE side of Spithead Channel.

The coral on the lee side of the channel is a vertical wall, and it is clearly distinct from the color of the water. On the windward side, however, the bottom goes up gradually. You think you are in deep enough water and then—CRUNCH!—you hit a coral head. As noted above, the channel appears at first to have a solid line of reef, but it has a zig in it. As you reach the end of the western reef, you must bear off to a course of 210° magnetic to clear the western end of the eastern reef.

Remember that the breakers you see before you when you are at the northern end of the channel are on the eastern side of the channel. It is very important that the helmsman and the reef pilot on the bow (or on the spreaders) review the game plan *before* entering the channel. Make sure everyone understands the situation. In one instance when I was helmsman, lack of good communication between the reef pilot and me caused us to bounce on the windward side of the channel. I had not listened to my pilot—who was correct!

Once you are clear behind the solid part of the windward reef (the north end), place the reef north of Conk Point slightly open to the east of Conk Point. This course of 210° magnetic is basically correct, but you will have to zig and zag to avoid the detached coral head northwest of Little Bird Island. Bear off and pass between the two coral heads—strictly a matter of eyeball navigation in calm weather. From here on, there is little likelihood of getting in serious trouble. You may get parked, but you won't run aground. Once safely inside Nonsuch Bay, you can happily spend a week!

INDIAN TOWN CREEK

(Chart 29; II A, A-27, A-271)

This is a small harbor seldom used by yachts, but it offers complete shelter and the facilities of the Long Bay Hotel, which serves lunches and dinners (telephone: 463-2005; reservations required). The first time you go in, it is advisable to take a pilot. So radio English Harbour on channel 68 and ask them to call the hotel. If you provide an approximate ETA, the hotel will send a Whaler out to meet you.

The entrance to Indian Town Creek is 12 to 15 feet deep in the channel, decreasing gradually to five to eight feet. If the wind is in the northeast, the swell roars in through the narrow channel—no more than 40 or 50 feet wide. Once you spot the break in the channel, you will see a low, clean bluff and a low but conspicuous rock, about four feet high, centered against this bluff. A course of about 220° magnetic will lead through the channel, but I strongly advise not doing this until you have done it once with a pilot.

Once inside the harbor, the bottom is none too clear, so proceed with caution. The water at Long Bay dock is three to four feet, and an engine is necessary. (David Simmons in *Bacco* seems to be the only person who is able to beat to windward out of Indian Town Creek—and even he grounded once.)

BELFAST BAY

(Chart 30; II A, A-27, A-271)

Seldom visited by cruising yachts until recently. Now more and more have investigated it and have found it to be an excellent and sheltered harbor, wonderful for small-boat sailing and with many coves that make almost-perfect hurricane holes.

To approach Belfast Bay, round Indian Town Point close aboard, then Dians Point (Chart 29), and head for the east end of Guana Island. As Pelican Island comes abeam and the water shoals, stand in, stay in the blue rather than the green, and leave the *detached* coral heads north of Pelican Island *to port*. Then come to port, eyeballing your way past the inner reefs on a course of approximately southwest. Turn south between the reefs, using eyeball navigation to avoid the rock in midchannel after the reefs at the entrance.

The above entrance route is preferred by David Simmons, but Des Nicholson and Joel Byerly have another route. They pass close aboard Indian Town Point and Dians Point and then head for Pelican Island. As the water shoals, they head up, staying in deep water and leaving the *detached* coral heads off Pelican *to starboard*, passing between them and the reefs on the north end of Pelican Island. As the channel opens up, head west, following the blue water, and then southwest, avoiding the rock in midchannel.

Once inside the bay, there are coves too numerous to mention. Rely on eyeball navigation in the clear water. In the murky water, it is strictly a case of sending the dinghy ahead with a leadline or sounding pole. As in Nonsuch Bay, more water is available at the heads of the coves than is shown on the chart.

When leaving, be prepared to power out unless you and your boat are especially handy under sail.

GUANA BAY

(Chart 30; II A, A-27, A-271)

Approaching Guana Bay from the east, proceed as above, but do not turn southwestward into Belfast Bay. Instead, skirt the reef and run down into the harbor, leaving Crump Island to port—strictly eyeball navigation. Once inside the harbor, be careful, since there are hundreds of protruding coral heads. Fortunately, these are easily spotted and avoided, while the reefs give perfect shelter. The good anchorages in Guana are also too numerous to mention.

Sailing Directions for the Northeast and North Coasts of Antigua (Charts 31, 32)

After sailing all these waters for 35 years or so, I stand on what I said a long time ago: This is one of the most dangerous and treacherous coasts in the Eastern Caribbean. (I wrote about my own troubles here in the article "Crunch," in *Sail*, October 1982, and in *Yachting World*, December 1983.) But this part of Antigua provides wonderful cruising, and if you read these sailing directions carefully, stay on your toes, and don't become careless, you'll not come to grief.

The previous sections described the splendid harbors of Belfast Bay and Guana Bay. Now let's assume that you've come from Nonsuch Bay and are planning to bypass Mercers Creek and go directly to Parham and North Sounds. Here's the drill.

Round Indian Town Point and steer a course of approximately 350° magnetic, but remember that you may be making leeway and that the current may be setting you down; look over the side, and the moment you see the bottom harden up, adjust course accordingly.

The first entrance to North Sound is through Bird Islet Channel. This is something I wouldn't do myself, because the channel is very narrow. Also, it is hard to spot, because this whole northeast corner is low, with few distinctive landmarks. But several experienced sailors, including Dave Ferneding of the yacht *Whisper*, say that with a crew member in the rigging, you can use this entrance in normal conditions. *Do not, however, try it in heavy weather.*

To find the entrance to Bird Islet Channel, sail northwest until the big dish aerial east of the airport lines up with the easternmost point of Long Island, appearing over Cistern Point (which has a distinctive red-roofed building), on a bearing of 249° magnetic (see Chart 31). Come left and steer this range, which will lead into the channel. Once in the channel, you will have to turn to port sharply and come to almost due south and then to starboard again to

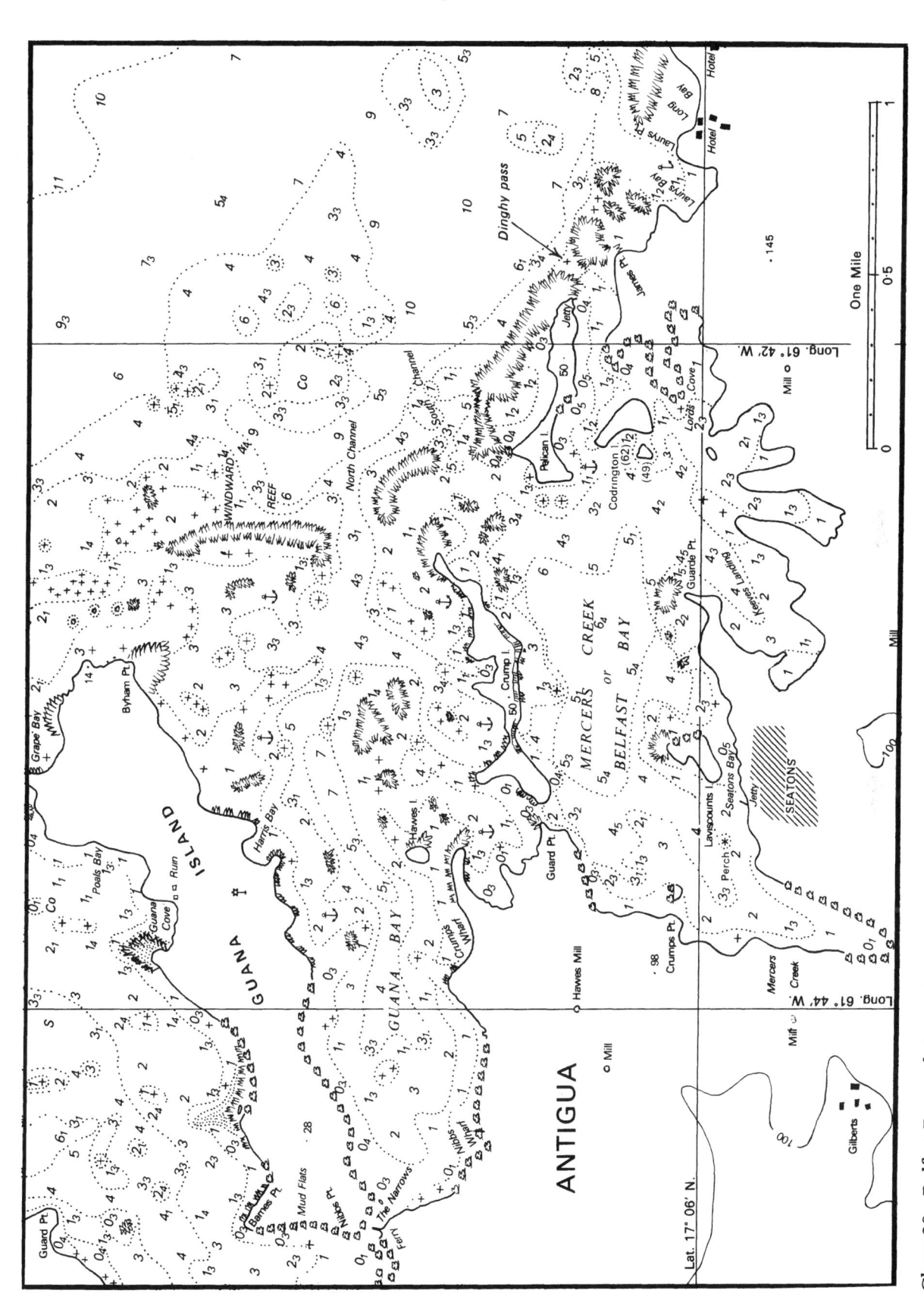

Chart 30 Belfast Bay and Guana Bay

southwest to get into deeper water; you'll leave North Whelk to port on your way into North Sound. I repeat that this route is only for the experienced reef pilot, with a person in the rigging, and in good weather.

The more sensible route, in my view, is to continue on northwest for another four miles or so, and go through Horse Shoe Reef. When the dish aerial comes out from behind Pasture Point, the northernmost point on Long Island, come to port to west-northwest, staying in blue water and keeping a careful lookout for the reefs to leeward. Hold this course until Prickly Pear Island bears 205°. (Boggy Peak in Antigua's southwest quadrant will bear 216°.) Jibe over and steer 205° magnetic toward Prickly Pear Island—but be sure you pick up Horse Shoe Reef on your way in, and keep it close aboard to starboard, as there are two coral heads east of the course that are hard to spot.

Ideally, there should be a physical range to mark this entrance; how many of us can sail exactly 205° magnetic in a seaway without a few reference points to go by? Anyway, do your eyeballing carefully, and make sure you find Horse Shoe. Do not attempt this entrance after 1500, and remember that in the winter, when the sun is south of the latitude of Antigua, it will always be ahead of you when you pass south through this passage, no matter what the time of day. It's much easier in the summer, when the sun is north of Antigua.

Once past Horse Shoe Reef, continue on toward Prickly Pear and then come left to course 153°. Stand on into Parham Sound and pick up the entrance buoys to the Maid Island dredged channel (see Chart 32).

Now that freighters and fuel tankers to supply fuel for the distillation plant are regular visitors to North Sound, the buoyage leading through the channel should be excellent—but it isn't!

In the 1980s, the new IALA Buoyage System was introduced, and for a while, confusion reigned. The European system was red/left/returning, while the American was red/right/returning. Some of the Latin American countries followed the European system, some followed the American one. Similarly, the Eastern Caribbean was a patchwork—some red/right/returning and some red/left/returning—most confusing! Around 1988, ALL buoyage systems in the Western Hemisphere (i.e., all of North and South America, plus the Lesser Antilles) were changed to red/right/returning. There is, however, one exception—namely, the entrance to North Sound/Parham Harbour, which is buoyed red/left/returning! This just serves as a further illustration of my contention that the buoyage and light system in the ex-British islands is designed to keep harbor pilots, ship wreckers, and salvage men from starving to death.

Also, there is more water off the North Sound distillation plant than the charts show, because the tankers have run aground a few times, and each time the authorities have to do more dredging to free the tankers!

Do not come left of the 153° course or you will clip Scott Shoal or the reefs southeast of it.

If you don't want to take a chance with Horse Shoe Reef, you can keep on sailing west-northwest and go through Diamond Channel, which is an easy range to pick up: Boggy Peak in line with Great Sister, bearing 190° magnetic. Once inside, you can work your way eastward through Boon Channel.

Or you can keep going west and sail all the way around Diamond Bank to get into Boon Channel. But leave the miniature Texas tower on Diamond Bank at least 200 yards to the east, as the reef extends west of the tower; there is also a wreck west of the tower. Some experienced local sailors urge leaving the tower 500 yards to the east, but it is a matter of eyeball navigation, and it also depends on your ability to judge "distance off." In any case, be extremely careful.

These directions to Parham and North Sounds are fine if you are coming from nearby Nonsuch Bay or the Belfast Bay area. But all experienced Antigua hands advise strongly against trying to go all the way to Parham/North Sounds eastabout from English Harbour unless you have a large boat that is extremely good going to windward. After leaving English Harbour, it will be a hard slog to weather in a big sea all the way to Nonsuch; by the time you reach Bird Islet or Horse Shoe Reef, it probably will be late in the day and the sun will be wrong for reef navigation. Since the actual sailing distance is about the same either way, *it is much better to go westabout to Parham Sound from English Harbour.* Below are the westabout (or clockwise) sailing directions.

Leave English or Falmouth Harbour early in the day and run downwind to Curtain Bluff; there will be a big sea, but it will be on your stern. Then duck inside Cade Reef, run down a course of 292° magnetic (the range is the white roof of the Curtain Bluff Hotel in line with the second valley north of Old Road Bluff), which will lead you through to Goat Head Channel (Chart 34). See Sketch Chart

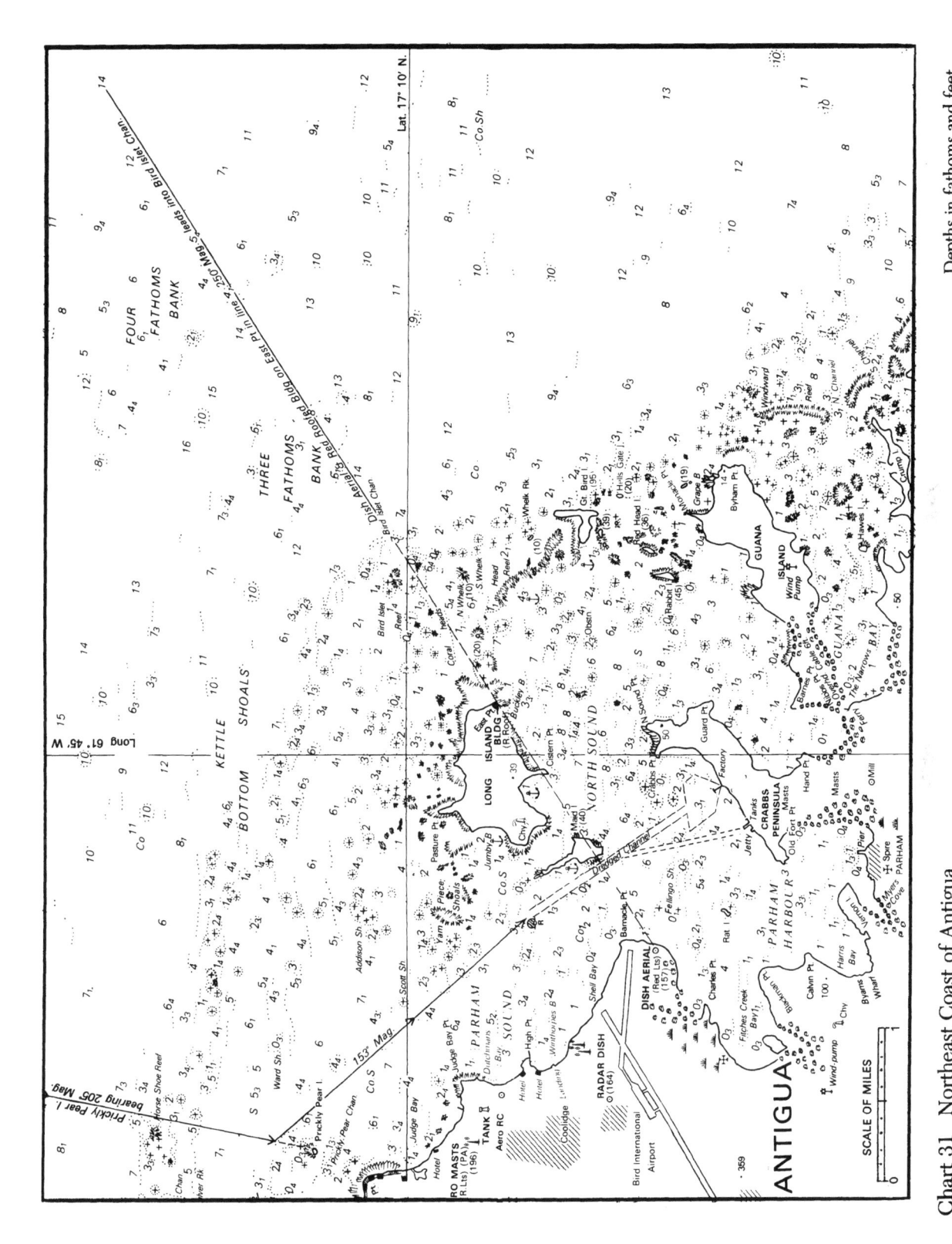

Chart 31 Northeast Coast of Antigua Depths in fathoms and feet
CAUTION: Many experienced yachtsmen consider that Antigua's northeast coast from Indian Town Point to Horse Shoe Reef is the most dangerous area in the Eastern Caribbean. It is low and featureless, with reefs extending up to five miles from Parham Harbour.

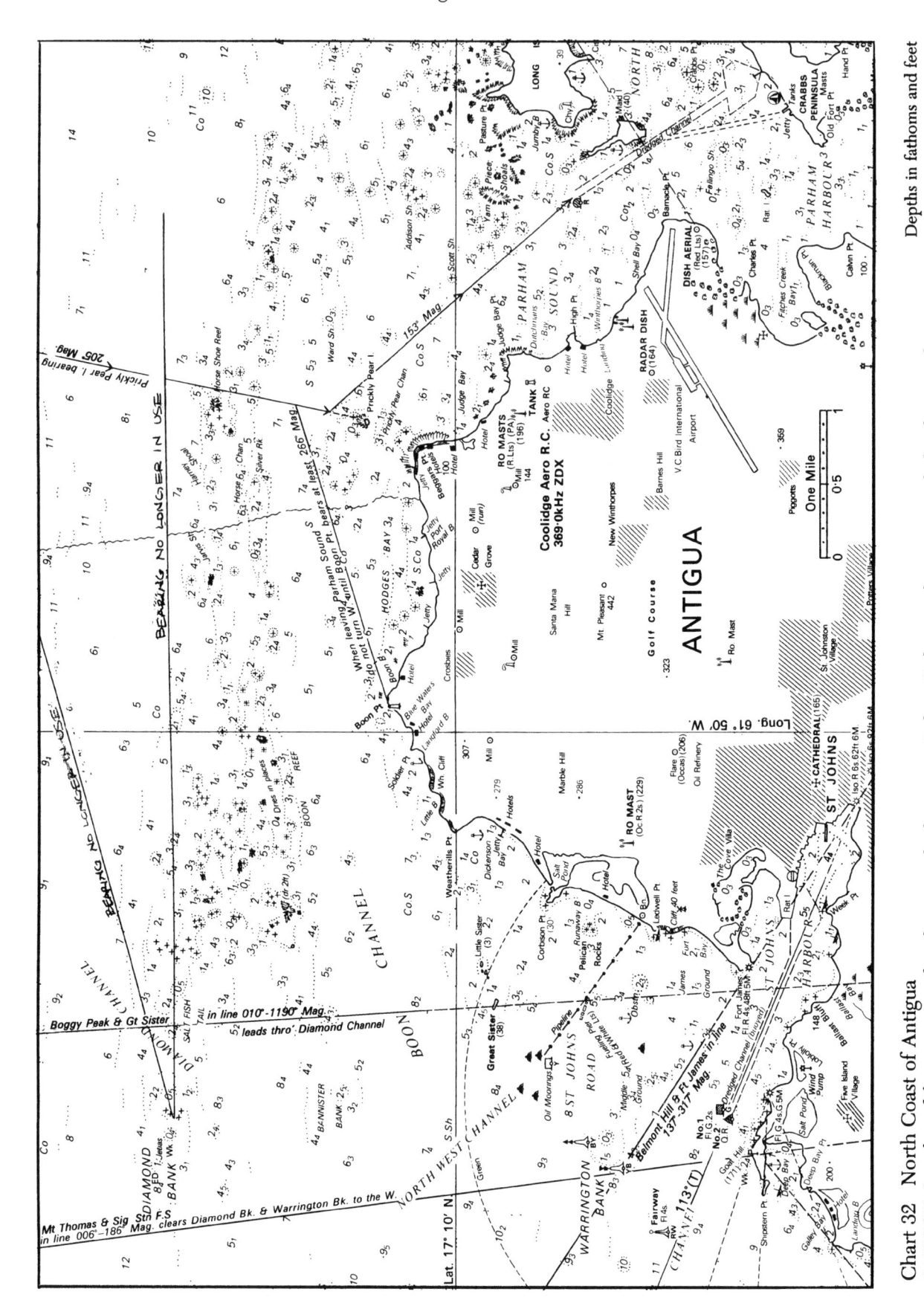

Chart 32 North Coast of Antigua
CAUTION: Stay clear of the area surrounding the cement loading pier in Parham Harbour, as there are unmarked underwater obstructions. Dredging continues in the harbor. Proceed with caution.

Depths in fathoms and feet

25 for various ranges helpful for sailing up the west coast of Antigua, and also read the southbound sailing directions for the west coast that follow the Deep Bay entry (see below).

Pass inside Five Islands and Pelican Island—but only with care and in good light. Stay close to shore and you will have a glorious reach in smooth water. Tuck up tight against Hawks Bill Rock (don't go inside it), Guard Point, and Shipstern Point. If the wind is from the north, tack inshore and pass inside the fueling pier off St. Johns and its inboard mooring buoys, then go inside Little Sister; hug Weatherills Point and go on up Boon Channel.

It may be windy as you beat up Boon Channel, but there never is more than a large chop, since the reefs to the north and east break the Atlantic swells. Favor the Antigua shore, but watch out for nobbies (coral heads) in Hodges Bay. Pass either side of Prickly Pear Island—it depends on the handling qualities of your boat and your skill as a reef pilot. You should have timed your departure from English Harbour so that you arrive at Prickly Pear *no later than 1500*. Work your way down to the 16-foot-deep dredged channel at Maid Island, as described above. Stand down this channel, keeping a bearing of 153° magnetic on the cement factory on the Crabbs Peninsula. (Off to the west is the wreck of Tony Garten's 79-foot converted motor gunboat *Warrior Guerroyant,* which went up with a big bang one day when Tony was cooking a curry lunch—the curry must have been a little too hot!) Once in North Sound, use eyeball navigation to get to wherever you'd like to be.

Obviously, if you are coming to the north and northeast coast of Antigua from the northwest or from Barbuda, you can choose any of the various entrances I have described above. The specifics of this wonderful cruising ground appear below.

PARHAM SOUND

(Charts 31, 32; II A, A-27, A-271)

Long Island/Jumby Bay is a resort that was a long time "a-borning." It staggered along for the better part of 25 years—until the middle of the 1980s, when it took off as a great place for the very, very wealthy. It is essentially an exceedingly upmarket resort—not necessarily the kind of place that the average yachtsman wants to visit. There is, however, good anchorage under the lee of Long Island in Jumby Bay. Just make sure that the ground swell is not rolling in. Dredging has been done, but, basically, the controlling depth of the bay is about eight feet. Any boat drawing more than that should approach with extreme caution. Shoaler boats that are trying to get as close as possible to shore should keep the leadline and fathometer in use, and all crew members should keep their eyes peeled!

NORTH SOUND

(Charts 31, 32; II A, A-27, A-271)

North Sound, with its countless anchorages inviting exploration, is becoming more and more popular. However, be sure you have Imray-Iolaire Chart A-271. The harbor charts in this guide, and Imray-Iolaire Chart A-27, are just not detailed enough for exploring North Sound.

Formerly, the only way to get supplies here was to go all the way back to the south coast of Antigua, but that changed when Mike and Yori Piggott built Crabbs Marina in 1980. At first, it looked as though it would take off immediately and be a very popular marina and repair facility. There was plenty of space, buildings were erected, and excellent heavy-duty machine-shop equipment was installed, along with a 50-ton Travelift. One thing led to another, however, and even though it started off quite nicely, it reached an efficiency level that was just acceptable and then stopped. (Some say it actually retrogressed.) When Crabbs Marina opened, they had lots of extra bits and pieces for their heavy-duty equipment, but gradually the extras went missing, and now only the equipment remains. Theoretically, they should be able to machine just about anything a yacht might need, but in fact that is impossible without the attachments. A real tragedy. Perhaps in the future, some entrepreneur will assess the situation and establish a good machine shop. The potential certainly is there. A yard minus a machine shop is extremely frustrating to anyone hauling or doing repairs there.

Just as with Grenada Yacht Services, the docks at Crabbs Marina are in a state of disrepair, and the marine store is as bare as "Mother Hubbard's cupboard"! Why do they waste their money paying the wage of a clerk to staff the chandlery when he has nothing to sell?

A big problem with the marina is that the owners failed to establish a reliable transportation system to and from town. Thus, if you have to go to English Harbour for supplies, it is a major undertaking if you don't have a car.

When Crabbs Marina opened its doors, *Iolaire* was one of the first boats hauled, and two major refits were done on her during the marina's early years, so we spent a lot of time at Crabbs. As a result, Mike Piggott, the major stockholder, recruited me as "unofficial adviser." If the Crabbs people had taken to heart the suggestions and advice I offered in the early and mid-1980s, I feel sure that the marina would not have the problems it is facing today. In the old days, before the Pier 5 Restaurant was built here, the problems of the world were solved between 1700 and 1900 while sitting on empty food cases in Hildred's commissary.

One evening I sat down with Theo Francis, the contractor who built Crabbs and who now manages the marina. Using Theo's figures, we estimated that if the roof area of Crabbs were guttered and all the rainwater from the roofs were led to cisterns, this investment could be paid off in three years. (These calculations were based on the price of water at seven cents a gallon and an average annual rainfall of 36 inches. Water is now 18 cents a gallon at the yard!)

Unfortunately, this scheme was never carried out. Now a ridiculous situation exists. When your boat is hauled at Crabbs, you must pay 25 cents a gallon for water to clean the boat! This happens despite the fact that the island's large desalination plant—which is adjacent to the marina—continues to pump into the sea about half of the fresh water that it is creating!

To compound the paradox, people are taking long showers (using 10 to 40 gallons of water at a time) at the marina for absolutely no fee. You have to pay to clean your boat but not yourself! It is worthwhile comparing this situation with that of Jolly Harbour (see description later in the chapter). Crabbs Marina is a perfect illustration of the point made by the radio announcer I mentioned earlier, who said, "What Antigua needs is BRAIN, not RAIN!"

Regarding electricity, I recommended early on that Crabbs Marina install meters all around the yard so that yachts could plug into power sockets and be charged according to use. At the moment, as soon as you plug in, you pay EC$25 a day—whether you operate a little electric drill once or have four grinders running all day long. The guy who uses a lot of electricity is getting off lightly, and the guy using a little is being robbed.

One result of this inequity is that a lot of boats, when they haul here, acquire a gasoline generator rather than pay an extortionate fee for electricity. The hauling charges at Crabbs are reasonable, but you may end up spending more for water and electricity than you do for hauling.

Finally, there's the Travelift (or, rather, its operator). In 1980, when the marina opened, Travelifts had bad reputations for mishandling wooden boats. It can be tricky—if wooden boats are not slung properly, they can suffer major structural damage, especially if they are weak already. Even a boat with a strong hull can be lifted back into the water improperly and then strained. Paint can chip off or crack and suddenly all the seams show. David Simmons, senior Lloyd's surveyor at the time, was strongly opposed to hauling any wooden boat in a Travelift. Other people felt the lifts were perfectly acceptable—*provided that* the boats were slung correctly. This, in practice, can mean having three (sometimes four) slings, as opposed to the normal two.

In the early days of Crabbs, the Travelift operator was an eager young Antiguan named Wingrove, who had a winning personality and was willing to learn. During one of *Iolaire*'s refits, Mike Jarrold (owner of *Lily Maid*, one year older than *Iolaire*) and I spent time coaching Wingrove on the correct procedures for hauling a wooden boat—i.e., with slings under the ballast and structural keel and no slings at the ends of the boat. All went well for a few years, but then Wingrove went off to bigger and better things, after training his replacement. Then his replacement trained the next one, and so on. Each time, a little of the expertise was lost. By now the hauling procedures at Crabbs have definitely gone downhill, as is illustrated by the story that follows.

I requested that *Capadena*, my son's 32-foot J. Francis Jones—designed sloop, be hauled at Crabbs in my absence. Then I spent about two weeks working on the boat, along with Dale Mitchell and a couple of Venezuelan crew. When the time came for her to go back in the water, the Travelift arrived and the operator put one sling under the ballast keel and the other under the stem. Now this is about the fastest possible way to "break a boat's back," or open up the keel/stem seam, which would have completely ruined all our hard work! So I pointed this out firmly to the operator and requested that both slings be put under the keel. The operator insisted that that would make the boat take a nose-dive. So I told him that if he was worried about the boat nose-diving, he should use a double sling forward—one under the forward end of the keel to take the weight and the other to serve as a safety sling. No luck. *Capadena* was picked up with one sling under the keel and one under the stem. Luckily, she is a very strong boat and no serious damage resulted. Needless to say, I was livid. When Theo Francis arrived an hour later, I complained loudly. He agreed that I was completely justified to be irate, and he admitted that other wooden-boat owners have had cause for being angry about the treatment of their boats here.

If I were in charge, I would have fired this incompetent employee on the spot, but Theo promised to give the man a serious lecture. If you have a wooden boat and want to haul at Crabbs, my advice is to sit down with Theo and agree on exactly how the boat will be slung. Make a sketch of the boat and show where you want the slings rigged. Make sure that the operator sees the sketch and that both he and Theo initial it. Then, any possible confusion will be eliminated. (With a wooden boat, this is a good practice no matter where you haul.)

Despite all of the above, there are lots of pluses about being at Crabbs. For instance, the land is low and flat, and the wind keeps it much cooler here throughout the year than in the English Harbour area. In fact, you almost get blown away at times! Another bonus is that since Crabbs is "out in the middle of nowhere," you will not be pestered by all the hangers-on who are inclined to cluster in the English Harbour area.

The marina has a commissary that stocks basic supplies; car rentals are available; taxis can be summoned; water, electricity, fuel, and ice are available; the showers are clean; and the trash-disposal system is excellent.

There is plenty of hauling space at Crabbs, which is built on filled land that is well packed yet still easy to dig into. When Hurricane Hugo came through in 1989, something like 30 boats blew out of their cradles, so now, if you are in for long-term storage, they dig a hole for the boat! The rates are, as far as I can ascertain, the cheapest in the Eastern Caribbean. (The word seems to be out: There were 150 boats hauled for long-term storage in the summer of 1992.) You can also pull your mast here for a very reasonable fee. Theo is a qualified crane operator, and one of the best I have ever seen.

If you like to do your own work, this is a good place to haul—as long as you have most of the bits and pieces you think you'll need, and as long as you supervise the Travelift operation. You can make arrangements with an independent contractor to do painting and engine repairs. Carpentry can be done by my old friend Bajan. Just ask someone at Crabbs where to find him. For complicated repairs, contact Mike Flori at PEM Marine in Parham (telephone: 463-2148 or 3575; fax: 463-3576). He is a man of many talents, and there seems to be nothing on a boat he cannot fix. He can weld aluminium and repair engines; he has a fairly good carpentry gang; and he is excellent at fiberglass repair.

At Crabbs, you will find Customs and Immigration, as well as the Pier 5 Restaurant. This may not be the finest eating establishment in Antigua, but it does have a very friendly atmosphere and reasonable prices, which appeal to the average yachtsman.

If you are doing a major refit on your boat, there also are some housekeeping cottages for rent at reasonable rates.

Unfortunately Crabbs marina which was a great little marina with wonderful hauling facilities and situated in the right place, at the right time was so badly run that it never made money and finally went bankrupt. Some yachtsmen wanted to buy it at the bankruptcy sale to reorganise it and keep it going as a hauling facility and marina. However, they were outbid and now it appears that it will be used as a storage facility for containers. A real tragedy.

If the government of Antigua would spend some of its development money dredging two short channels—between Guana and Crump islands and the mainland—it would open up the largest sheltered cruising ground in the Eastern Caribbean. This would be a gorgeous area providing eight times as many anchorages as there are in the ever-popular Virgin Gorda Sound in the British Virgins. Yachts could get into incomparably beautiful Guana Bay, Belfast Bay, and Mercers Creek from North Sound—through the back door, as it were—and they would come in droves. Boats based at Crabbs could spend a week here in these interconnected cruising grounds, anchoring twice a day and never repeating. The project—which would require about 500 yards of dredging—would provide a maximum economic return on minimal investment.

While sailing around the North Sound area, you should have Imray-Iolaire Chart A-271 in front of you, sail only in good light. and keep your eyes open. There are a few coral heads on which you might get parked, although the area is so well sheltered that you would seldom be hard aground.

The most popular anchorage in the North Sound area is off the western end of Great Bird island, where you'll find complete shelter, beautiful white-sand beaches, a whole island to explore, and enough reefs to keep snorkelers busy for weeks.

Another favorite anchorage is right up behind Head Reef; put your anchor practically on the reef, then run a stern anchor out so that if the wind dies, the current, which sometimes sweeps across the reef, won't push you onto the reef. You can snorkel directly from the boat.

Other anchorages are too numerous to mention; just start exploring with the chart and eyeball navigation.

It is possible to power out through Bird Islet Channel, but only experienced reef pilots should do this in boats that have plenty of power. Once you are out from behind the reef. you will be facing the Atlantic swell, with nothing between you and Africa; an engine failure here would be a complete disaster. Yet small, handy boats skippered by good sailors can tack out through that channel, as Julian Guildersleeve and Bernie Wong have proved many times. Both feel that the easiest way to get to English Harbour from Crabbs Marina on North Sound is out through Bird Islet Channel. They point out that it is a short, smooth-water beat out through the channel, then a short beat around the corner to Nonsuch Bay. Then it's just a downhill sleighride to English Harbour or Falmouth.

Others, however, myself included, feel that the best way to go is to head westward from Crabbs (see sailing directions above) and then counterclockwise, around the western side of Antigua, to English Harbour. The route through Bird Islet Channel is strictly for experienced sailors—and then only when it is not blowing too hard.

The great feature about North Sound is that all the anchorages are within dinghy distance of Crabbs Marina. If you need supplies, you can send out the dinghy without having to move the mother ship.

PARHAM HARBOUR

(Charts 31, 32; II A, A-27, A-271)

Parham Harbour gives excellent shelter in all weather. Generally you'll find nine feet of water, but watch out for a shoal due south of Umbrella Point and the shoals east of Clark Point. Once past the Umbrella Point shoal, favor the eastern side of the harbor. You can anchor off the jetty in 10 feet of water, but proceed slowly, as the water is not clear and there is a one-fathom spot off the jetty. Basic supplies can be bought in town, where you can also get a taxi or bus to take you directly into St. Johns. The old Anglican cathedral that overlooks Parham town is a magnificent example of old West Indian architecture. (Parham was the original capital of Antigua.) There is also a small Catholic chapel that has one of the best folk masses I have ever attended. Take a tape recorder, ask permission, and tape this excellent folk mass to play at your home parish.

Mike Flori of PEM Marine has a small yard in Parham with eight feet of water at his dock. As noted above in the North Sound section, Mike is an amazing person who can fix anything that needs fixing! For instance, he did a splining job on Frank Lepard's 40-foot cutter *Pedlar* that completely solved *Pedlar's* leak problems. Frank claims he now uses only a sponge in the bilge. Mike also has done massive deck-repair jobs; has rebuilt fiberglass boats; has straightened a number of bent masts; and has cut and welded in new plates. He also does electrical repairs and is a superb engine and outboard mechanic. Needless to say, with all these talents, he usually is snowed under with work, so he cannot always accept every job, but it is well worth calling him to check. Mike Flori of PEM Marine is no longer in business.

East of town is a large mangrove area. If you head eastward in the dinghy, you will find a river that leads up through that area. If you draw five feet or less, you can easily take the boat up into the mangroves and moor in perfect safety if there is danger of a hurricane. A boat drawing six feet of water with a powerful engine at high tide probably could power through the mud and get into the mangroves, but I think it is impossible for a boat drawing more than six feet to get across the bar—unless someone discovers a deepwater channel. Despite extensive soundings with my sounding pole, I have been unable to find any such channel.

Now here's what you will find if you retrace your steps west and south from Boon Point.

Leaving North Sound and Heading West

When leaving North Sound, you must be very careful—it is very easy to get your tail in a wringer, as we once did here on *Iolaire*. If you are heading westward through Boon Channel, you can pass either north or south of Prickly Pear Island. If you decide to pass to the north, hold a course of 333° magnetic from Maid Island Channel until north of Prickly Pear Island, but don't swing west until Boon Point bears at least 265° magnetic. If you turn west before Boon Point reaches this line of bearing, you will come to a sudden stop (as did *Iolaire* and two other boats) on the reefs northwest of Prickly Pear. Then, once you have turned west, favor the Antigua side of Boon Channel until you are clear of the reefs forming the north side of Boon Channel and the tower marking the western end of Diamond Bank. If you decide to pass to the south of Prickly Pear Island, steer a course of approximately 320° magnetic from the outer end of Maid Island Channel, aiming for a point midway between Beggars Point and Prickly Pear Island. Eyeball your way through Prickly Pear Channel in good light, then swing westward, sailing down the coast of Antigua and keeping clear of the isolated coral heads in Hodges Bay.

DICKENSON BAY

(Chart 32; II A, A-27. A-271)

A beach runs for a mile along the shore. Hotels are scattered throughout. This is a likely spot to visit if you crave a little night life. The bay is none too deep. Ease your way in with the leadline and anchor in a convenient depth. This bay is also open to the northwest and apt to be rough in certain kinds of weather, and it is always poor holding.

ST. JOHNS HARBOUR

(Charts 32, 33; II A, A-27, A-271)

The capital of Antigua, the largest town, and the point of entry is St. Johns, which is seldom visited by yachts—there are no appropriate facilities. The harbor—which used to be shallow and muddy—has recently been dredged to 35 feet to allow cruise ships to berth at a dock right in the middle of town. A 30-foot turning basin has been created, and the remainder of the head of the harbor (which in years gone by was eight feet or less) has been dredged to 12 feet.

St. Johns is an exception to my oft-repeated caution about not entering strange harbors at night. The channel is buoyed-plus! For the average yacht, the shoals on both sides of the channel are not bothersome. If approaching at night, it is best to anchor northwest of the main ship jetty, wait for morning, and then take your dinghy ashore to clear Customs and Immigration. If you wish to visit the town, pick up your anchor and put it down close in, but be sure to leave room for the cruise ships, which visit regularly.

Before moving from the shipping pier to town, check out the supermarket, which is about 200 yards east of the main commercial dock. The best anchorage for visiting the town is in the northeast corner of the harbor, north of the cruise-ship dock. Check the depth with a leadline or your fathometer. Make sure you are not in the turning basin, but rather in 12 feet or less of water. Then you will not have to worry about the cruise ships maneuvering on and off the dock. It is not advisable to spend the night anchored off town. Move elsewhere.

Near the post office are two stores—Drew's and Bryson's—for major supplies; across the street, outside the post office, are roadside stalls where ladies sell a moderately good supply of fresh fruits and vegetables. The other option is the main outdoor market, but it is a long walk away.

For many years, there was an ongoing debate about which town deserved the title of "The least attractive town in the Eastern Caribbean." It was a toss-up between St. Johns, Antigua, and Roseau, Dominica. Recently, however, St. Johns has picked up considerably, and now it boasts a restored and reopened Redcliffe Quay—a pleasant setting for exclusive shops, an art gallery, and restaurants. If you are anchored in St. Johns Harbour, I recommend exploring the town. Don't miss the museum in the old courthouse in the lower end of town.

DEEP BAY

(Charts 32, 33; II A, A-27, A-271)

South of St. Johns, Deep Bay offers fine anchorages and beaches. Two fathoms will carry quite close to the beach at the head of the bay. It may be rough, however, when the ground swell is running. When entering, watch out for the wreck that is awash due south of Shipstern Point. It provides good fun for snorkelers, and you used to be able to find lobsters in its mast stumps.

In past years, I recommended not anchoring in Deep Bay because yachts had been boarded and attacked at night. Now, however, since the Royal Antigua Hotel has been built here, this problem seems to be a thing of the past. The bay is an attractive anchorage for yachts, and the hotel does not encroach too drastically on the fine beach. Check out the fine view from the old fort up on the hill. Although Deep Bay is not deserted, it certainly is not overcrowded with yachts.

Sailing Directions for the West Coast of Antigua

You'll have superb sailing passing south along the west coast of Antigua, provided you stay on the ranges. The American chart notwithstanding, there is no water inside Hawks Bill Rock. Beyond this rock, hug the shore. Ten feet can be taken inside Pelican Rocks and the rocks past Fullerton Point. Favor the Pelican side of the channel. Then put Fullerton Point in line with Hawks Bill Rock, a range that will lead you through Five Islands Channel to the east of the highest of the Five Islands. The depth is 10 feet. Or you can pass inside all of the Five Islands, again in 10 feet of water, but Cook Shoal is on a direct line between Fullerton Point and Five Islands Channel. Let's hope that Jolly Harbour will mark Cook Shoal, as it is hard to spot, and the salvage men and yacht yards will have plenty of work. With all of the yachting development at Jolly Harbour, boats are bound to hit Cook Shoal!

Once past Five Islands Channel, place the highest of the Five Islands in line with Sandy Island; the range will lead clear of all dangers. Once you have

Chart 33 Saint Johns Harbour

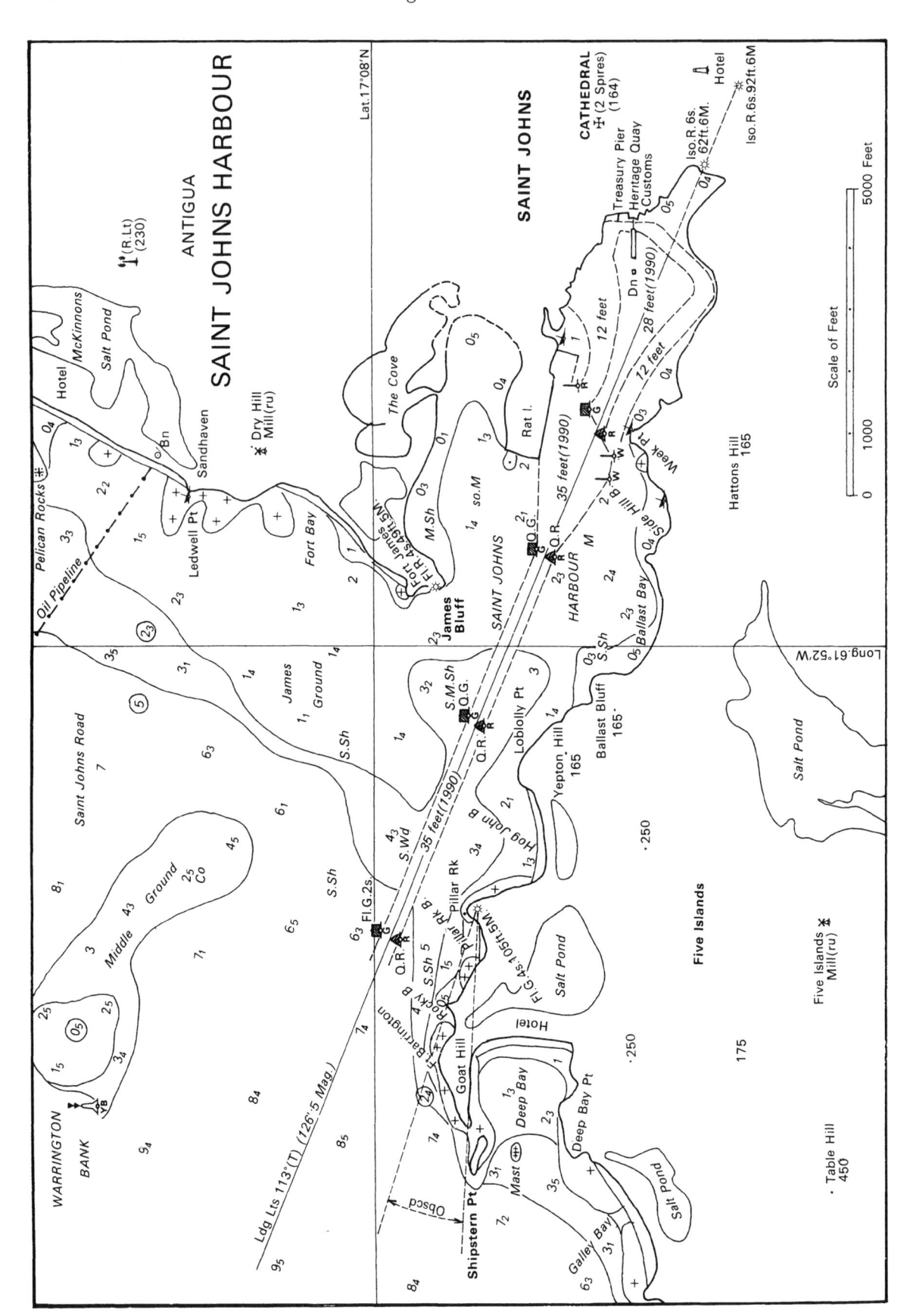

cleared the shoals off Johnson Point, you can lay a course inside Middle Reef (Chart 34). There are numerous anchorages along this western shore, but all tend to be shoal, so ease your way in to a suitable depth.

WARNING: One major danger in this area is a roughly circular shoal, about 20 yards in diameter, with no more than three feet over it, located seven-tenths of a mile, bearing 257° magnetic, from Ffryes Point. It is a great place to find if you want to go diving, a very poor place if you are merely cruising in the area and come to a sudden stop. A few boats have hit this shoal and been pulled off by John Bentley, who states that the reef is exactly where the chart shows it is, but it is very difficult to spot—as is illustrated by the fact that the new Antigua Coast Guard boat bounced off it, damaging propeller, strut, and shaft. The boat had to be given an expensive haul and repair job! The only good range for avoiding this hazard is Range E on Sketch Chart 25.

This danger was less problematic in the past because relatively few boats were in the area, but now that the huge Jolly Harbour complex has been built, I predict that unless someone marks this shoal—preferably with a solid post driven into the rock, because buoys tend to go adrift—Antigua's salvage men are going to love this rock and all the business it will generate.

FIVE ISLANDS HARBOUR

(Chart 35; II A, A-27)

This is one of numerous anchorages along the western shore of Antigua. Anchor off Maiden Island and avoid the eastern half of the bay, which is shoal- and mosquito-infested.

MOSQUITO COVE/JOLLY HARBOUR

(Chart 35; II A, A-27)

Mosquito Harbour is no more. The Jolly Beach Hotel has now opened up the old salt pond behind Mosquito Cove and created Jolly Harbour. This is the newest and largest marine-oriented land-development project in the Eastern Caribbean since Dr. Daniel Camejo developed El Morro on the north coast of Venezuela in the late 1970s and early 1980s.

The developers here have dredged a 13-foot channel from the salt pond into Mosquito Cove. Miles of bulkheading have been installed, creating a 148-acre basin, a 150-slip marina, and 500 two-bedroom, two-story, waterfront apartments. Everyone who purchases an apartment has the use of a short dock and the right to tie up a boat bow-on to the dock.

As of June 1993, you could not clear Customs and Immigration at Jolly Harbour, but most likely you will be able to do so by the time you read this—check on VHF channel 68.

The entrance to Jolly Harbour is southeast of Five Islands. Pearns Point, at the outer end of the channel, is marked by a large post with a flashing red light. Leave it to starboard; axis to the channel is 100° magnetic. The channel is marked by some rather small buoys (buoyage may be improved as time goes by). At the head of the channel, the turn is marked by another day marker. Leave it to starboard, course approximately 148° magnetic, to head into the inner harbor. The channel was dredged to 13 feet in April 1992, but there is always the problem of shoaling. We found slightly less than 12 feet in one short stretch at low water in May. In June, July, and early August, the Caribbean is likely to be a foot lower, so the depth might be down to 11 feet at low tide. Deep-draft boats should check with Jolly Harbour Marina via VHF channel 68 to verify the depths. Let's hope Jolly Harbour management will mount a tidal gauge on the outermost post, and also a tidal gauge in their office, so if you cannot read the gauge on the post, you can always contact the office for the depth at the shoalest point.

The narrow entrance to the dredged lagoon should keep out any hurricane-generated swells. If Jolly Harbour does not become overcrowded, this could prove to be one of the best hurricane holes in the Eastern Caribbean. The sheltered 148 acres of water will be ideal for recreational rowing as well as cruising in electric launches such as are used in the rivers and broads in England. To me, these launches are perfect. They are long and narrow; dead silent; generate no wake, no fumes, no pollution; and come equipped with a fabric sunshade reminiscent of the Edwardian era. To recharge the electricity, you just plug it in to normal household current—and an overnight charge allows the launch to be used the next day for up to 18 hours. Because the west coast of Antigua is sheltered from the trades, you can use launches of this type to explore the entire coastline—from Dickenson Bay on the north coast to Curtain Bluff on the south. (Just be sure that when you go around Johnson Point, you stay *inside* Cade Reef.)

Because of the layout of the apartments at Jolly Harbour (many of them are at the tips of long fingers of land), I suspect that for some tenants it

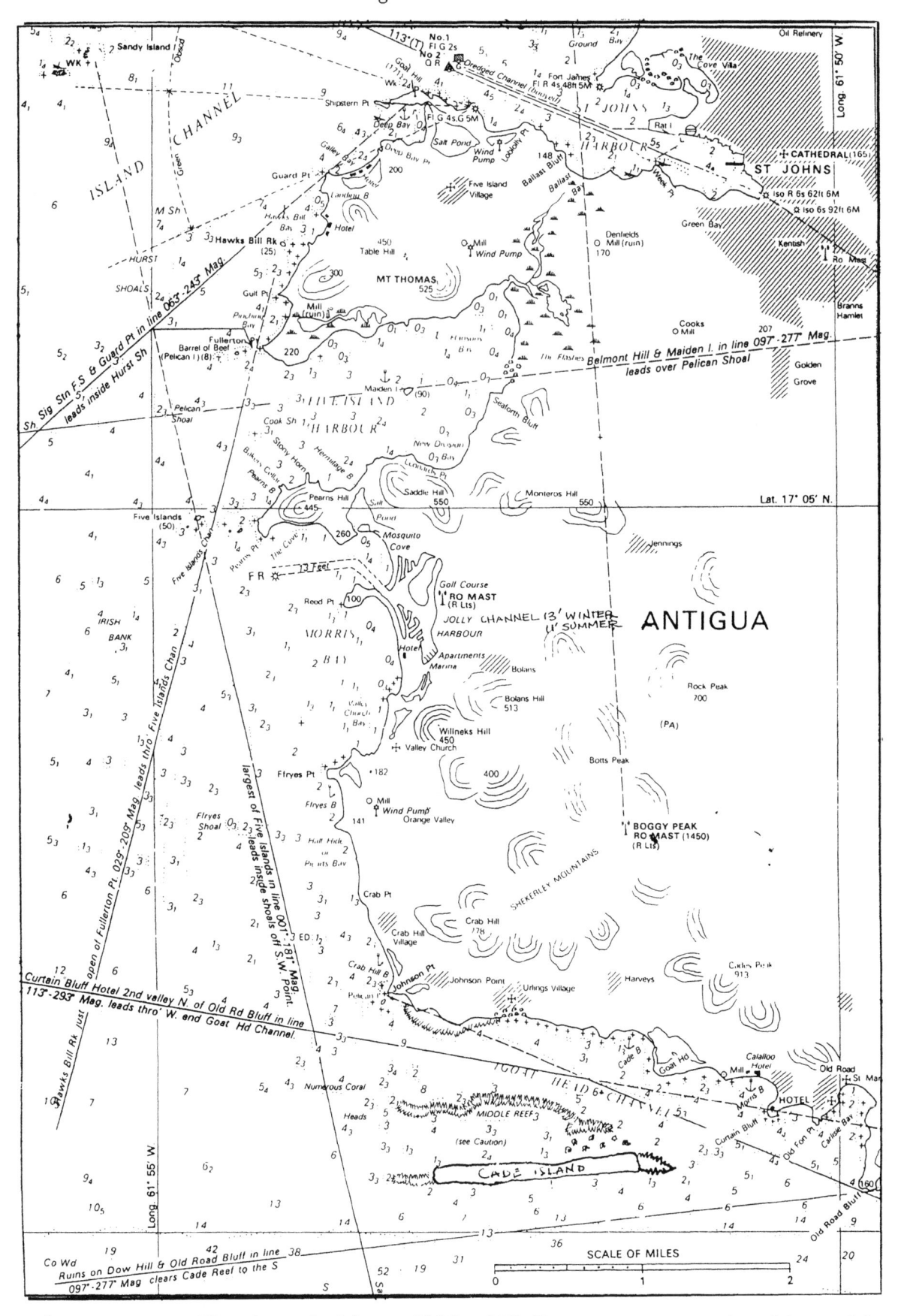

Chart 34 Antigua, West Coast: St. Johns to Old Road Bluff   Depths in fathoms and feet

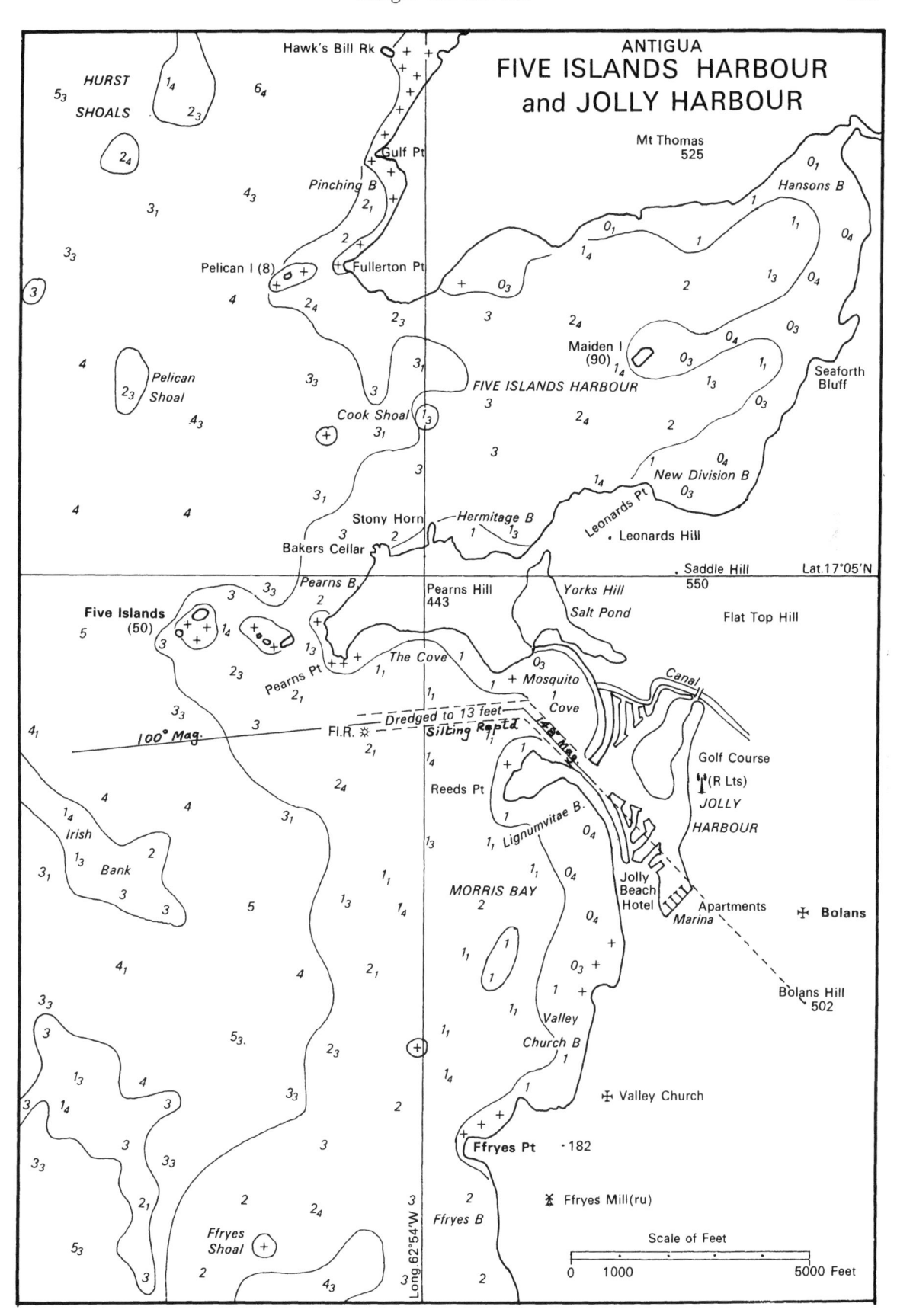

Chart 35 Five Islands Harbour and Jolly Harbour

might be easier to hop in a dinghy rather than a car to go shopping. The dinghy distance is shorter.

Such a situation reminds me of my days in Grenada, where I won quite a few beers by betting people that I could hop in my rowing dinghy and row from the Nutmeg Restaurant in town to the end of the Grenada Yacht Services dock faster than my drinking partner could do by jumping in his car, racing through the traffic, and running down to the end of the dock!

The Jolly Harbour development is in good hands—those of Geoff Pidduck and Hans Lammers. Both are experienced yachtsmen who have witnessed the mistakes made in other developments. One of the first points they stipulated was that there will be a five-knot speed limit in the lagoon. How they will enforce this is not clear, but Hans is imposing enough and determined enough to make it work! No anchoring will be allowed inside Jolly Harbour; all boats must be alongside a dock. Hans also plans to ban jetskis and waterskiing—the "sports" that really have ruined Venezuela's El Morro Marina. On weekends there, it is worth your life to try to cross the main channel. If you are tied up to the seawall, you will hobbyhorse so badly in the huge wakes that, at times, you bury your bow!

These rules can be issued because Jolly Harbour is a manmade harbor, so the owners have the authority to regulate all affairs within the harbor.

The marina is at the head of the harbor—the southeast corner—where there is a very attractive shopping center that eventually will have all the facilities and supplies that yachting folk could require.

All of the slips have water and electricity; many also have telephones and cable-TV hookups. (I must say that when I sail *Iolaire* into this marina, I doubt I'll make use of the cable-TV hookup!)

The Jolly Harbour buildings have been designed in an attractive pseudo-Spanish style, with overhanging porches offering plenty of shade. The roofs are used for collecting water—the most advanced water-collection scheme I have seen anywhere in the Caribbean. The roof water is led into cisterns, where it is mixed with "city water" via a huge header tank on the hill that holds half a million gallons of water. If the St. Johns central water system breaks down, Jolly Harbour can fall back on its own supply—which, in such a situation, would last for approximately five or six days.

Not only is all the water gathered from the roofs, but the "gray water" from the sinks, laundry, and showers is collected, filtered, and used on lawns and the golf course. If only other developments in the Caribbean could have been so meticulously planned as Jolly Harbour, many of the island water-shortage problems certainly would have been alleviated.

All the sewage from the hotel, the marina, and the apartments is fed into a private sewage-treatment plant—we can only hope that the plant will be well maintained and not become overloaded. Too often, a plant may be good at first, but then expansion puts too much strain on the system and someone in charge decides simply to pump the surplus raw sewage straight into the harbor or sea. This unhappy state of affairs has caused the pollution of many large towns in the Caribbean—notably in St. Thomas and at Grand Anse, Grenada. In the latter case, the hoteliers have blamed the pollution on visiting yachts. Let's hope that the planners at Jolly Harbour have provided for the inevitable growth of the area so that the sewage plant will not become overloaded.

The north side of the harbor has a hauling and storage facility—60,000 square feet of hard standing and another 30,000 square feet of soft (hard-packed sand) standing. When I haul out *Iolaire* there, I will have her put in the soft-standing area, because that makes it easy to chock and easy to dig into when you want to remove keelbolts, the centerboard, or the rudder. Also, if you take a fall from the scaffolding (as I did several years ago at Crabbs Marina), you have a better chance of ending up relatively unscathed if you land on packed sand than if you hit hard concrete! But that is just my opinion. Other experts will spout off their own myriad reasons why they favor a hard-standing area. At least Jolly Harbour offers both options.

Jolly Harbour's hauling facility is expanding rapidly. They have a 70-ton Travelift with an extra-wide 22-foot beam—and this is a lift with a history. It started its career in Derecktor's yard in Mamaroneck, New York; then, many years ago, it was sold to Bobby of Bobby's Marina in Philipsburg, St. Martin, where it was used until it was replaced by a 90-ton lift. The marine store at Jolly Harbour is a division of Robbie Ferron's Budget Marine, so I am sure it will be excellent in years to come.

Eventually there will be a complete repair facility here, with paint shops, machine shops, engine, sail, and electronic repair—the works. Needless to say, it will require some effort to persuade businesses to relocate from the English Harbour/Falmouth area, or to open a new division of their operation at Jolly Harbour. Given time, however, this certainly will come to pass, since the apartments are sure to attract a large number of the yachting fraternity; the 150 slips will create considerable demand for hauling, repair, and storage facilities; and the managers have built two large sheds to accommodate businesses and storage lockers for apartment owners and visiting yachtsmen.

The biggest hurdle facing Geoff and Hans at the moment is the fact that all the marine services are congregated in the Falmouth/English Harbour area—a 30-minute drive from Jolly Harbour on a rough road, or an expensive taxi ride. Admittedly, there is bus service to English Harbour, but you have to take one bus to town and then another one to your destination—using up 1 1/2 hours of your time. Much of the success of Jolly Harbour in its early days will, I believe, rest on the ability of the management to provide a reliable, regular, and affordable transportation system for yachtsmen until such time as they can persuade businesses that it would be profitable to relocate or to open another outlet.

A major advantage of Jolly Harbour is its proximity to dozens of beautiful white-sand beaches. You can easily find yourself a bit of deserted (or semi-deserted) beach within a half-hour or an hour's sail from Jolly Harbour. In the English Harbour/Falmouth area, the beach story is totally different. The only options are Freeman Bay and Pigeon Beach, which most certainly are not deserted.

Exactly how far along Jolly Harbour will be when you arrive is hard to predict. I advise dropping by to investigate the situation before deciding to fight your way around the southwest coast of Antigua to English or Falmouth Harbour.

Sailing Directions for Jolly Harbour Area

When proceeding north from Jolly Harbour or approaching Jolly Harbour from the north, you can sail inside the easternmost of the Five Islands and inside Pelican Island. However, don't attempt this unless the light is good and you are an experienced reef pilot. While crossing Five Islands Harbour, BEWARE of Cook Shoal, as it is on a direct line between the above-mentioned channels! Swing to the west to avoid Cook Shoal, then harden up to enter the channel between Fullerton Point and Pelican Island (if going north) or to use the inside channel of the Five Islands (if heading south).

MORRIS BAY (WEST COAST)

(Charts 34, 35; II A, A-27)

This is a bit confusing, as there are two Morris Bays in Antigua—one just south of Mosquito Cove and the other on the south coast near the Curtain Bluff Hotel.

The Morris Bay on the west coast is not a very popular yacht anchorage, because you must anchor well offshore and also because there is a six-foot shoal in a line between Reed Point and Ffryes Point that sometimes provides excellent surfing in periods when the ground swell is rolling in. The Lighthouse Radio beacons behind the Jolly Harbour complex provide excellent landmarks when approaching Antigua from the west. This area does provide an anchorage, but any boat drawing more than five feet must be very careful.

FFRYES BAY AND CRAB HILL BAY

(Charts 34, 35; II A, A-27)

These are viable short-term anchorages, with a tendency to shoal. Both are pleasant lunch spots off deserted white-sand beaches.

MORRIS BAY (CURTAIN BLUFF)

(Chart 34; II A, A-27)

Goat Head Channel offers a smooth passage to the east when the light is favorable. Ranges are of no real use since, tacking to windward, you will be criss-crossing all the way. If the light fails before you have cleared the reef, there is an anchorage of sorts in Morris Bay. If the wind is north of east, the anchorage, at the Curtain Bluff Hotel, can be good, but there always will be a slight roll. (Remember my oft-repeated caveat: When you see a beautiful white-sand beach, beware of swell.) Also, the bottom here is full of weeds, and holding is poor. It once took me five tries to set a 50-pound fisherman anchor before I finally dove down and shoved the fool thing in!

The Curtain Bluff Hotel on Morris Bay is one of the best on the island. The owner, Howard Hulford, used to throw an enormous party that was one of the high points of Antigua Sailing Week. He always ran an excellent launch service, not only in Morris Bay but also around the corner to the yachts anchored in Carlisle Bay—a real boon to the yachtsman, as the anchorage off Curtain Bluff became too crowded during Sailing Week. I predicted that some night a squall would come in from the south during Sailing

Week and create major havoc, but it never did. Now Jolly Harbour has replaced Curtain Bluff in the Antigua Sailing Week schedule.

CARLISLE BAY

(Chart 34; II A, A-27)

A beautiful, palm-lined anchorage. The shores are rimmed with coral, but the center of the harbor is clear of hazards and calm as long as the wind is not south of east. But Rendezvous Bay, the next one to the east, is wide open and frequently untenable. Still a nice anchorage but, on 'the deserted Palm lined beach' there is now a hotel

In conclusion, I want to emphasize that because of all the excellent features I have mentioned, Antigua has the potential to become one of the outstanding yachting areas in the Caribbean—not just a departure point or a place where yachtsmen come for a big bash during Antigua Sailing Week. But before that transformation can occur, a few problems have to be solved.

First, I think that the government does not take yachting seriously enough as a source of tourist income and goodwill—past, present, and future—and that whatever money the government *is* willing to spend to improve the yachting situation is not being spent wisely. If the bureaucrats would sit down with knowledgeable sailors and marine-oriented business operators and work out an integrated plan for improving navigational aids and developing yachting facilities, Antigua's reward in money and prestige would be tremendous. Also, as mentioned earlier in this chapter, Nicholson's Agents Week and Antigua Sailing Week and the Classic Yacht Regatta generate millions of dollars worth of business for Antigua. Many of us feel that the government of Antigua, the hotel owners, and the bar and restaurant owners should give the yachtsmen a fair shake.

Second, the Immigration officers at the airport and at English Harbour have never distinguished themselves with their courtesy or helpfulness. Most people's first impression of a country comes from its Immigration staff, and the Antiguan officials at times have appeared downright rude and obstructionist. This is a big problem for an island nation where tourism is the only real industry, and everyone hopes that someone will have the sense to do something about it soon.

Happily what used to be a major problem here seems to have been resolved. Crime inflicted against yachtsmen in English Harbour, if not completely eliminated, certainly has been drastically curtailed—to the point that, from the yachtsman's standpoint, it is one of the most crime-free areas in the Eastern Caribbean. This is a welcome and very pleasant change from the late 1970s and early 1980s, when English Harbour was probably one of the most crime-ridden areas for yachtsmen in the Eastern Caribbean. Hats off to whoever is responsible for this improvement. The government of Dominica should take note!

Barbuda

Do not navigate around Barbuda unless you have on board Imray-Iolaire Chart A-26. Chart 36 in this book is an aid, NOT a replacement for the Imray chart. Use the chart when navigating in the area between Cocoa Point and Spanish Point.

When laying your course to and from Antigua, be sure to use Imray-Iolaire Chart A-3; Chart A is the wrong scale and not detailed enough. Be aware that for the area east of a line from Spanish Well Point to the eastern part of Dodington Banks, the charts are sketchy. Only experienced reef pilots should navigate through this area—and only in ideal conditions. If the sky is overcast or the sun is low in front of you, don't try it.

In the early days of the Imray-Iolaire charts, Sun Yachts had just established its fleet of charter boats at Crabbs Marina, and both organizations were interested in having a charter-boat fleet that would popularize the north coast of Antigua and Barbuda. I pointed out that it was not profitable for me to spend a week exploring the island of Barbuda because we'd be unlikely to sell many charts for that area. Thus, the two charter organizations decided to get together and hire Imray to do a chart of Barbuda. So we sailed over to Barbuda and spent a week exploring the area, with me standing on *Iolaire's* lower spreaders for hour after hour!

It was a very good exercise, because we discovered some interesting bits of information: It appeared that if you drew a line northeast-to-southwest across the island, many things east of that line were fouled up and everything west of the line was dead accurate. I can only guess that there were two survey crews operating from the same survey vessel and that one of the crews was good and the other was not! We proved that the British Admiralty chart of the reefs off the southeast corner of Barbuda was completely inaccurate. We also discovered why, from the deck of a boat, you can never spot the Highlands, described as a range in all the old guides and on the British chart and the American DMA chart. The

Highlands are still described as 220 feet high. However, the modern topo map, which had been available to the Admiralty and the Defense Mapping Agency since 1956, showed the Highlands as being only 114 feet high—quite a difference!

After surveying the entire area from the mast of *Iolaire*, we feel we produced an accurate chart (Imray-Iolaire Chart A-26). With the aid of aerial photography (becoming increasingly popular) to pinpoint all the coral heads in and around Barbuda, we hope to be able to improve the chart.

When people ask me about the Barbuda chart and its accuracy, I am reminded of the Maine pilot who was leaning over the bridge taking a supertanker up through Penobscot Bay. The tanker skipper was becoming progressively more nervous and said, "Pilot, do you know where every rock in Penobscot Bay is?" The pilot looked at him and, in typical Maine fashion, calmly replied, "Hell, no!" The skipper blurted out, "Well, if you don't know where all the rocks are, how the hell can you call yourself a pilot?" To which the pilot replied, "I don't know where all the rocks IS, but I sure know where they AIN'T!"

If you follow the directions on the Imray-Iolaire charts and stay on the ranges, you will be safe. However, if you get off the ranges, you are on your own!

Barbuda lies 25 miles north of Antigua—to which it belongs—and is well off the beaten track of customary interisland cruising. It is low, flat, and featureless, and thus cannot be seen from Antigua. Somewhat inhospitable looking, it was never heavily colonized. For many years, a settlement was maintained on the island for the sole, grim purpose of breeding slaves. The Codrington family owned the island for almost 200 years, and, after the slaves were freed, continued to use the island as a game-hunting ground. The accounts of nineteenth-century visitors to the island speak in a single voice of its abject poverty.

Until very recently, the economy of Barbuda had not improved much, but times are rapidly changing. Many years ago, the establishment of the Coco Point Lodge provided some employment. Then a guest house was built nearby and expanded into the K Club, which certainly has aided the situation. Now the whole area from the Martello Tower westward is nothing but one-story houses, which are very well lighted! The construction of all these houses, and the labor to maintain them, has radically changed the employment picture.

In the planning stages are a number of multinational hotel projects slated for the beach west of Palmetto Point. Happily, though, development is being concentrated in the southwestern corner of the island. No development seems to be in the works in the Spanish Point area. If you really want to enjoy the empty beaches on the west coast of Barbuda, you'll need to hurry there soon.

You must clear Customs in Antigua before sailing for Barbuda. Antigua will give you coastal clearance to Barbuda. The police in Barbuda told me that it was not necessary to go into Codrington to clear in Barbuda, but if you happen to go ashore, take the coastal permit with you.

Barbuda has some superb beaches and is a quiet, attractive cruising ground—provided you maintain a healthy respect for the potential inaccuracy of the charts. Best to arrive there early in the day and rely on your vision and good light. If a squall springs up, it would be well to stand south until the weather clears.

You can approach Codrington Village via several routes. There is a channel through the shoal reefs on the northwest corner of the island leading down into a large lagoon west of town. Only an experienced reef navigator—preferably with a local pilot aboard—should attempt this, and then only in good light. Exactly how much water can be carried through this channel is subject to much debate, but it would appear that four feet is the maximum draft that will succeed. However, I have heard some say that as much as eight feet can make it.

In years gone by, Des Nicholson's favorite procedure was to put a crew member in the rigging and approach Barbuda from the west. The person aloft had two jobs: to eyeball navigate and miss Tuson Rock, and also to spot the village (Codrington) over the low sandspit that forms the western side of the lagoon. The anchor would go down due west of town; the dinghy would be launched, run in to the beach, picked up and manhandled over the tops of the sand dunes, and placed in the lagoon. The party then would row into town.

There are three dangers in this method. First and foremost is Tuson Rock, which lies half a mile offshore and is unbuoyed and difficult to spot. It is almost impossible to find by bearings, since the western shore of Barbuda is so low and featureless that there is nothing from which to take a bearing.

Second, there is the danger of being anchored off this beautiful sandy beach and having the ground swell come in—which of course is very likely in winter. Whenever you see a beautiful beach with nice, big dunes, remember that the sand was tossed there by the swell. In this case, the anchorage during the winter months could be either uncomfortable or downright dangerous.

Third, there is Stampede Reef, so-called because

the yacht *Stampede* found an uncharted coral reef off the west coast of Barbuda between Palmetto Point and Tuson Rock. Where this reef is, no one seems to know. The crew members of *Stampede* were so embarrassed about running aground that they never told anyone where they hit—much less sent the information off to Imray or me so that we could mark it on the chart. Thus, all I can say is that a shoal exists there that is not on the Imray-Iolaire chart.

Imray-Iolaire charts are the most accurate ones available to yachtsmen today, but they can only continue to be accurate if mariners will do their part by sending us information on any inaccuracies they may discover. It is impossible to cover an arc well over 1,000 miles long—from the western end of Puerto Rico to the western end of Venezuela—and keep all of the charts absolutely accurate unless we have the help of yachtsmen who use the charts. Perhaps one day the crew of *Stampede* will reveal just where they hit that uncharted rock!

Approaching Barbuda from the South

Things have changed. The Highlands can be very difficult to spot, because, as mentioned above, they are only 114 feet high (not the 220 feet specified on British and American charts). The area around the Martello Tower, which for many years was so overgrown that it was almost impossible to spot, has now been cleared, and a hotel has been built around it. I am told it is now distinctive. However, the crane at the sand jetty is by far the best landmark. Other landmarks are, of course, the Coco Point Lodge and the newer K Club. The old Imray-Iolaire charts indicated "guest house, conspicuous white roof," but now there is a whole series of roofs, and they are easy to spot. Further, it is easy to pick out Palmetto Point, because there is now a long row of houses on the beach running east of the point. Big Willie the Dutchman actually sails into Barbuda at night (most of us think he is nuts!). He maintains that the houses of Palmetto Point have so many lights that you can already see them when you are only halfway across from Antigua. He homes in on that area, picks up the lights of Palmetto Point, makes a right-angle turn, proceeds eastward until he reaches sheltered water, and anchors until dawn.

My advice, however, is: Do not enter Barbuda except in the middle of the day with good light. However, the fact that Palmetto Point is well lighted means that if you are working your way eastward from St. Barts and you get near Barbuda, you will see the lights. In the old days, you could run aground without seeing a thing.

As you approach Barbuda, one of the coral heads of Codrington Shoals has as little as nine feet of water over it, while East Codrington Shoal has only seven feet over it. These heads are accurately charted.

If you draw six feet or less and want to anchor in a harbor, you may stand north for the crane until you see a big breakwater; bear off and pick up the channel markers, keeping the red buoys on the starboard hand on a course of 025° magnetic. THE CRANE IS NO MORE. The harbour is there, but proceed with caution as the frequent hurricanes of the late 1980's have moved things around considerably.

COCOA POINT
(Chart 36; II A, A-26, A-3)

If you would rather anchor up behind Cocoa Point, come up hard on the wind, carefully following either the Imray-Iolaire chart or Chart 36 in this book. As you approach the Cocoa Point area, bring the hotel that is two-thirds of a mile north of Cocoa Point to bear 052° magnetic, stand in on this line of bearing until you have passed north of the reefs to the west of Coco Point Lodge, then tack and stand south. Go as far as your draft will permit. You will see that the beach by the southern point is much flatter than it is in front of and north of the lodge. The steeper the beach, the more the likelihood of ground swells. Good anchorage can be had in 12 feet of water, with Coco Point Lodge bearing about 120° magnetic. Boats that draw five or six feet can move even farther south and anchor in behind the reef, with the hotel bearing 080° to 090° magnetic. In fact, a good reef pilot can enter through the break between the north and south reefs off Cocoa Point; David Simmons does this regularly in *Bacco*.

Two-thirds of a mile north of Coco Point Lodge is K Club, which unfortunately is not set up to cater to the needs of the average yachtsman, although it is not quite as unfriendly as Coco Point Lodge. K Club is another of those all-inclusive establishments where guests play a flat fee that covers everything—transport, bed, drinks, entertainment, and so forth.

In the winter months, this can be a rocky and rolly anchorage, and you may have to anchor bow-and-stem. However, once the ground-swell season has ended—generally by mid- to late April—this anchorage can be beautiful and calm. The advantage of this southern anchorage in the summer is that once the Coco Point Lodge is closed for the season, you can go ashore and enjoy the fabulous beach. In the winter, when the lodge is open, the beach is

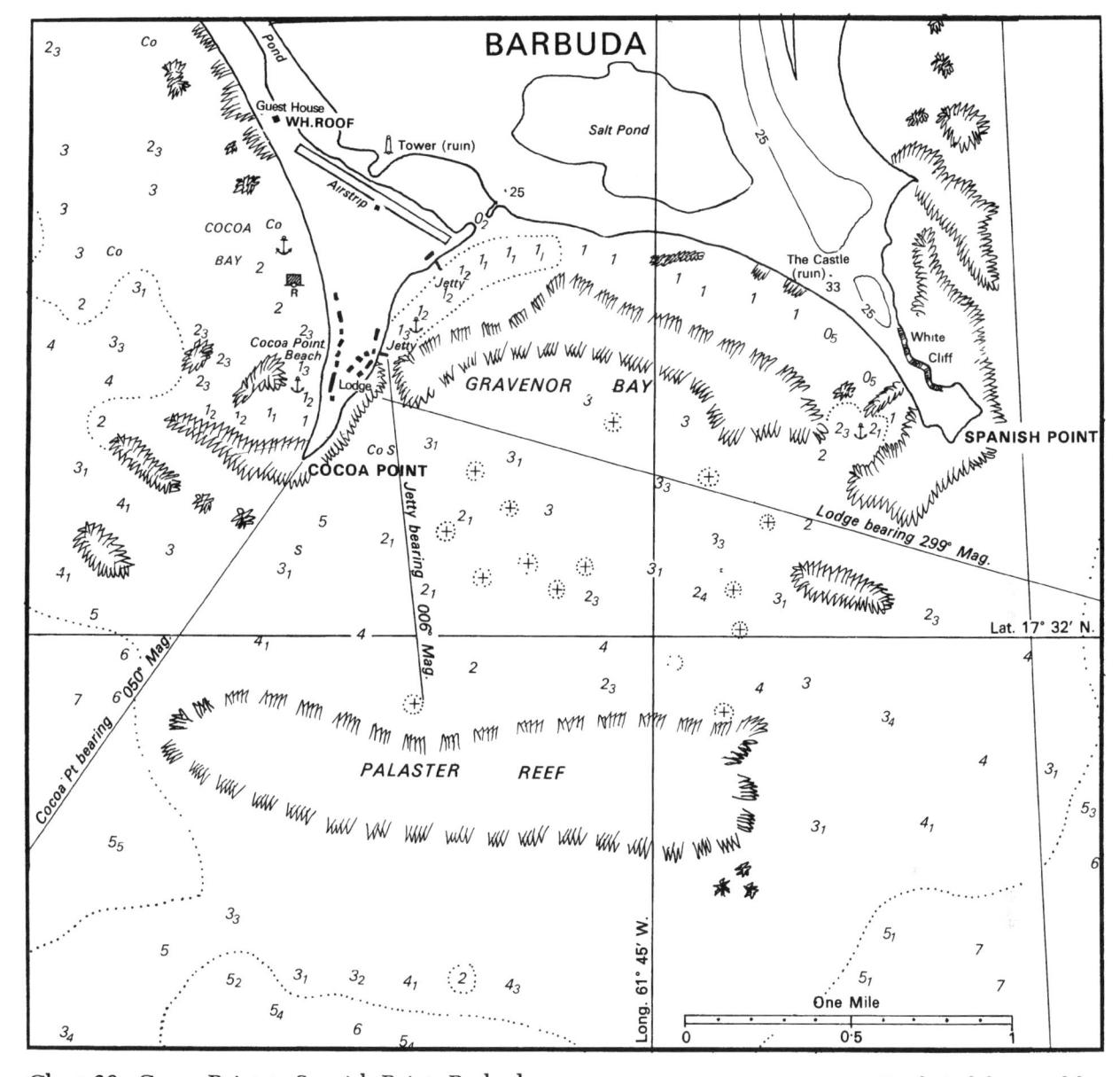

Chart 36 Cocoa Point to Spanish Point, Barbuda

Depths in fathoms and feet

1. Palaster Reef consists of large patches of coral with deep, two-to-three-fathom passes between them. The experienced pilot can thread between the heads and anchor inside Palaster Reef.

2. Approaching Spanish Point, stand north, keeping Pigeon Cliffs open from Spanish Point bearing approximately 010° magnetic until the roofs of Coco Point Lodge bear approximately 298° magnetic. Then turn west to run down this line of bearing, keeping the broken and shoal water close aboard to starboard. Slowly rounding the reef, turn northeast and work your way northeastward, anchoring in a suitable depth. This entrance can be used only between the hours of 0900 and 1400, and then only by experienced reef pilots with a reliable lookout stationed in the rigging.

3. The east coast of Barbuda may be approached only in calm weather, by small boats, dinghies, Boston Whalers, and inflatables skippered by someone with local knowledge.

4. The area from Spanish Point to Cocoa Point is encumbered with numerous coral heads with 2 1/2 to 3 fathoms or more. There is no single course that will lead through this area. Put someone in the rigging and use eyeball navigation.

5. The anchorage west of Cocoa Point is exposed to the winter ground swell (November through April). The best anchorage is as far south as you can get eastward of the reef of Coco Point Lodge.

6. In vessels drawing five feet or less, remember that the skillful reef navigator can work from Cocoa Point to Spanish Point, or the reverse, inside Gravenor Bay. Favor the shore rather than the reef.

7. Cocoa Point bearing 049° magnetic is the entry for yachts proceeding to anchorages east of Cocoa Point, Gravenor Bay, or Spanish Point, passing north of Palaster Reef.

closed to visitors; yachtsmen are encouraged to anchor north and west of a red buoy about 3,000 feet north of Cocoa Point.

SPANISH POINT

(Chart 36; II A, A-26)

If you sail for Barbuda from the east coast of Antigua, leave Nonsuch Bay early in the morning and throw out a fishing line as you pass Indian Town Point; you undoubtedly will catch a few fish before clearing Antigua.

Lay your course for Spanish Point, 28 miles to the north. Remember, though, to allow for the westerly set of the current, which may be reinforced by the tide and the leeway of your boat; you should sail about 015° magnetic and will enjoy a glorious beam reach.

As you approach Spanish Point, stay far enough to windward of the rhumb line to keep Spanish Point open on Pelican Point. Sail on in to Spanish Point, course approximately north magnetic, until you see the breakers off Spanish Point. Then bear off, run down to the west with Coco Point Lodge bearing about 300° magnetic, keeping the breakers on the starboard hand. Round up behind the breakers and work your way as far inshore as your draft permits.

Here again, the British Admiralty and US charts are wrong—they show a continuous reef that extends one-half to three-fourths of a mile out from Spanish Point. It does not. As Chart 36 and Imray-Iolaire Chart A-26 both indicate, there is a break a couple of hundred yards wide in the reef that extends one-half or three-fourths of a mile out from Spanish Point. Most experienced yachtsmen know about this, and we confirmed it while exploring Palaster Reef in June 1982 while obtaining data for the Imray-Iolaire chart.

Most sailors knowledgeable about this area like to approach Spanish Point to windward of Palaster Reef, as described above. However, some other good sailors prefer to come in from the west by passing to leeward of Palaster Reef. (The reef extends a lot farther to the west than the Admiralty and DMA charts show.) On this route, you pass west of Palaster Reef and then short-tack up through the coral heads and approach Spanish Point from the west. It is perfectly possible. We have done it a number of times with the engineless *Iolaire*, but I have always been in the rigging. You don't really need to man the rigging if the sun is overhead or in the west with good visibility, but if you have any doubt, put someone aloft. In any case, don't try it before noon.

Once behind Spanish Point, work your way in, using a long boathook or a leadline, but do not anchor too close inshore, because there is an 18-inch rise and fall of tide. If you anchor with one foot under your keel, you may be bouncing off the bottom at 0200.

GRAVENOR BAY

(Chart 36; II A, A-26)

You can enter either end of Gravenor Bay. To come in from the west, bring the dock to bear 005° magnetic, then run on in; you'll find nine feet of water in the channel, which shoals to seven or eight feet just inside the reef. With care, five feet can be carried almost anywhere in the bay; most water apparently is close to shore. In fact, five feet of water can be carried all the way from the west end of Gravenor Bay along the shore inside the reefs right up to Spanish Point. You can anchor anywhere in the bay. I think that in all except the most extreme conditions, the offlying reef would reduce any swell to nothing more than a minor chop.

To get to Gravenor Bay from the Spanish Point end, just bear off, run downwind, and anchor at a depth suitable for your draft. Proceed slowly, though, because of those five-foot areas.

PALASTER REEF

(Chart 36; II A, A-26)

This is a series of reefs with breaks that permit entry or safe anchorage inside with plenty of water in between the coral heads. Use a Bahamian moor, and if the wind picks up, use two anchors off the bow and one off the stern. This is an ideal spot for the adventuresome in settled weather and good light. Remember that Palaster Reef extends much farther west than the BA and DMA charts indicate.

PALMETTO POINT

(II A, A-26)

Palmetto Point seems to have extended southward from its old charted position. The Imray-Iolaire charts should be correct, but it is difficult to verify them absolutely. Visual sightings indicate that the bottom is fairly steep-to, so stay 200 yards offshore and you will not get in any trouble.

Sailing up the west coast of Barbuda is glorious, but be warned that Nine Feet Bank is indeed only nine feet deep. We have checked it carefully with the leadline and sounding pole. Go on up the coast,

100 yards offshore, and you'll find good anchorage between Tuson Rock and the mainland. However, during the winter, the ground swell might come in, so be sure to moor securely bow-and-stern. Also, there is a very strong northerly current along this shore. When one yacht lost her Boston Whaler off Spanish Point, the boat was retrieved a day later off the northwest coast of Barbuda! It had drifted west around Cocoa Point, along toward Palmetto Point, and was then carried northward up the west side of the island. We saw proof of this northerly current on *Iolaire* in June 1982, when, despite having the awning and the mizzen up (which should have kept us facing east), we faced south instead.

In 1982, we also doublechecked the location of Tuson Rock and the two unnamed shoals southwest of it. They all appeared to be where the charts showed.

The whole lee coast is just one magnificent sand beach with absolutely nothing on it. If you wish to get to town (Codrington Village), you can take the dinghy down to the canal—easy to spot, as it is the only place with no bushes. Upon landing, carry the dinghy across the narrow bit of land, no more than 50 yards wide, and go on across to Codrington.

The government of Antigua now owns a large sand dredge, and I wonder whether they will dredge a deepwater channel through this narrow sandspit and open up Barbuda's lagoon to the sea. This certainly would simplify the transportation of supplies from Codrington Village, and it would make the lagoon suitable for yachting. What a magnificent place to sailboard and race small cats! A dredged channel could make it possible to develop Barbuda as a major tourist island and could convert the lagoon into a large, hurricane-proof yacht harbor.

Barbuda is not a place for dressing up and going ashore for dinner. It is an ideal place for enjoying wonderful beaches, excellent snorkeling, and solitude.

The west coast of Barbuda the best anchorage appears to be north of the jetty with the houses and palm trees in Low Bay as far north as you can get without getting mixed up with the shoal water and coral heads. The reef to the west of you will do a lot to keep down the swell, but it must be admitted that if the ground swell starts rolling in it is time to leave the west coast of Barbuda.

When approaching Low Bay make your approach south of Tucson Rock—stand in shore—then turn north passing east of the coral head north of Tucson Rock. Although there are passages between the coral heads north of Tucson Rock the passages are difficult to find—follow the above directions.

This information is the result of exploration on *Li'l Iolaire* April 2000.

NOTE: there has been no exploration of Barbuda north of Low Bay since the original survey was done in 1848!!!

Further there are so many coral heads north of Tucson Rock it is impossible to chart them.

Navigational Warnings

2. ENGLISH HARBOUR

The new range installed was discontinued as unsatisfacrory and they have gone back to the original range with two range marks—039° magnetic. This is now easy to pick up as in line with the two range marks there is a large 100-foot+ tower which at night exhibits a flashing red light. It has a one second red flasher at night, and in daylight a white strobe appears at the top of the light. This light can be confusing to a boat approaching from the east, as it is so high that it is visible all over the eastern coast of Antigua.

3. FALMOUTH

Falmouth range is correct but is very difficult to pick up as the range marks are well to the east of the Catamaran Club and the range marks are on completely different elevations. Thus they are rather difficult to line up. But if you stay on this range you can carry fifteen feet all the way in to the Catamarans Club. We checked this out with a lead line April 2000—May, June and July you will have eighteen inches to two feet less!!

APPROACHING ENGLISH HARBOUR/FALMOUTH HARBOUR

Now when approaching from the south Falmouth Harbour it is very easy to spot as on Monks Hill east of Great George Fort is a tower flashing red—a two second light at night. Equally visible during the day are two towers. The western most one is a 100-foot thin pole with a fixed red light. The eastern most tower has a 100-foot+ red and white light. If the western tower is brought to a bearing of 030° magnetic that will lead in to the entrance of Falmouth Harbour. Once Proctor Point is abeam pick up the Falmouth Harbour range, if heading for the Catamaran Club. Otherwise, leave the Bishops Shoal buoy to starboard, leave the Bougham buoy to port and follow the buoy channel to the eastern side of Falmouth Harbour.

The other landmark when approaching from the south—and may be more visible than the towers—is a great gouged ravine leading down from Great George Fort on Monks Hill. The gouge was created by the deluge of hurricane Lenny. As the years go by that gouged ravine will become deeper and wider, and more visible. The landmark that will be there for 100 years.

NOTES

ENGLISH HARBOUR
(Chart 26; II A, A-27)

No problem at Limey's Bar as the Park Department has taken over the dock yard and is now enforcing noise pollution.

In recent years with the building of Antigua Yacht Club Marina, Falmouth Harbour Marina and the Catamaran Marina in Falmouth haroubr, so many boats have moved from English Harbour to Flamouth so that there is never any problem finding stern to berthing in Helsons dock yard.

As soon as you check in with Customs & Immigration make sure you pick up the Antigua Marine Guide. This is much more up to date than any cruising guide could possibly be as it is locally produced every year and is kept absolutely up to date.

Antigua has just about everything a yacht needs for repair, refit or general maintenance. The electronics are provided by many companies. The two oldest being John Eyers at Cay Electronics and Cap Green at Signal Locker. Between the two of them they have trained half a dozen Antiguans as electronic engineers, electricians, and refrigeration experts. Many of their trainees have gone off and formed their own companies.

There are, as of April 2000, two different rigging services. Two sail makers. A couple of refrigeration repair and installation firms. Watermaker services to keep your watermaker going. You can consult the Marine Guide regarding the machinists. Antigua Slipway, Budget Marine and Outfitters all are able to order anything they don't have, from abroad and get it shipped in very rapidly. Wayfarer Marine of Camden, Maine and Hinckleys also of Maine have agents in Antigua.

For hauling facilities Antigua Slipway has a railway the capacity of which goes up and down by the year, depending on the condition of the underpinning. But generally it is around 100 tons, sometimes it is considerably more. Also they have a 25 ton hydraulic trailer. Jolly harbour has a 60 ton lift.

7

Montserrat and Redonda

(Imray-Iolaire Charts A, A-25, A-3)

Montserrat

Montserrat has long been a bridesmaid but never a bride. The island lies 35 miles south-southeast of Nevis, 35 miles southwest of English Harbour, and 35 miles northwest of Guadeloupe. Hence, many yachts stop there en route from one place to another, but seldom do they remain long on the island. Like Dominica, Montserrat is a farmer's delight and a sailor's nightmare. It is high, beautiful, and lush, but has no harbor. The only port of entry is Plymouth, and that is the merest excuse for a harbor.

The island is famous for the friendliness of its black citizens, who speak English with an Irish brogue. And the island even has an Irish connection—the immigration stamp being an Irish shamrock. We also found the Irish connection in the person of Carol Osborne, wife of Cedric Osborne of the Vue Pointe Hotel. Carol is Boston-Irish and has strong family ties with the Skibbereen area, only a few miles from Glandore, where Trich and I spend the summers. We also discovered that she probably is related to Aileen Calnan, a former secretary of ours, through the numerous Calnan cousins in County Cork.

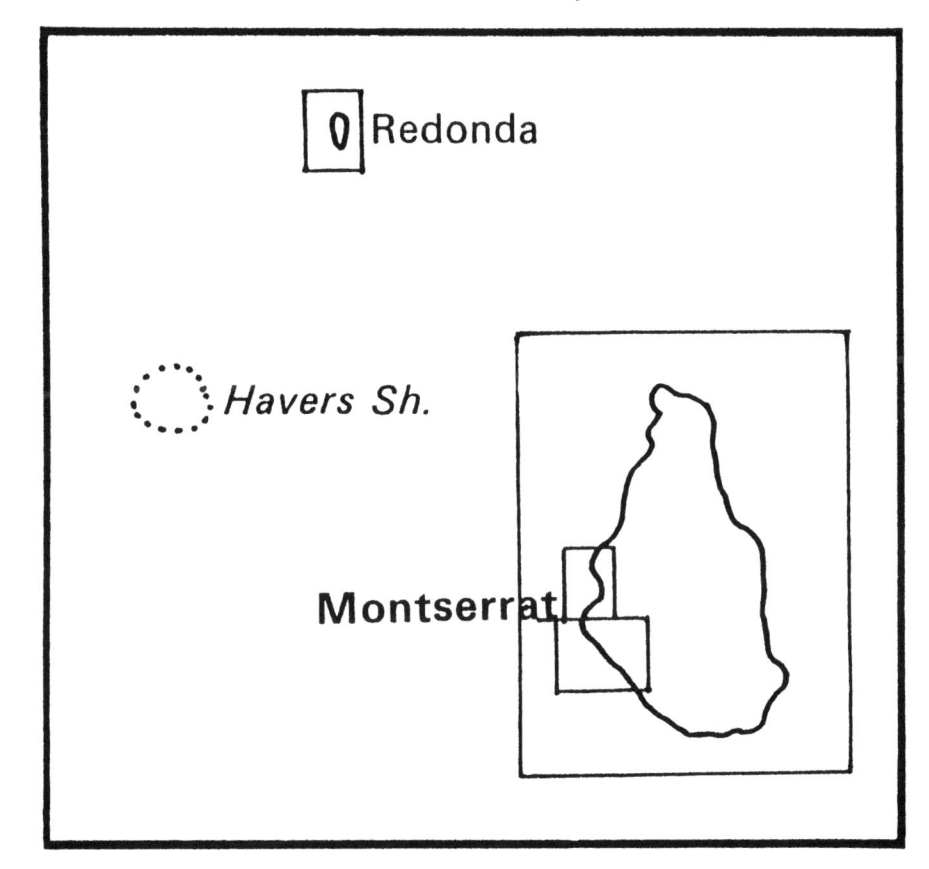

Chart 37 Montserrat

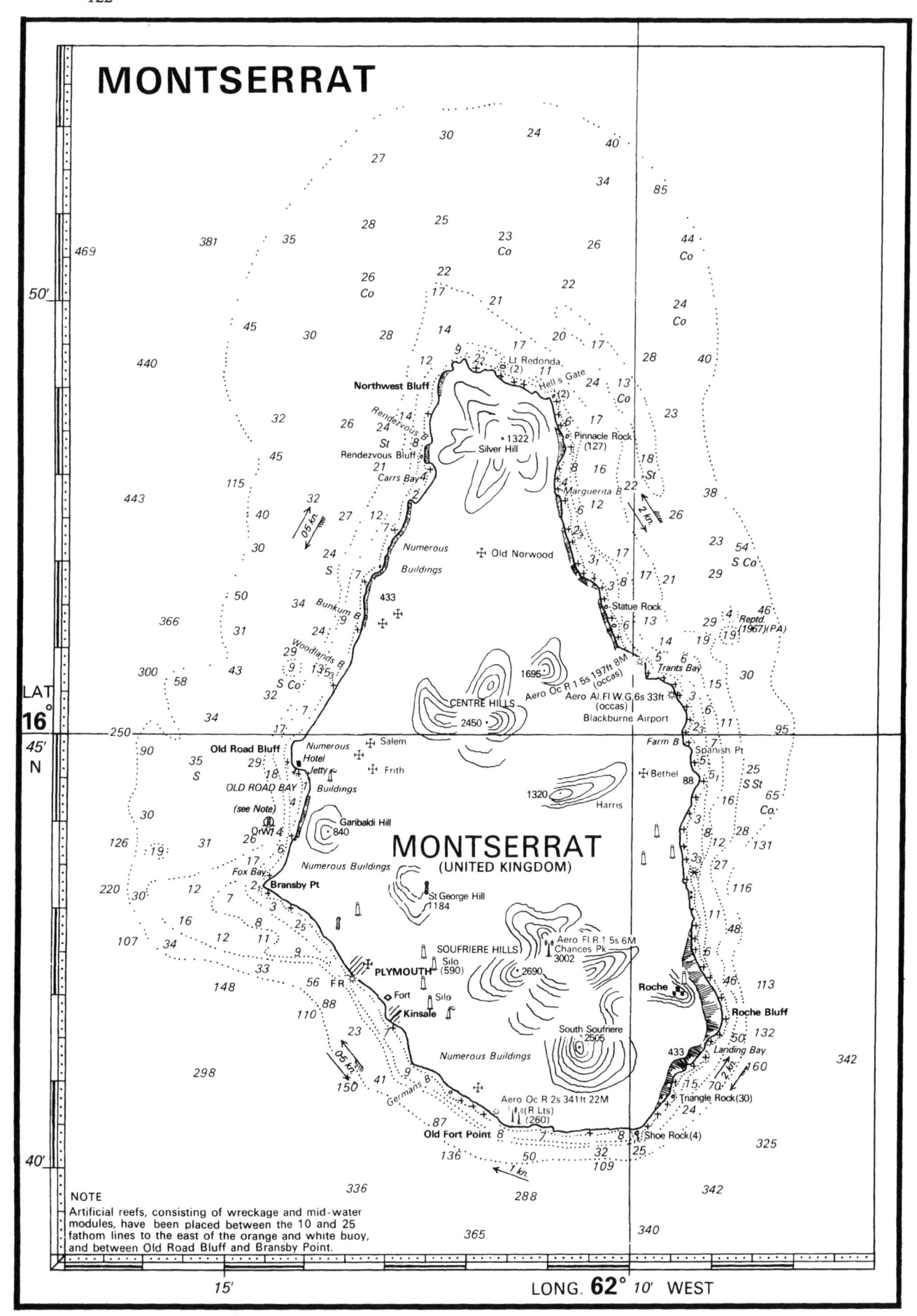

Montserrat is also known for the difficulty of landing on its open beaches. I have read four books written between 1830 and 1900 on traveling in the West Indies. All register the same complaints about Montserrat: a great surge on the beach; the boatmen not being experienced seamen; and everybody arriving ashore soaked to the skin. Wandering across the island in wet woolen clothes did not improve the temper of the nineteenth-century tourists, and it will not improve yours—so be forewarned.

Take your dinghy to the north side of the steamer dock, where there are some steps. Jump ashore, push the dinghy off, and run a stern anchor to hold it off. (The dock itself was cleaned out by Hurricane Hugo in 1989.) In March 1992, there was a 150-foot steel barge moored to the end of the seawall. We were told that construction would soon start on a 300-foot steamer dock extending in a southwesterly direction. Seeing, however, is believing!

The Customs and Immigration officials at the dock are friendly, helpful, and inexpensive, but DO NOT ENTER after hours, as the fees for that privilege are now very high.

One anchorage in the Plymouth area (see Chart 38) is about 500 yards south of the dock—sand bottom and 30 feet of water with some roll, but not too bad considering how open it is. It can certainly vary from day to day. If you want to try surfing ashore in your dinghy, land by the Yacht Club, where during the week you will find an excellent restaurant serving lunch every day and dinner on request. Over the weekend, the club is populated by the Montserrat sailing community. Sailing is restricted almost entirely to Sunfish, which they race enthusiastically, if not with world-class skill. They are very hospitable hosts.

Another anchorage is north of the dock on the shelf. Anchor on a Bahamian moor, as you could run the risk of swinging ashore if the wind died down. Once you are anchored, there are a number of permanent moorings used by the local fishing boats—run a light line over to one of the heavy buoys to keep you from swinging. The fishermen are friendly and don't seem to object. The one disadvantage of this anchorage is that you are immediately downwind of the propane-gas plant, which exudes a terri-

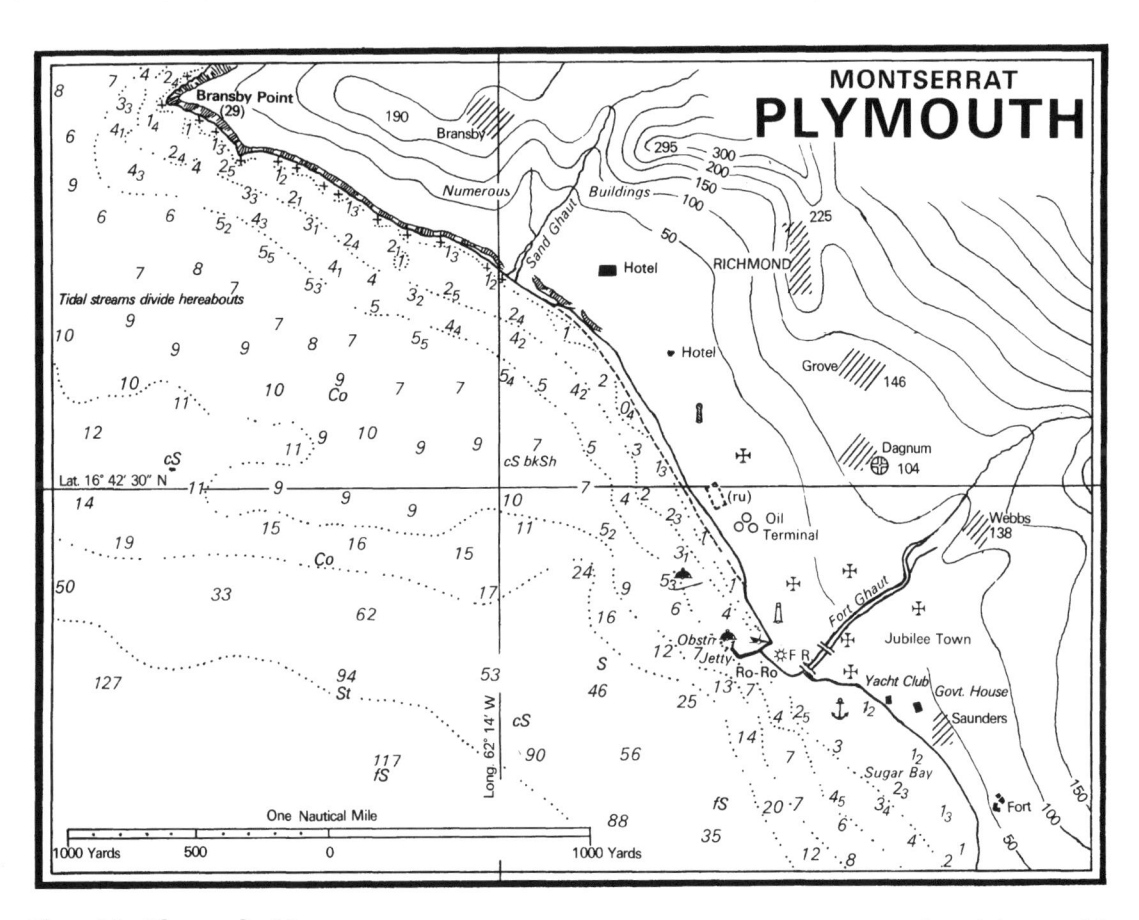

Chart 38 Plymouth, Montserrat   Depths in fathoms and feet

ble stench because of the unpleasant-smelling additive that is put into propane as a safety measure (pure propane is odorless). Usually it serves as a warning that you are in danger of blowing your boat sky-high—if you can smell "gas," you are in trouble! In the case of the anchorage, there's no danger—only a heavy assault on your olfactory senses.

The little town of Plymouth is worth a walk around; there are a few small restaurants and a market that is open every day, although the best days are Friday and Saturday, beginning a little after six in the morning. The town has many shops, the most interesting to my wife being the one near the taxi stand where you can buy sea-island cotton by the yard. The shops are definitely not "high fashion," but they are run by interesting, friendly people. Few have more than one clerk, so store operations and selling are very slow and low-key. It's actually very pleasant—rather like the pace in the islands 20 to 30 years ago.

Several small supermarkets seem to have an amazingly varied collection of supplies—much greater than one would expect for an island with a population of only 12,000. But, then again, Montserrat is a rather amazing island. Dale Mitchell, who was sailing with us in 1992, was living on St. Martin and investigating the possibility of setting up a recycling plant for the islands of the Eastern Caribbean. In assembling the statistics on how much trash each island produces, he came across the astounding information that Montserrat consumes more Heineken beer, per capita, than ANYWHERE ELSE in the world! Each month, Montserrat consumes no fewer than 14 containers of Heineken. (Each container holds 28,000 beers!) This would mean 33 bottles of Heineken a month if every citizen consumed it. Leaving aside the children and a small percentage of teetotalers, it is clear that the adult population of Montserrat is doing some serious drinking of what this author considers to be the world's finest beer!

Block ice can be bought from the fishermen's co-operative. Just walk along the waterfront and head north about 150 yards. The road ends at a green building next to a pile of fishing nets—this is where you can get the ice. You can refill gas bottles by taking them to the Texagas facility near the police station. Forget about fuel and water! Perhaps they are available, but it's so difficult that it's not worth the effort!

The LIAT air service on and off the island has been supplemented by Montserrat Air Services, which has five flights a day from Antigua and will add extra flights if necessary. Landing on Montserrat is an experience, because the flight path leads you right along the vertical cliffs on the windward side of the island. The runway axis is northwest-southeast; how the pilots land when the wind crawls around to the northeast and creates a 90-degree crosswind is beyond me. But the pilots are good, and the DeHavilland Otters can land just about anywhere. Because all the airlines are in the habit of losing baggage, be sure when changing planes to fly to Montserrat that you carry at least two days' clothing in your hand luggage.

There are two other anchorages in Montserrat. The nearest one to town is Old Road Bay, south of Old Road Bluff, the site of the Vue Pointe Hotel, owned by the Osbornes. The best anchorage here is south of the new dock in the northeast corner of the harbor (see Chart 39). Anchor in four to five fathoms of water and use a good-size anchor, as the shelf drops off rather sharply. A swell is always present, but landing a dinghy is not as difficult as it appears to be, looking from seaward. Row your dinghy in behind the stone dock, where there are some steps. Use a stern anchor to hold the dinghy off so it won't bang on the dock. Even with a swell breaking on the beach, the northern corner of the dock is fairly calm.

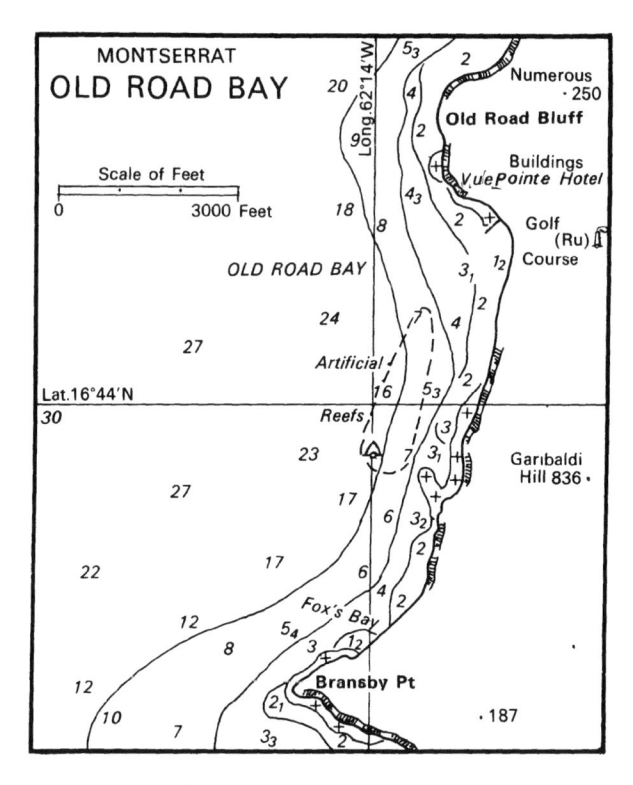

Chart 39 Old Road Bay, Montserrat   Depths in fathoms and feet

If you anchor at Old Road Bay (Vue Pointe Hotel), the easiest way to get to town is via fast dinghy. It is only a three-mile run into Plymouth by water. In a taxi, it is a long haul over hill and dale, and the published fare is EC$42—one way! At that price, I'd almost be willing to row *Iolaire's* dinghy from Old Road Bay into town!

David Blake, who has worked for various bareboat charter companies and who now lives on the northern end of the island and runs the dock and watersports concession, says that there are plans to extend the dock almost 100 yards to the south. They want to put in water, electricity, and proper yacht services, but it is up to the government of Montserrat to complete this project. When will that happen?

Nowadays, when you come ashore in Old Road Bay you will find a small and pleasant beach bar, good swimming off the black-sand beach, sailboards and Sunfish for rent, a shower on the beach, water available at the dock (sea conditions permitting), and an excellent restaurant at the top of the hill (Vue Pointe). Arrangements can be made to use the hotel tennis courts and golf course.

Carrs Bay, in the northwest corner of the island, is the island's third anchorage. It is rocky and rolly in winter, but I am told it is frequently good in summer.

From our observations of the islands, Montserrat appears to be one of the most prosperous islands in the Eastern Caribbean—despite the devastation caused by Hurricane Hugo in the fall of 1989. Hugo came through and cleaned the island out. Some places, like the Vue Pointe Hotel, were completely flattened. But, like a phoenix, Montserrat has risen from the ashes. By 1992, everything was so completely rebuilt that it was hard to believe that disaster had struck only two and a half years earlier! The roads are smooth and well paved, water supplies are excellent, the electrical supply is adequate, and—wonder of wonders—there seems to be a phone system that works! Foreign exchange comes in from a variety of sources. Although there are only about 100 first-class hotel rooms, there are nearly 100 houses with small swimming pools available for rent. In the 1970s, a large group of Americans and Canadians retired to Montserrat and built houses, giving the island a large construction boom. This has tapered off, however, as most of the land that was set aside for residential development has been purchased and built on.

One possible reason for the prosperity of Montserrat is the fact that it still is an associated state tied to the United Kingdom, which handles all of Montserrat's foreign affairs. The other islands that gave up their associated-state status and gained their independence are now saddled with top-heavy bureaucracies that they cannot afford and cannot make function.

For years I have been hearing stories about marina developments in Montserrat. The first and most logical of all these plans was to bulldoze out a marina on the flat land north of Plymouth; then, once the whole thing was dug out and docks constructed, blast a channel and let the water in. For one reason or another, this never came to pass.

Then a group of English "experts" (x = an unknown quantity; the "spurt" is a drip under pressure!) came to Montserrat and drew up plans for a totally unworkable marina. It was to have slips for 200 30-foot boats (where are you going to find that many 30-foot boats to come to Montserrat?) and was laid out in such a way that a 50-foot boat would have difficulty turning around in the space available. Not only that, but the area designated for dredging turned out to be solid rock. The total cost of this engineering "expertise" was £250,000—roughly EC$1 million—and Montserrat has nothing to show for it! If just one engineer had come out and taken a good look at the situation and recommended that the money be spent extending the existing dock at Old Road Bay, there could have been a big, usable dock for yachts and local fishermen alike.

The latest bright idea for a marina in Montserrat is supposedly going to be bankrolled by the World Bank. The scheme is to blow up the cliff on the north end of Carrs Bay, drop it into the sea, and use the rubble from the cliff to build a long breakwater extending southwestward from the point to create a sheltered cove inside the breakwater. It sounds like more pie-in-the-sky, although in March 1992, I was told that a Carrs Bay marina would definitely exist within the next 12 months. I'll believe it when I see it! I still maintain that if they had taken the money spent on the fancy engineering studies and just told the construction authorities to keep dumping rock in a southwesterly direction from the existing small jetty in Old Road Bay (Vue Pointe Hotel), it would have been better than all the studies done for marinas that have never been built!

As everyone knows Montserrat has a volcano that had not been active for 500 years, it exploded in 1990 and has been blasting away ever since. The entire southern half of the island has been made uninhabitable. The town of Plymouth is completely buried under ash. The harbour is destroyed and in fact the anchorage at Old Road Bay is largely filled in with volcanic ash. Yachts are not encouraged to anchor there but some do. The local fishing boats lie in Old Road Bay as the only other anchorage is up at Carrs Bay, which is frequently absolutely untenable in winter. At Carrs Bay a small jetty has been built for off loading supplies for the island. A few people still stay on the island of Montserrat. There is a regular ferry service from Antigua to Carrs Bay where you will find the Customs & Immigration, but unless the conditions are absolutely perfect anchoring at Carrs Bay is one step away from impossible.

Redonda

Midway between Montserrat and Nevis is the pinnacle rock of Redonda (Sketch Chart 40). Until recently, Redonda was uninhabited and a dependency of Antigua, 25 miles to the east. It has an intriguing and little-known history.

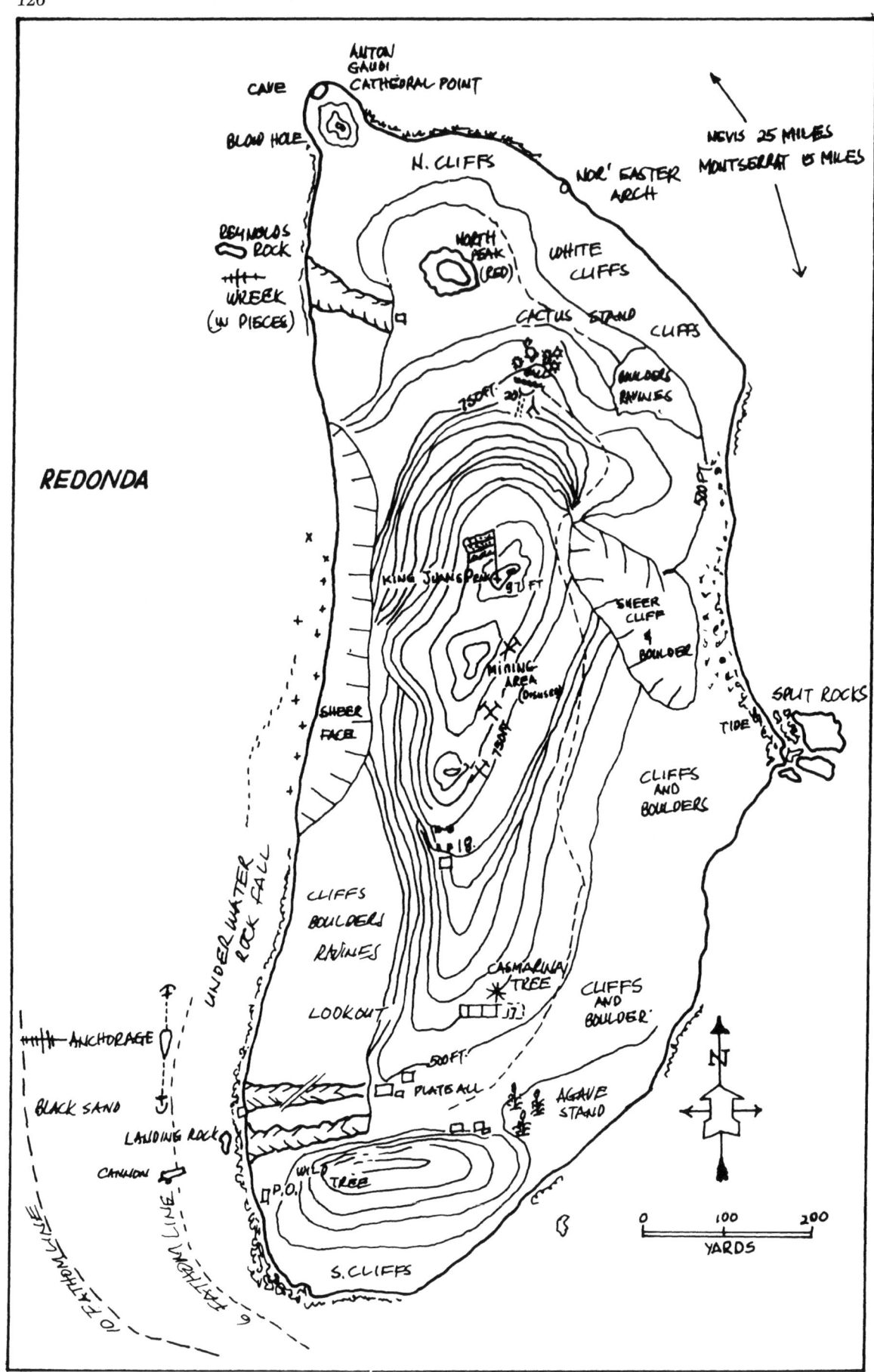

Sketch Chart 40 Redonda

Redonda was first discovered by Christopher Columbus in 1493 and named Santa Maria Redonda. Phosphate mining started in 1865, and it was not until 1872 that the island was annexed to Antigua. The mining operation was quite something—the mines were right at the top of a mountain 750 feet high. The phosphate was carted to a cable car, then carried down a steep ravine and off-loaded onto ships.

In 1899, hurricanes destroyed most of the buildings, and, finally, phosphate mining stopped with the outbreak of World War I in 1914. Blockades made it impossible for ships to get through to Germany, which reputedly was the island's main market.

Caretakers lived on the island until 1929, the mining lease was given up in 1930, and the island was abandoned until the summer of 1978, when the Antiguan government decided to establish a post office in Redonda! Sailing philatelists should take note of this, since letters not only get Redonda stamps but also a Redonda postmark. But why Antigua decided to set up a post office on this tiny island is beyond me!

Another interesting fact is that Redonda has had a "king" ever since 1880, when M.P. Shiel, science-fiction author *(The Purple Cloud,* etc.), was crowned King Philip I of Redonda. Upon his death, his literary executor, John Gawsworth, became King Juan I and appointed various "literary dukes." In turn, his literary executor became King Juan II of Redonda and actually visited the island on 13 April 1978, with a group of scientists who planted an ecological flag on Redonda. Accompanying the group was the ever-inquisitive Desmond Nicholson.

Desmond, who has sailed in the Caribbean for some four decades, reported the anchorage to be excellent: black-sand bottom, in six fathoms, moored bow-and-stern, facing north-and-south. After a day in Nevis, where they had rolled their guts out, it seemed like bliss. The group spent three days in Redonda, and although the wind was blowing like mad outside, the anchorage was calm. Desmond warns that the only access to the mountain is via a gully—probably the track of the old mining cable car—but it is treacherous, so you need good, stout shoes when you climb it.

AVES ISLAND

For want of a more logical place, uninhabited Aves (or Bird) Island, 125 miles west of Dominica, appears on the chart for Puerto Rico-to-Martinique (Imray-Iolaire Chart A). Less than half a mile long, some 300 yards wide, standing no more than 12 feet high, and changing size and shape with every storm, it gives me the willies just to think about it. Some say it is the eeriest, most desolate spot in the world; others claim it is the most beautiful. Although it has been nightfall every time I have passed it (lying as it does on the direct route from St. Thomas to Grenada), I tend to agree with the former view. An anchorage of a sort can be made in sand and coral in the island's lee. It will be rough, though, since the swell hooks around both ends of the reef. Eyeball navigation is absolutely essential.

Owned by Venezuela, Aves is now a turtle-and-bird sanctuary, but it has a long history of tragedy and near-tragedy. During the hurricane season, turtles go there to lay eggs, and the reptiles are pursued by hunters and naturalists. Any number of West Indian turtle schooners have been wrecked on its shores. They would anchor in the lee, relying on the trades to keep them off, and when the wind died out, the swell would pitch them high and dry on the beach. In the late 1960s, the famous Norwegian lifeboat *Ho Ho,* which had sailed around the world in the 1930s, went out to Aves in the hurricane season to gather turtles. Nothing has been heard of boat or crew since. Even more recently, a young French couple anchored and went ashore to study turtle life at night. At dawn, they discovered that their boat had drifted out of sight. Two nights later, they were able to signal a passing freighter. Lo and behold, what was being towed astern but their yacht! Some people are very lucky.

Others, however, are not. Perhaps one reason Aves has such a bad reputation is that the charts have positioned it wrong. Actually, it is roughly three miles to the northwest of where it is shown on many charts. In any event, be sure to give it a wide berth at night and keep a sharp lookout for it by day. The latest corrected position of Aves Island, according to the British Admiralty, is 15°45′ North, 63°36′44″ West. (The US chart makes it 15°42′ North, 63°38′ West.)

Aves Island is no longer simply a breeding ground for turtles and birds. In April 1979, the crew of the catamaran *Canowie* visited the island and reported that it had become some sort of Venezuelan naval base. They were unable to find out exactly what was going on and were unable to obtain permission to go diving. Thus another offbeat and deserted island has succumbed to the flood of civilization.

The most recent information indicates that the Venezuelan government now has a permanent military establishment here—including a hurricane-proof, Texas tower-type building on stilts at the water's edge. The mystery of exactly what they are doing there remains unsolved, but troops are stationed there for 60-day stints, then rotated back to Venezuela. Thus, the greeting that yachtsmen receive at Aves varies from month to month. Some yachts have visited and have been entertained royally, while others have been ordered away in no uncertain terms.

The well-known charter skipper Hans Lammers, aboard his Nicholson 52 *Rumours,* sailed to Aves Island with a group of amateur radio (ham) operators who wanted to be the first ham operators ever to transmit from Aves Island. They cleared the whole operation with the Venezuelan government, obtained all the necessary permissions, were royally greeted by the military establishment on the island, set up the base camp ashore, and commenced transmitting. Within a few hours of the first transmission, Venezuela's ham radio operators were infuriated to discover that a bunch of "gringos" were transmitting for the first time from Aves—a Venezuelan possession. They raised such a fuss in Caracas that the group's permission to transmit was rescinded. The military representatives on the island were told to see that the crew of *Rumours* packed up their gear and left. Needless to say, the troops had to enforce the order, but they certainly did it with no enthusiasm.

Aves also figures in an intriguing archaeological mystery. On the evening of 4 May 1697, a certain Comte Jean d'Estrées, with a fleet of eight ships-of-the-line, three transports, and eight frigates en route to capture Curaçao, ran up on the windward side of a so-called Aves Island, losing 13 of his ships. Diving in search of these wrecks obviously would be fascinating. The problem, though, is greater than the Venezuelan naval base or even the lack of protection from weather and sea. No one seems to be sure which Aves Island was the site of the disaster—this one, which lies 125 miles west of Dominica, or Ave de Barlovento, 90 miles east of Curaçao.

It seems to me that the solution lies in finding out where d'Estrées went after leaving Brest, France, on 7 October 1696. What was his last anchorage or landfall before 4 May 1697?

Venezuelans who are divers have told me that Comte d'Estrées' fleet piled up on the east coast of Ave de Barlovento. That area is so rough that despite the large number of ships that sank, little of the wreckage has been recovered—but cannons are definitely down there! If any reader can throw more light on this whole subject, I'd like to hear about it.

8

Guadeloupe

(Imray-Iolaire Charts A, A-28, A-281, A-3, A-4)

Note: It is reported that all buoys in Guadeloupe have been changed to the IALA US system—green to port when entering.

Aside from occasional bouts of political unrest, Guadeloupe is one of the most interesting islands in the Caribbean. It offers visiting yachts an excellent chance to stock up on French bread, cheese, fruit, and fresh vegetables—items that are hard to find in Antigua to the north and more expensive in Martinique to the south. Beyond that, though, Guadeloupe is a fine place to do some exploring.

But first there are a few problems that bear mentioning. The whole west coast is extremely steep-to, and it is very hard to find an anchorage except in the marina south of the town of Basse Terre in the southwest corner, or at Deshaies in the northwest corner. Tom Follett likened anchoring on Guadeloupe's lee coast to throwing an anchor against an 86th-floor window of the Empire State Building and expecting it to hold.

I realize I am biased, but I think that the best charts for Guadeloupe and its offlying islands are Imray-Iolaire Charts A-28 and A-281; on those two charts, you will find every place you could possibly think of anchoring—unless you decide to explore Grand Cul-de-Sac Marin, the reef-strewn area between the two northern tips of the "butterfly wings." The other existing charts on this area are very poor. A new French chart has been promised ever since a survey was undertaken in 1983, and it certainly will be worth buying, but, incredibly, it had not appeared as of March 1992.

For many years, Guadeloupe could be approached from the north, and yachts could pass from Rivière Salée right through to Pointe-à-Pitre, but then, in the early 1970s, the bridge stopped opening. A new bridge was built, but passage could not be made through Rivière Salée until further alterations—i.e., raising the drooping high-tension wires and burying the water lines that had been built across the river when it was impassable due to the inoperative bridge.

Thus, it was about 10 years after the bridge had been built that the river could again be used by yachts. For a while, it was perfect—the entire length of the river was dredged down to 12 feet. However, at its northern end, the river has always been subject to shoaling. In March 1992, the northern end of the river seemed to have a minimum draft of about 6 1/2 feet. (See further discussion of this situation under Grand Cul-de-Sac Marin, later in this chapter.)

Passing through the Rivière Salée is very worthwhile when heading south, as it puts you right in Pointe-à-Pitre. The excellent marina at Bas-du-Fort is within easy dinghy distance from town, and it also provides access to the supermarket at the Mammoth shopping center—without a doubt one of the best supermarkets in the Eastern Caribbean (especially when you contemplate all the French "goodies" available). Be forewarned, however, that the high quality means prices to match.

If you are not keen on paying for a marina, there is an anchorage off Pointe Fouillole.

Customs formalities have a roller-coaster history in Guadeloupe, but things are now quite straightforward. There was a time when everything was typically French—free and easy; they would glance at the passports, say, "Bonjour, monsieur," and that was that. But since Guadeloupe is the capital of the French West Indies, officials periodically would arrive from France and try to enforce French Customs laws. When this happened, yachts could be in trouble. A thorough examination of these laws will reveal that if a Customs officer takes a dislike to you and wants to "get" you, it is just about impossible to stop him from finding *something* "illegal" on your boat!

The American yacht *Jaguar* learned this lesson in 1982, when she was held for several months. If I remember correctly, it cost more than US$15,000 to buy her out! An interesting French type of rule was violated: officially, the owner MUST be aboard any yacht in French waters (luckily, this is seldom enforced!). The only exception to this rule appears to be the owner's registered concubine! What a chance for a female skipper to operate a charter boat in French waters—all she has to do is tell the Customs officials that she is the owner's registered concubine! (Incidentally, a good French-English guide to Guadeloupe, put out by Françoise Virlogeux, has a summary of the French Customs laws.)

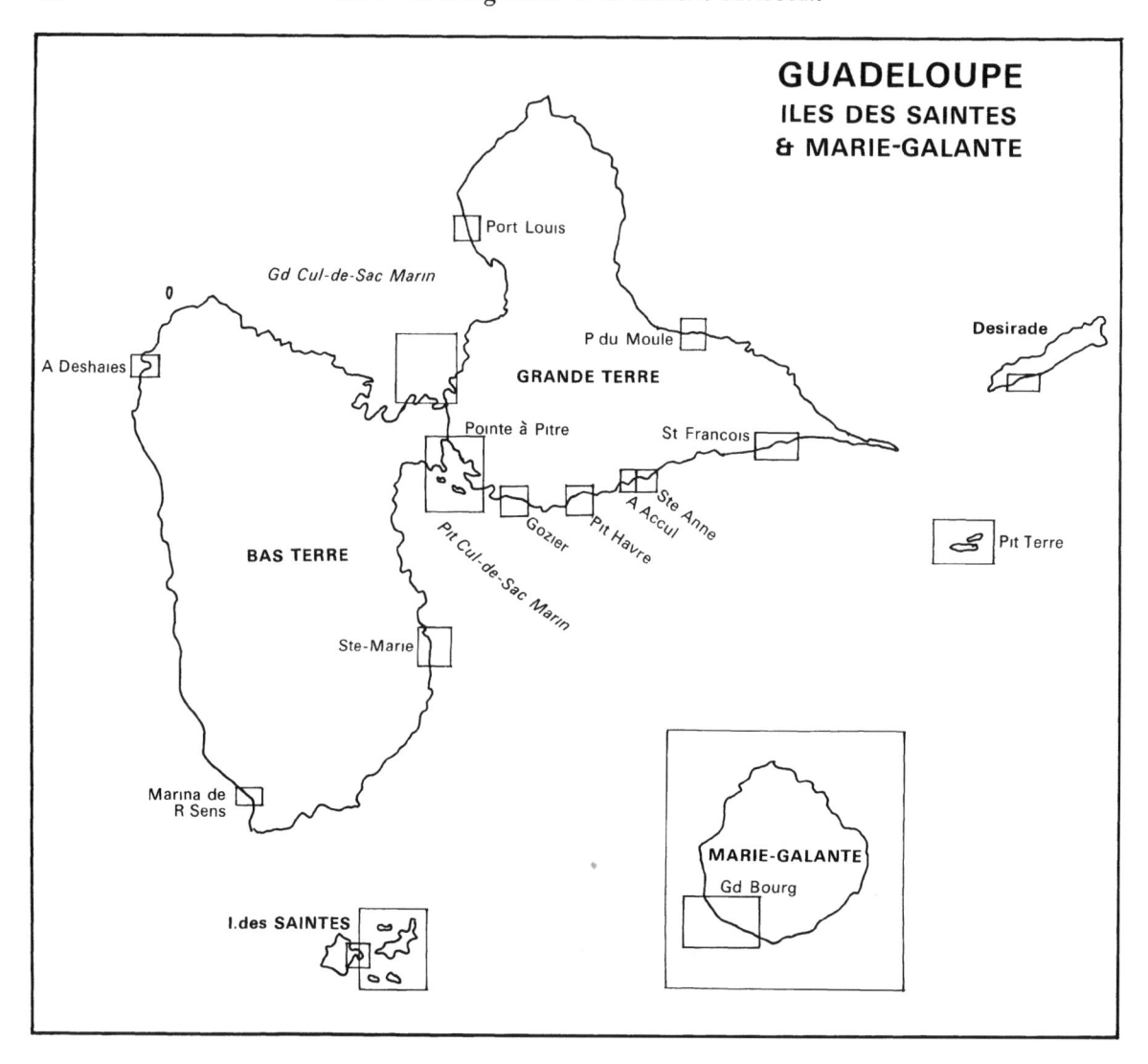

In 1992, entrance and clearance were a cinch. These days, any member of the crew just has to take the ship's papers and all of the crew's passports to the Port Captain's office at the marina in Pointe-à-Pitre.

The names of Guadeloupe's two islands (the "wings" of the "butterfly") cause some confusion. Grande Terre, the eastern island, literally means "big land," but it actually is low and flat; Bas Terre is in fact the highland. The same holds true in the name of Iles des Saintes, just south of Guadeloupe, where the lower of the two islands is Terre d'en Haut and the higher Terre d'en Bas (in sailor's terms, "upwind" or windward land, and "downwind" or leeward land).

Bas Terre is most interesting to explore, since it is high, lush, and covered with jungles, forests, rivers, and waterfalls. It also boasts Soufrière, a 4,869-foot live volcano. If you walk south from Deshaies, you will come to a small river. Upstream are excellent places to swim and bathe. If you wish to explore farther with the aid of a road map and tourist guide, you can get to the double waterfall at Carbet—twin torrents that drop 377 feet down the side of a cliff.

Grande Terre, separated from Bas Terre to the west by the Rivière Salée, is low, flat, and covered with sugar cane. Until 1992, I always felt that it held little interest for the tourist, since most of what you see is mile after mile of waving sugar cane. However, when we rented a car to visit all the ports of the southeastern coast of Guadeloupe (plus Port du Moule and Port Louis), to our delight, we discovered some good Guadeloupian restaurants that probably had never seen a single tourist. From the road, we could also see a large number of old estate houses, some of which have been restored magnificently. It's not a bad three- or four-hour drive if you want to get off the beaten track.

One excellent way to see Guadeloupe—especially if you are anchored in Pointe-à-Pitre—is to fly on Air Guadeloupe. The airline has a flight that takes off from Pointe-à-Pitre and goes over the mountains to a scary landing on a little grass strip at Bas Terre. Then it goes on to Iles des Saintes, Marie-Galante, Deshaies, and back to Pointe-à-Pitre. In a few hours, you can have a beautiful aerial survey of Guadeloupe and its surrounding dependencies. The plane flies with no copilot, so if you arrive early and speak to the desk attendant or the pilot, you might even be able to sit in the copilot's seat—which, of course, provides a fabulous view.

A point to remember in Guadeloupe is that even though shopkeepers and the educated citizens speak proper French, the majority of the islanders speak in a very difficult-to-understand *patois*. Almost no one speaks English in Guadeloupe. The few exceptions are some of the black people working in the market who have emigrated from Dominica. They will often be willing to serve as guides for a nominal fee.

In general, then, this large, lush, mountainous, well cultivated, civilized, and heavily populated capital of the French West Indies is well worth investigating. Its geography is varied and it abounds with history, most of it bloody. The carnage during the French Revolution and the Napoleonic Wars was unbelievable. The infamous Victor Hugues established his headquarters in Guadeloupe while he "visited" the other French islands in the name of the Revolution. He traveled well equipped, carrying his own portable guillotine to do in on the spot anyone to whom he objected.

Guadeloupe has numerous small hotels that are comfortable and charming and serve outstanding meals. Since the mid-1960s, a number of large, so-called modern hotels have been erected, but I prefer the older type: The food is better, the prices are much more reasonable, and they usually have a more congenial management. In any case, I tend to be suspicious of any ostensibly French restaurant that prints its menu in English.

Air communications are good, and reputedly some of the cheapest flights in the Caribbean are from Paris to Guadeloupe. The telephone system is now excellent if you have a phone card, but do not try making a call via an operator—that is a dead loss! Mail service is no better or worse than on any of the other Caribbean islands.

As mentioned above, Guadeloupe is a good place to provision, and it's easy to find ice cubes. Block ice is also available, but at tremendous expense—we did buy some in a corner shop. Apparently a truck goes around the island delivering the ice, but we were never able to find out where it starts out! Must be a military secret!

BASSE TERRE

(Sketch Chart 41; II A-28, A-3, A-4)

In the southwest corner of Bas Terre is the town of Basse Terre. Formerly, it was used by yachts to pick up supplies or drop off guests, but nowadays I recommend sailing on south past Basse Terre to the new Marina de Rivière Sens. It's approximately one mile south of Fort Richepanse, on the flat land just before the shoreline rises to a cliff with a rock quarry on it.

I first discovered this marina in May 1977, when I flew north from Grenada to St. Thomas, and I visited it by dinghy in May 1978. The facility was not publicized at all while it was under construction, and it staggered along, half-completed, until the mid-1980s. Once it got underway, it was damaged regularly by a number of hurricanes that passed north of the island, creating a swell that damaged the breakwater. Needless to say, Hurricane Hugo devastated it in 1989, but it has been rebuilt.

The marina is earning a good reputation as an excellent operation with very helpful staff, reasonable rates, free water and electricity, showers, a "capitainière," Customs and Immigration offices, and a restaurant overlooking the harbor. There are also a few small shops for outboard repairs. Although the marina usually is crowded with local yachts, there are berths available. The yacht *Phoenix* grounded here with eight feet (she probably passed too close to the end of the breakwater), but I have been assured that nine feet can be brought alongside at the fuel dock. However, give the end of the breakwater a wide berth, as it still has some damage from Hugo. Inside the marina, you are limited to about 6 1/2 feet. Getting from the marina to Basse

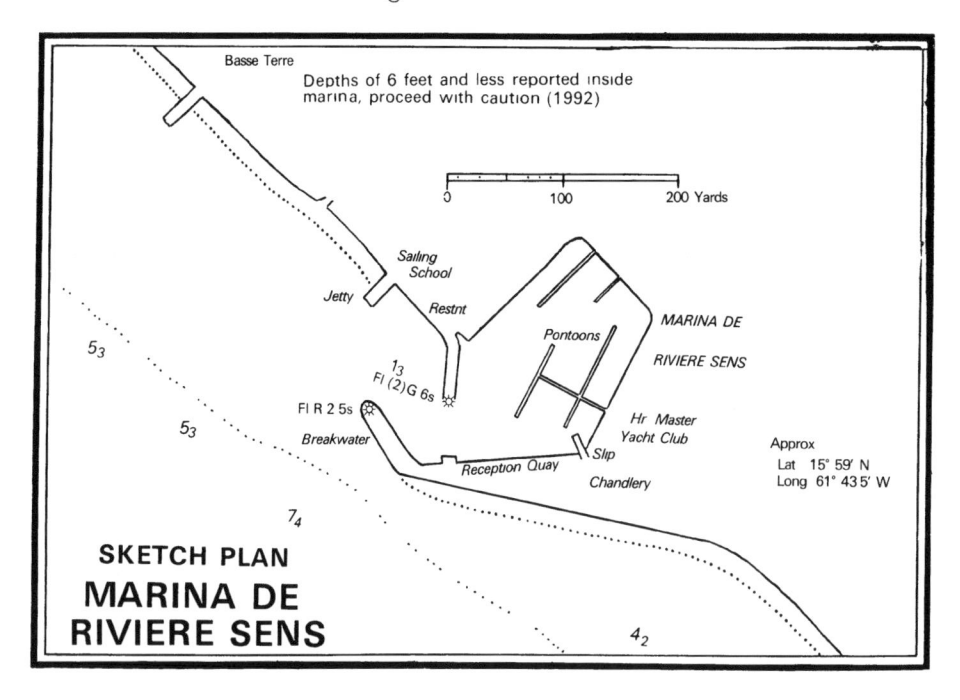

Sketch Chart 41 Marina de Rivière Sens, Basse Terre

Depths in fathoms and feet

Terre means either a long walk or a short taxi/hitchhike ride.

In addition to the marina, this area offers one of the few decent natural anchorages in the southwest corner of Guadeloupe—a shelf off the marina where you can anchor in 2 1/2 fathoms on a sand bottom. A Bahamian moor is advisable, since early in the morning a wind can come in with authority from the southwest; it can also swing back suddenly to the east. Without a Bahamian moor, you are likely to foul (and then drag) your anchor as the boat waltzes around in the variable winds.

If you do not reach the marina by dark when coming south from Antigua, don't worry. The coast is practically a vertical wall, and you can safely work your way past Basse Terre and Fort Richepanse. Then look carefully with night glasses until you see the boats moored off the marina. Sail on into the anchorage area and use a tripping line when anchoring to avoid fouling the permanent moorings. Anchor for the night, since the wind should be offshore the whole night, allowing you to get a sound sleep before rigging the Bahamian moor. In the morning, row the dinghy ashore and hitch a ride to town for shopping.

The town of Basse Terre is far more stimulating than its harbor. It is strictly nontouristy and geared to the needs of the local Guadeloupians. The market is excellent. If you need an interpreter, look around for "a *really* black mon," as the West Indians say—he is likely to be from Dominica and able to speak both English and French. Most are happy to interpret for you.

There are several small supermarkets that carry everyday needs, and the numerous restaurants throughout the town cater to all budgets—from little "holes in the wall" patronized by the working men to large, fancy restaurants geared toward the upper class. A good test is to stick your head in the door—if the place is filled with locals (as opposed to tourists), you are likely to receive good value for your money, as the French West Indians insist on this.

Basse Terre is also a fine shopping town. Many years ago, I stopped at a small boutique to buy some shorts for my late wife, but I didn't know her size in French. I tried to describe her to madame, who suddenly halted my gestures and summoned six girls who had been busy sewing in the back room. I pointed out one who appeared to be about Marilyn's size, and for the next half hour she happily modeled various shorts for me. I bought a few pair, and they turned out to fit perfectly! Only on a French island could you get free modeling service!

For many years, Fort Richepanse was barred and bolted, and no one was allowed in. I used to speculate that perhaps Charles de Gaulle's *force de frappe* included missiles stationed at top-secret forts in the French West Indies with their warheads pointed at Washington, DC! Now that De Gaulle is long gone and the cold war is history, the French have opened up and restored the Caribbean forts as tourist attractions. They are worth visiting.

From Basse Terre, buses run to all parts of the island, but most leave rather early in the morning. The ride to Pointe-à-Pitre takes a couple of hours. You can also hire a taxi, but if you want to visit Pointe-à-Pitre, it is better to set out from Deshaies, at the northwest corner, since the ride is shorter. Some people like to get off at Basse Terre, taxi around the island, and meet up with their boat at Deshaies.

ANSE A LA BARQUE

(II A-28, A-3, A-4)

Six miles north of Basse Terre lies what used to be a beautiful and quiet cove. Now, however, I have been told that there are so many small yachts moored permanently at its head that it is almost impossible to get in far enough to find bottom for anchoring. Also, the two steamer buoys to which you used to be able to moor are no longer there. All this is academic anyway, since heavy traffic along that coast makes sleep nearly impossible. If you do decide to have a try, the cove is small but easy to spot. Anse à la Barque is marked by a fixed green and group flashing white. In the daytime, you will see a concrete dock with a number of small boats moored nearby. If you can't get in close, remember that the cove is very deep and you will need lots of line out.

Running north from Anse à la Barque, hug the coast within two pistol shots. With luck, you will hold a breeze, and if you don't, the water will be calm enough for easy motoring. There are two dangers that must be avoided. North of Ilots à Goyaves (Pigeon Islands) is Pointe Malendure, which has a six-foot shoal slightly north of it. A mile north of Goyaves lies Pointe Mahout, with a four-foot spot 200 yards offshore. For what it's worth, I have also heard of a few boats that either have had the living daylights scared out of them or actually have suffered a bullet hole through a sail. It seems that there is an army firing range along this sector of the coast. It is seldom used, but when it is, the soldiers are less than careful about their aim.

ILOTS À GOYAVES (PIGEON ISLANDS)

(II A-28, A-3, A-4)

For many years, I wandered by these islands and speculated that there might be an anchorage, but I never stopped. Frick Pottiger was, I believe, the first foreign yachtsman to investigate the possibilities. In the early 1970s, he found an anchorage under Pointe Malendure, took his dinghy over to Ilots à Goyaves, and discovered an excellent spot for snorkeling and diving. Since that time, others have also discovered the area, and it is now a national park. Several Guadeloupian dive shops take expeditions out there, but spearfishing is banned in the national park. Because of potential damage to the coral—which takes hundreds of years to replenish itself—there is no good anchorage. It's best to anchor on the "mainland" at Pointe Malendure, where there is a small sand shelf. Anchor carefully, however, as the bottom drops off very steeply. Ashore you will find a beach bar that offers drinks and snacks, and it is only a short dinghy ride from the beach to the islands.

DESHAIES

(Chart 42; II A-28, A-3, A-4)

At the northwestern end of Guadeloupe, this is the ideal landfall when coming south from Antigua, and likewise a good departure point when leaving for Antigua. As a port of entry, it used to be unique. You rowed your dinghy ashore and walked to the northern end of town. There you found a small bar, where the barmaid not only served you a drink but also gave you all the necessary forms to fill out. You wrote out a crew list, had a glass of wine, and all was done! In the years before that, you had to climb up the hill to the gendarmerie to do the paperwork. It was a long, hot climb, but the view was worth it. However, evidently the gendarmes didn't like being disturbed by yachtsmen, so the bar routine was adopted.

By 1990, we were told to head south up the hill, where we found a very sleepy French official awakening from his afternoon siesta. He looked at the passports, scribbled a few notes, and wished us "Bonjour." Exactly what the situation will be when you arrive, who knows? Just go into a bar, order a beer or wine, and ask what the regulations are for clearance.

When anchoring in Deshaies, stay clear of the dock, as it is used by passenger catamarans. Check the swell on the beach—sometimes the northeast corner of the harbor is best, and at other times the southeast corner is better. Stay fairly close inshore, watching out for fish pots. The water is crystal clear.

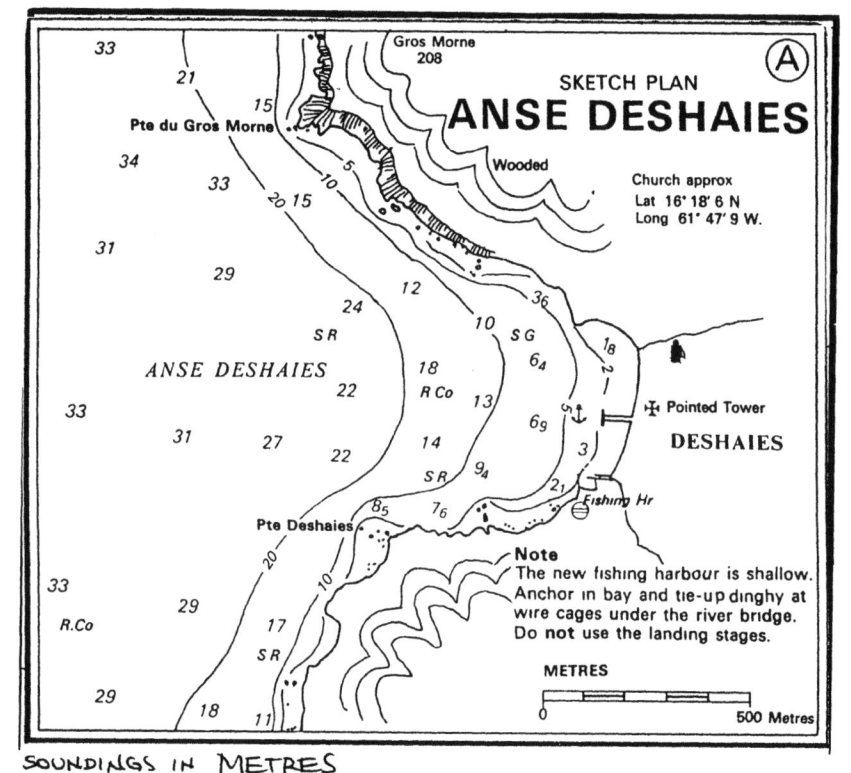

Check carefully when you drop your anchor, and if it won't set, dive down and reset it. There are a couple of old ships' anchors in the outer part of the harbor in water too deep for normal diving, and your anchor will be lost if you foul these anchors, since they are too big to be lifted off the bottom by an anchor windlass.

The ground swell can roll in, but not dangerously. If the swell is running, all anchorages in this area will be uncomfortable. One word of caution, however: If approaching from the south, do not round up too close to Pointe Deshaies at the southern end of the bay; rocks extend from the shore farther than you might expect. I found this out the hard way!

The town itself is unusually picturesque, with numerous fishing boats drawn up on shore, nets drying, small boys sailing model boats, and an assortment of workshops producing decidedly tasteless furniture from beautiful wood. One such shop is almost completely filled by the largest and most complicated woodworking machine I have ever seen. Its operator, however, evidently knows how to operate it well. Stan Young of *Limley* had him lengthen his cabintop by four feet, and the man did a beautiful job of it in six days.

There is not much available in the way of supplies, but a visit to the bakery late in the afternoon will be rewarded with bread hot out of the oven. South of town is a small stream with a two-track road paralleling it. Follow the road along the stream, and when it ends, start climbing. You will find small waterfalls, exquisite little pools suitable for freshwater swimming, and some excellent birdwatching. Chances are you will be completely alone, as there is no habitation along the stream.

In the south east corner of the harbour by the River Deshaies a small new harbor for fishing boats has been built. However, do not tie your dinghy up among the fishing boats, as they take a dim view of yachtsmen that do.

Hard dinghies are likely to be cast adrift. The next stop is Panama. They are likely to stick an ice pick into inflatable dinghies. If you are bringing a dinghy into the south eastern corner of the harbour to visit customs take the dinghy up the River Deshaies, above the bridge and tie it off above the bridge. There purportedly it will be safe.

GRAND CUL-DE-SAC MARIN
(Chart 43; II A, A-28)

The northern waters of Guadeloupe—the great reef-encumbered bay between the two "wings" of the "butterfly"—are covered in detail by French charts 3287, 3422, and 3367. For some unknown reason, however, they ignore the details of Port Louis, the only real town in the area.

From the look of the charts, these reefs must have some of the best diving and their shores some of the best exploring in the Antilles. A boat drawing six or even eight feet could go most places—with care. Shallower-draft boats can navigate Grande Rivière à Goyaves without danger, since it's all soft mud (and

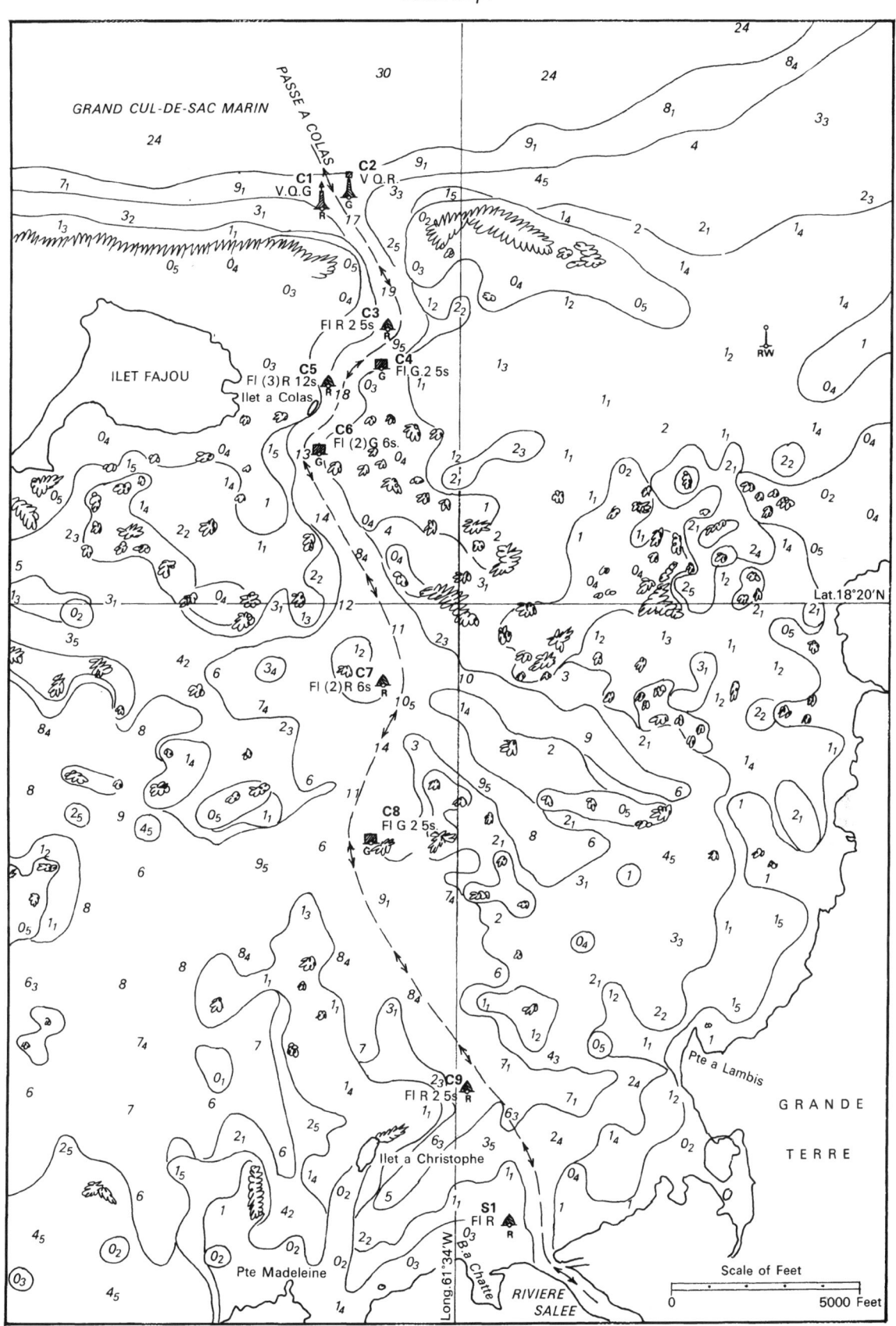

Chart 43 Rivière Salée, Northern Entrance (Grand Cul-de-Sac Marin)   Depths in fathoms and feet
Course from C1 to C3, approximately 180° magnetic; C3 to C5 and C6, 235° magnetic; C6 to C7, 180° magnetic; C7 to C8, 215° magnetic; C8 to C9 and S1, 160° magnetic.

great exploring). But why explore the river in a yacht? A dinghy would be much more practical and less nervewracking. I suspect that Canal Desrotours also is passable. Birdwatchers probably would have a field day (as it were) exploring Guadeloupe's many small rivers in a rowing dinghy or a kayak.

When I first arrived in Guadeloupe in the early 1960s, the sugar factory was still operating at Pointe-à-Pitre and spewing great clouds of black smoke and burnt sugar cane onto all the yachts anchored there (hence my dislike of the town in those days). Much of the sugar cane was still transported to the factory on steel barges that were towed through the Rivière Salée and up through the various other rivers to the sugar estates.

On the western shore of Grande Terre are numerous waterways leading back into towns, villages, and cane fields. Someday I would like to poke along some of them, since I suspect there are many ruins dating back to the days when sugar was the area's prime asset.

As scary as exploring may seem from the chart, there is a local system of rudimentary aids to navigation. When proceeding eastward, leave all red buoys on the starboard hand and white ones to port. What you do when you are going north or south, I can't say. If the buoys are there at all, I'm sure the white ones will be so rusty that they will appear red.

Paul Johnson, who now sails the large fiberglass gaff ketch *Venus*, emphasizes that although this area between Grande Terre and Bas Terre is extremely interesting and a lot of fun to explore, it should be done only by people who are experienced with reef navigation—and even then only when the sun is high. Apparently this is one area where the French charts are no longer reliable, since they were produced in World War II and have not been updated. As mentioned at the beginning of this chapter, a new survey was done in 1983, but, as of 1992, no new charts had been published. During the last 30 years, a number of hurricanes have come through Guadeloupe, and many more have passed nearby, creating huge ground swells that tend to change the locations of mudbanks and islands. The coral has grown and banks have built up from the runoffs of the various rivers. This is an area that you can enjoy completely by yourself, but ideally you should have at least one person on board who is used to exploring shoal waters in the tropics.

Now that the Rivière Salée is open to navigation, this area has become increasingly popular with the locals on weekends. During the week, however, you probably will have the whole area almost completely to yourself.

Grand Cul-de-Sac Marin can be entered in a variety of ways. If you are an experienced reef sailor, want to do a lot of exploring, and are in the Deshaies area, you can beat eastward—which may be a bit difficult, as it can get rough on the northwest coast of Guadeloupe—and enter through Passe de la Grande-Coulée. Do not enter this area until the sun is high, and remember that the northwest coast experiences an early morning calm that lasts until about 0830 or 0900 (slightly after the starting time of the annual Antigua—Guadeloupe Race, which tends to foul up the first part of the race). You can leave Deshaies at 0730, arrive at the buoy at Passe de la Grande-Coulée about 0900, and get inside. Follow the buoys, heading eastward, until 1100, when the sun is high. Then work your way eastward behind the reefs—an area where you will find either plenty of water or no water at all! If you proceed with care, constantly eyeballing the shoal bottom, you should be safe, as you are completely sheltered by the outer reef. There are plenty of places where you can anchor and dive on the reef in complete solitude. Just be sure not to drop your anchor into the fragile coral.

If you are approaching from the north—and particularly if you are intending to use the Rivière Salée—head for Passe à Colas, which is marked by two large sea buoys, C1 and C2. If a big sea is running, it may be difficult to find these buoys unless you pick up the range marked on the old Imray-Iolaire charts as 179° magnetic on the 20-story buildings in Pointe-à-Pitre. A lot of new buildings have been built; the relevant ones are the two tall westernmost structures. In 1992, we checked this range by dinghy (I cannot take *Iolaire* up the Rivière Salée, as she has a draft of seven feet six inches and no engine). While bouncing along in the dinghy, I came up with a bearing of 181°/183°, but who can take a 1° bearing? I advise putting the bow on 180° magnetic and steering toward the westernmost skyscrapers. Then keep your eyes peeled and you will pick up the sea buoys. Continue on the same course and you will pick up C3; then turn to starboard to a course approximately 235° magnetic, where you will pick up C5 and C6. Remember that you are entering Pointe-à-Pitre, so it is red/right/returning. Once you have reached C6, go back onto a course of about 180° to C7. Come to a course of approximately 215° magnetic to C8. Then there is a long shot of approximately three miles (course about 160°) to C9 and S1, which should be left to starboard. At the northern entrance of the river, proceed dead slow, as there is always a shoaling problem. Not too many years ago, the river entrance was dredged to a full 12 feet, yet nowadays this northern entrance has shoaled to 6 1/2 or seven feet. If you have any doubts, send the dinghy ahead. Once you are actually into the river, there is greater depth and all is well.

You will have no problems going down through the river—lots of scenic mangroves and the option of dinghy exploration of the rivers and lakes off to the sides. Fortunately, the overhead wires are now a full 85 feet. In the 1960s, the overhead clearance was listed as 110 feet, but then some lower wires were strung, and one yacht nearly met disaster. Either it was raining or the boat touched the wire, but they passed underneath the wire close enough for the mast and rigging to become a giant spark plug. Lightning jumped from the high-tension wire to the yacht's rigging and blew a couple of holes in the waterline where the chainplates ended. Luckily, the skipper reacted quickly and managed to plug the holes before the boat sank. In writing to me about this incident, he admitted pouring himself four stiff shots of Scotch right after it all happened.

Because of the draft limitation, I cannot imagine how any yacht that is able to pass through the Rivière Salée can have a mast anywhere near the 85-foot overhead clearance, but if the situation should arise, remember that your mast can act as a giant spark plug with horrendous and possibly fatal results.

The bridge opens up every day except Sunday at 0530 and stays open only long enough for boats to pass through. (Double-check this when you arrive, as there has been considerable pressure to have it open seven days a week.) It's worthwhile anchoring (bow-and-stern) north of the bridge because although the current is from the north most of the time, it occasionally reverses itself. You don't want to find yourself waltzing around. It's also a good idea to get a crew member into the dinghy to check out how many boats are on the other side of the bridge waiting to go in the opposite direction. This is definitely not a two-way bridge channel, and there is no official control. The distance between the piers is only 33 feet. The bridge does not open to full vertical position, so favor the east side. (Better to scrape a pier than to hook your rigging on the bridge!)

The local traffic authorities do not like to open up the bridge for any longer than necessary, as it brings all traffic to a complete halt, but they have a strange modus operandi. At 0530, not many people are using the footbridge, yet they open up the main bridge and stop all the traffic, and then they open the footbridge, which takes about four times as long to open as the vehicle bridge. Why don't they open the footbridge first and then the main traffic bridge?

Once in a while, for reasons known only to the island's Highway Department, they decide not to open the bridge for a considerable period of time. In December 1990, for instance, a boat heading for Nicholson's Agents Week in Antigua arrived at Pointe-à-Pitre and discovered that the bridge was not opening. The skipper inquired at the harbormaster's office and was told by an apologetic harbormaster that the Highway Department was in charge of the bridge, and those officials were the ones who had decided to stop opening it. The skipper was able to obtain no further information about why the bridge was nonoperational or how long he would have to wait for it to be operating again! Then, instead of taking a short sail through a three-mile passage on the Rivière Salée, followed by a beam reach through the channel in Grand Cul-de-Sac Marin and a lazy 40-mile beam reach to English Harbour, Antigua, he had a 30-mile beat against wind and current to the eastern end of Guadeloupe, followed by a 60-mile reach to English Harbour—a sailing distance of about 120 miles versus about 50 miles the other way. He was most definitely NOT a happy skipper by the time he reached Antigua!

When passing the bridge and heading south, watch out, as there is a French booby trap. (Incidentally, other guides have not picked up this anomaly!) When coming out of the river at the southern end and heading into Pointe-à-Pitre, there are two buoys. Despite the fact that the first buoy is red and the second buoy is green, you must leave BOTH buoys to starboard (i.e., to the west). Why the green buoy is where it is, I don't know, but I have been told that many boats have run aground in that area. Not wishing to rely on secondhand information, I sounded the area in a dinghy and confirmed this (see Chart 47, Pointe-à-Pitre).

Although the buoys marking the entrance to Rivière Salée in Grand Cul-de-Sac Marin are all lighted, I would not try negotiating the river at night. If you miss a buoy, or you can't locate one against the shore lights, or one of the buoys is unlighted, you would come to a sudden stop on hard coral. You would be another salvage client for the Lemarie brothers of Pointe-à-Pitre.

When coming in from the north, try to time your arrival at the northern entrance (Passe à Colas) for no later than 1500. This leaves you time to reach the northern side of the bridge and be secured before nightfall. Then you will be able to relax and watch the white egrets at their nesting site north of the bridge. Be sure to have plenty of mosquito coils, though, as these pests tend to attack with a vengeance when the wind dies down at night!

If you realize you are going to arrive late at Passe à Colas (i.e., after 1500), my advice is to trim sheets, head east, anchor off Port Louis, go ashore and look around, have a good French meal, and relax. Then, the next morning, go through Passe à Colas, anchor inside Grand Cul-de-Sac Marin, and enjoy some swimming and diving. In the afternoon, head south through the Rivière Salée and anchor north of the bridge in order to be ready for the 0530 opening.

PORT LOUIS

(Chart 44; II A-28, A-3, A-4)

If you are heading for the entrance to Passe à Colas and it is late in the day (any time after 1500 would be too late to enter the Passe, as the light would not be good), go into Port Louis. Although this is an open roadstead and not a harbor, it is a satisfactory anchorage in normal conditions with the wind from the east. Anchor at the south end of the village off the fishing port, which is a good place to leave the dinghy while you explore the town.

The small harbor is strictly for shoal-draft fishing boats and dinghies—I have not anchored here, only viewed it from shore, but I recommend anchoring due west from the south end of the fishing harbor.

From the look of the old buildings, it's easy to imagine that the town once must have been quite prosperous. The magnificent cast-iron streetlamps are an impressive sight and make the stop worthwhile. As in every town in the French Antilles, you can always find restaurants if you poke around a bit. It's just a matter of selecting one that suits your pocketbook and taste!

There are no big supermarkets, but the small shops certainly can supply basic needs.

PORT DU MOULE

(Chart 45; II A-28, A-281, A-3, A-4)

The northeast coast of Guadeloupe is bold and steep-to, and only this harbor warrants discussion. The British Admiralty's Sailing Directions—which, of course, is published for large vessels—warns of difficulty of entry and states that it is unsafe from October to March, presumably because of the ground swell.

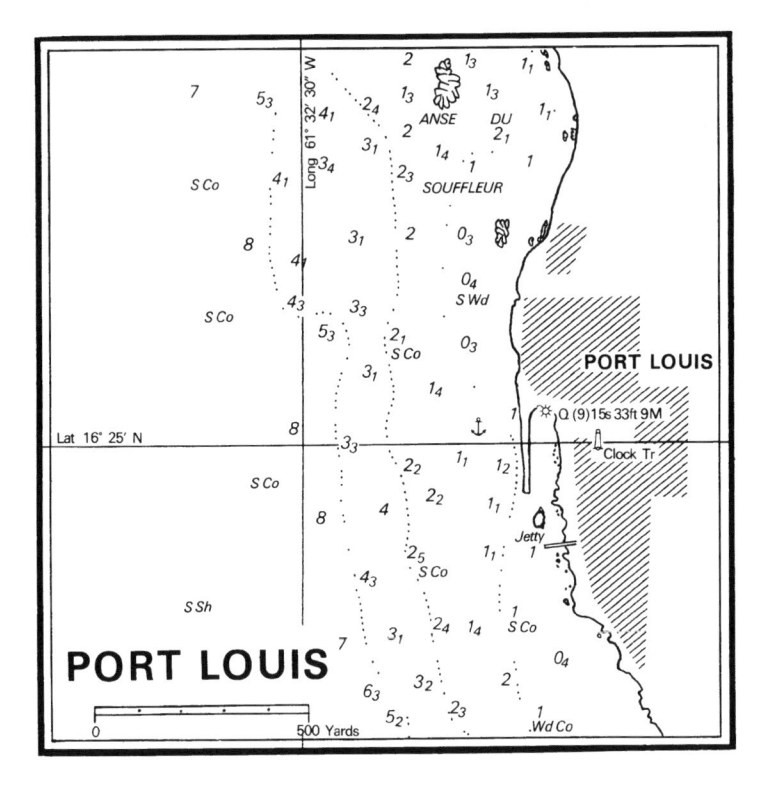

Chart 44 Port Louis   Depths in fathoms and feet

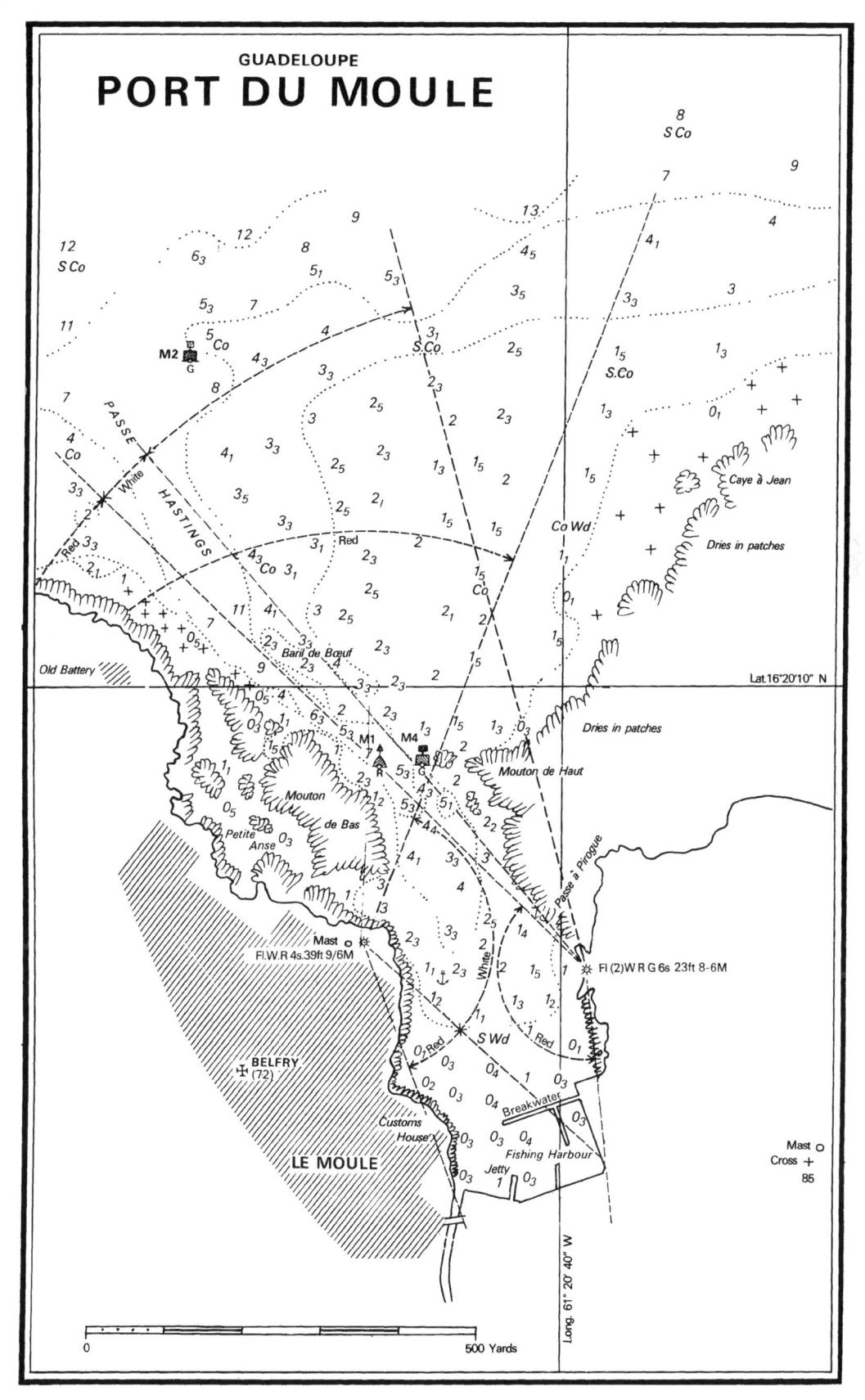

Chart 45   Port du Moule   Depths in fathoms and feet

The wind also can come directly out of the north during those months. Both of these factors would conspire to make a large power vessel unmanageable in restricted quarters. I have attempted a visit some four times now, but I have always been rebuffed by the weather and the swell. However, Hank Strauss of *Doki* reported that he was most intrigued by the harbor when he sailed in during the summer of 1972. He cautioned, though, that it should be attempted only when the rollers are not running.

In April 1993, I discovered that the ever-adventurous Hans Hoff of *Fandango* took this 90-foot Rhodes-designed motorsailer into Moule. He reported that he had had no problem—just followed the range. Once inside, he rounded up, dropped anchor in shoal water as close as possible to the reef, backed down on the anchor, and launched his dinghy. His ever-faithful mate, Eddy, ran a line off to one of the big ship anchors embedded in the reef to windward. Then he ran a stern line to the bollard over on the town side. He pretty much blocked the harbor, but Hans said the fishermen didn't seem to mind. They just ducked under his bow line, waved at him, and headed out.

Once you have identified the town of Le Moule, pick up the light tower on the eastern side of the harbor. Bring this to a bearing of 150° magnetic and run in on this bearing until the old battery is abeam to port, then bear off to 180° magnetic to pass to leeward of Baril de Boeuf, which has only 15 feet of water over it—the channel has 35 feet or more. Hold this course for about 100 yards, then harden up to 145° to pass between the buoys. Round up and anchor anywhere you like in the inner harbor. This definitely calls for a Bahamian moor or a bow line tied to shore with a stern anchor out. Otherwise, you will be swung onto the reefs when the current reverses.

In March 1992, when we were there, the inner buoys were in place and the light towers were there, but the sea buoy was missing. Considering its exposed location, I suspect it often is torn adrift! Under no circumstances should you attempt to follow one of the small fishing boats in, since they snake their way through chinks in the reefs that will not tolerate deeper-draft boats.

Once anchored, you might consider taking a diverting side trip via dinghy to the head of the harbor and on up the river, which extends well into the center of Grande Terre. Along the way are the skeletal remains of the once-flourishing sugar-cane industry.

The town of Le Moule itself is not without interest. An old battery, off the beaten track on the west side, is definitely worth exploring. Lying on the ground alongside the battery are two cannons—among the largest muzzle-loading cannons I have ever seen in the Eastern Caribbean! They are a full nine feet long, with a bore diameter of nine inches. How many pounds would that be? Maybe 48? With guns like that, Le Moule must have been a strategic port in its day!

Nowadays, it is a picturesque town that time has passed by—rather like the French Antilles of 30 years ago. There are a number of good restaurants, which obviously cater to local Guadeloupians, not to tourists.

South Coast of Guadeloupe

SAINTE MARIE

(Chart 46; II A-28, A-281, A-3, A-4)

From Bas Terre, you might admire the perfect shelter offered here by the two rows of reefs and detached coral heads, but it seems to be a flip of the coin as to whether or not you can gain entrance by sea. I know of two yachts that have sailed in successfully, yet townspeople talk of three yachts lost there within six months. The Lemarie salvage tug, based in Pointe-à-Pitre, is kept busy with yachts that ground out in this area. If the sun is high and the water clear, you might feel bold enough to venture around the numerous reefs. Reports are that the entrance is buoyed, but also that it often is murky. The rain squalls that frequently blot out the town also flood the rivers, which in turn carry mud into the harbor—with the result that you cannot see the reefs. It is a reach in (and a reach out), and there is anchoring anywhere the depth looks good. Le Gros Loup gives excellent shelter from the sea, providing a beautiful, cool anchorage.

As each year goes by, and more and more yachts flock to the Caribbean, adventurous yachtsmen are going farther and farther off "the beaten track." In March 1992, as we sailed south from Pointe-à-Pitre, from Frégate de Haut to Sainte Marie, we continually spotted masts of boats tucked away behind the reefs. This looks like a new area ripe for exploration. I would not try it, however, without the aid of a detailed French chart or the new Imray-Iolaire Chart A-282 (available 1993).

POINTE-A-PITRE

(Chart 47; II A-28, A-3, A-4)

Guadeloupe's main city and the capital of the French West Indies. The harbor is well buoyed, well lighted, and well sheltered. Best of all, you no longer

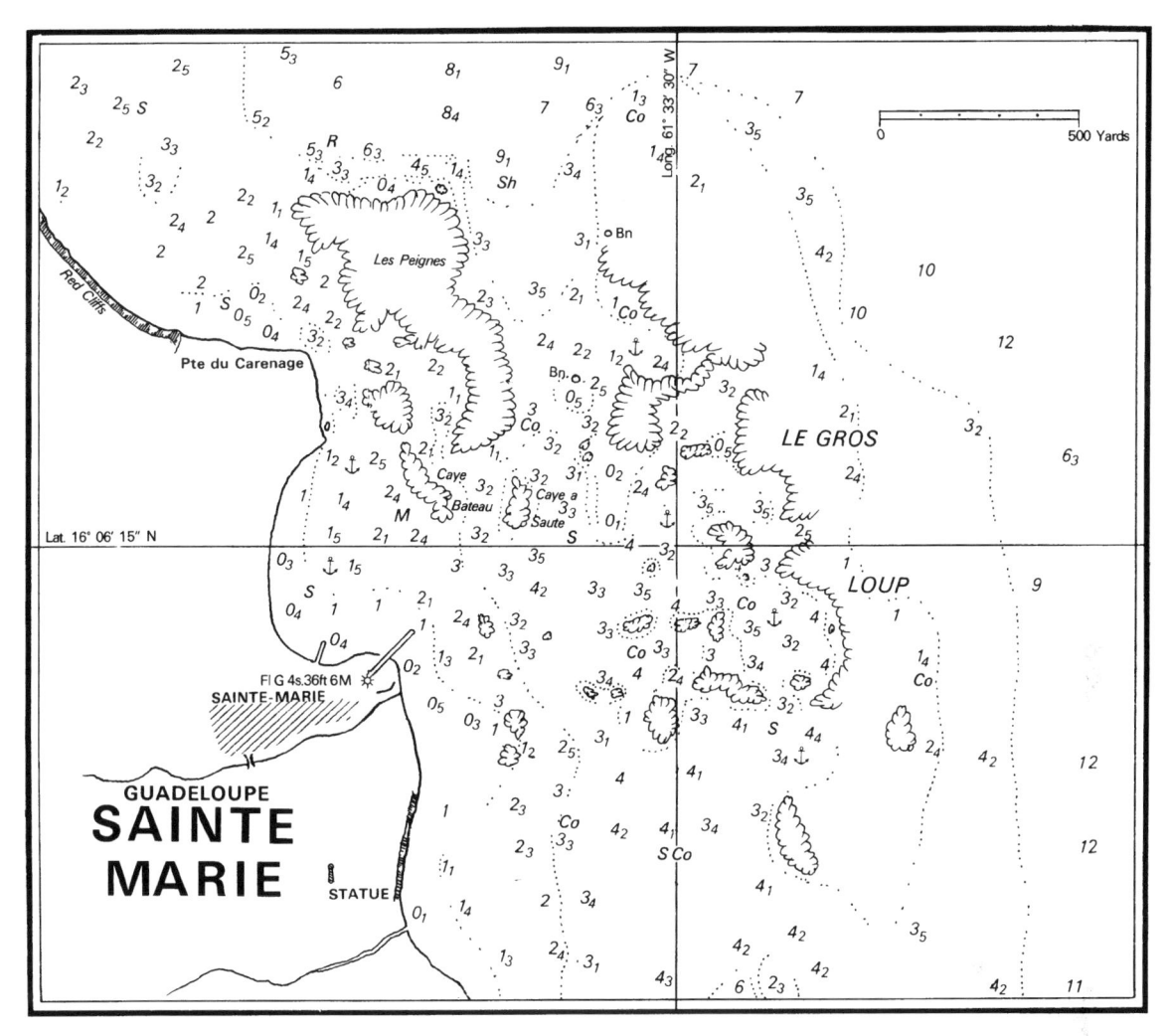

Chart 46 Sainte Marie   Depths in fathoms and feet

have to anchor in the filthy, noisy, commercial harbor—a place beset with pilferage problems (plus it used to have the smoke and stink from the now-abandoned sugar factory). Instead, there is the Bas-du-Fort Marina (described below).

The entrance to Pointe-à-Pitre is very deep and buoyed, but buoys are placed precisely at the end of the shoals they mark, so that it is impossible to cut them even by a few feet, and the channel is so narrow that if a ship is going through it, there is no room left for a yacht.

Two things about entering Pointe-à-Pitre are worth mentioning:

1. The white 13-mile range lights at Monroux and Pointe Fouillole that line up on a bearing of north magnetic are visible only 2° either side of the bearing. Thus, they will be invisible if you are not bang-on the range. Furthermore, the rear light is only 20 feet higher than the near one, so it is difficult to line them up from the deck of a yacht.

2. On the outer approaches of Pointe-à-Pitre, two miles south of the harbor entrance, is a series of buoys for the main deepwater shipping channel, which yachtsmen generally would ignore. However, at the northwest section of this channel is a shoal spot east of the channel with only 10 feet of water; avoid this area, because the Atlantic swell can produce a dangerous breaking sea over the shoal. And in the crystal-clear water, the bottom can look awfully close to the top.

Pointe-à-Pitre has much to offer. First of all, it has the Lemarie clan, which used to operate a pictur-

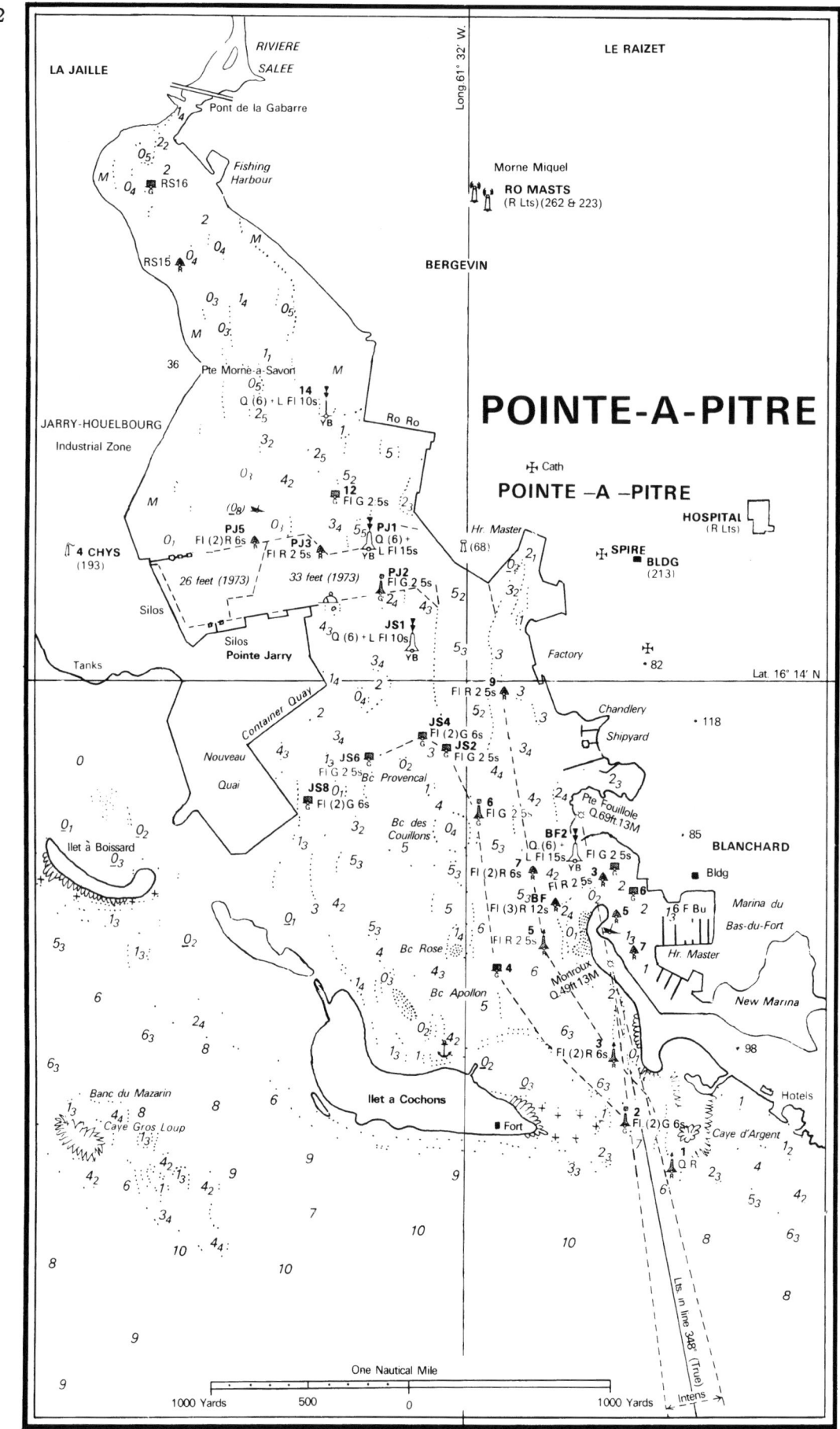

Chart 47   Pointe-à-Pitre   Depths in fathoms and feet

esque and friendly marina just north of Pointe Fouillole. Pierre was a French Canadian from Quebec and his wife and five sons helped him run the business. The marina is pretty much closed down now—because of the new one at Bas-du-Fort and because Pierre, after a lifetime at sea, was killed in a car accident. (Seamen should stay at sea!) But the sons still run a thriving salvage business. Their small tug (only 16 feet long) with a 120-hp diesel and a huge prop is kept busy pulling people off the reefs at Sainte Marie and Petit Havre. After they rescue you, the Lemaries can haul your boat in their dry dock—which can handle up to 120 feet—and fix whatever needs fixing. They can be contacted on channel 16 or by telephone: 903447. Next to them is Chantier Naval Forbon (telephone: 832134), which has two small slipways and a dry dock under construction. Alongside these two high-tech yards is Club Angelina, where an old-fashioned French boatbuilder still turns out the traditional Saintes-style boats with frames cut from natural crooks.

The traditional Saintes fishing boats have gone by the board, and now they are all powered by huge outboards, but the old design lives on as a racing class. They are about 21 feet overall, with a short bowsprit; high, flared bow; slack bilges; a fairly deep keel; and a draft of about 3 1/2 feet. Most have no outside ballast, but rather ballast blocks cast to fit in the bottom of the bilge. Stability is provided by four or five men hiking out with hiking straps. The boats are magnificently constructed and have such a high-gloss finish that they look like fiberglass. All are supported by clubs or local businesses. While in the Saintes, we watched eight of the boats racing, and when I went to Club Angelina to buy a piece of wood for our sailing dinghy, *Sinbad*, I saw the racing schedule—a match-racing series that had three professional, high-priced French yachtsmen competing against the locals. Unfortunately, we missed the series—I imagine it would have been most interesting. (See chapter 4 for more on these original and exciting craft.)

The new marina at Bas-du-Fort is easy to spot when entering from the south. It is the first cove on the right-hand side of the channel and is well buoyed and well lighted; you can even enter at night. It has an impressive variety of facilities: fuel, water, electricity, showers, telephone, telex, a number of good marine-supply stores, a sail-repair operation (Atelier Voileril), charter agencies, brokers, electronics repair, a 30-ton (but rather sick-looking) Travelift, a whole string of excellent restaurants, a small but well-equipped supermarket, and dockage space for about 600 boats. You can contact TCS Ship Chandler (telephone: 268050; fax: 268020) and deal with office director Baudouin Morat, who can supply duty-free beer, wine, liquor, and cigarettes—which, on the French islands, is a considerable saving. I have never done business with him myself, but if he is half as good as Philippe Vatier in Martinique, it would be well worth contacting him.

The entrance channel at Bas-du-Fort allegedly is 10 1/2 feet, and that same draft seems to be available at the outer docks; inner docks get shoaler. If you have a deep-draft boat, I recommend going alongside the fuel dock and inquiring where there is a berth with enough water for your boat.

From the marina, you can get a taxi to town—or walk outside the marina and pick up a bus. If you would rather go by water, it is a mere 10-minute dinghy trip. Once there, however, you have a problem. The Yacht Club de Guadeloupe extends guest privileges to absolutely no one. Only club members may use the facilities or tie a dinghy up to the dinghy float. This attitude is rather astonishing, especially since Guadeloupe is fast becoming a yachting center. At the moment, the club feels like a morgue; if they would consider extending guest privileges to yachtsmen who are members of other clubs, they might well have a vibrant and probably profitable club and bar.

So, you have to tie up your dinghy just south of the yacht club, off the harbormaster's office, then walk to town through the main dock area. The dinghy will be perfectly safe, but it is a long walk back with supplies. Straight ahead from the dockyard, on rue Schoelcher, is a market where you can get fresh produce. Continue along the same street and you will find small butcher shops selling veal and pork roasts, legs of lamb, *escalope de veau*, and the like. There is also a produce and fish market right at the north end of the basin near the abandoned sugar factory. Local freighters no longer come in there, so I think it would be perfectly safe to take your dinghy right up to the market, tie it up, load your produce into the dinghy, and leave it there while you are off in town doing more shopping. Across the street is the Office du Tourisme, which has all sorts of interesting FREE brochures on Guadeloupe and its offlying islands. (The material is in both French and English.)

For one-stop shopping, however—everything from soup to nuts-and-bolts—take a bus, a taxi, or a *taxi collective* (one that runs a set route and you buy a seat) to Mammoth, one of the biggest supermarkets I have ever seen. (While shopping for food in this emporium, I even bought Trich a terrific bikini for US$3.50! The place even takes credit cards!)

Mammoth is closed from 1300 to 1500, but that's no problem, because you can leave your unfinished shopping there and go across the street to eat lunch in an excellent small French restaurant: good food, reasonable prices, personable owner, and immaculate bathrooms. The shopping mall surrounding Mammoth has banks, boutiques, and much more; a stop in Guadeloupe is not complete without a visit to this area.

Another plus for Pointe-à-Pitre is that prices are substantially lower than in Fort de France in Martinique. There are numerous good restaurants scattered all over town that obviously cater not to the tourist but to the average Frenchman, who has high standards for food and wine. Also, the open-air market, though not as picturesque as the one in Martinique, is considerably cheaper.

On rue Gaspail is ElectroNautic, Henri Martin's fabulous marine-supply establishment. It is very convenient, because it is in the cove north of the old sugar factory, and you can go there by dinghy en route to town or by taxi. You can walk in the back entrance of the establishment and see literally hundreds of outboards, plus Del Quay dories, Boston Whalers stacked up by the half-dozen, Sailfish by the dozen—you name it, he has it. He also carries the complete set of French charts for the area. But remember, if you are in Martinique and headed for Guadeloupe, buy your Guadeloupe charts in Martinique, since Henri, because of the demand, may be low in stock for the Guadeloupe charts.

ElectroNautic also carries the Street guides and the complete line of Imray-Iolaire charts. The manager, Mr. French, is very helpful and speaks excellent English.

In the marina is a chandlery called Karokera (telephone: 909096; fax: 909749), which is one of the better ones in the Eastern Caribbean. The manager, Mr. Guisbert, speaks superb English and is most accommodating. He, too, maintains the full line of Street guides and Imray-Iolaire charts.

When in Pointe-à-Pitre and heading north to Antigua, the logical route is through the Rivière Salée, as long as your boat draws 6 1/2 feet or less. Before you make your decision, inquire locally about the depths at the northern end of the river, since shoaling is always a problem. Who knows when the river will be dredged again.

Details on negotiating the river from the northern end were given above under Grand Cul-de-Sac Marin. Here's what you'll need to know about heading up the river from the southern end.

The day before you plan to go through the river, head north through Pointe-à-Pitre Harbor until you are north of town. Anchor in the dredged area just south of the river estuary off the fishing port. Be sure to leave the green buoy at the southern end of the river to the west, or you will go aground. (See Grand Cul-de-Sac Marin section for discussion of bridge hours and traffic patterns.)

Once through the bridge, anchor and wait until you have enough light. In the winter, this means about 30 minutes after the bridge's 0530 opening. Proceed through the river, but go slowly when exiting the northern end so that if you touch bottom (it is soft mud), you can back off. Follow the buoys through Grand Cul-de-Sac Marin (reverse the directions given in that section). Once clear of the sea buoy, the rhumb-line course to English Harbour is 355° magnetic—39 miles—but allow for the westward set of the current and your leeway. Use Imray-Iolaire Chart A-3, as Chart A is not the proper scale to plot this course easily. This should be an easy reach rather than the tight reach it is likely to be from Deshaies to English Harbour.

Augie Hollen points out that if your boat is too deep to go through the Rivière Salée, you can have a wonderful day's expedition by dinghy—either a dinghy with an outboard or a good rowing dinghy with auxiliary sail. Pack bug repellents (just in case), ingredients for a picnic lunch, a bottle of wine (and also some ice water, since wine is great but does not quench the thirst). Chug on through the river and on out into the northern reef area, with all its rivers, creeks, birds, and fish. However, DO NOT make this trip on a Saturday or Sunday, as that is when all the powerboats in Guadeloupe tear northward through the river at top speed, headed for a day of swimming and diving in Grand Cul-de-Sac Marin. Then, of course, they return along the same route in the evening. All this makes the dinghy trip hair-raising, uncomfortable, and dangerous!

LA GRANDE BAIE

(II A, A-28; French 3375)

Southeast of Pointe-à-Pitre, this is a good sheltered anchorage as long as the wind is in the northeast. With the wind from the southeast, it becomes rough and uncomfortable. It shoals very gradually, so feel your way in. This area has long been eyed for development, so by the time you arrive, there may be a marina.

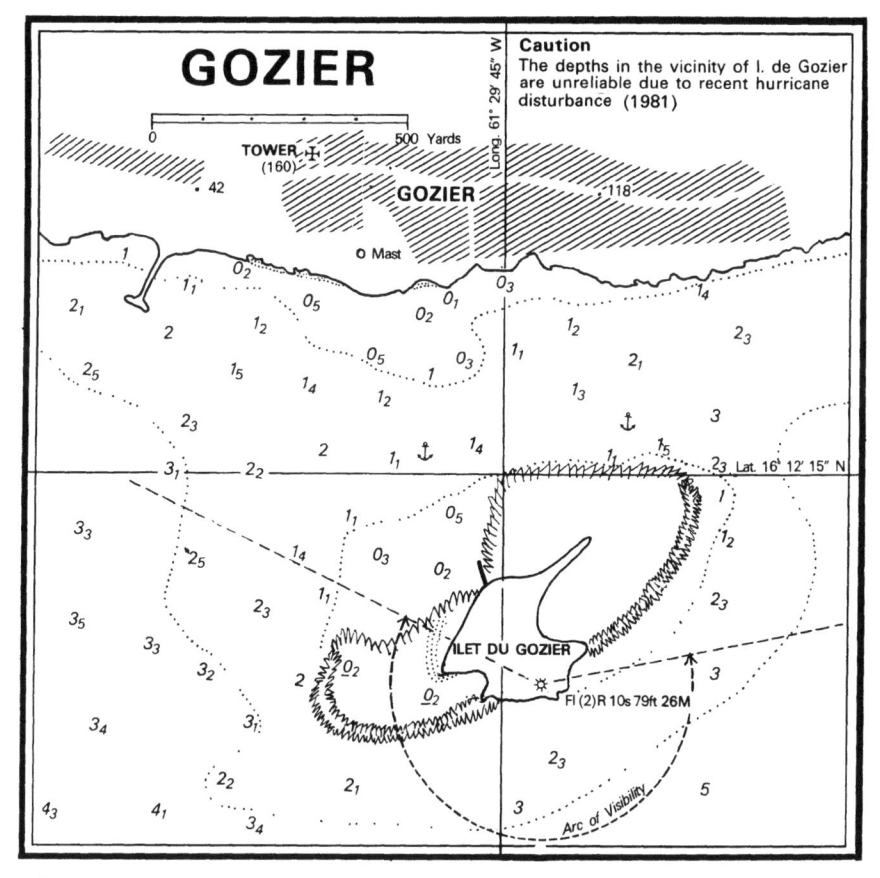

Chart 48 Gozier   Depths in fathoms and feet

GOZIER

(Chart 48; II A-28, A-3, A-4)

Four miles southeast of Pointe-à-Pitre lies this excellent anchorage and its surprisingly bustling village. The mainland and Ilet du Gozier give complete shelter to the northwest of the island on a sand bottom. There is plenty of water, with gradual shoaling. Feel your way in. The farther east you go, the less swell you will encounter. There is good snorkeling, and a number of hotels line the beach. It is only a short taxi ride to several towns along this part of the coast, and night life is active. This anchorage is also handy to the airport. If you anchor fairly far offshore behind the reef, there should be plenty of breeze and no bugs. Note that the current runs to the east at times, so you can become tide rode rather than wind rode—use a Bahamian moor. Several hurricanes have passed nearby, and Hurricane Hugo went overhead in 1989, so the area between Gozier and Ilet du Gozier has been subject to change in recent years. In the 1980s, we sailed *Iolaire* out through the eastern entrance (*Iolaire* drawing seven feet six inches) with no trouble. Whether or not that is still possible, I am not quite sure. I recommend that you approach from the west, anchor, and check the depths to the east via dinghy. Incidentally, for those who want an overall suntan, the beaches on Ilet du Gozier are dress-optional.

PETIT HAVRE

(Chart 49; II A-28, A-281, A-3, A-4)

There are other small harbors along the south coast of Guadeloupe that look enticing and reasonably accessible (at least on the charts), but I have found few sailing people who have visited them. However, Petit Havre, 2 1/2 miles east of Gozier, comes well recommended as an excellent anchorage in the winter months, when the wind is north of east and the swell is from a northerly direction. In the spring and summer, though, I would be careful, since if the wind goes into the south, the harbor will not be good.

The shoal off the coast here may or may not be

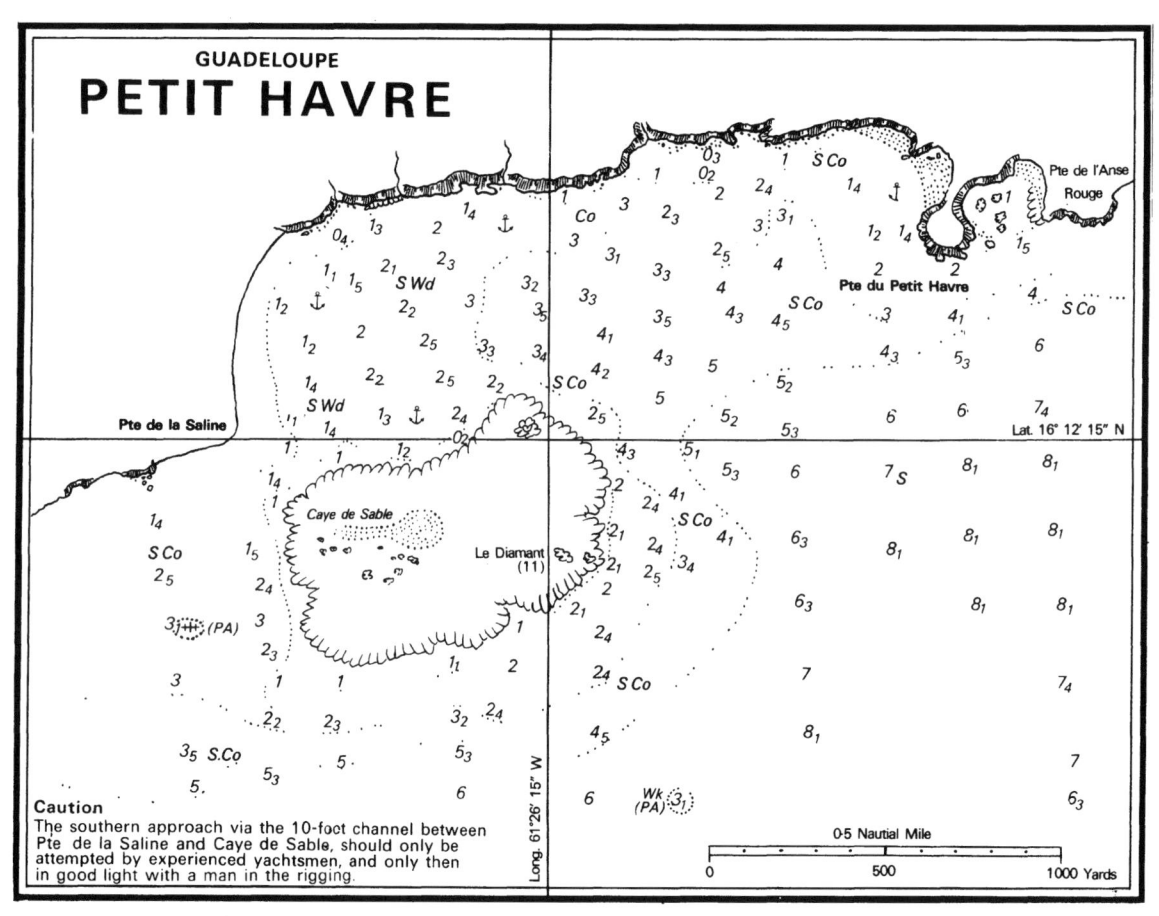

Chart 49 Petit Havre

Depths in fathoms and feet

visible. In 1983, most of it had disappeared because of ground-swell action; when you get here, it may look like an island again. In any case, there is a good anchorage in nine or 10 feet of water west of the shoal's northern rock. Tuck up close under the shoal; you should have calm water as long as the wind is north of east.

SAINTE-ANNE

(Chart 50; II A-28, A-281, A-3, A-4)

The harbor of this attractive town looks as if it were perfectly protected by the surrounding reefs, but it is not secure when the wind is south of east. There are two entrances, and even some buoys, but you still should not enter it except when the sun is high. The eastern channel affords the best entrance and the western channel the best exit. Shoal-draft boats can sneak up behind the reef to the east and gain complete shelter, but deeper boats should regard the harbor only as a daytime stopping place.

A new breakwater has been built on the western end of the harbor to create shelter for fishermen. You will find five or possibly six feet of water inside—send the dinghy ahead and check. It should be excellent for a shoal-draft boat. Anchor on a Bahamian moor so you don't swing around and take up too much space. The breakwater has a road on top, but it is not really a dock, just a wide riprap jetty. You cannot lie alongside.

Sainte-Anne is not officially a port of entry, but gendarmes there seem quite content to receive a crew list and wish you a good day. A number of hotels boast dining rooms serving French cuisine. Ice is available, and a small market is held each day. The beach in front of the town is lined with the Saintes boats typical of the south coast of Guadeloupe.

This gorgeous beach stretches eastward for about half a mile, providing tourists with a popular resort spot and yachtsmen with an unbeatable opportunity for bikini research. The equally extensive reefs out-

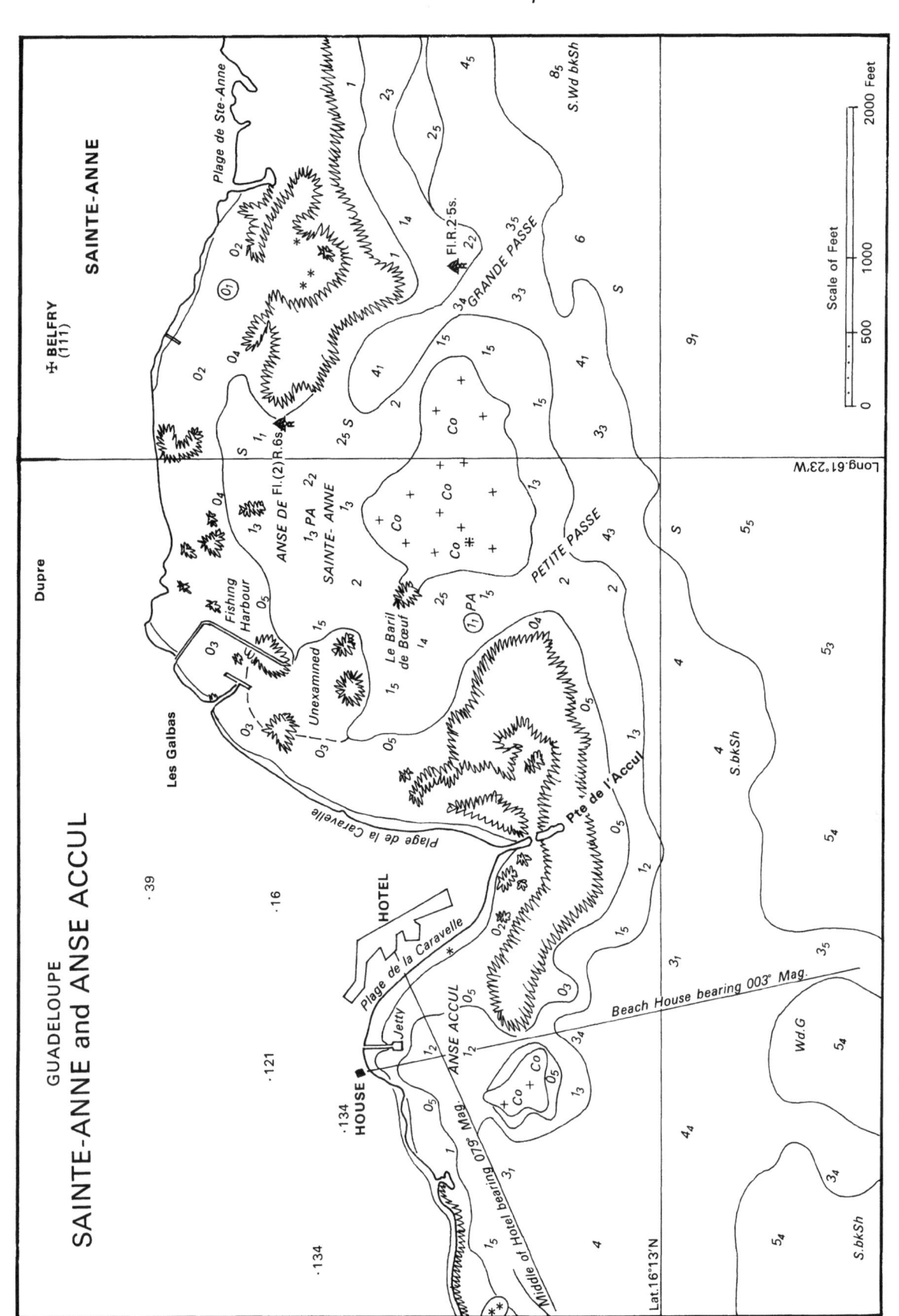

Chart 50 Anse Accul and Sainte-Anne

side offer outstanding diving. I have seen powerboats anchor off and fill up with fish in a few minutes.

ANSE ACCUL

(Chart 50; II A-28, A-281, A-3, A-4)

At the head of Anse Accul, high on a promontory, is a large building, formerly the Hotel Caravelle, now a Club Med. West of this point is a good anchorage. You enter by lining up the beach house with the large water tower on the hill behind it—range 003° magnetic. You can also come in from the west on a bearing of 079° magnetic on the middle of the hotel.

Club Med runs a busy sailboarding school, as well as all the usual Club Med activities. Remember, though, that the club is private. Don't go ashore and try to use its facilities unless you have been invited.

SAINT FRANÇOIS

(Chart 51; II A-28, A-3, A-4)

This small village-cum-harbor is frequented mainly by French fishermen from La Désirade who come to sell their catch. Like Petit Havre and Sainte-Anne, the harbor is open to the south, and therefore should be viewed with a jaundiced eye in spring and summer. In the winter, however, it ought to be comfortable.

The harbor's anchorage is small in the extreme. Buoys on the outer reef lead to the inner anchorage. To enter the anchorage, pick up the outer buoy, pass it close aboard to starboard, and steer 338° magnetic. There should be another buoy marking an inner reef. Round up when past this reef.

But why bother with all that? You can anchor behind Passe Champagne (see below) and come down to Saint François via dinghy. The dock at St. François is an excellent place to pick up fresh fish and lobster as it comes in on the fishing boats. The fishermen sell it right there or cart it off to one of the many nearby restaurants.

PASSE CHAMPAGNE

(Chart 51; II A-28, A-3, A-4)

This used to be a great spot for getting away from it all. Now it has a big resort complex—the Hotel Méridien—and a well-appointed marina. So now it's a different sort of place, but still worth a visit.

Use Chart 51 and Imray-Iolaire Chart A-28. To enter the pass, stand to the east until you can look all the way back down the channel. Run in on a bearing of 300° magnetic, leaving the outermost buoy to port and the buoy at the end of the eastern reef to starboard. *Do not cut it too close.* Round up around the next buoy to anchor, but watch out for shoal water between that buoy and the third one.

When going into the marina, use Imray-Iolaire Chart A-28, keep north of the buoys, and ease on in; nine feet can be squeezed in at high water.

The marina is either a long walk or a short taxi ride from the town of Saint François—but, as mentioned above, why bother? Take your dinghy around inside the reef and tie up to the fishermen's wharf; take along your stern anchor to hold the dinghy off. At the market, you can buy fresh fruit and vegetables and fresh fish from the fishermen. In the marina is a friendly restaurant that allowed us to freeze ice in buckets when all the ice factories on the island were on strike.

In and around the marina—as well as in town—are numerous small restaurants, as this area has developed as one of the major sailboarding centers in the Caribbean. On our last visit, we counted 60 sailboards inside and outside of the reef—there probably were even more that we didn't see.

There are many small apartment-type hotels that look like very basic accommodation—but what more would a sailboarder need? The deluxe Hotel Méridien is part of the French chain, but, unlike most chain hotels, it has character and individuality—huge porches, plenty of "gingerbread" trim, excellent landscaping, and all kinds of attractive boutiques. The planners succeeded well in duplicating the traditional French West Indian architecture and decor. The hotel's list of activities is vast: diving, swimming lessons, tennis, golf, and even an ultralight flying boat that buzzes around the harbor offering rides. (Flying instructions are also an option.) The sight of the pilot and passenger sitting in the plane's open framework is reminiscent of nothing so much as pre-World War I photographs.

The hotel has even piled some sand on a small reef just offshore and erected a small gazebo. Looks like no bar service there, though—I guess you just have to "bring your own."

Islands off the Coast of Guadeloupe

LA DESIRADE

(Chart 52; II A-28, A-3, A-4)

The name of this island means "desired one," but why anyone should call it that is beyond me. It has little or no fresh water, no timber, and its

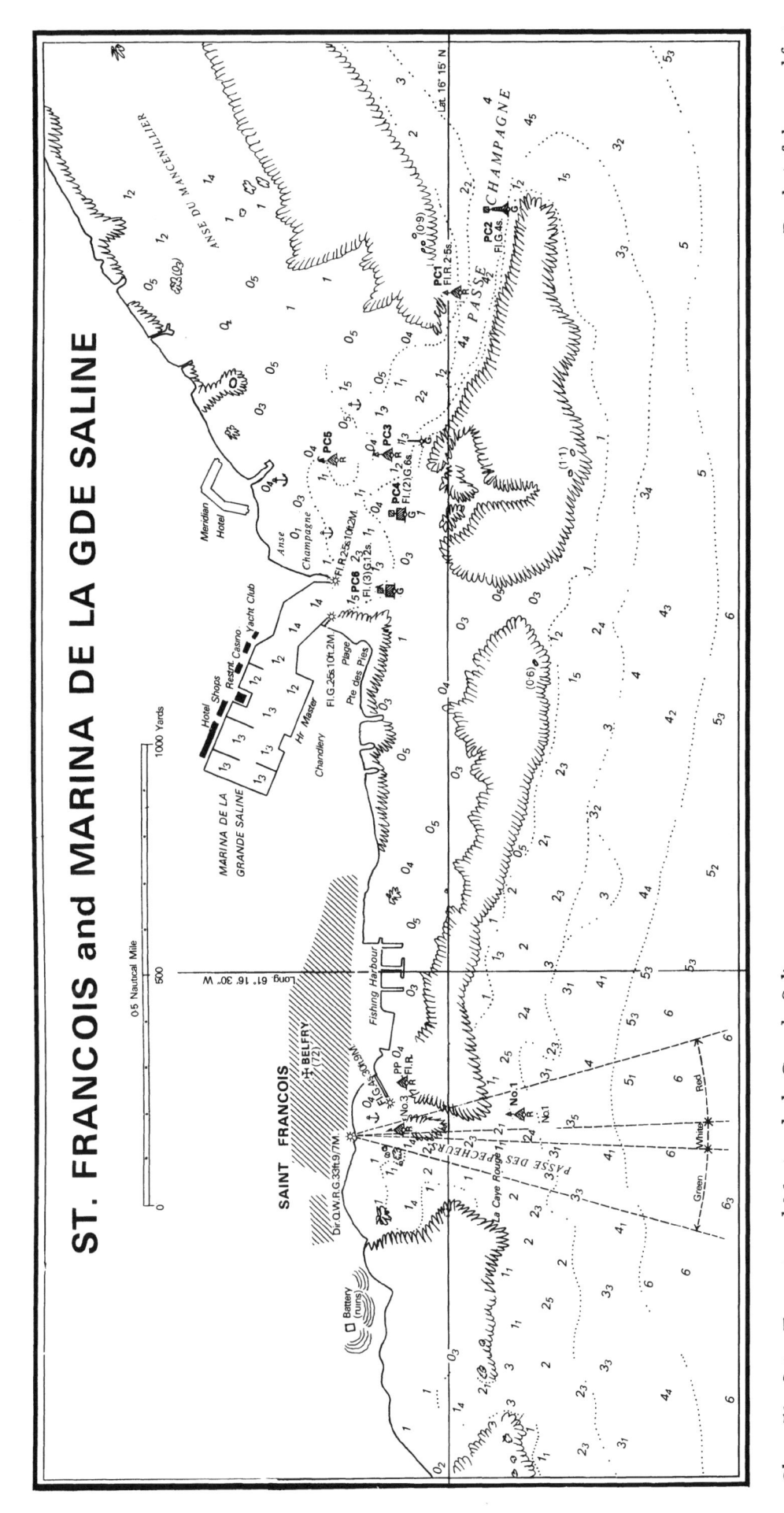

Chart 51 Saint François and Marina de la Grande Saline

permanent residents just barely get by. Maybe it is just as well that none of the French charts cover the island in complete detail. French 7102 at least is helpful to some degree in that it carries a plan of Grande Anse. The anchorage at Anse à Galet is long and narrow, lying in the same direction as the wind and sea. I don't think it would give much protection in normal trade-wind weather. And when the northerly ground swell starts rolling in, forget it.

I understand that if you have a shoal-draft boat, it is now possible to visit Grande Anse, on the south coast. The channel is buoyed. Leave both buoys to starboard—axis of the channel is about 348° magnetic. Proceed with caution and use eyeball navigation. According to the latest French chart, you can take five feet into the shallowest part of the channel, while the basin has been dredged to 6 1/2 feet. Inside the basin, you should find smooth water and a comfortable anchorage. Certainly this spot is off the beaten track for most yachtsmen. My information on this is secondhand, so I suggest that you heave-to in the outer entrance to the harbor by the outermost buoy and send the dinghy ahead to sound out the channel before attempting to enter.

The Pilot mentions another anchorage at the eastern end of the island—Baie Mahault—but cautions that it is accessible only with local knowledge.

The former lighthouse keeper on Petite Terre has kindly sent me some information on his neighbor to the north. La Désirade has a population of about 1,600, all of them fishermen and their families. There is only one road on the island, running along the south coast near the shore. Mahault has a restaurant, but no hotel. In the main town, Grande Anse, on the south coast, is a small inn that reputedly serves good French food. My informant agrees that only shoal-draft boats should enter the harbors—and then only with local advice. I suggest that if you really want to see the island, either fly over to it from Guadeloupe or charter a launch headed there from Petite Terre. The fastest one makes the trip in about 35 minutes.

Since the late 1970s, there has been a rumor that a marina would be built in Baie Mahault, but nothing has happened. Breakwaters have been built for

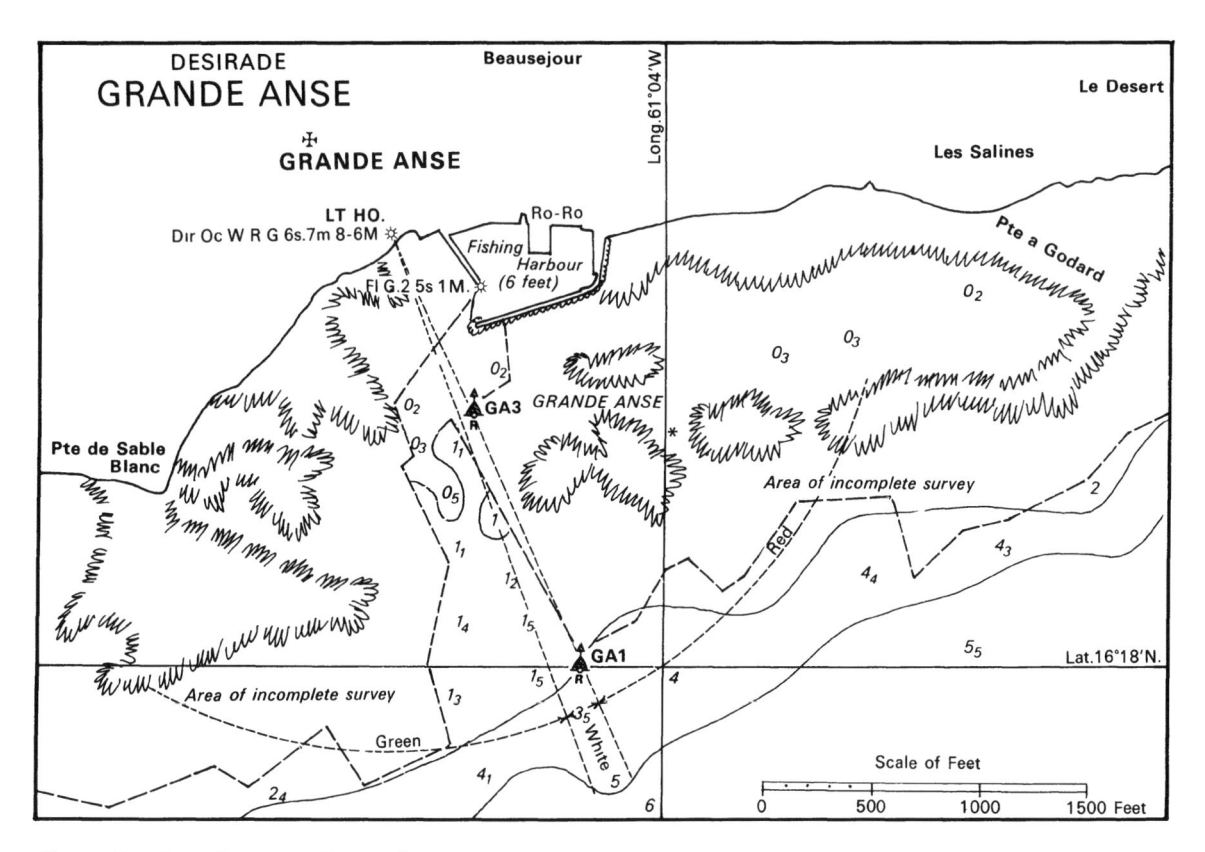

Chart 52 Grande Anse, Désirade

Depths in fathoms and feet

the fishing fleet, but the basin inside is only three or four feet deep—not a place for visiting yachts. There is always a ferry or a fishing boat in the basin, sometimes even a seaplane. A marina may never be built!

ILES DE LA PETITE TERRE

(Chart 53; II A-28, A-3, A-4)

Petite Terre is one of the most attractive anchorages I know in the Lesser Antilles—if the weather is right. It is well known and much appreciated by the French yachtsmen from Guadeloupe who visit on weekends, but no one goes there during the week except fishermen. When we first visited here around 1970, we were told we were the first foreign vessel ever to have anchored among these islands!

The islets show up quite well on French 3419, and Chart 53 provides more details. The western entrance to the channel between the islands is completely swept by breakers in heavy weather, and the eastern entrance is blocked by coral reefs. Don't attempt to enter in a northerly swell. Even in good weather, don't try it unless the light is perfect. Stand in on port tack with the western end of Terre de Haut bearing 137° magnetic until the break in the reef appears about due south. Make for this break, head south until the lighthouse bears 137° magnetic, and eyeball eastward into the anchorage.

There is nine feet of water between the coral heads, but the coral heads stick up a minimum of three feet from the bottom, so stay over the white sand as you work eastward. Favor the north side of the inner channel, where the coral heads disappear and the depth increases to around 15 feet. Continue eastward until you spot a small

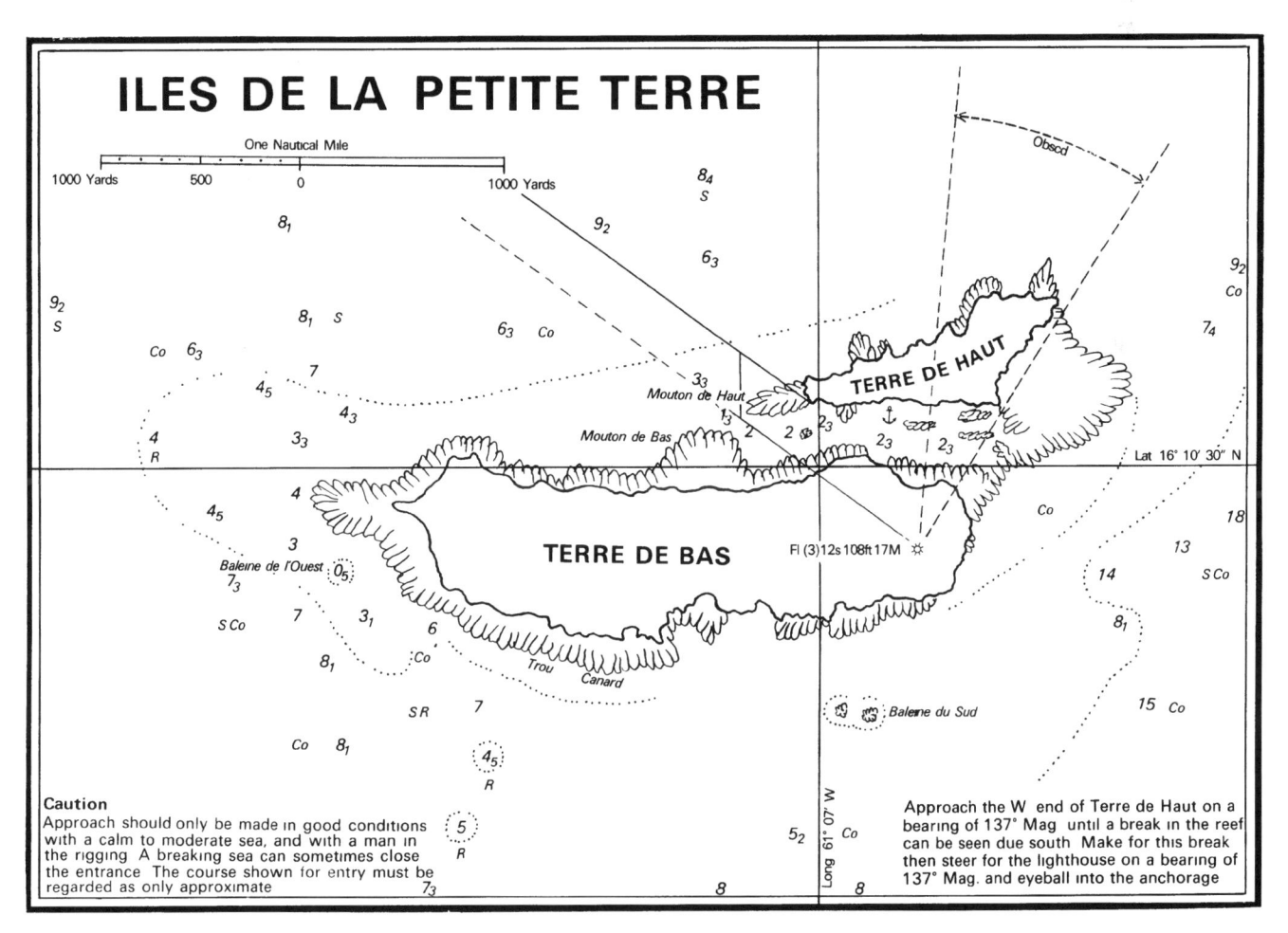

Chart 53 Iles de la Petite Terre   Depths in fathoms and feet

white-sand beach on the port hand. The beach is steep-to, practically vertical. Drop a bow anchor, run a stern line ashore, and warp in as close as you dare. If you anchor from the stern and run the bow in, you probably will be able to jump right onto dry land.

Naturally, there is great snorkeling between the two islands, and there is fine fishing on the exposed outer shore of Terre de Haut. A path conveniently leads from the white-sand beach to the outer shore. There's no dinghy landing out there, though, so it's a case of swimming from shore, catching your fish, and swimming back with it.

For those who like to explore ruins and see lighthouses, a tour of Terre de Bas is a must. The view from the top of the lighthouse is incomparable, but the light has been automated, so the tower is now locked and bolted—and you can no longer climb up and feast your eyes on the magnificent view. (For what it's worth, the structure is reputed to be the oldest lighthouse in the Western Hemisphere still in continuous operation, dating back to 1835. La Désirade Light is older, having been built in 1828, but it has since been completely rebuilt.) It is interesting to note that in the early nineteenth century, the French erected lighthouses on dangerous landfalls, whereas the British have yet to establish a light on Barbuda, despite the fact that the number of wrecks around Barbuda is well along in the hundreds. (They only established a light on Anguilla about five years ago.) Petite Terre's former lighthouse keeper insisted that there were no wrecks around either La Désirade or Petite Terre.

Terre de Bas once was a privately owned estate. The ruins used to be visible from the lighthouse tower, but now it is difficult to conceive of the extent of the estate unless you fly over the island in the ultralight seaplane from the Hotel Méridien. You might, however, be able to get a good view from your boat's mast in a bosun's chair. If you do go exploring here, be sure to get back to the boat before dusk, as the mosquitoes are rife. In the old days, the lighthouse keepers used to build huge bonfires during the rainy season to keep the mosquitoes at bay.

ILES DES SAINTES: TERRE D'EN HAUT

(Chart 54; II A-28, A-281, A-3, A-4)

The popular archipelago of islands 10 miles south of Guadeloupe is best approached and explored with Imray-Iolaire Chart A-281, which is the right size to use easily. There are two main islands, Terre d'en Haut and Terre d'en Bas, rising 1,000 feet out of the sea with numerous rugged peaks, plus countless little rocks and cays. There is an excellent anchorage off the town of Bourg des Saintes, lots of beaches, and attractive settlements populated by fishermen. These islands are a prime vacation spot for Guadeloupians, since the climate is always wonderful. But the breeze and dryness create the area's one major problem—lack of fresh water.

In each of the coves, you used to see the distinctive Saintes boats, with their high, flaring bow; low, heart-shaped stern; long, low mainsail; and genoa jib. At sea in the worst weather, they lay hove-to under oars, one man holding the bow to the sea and the remainder of the crew tending lines.

Today, unfortunately, you have to look hard to find these distinctive heart-shaped-stern fishing boats with a sailing rig, although there are a few around. The boats are still built in the old style: They still have the flaring bows and the well-fitted grown frames. But aft, to prevent the boats from squatting under the weight of the big, high-powered outboards that have replaced oars and sails, the beautifully proportioned heart-shaped stern has been replaced by a wider semicircular stern.

The boats still catch fish, but it is almost impossible to buy fresh fish in the Saintes. At the end of the day, all the fishermen sell their catch to a "buy boat" that lies in the main harbor. Then they take their money and purchase hard, dry salt cod that has been shipped from Nova Scotia! The reason they never bring fish ashore is that the boats are worked on shares, and each man is afraid that if anyone takes home a fish, it might unbalance the shares. Hence, they sell the catch for cash and split the proceeds.

Although the Saintes fishing boats are nearly extinct, their spirit lives on in the fleet of racing boats that are direct descendants of the old design and compete frequently in this part of the Antilles. In February 1992, when we were in the Saintes, we saw some of these craft racing. I noticed that the crews were young, athletic fishermen but the skippers were old, grizzled fishermen who appeared to be only two years younger than God. Obviously, these veterans were the experts on local wind shifts and tidal eddies. (More about these boats appeared earlier, especially in chapter 4.)

A small hotel that overlooked Bourg des Saintes used to be run by Al Cassino, who left Brooklyn in the early 1930s. He ran the hotel and the power plant, went through several wives, and sired countless children. For some reason, he and the priest

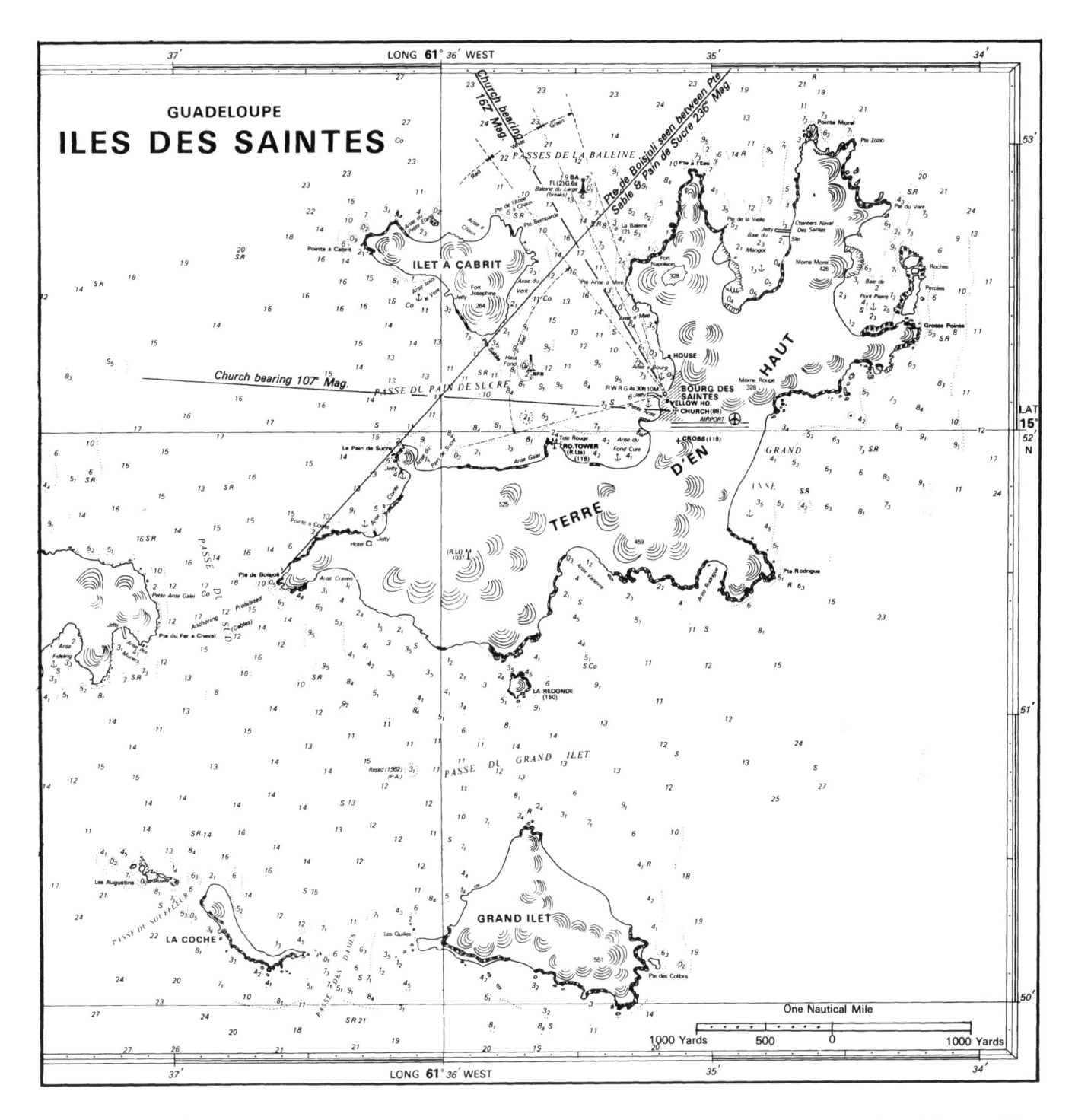

Chart 54   Terred'en Haut, Iles des Saintes

Depths in fathoms and feet

(the island's two most prominent figures) had a running battle going for years—they spoke to each other only through intermediaries. There was always an air of mystery about Al, but he never discussed his past with me. After he died, I found out that he had been on the losing side of a gang war just at the end of Prohibition, and a contract was out to fit him with cement shoes. He decided that the climate in the Saintes was much more salubrious than in the States, and he took hold in his new land so quickly that no stranger had a chance to approach without his knowing about it. When, indeed, "friends" arrived, they invariably found Al standing at the dock waiting to "greet" them. Instead of dying with weighted boots, he expired peacefully in bed.

At the head of the dock in Bourg des Saintes is a small restaurant, the Coq d'Or. With its balcony overlooking the harbor, this is a fantastic spot to sit and watch all the dockside activity. Along the main street that parallels the waterfront, you will find numerous small bars and restaurants. I wouldn't want to specify which one is best, but on the French islands almost all of the restaurants seem to be good—some are just a little better than others.

Underneath the Coq d'Or is a small bank that is open at very erratic hours. Not only that, but you cannot always withdraw money! They have a computer that seems to possess the infuriating characteristic of going completely functionless just when everyone crowds in and needs cash! However, all is not lost—you simply go to the post office, where you can obtain money against your MasterCard or Visa account! This is true throughout all of the West Indies, and it is a bit of information well worth remembering!

The majority of the larger houses are summer residences for the French from Guadeloupe, who come here to escape the heat and rain. There are a number of small grocery stores that are not large enough to stock a boat for a long cruise, but they do have the odds and ends that most cooks need. Excellent French bread is available, but you had better be there early, since it sells out quickly. Take cash, too, as it is not always cheap! In the old days, the bread was not so reliable. The first day it was excellent, the second day it was fine in soup, the third day it made a good wooden mallet, and on the fourth day you could drive nails with it!

The farther south you go in Bourg des Saintes, the cheaper the small grocery stores. The same is true of the restaurants. Those on the north end of town are by far the most chic and the most expensive. As you head southward, the restaurants become smaller, less pretentious, and, ultimately, less expensive.

Knowing the importance the French place on food, I imagine that you will still get excellent value for money despite outward appearances. A couple of the less expensive restaurants are quite difficult to find—a tiny sign, a little alleyway between a couple of nondescript houses, and—voilà—a cozy little two- or three-table porch overlooking the harbor. The kitchen won't look like much, but in the French Antilles, I have had some wonderful meals cooked in nothing but a couple of charcoal pots!

Except for outboard gas, fuel is unavailable in Terre d'en Haut unless you can make successful arrangements at the shipyard in Baie du Marigot (see below). You can, however, find fuel for both diesel engines and outboards in Anse des Muriers in Terre d'en Bas. Ice is strictly cubes—at considerable expense. Forget about water!

The main anchorage is off Bourg des Saintes, on the west coast of Terre d'en Haut. Its approaches are not difficult. If you enter west of Ilet à Cabrit, there are no dangers until Passe du Pain de Sucre, where the only hazard is Haut Fond, a pinnacle rock south of the eastern end of Ilet à Cabrit. This rock is well marked with a buoy. In approaching from the north and passing eastward of Ilet à Cabrit, there are the double dangers of Baleine du Large (just breaking) and La Baleine (two feet high). Chart 54 provides the ranges.

Baie du Marigot has a shipyard capable of hauling all but the biggest yachts. At the time it was built, I felt that a lot of money was being invested in the wrong place. This has proved true, as by 1992, the cradle looked very tired and the yard was almost bare. Adjacent to the shipyard is a derelict fish factory—again a large investment in the wrong place. I hate to think of how much money was wasted in these two ill-fated projects.

If you need to haul, then the yard may be worth investigating. A taxi will take you to Baie du Marigot, where you follow the signs for about half a mile on a path that is better suited for goats than people. (Instead of walking, you might try calling the shipyard at 895108 or 995315.)

From the sailmaker's standpoint, matters have retrogressed in the Saintes. In the 1980s, Michel LeDoz, a well-trained French sailmaker, was living here. He earned his reputation making sails for the likes of Eric Tabarly, Alain Colas, and other top French yachting pros. He decided to abandon the pressures of living in France and made a new home in the Saintes. As long ago as 1983, he was using a computer for sail design! This enabled him to calculate the sizes of all of the panels and build an entire sail without having to lay it all out for a final cutting.

However, he has now returned to France, and his place has been taken by a young sailmaker who works at Baie du Marigot (same phone number as the shipyard).

The best anchorage is north of the dock, in Anse à Bourg. Watch out for the shoal that extends out from the sunken ship whose bow projects out of the cliff. (She was going so fast when she hit the island that she went right through the mountain—or so it seems.) Anchor close to shore in three fathoms with plenty of scope; the bottom shelves off quite steeply. If it is blowing hard, put out two anchors; the gusts from the hills will cause you to sheer around badly. There is also an anchorage at Petite Anse, south of the jetty.

The northern anchorage is getting more and more crowded, so many boats now anchor south of the dock. The southern anchorage is acceptable—sand, good holding, and, except when the wind is from the north, it might be better than our original spot. However, old habits die slowly!

Take a crew list ashore to the gendarmerie, but don't tie up your dinghy to the main dock where it appears to be a dinghy landing. It isn't—we found that out the hard way. The ferry from Guadeloupe mashed our dinghy, and when we complained to the captain, he told us (in colorful French) where to put the shattered remains. We answered that if that was his attitude to visitors, we would complain to the ferry owner. He said *he* was the owner. We said, all right, then we would take the matter to the mayor. He said *he* was the mayor. When we applied for aid from the local constabulary, all this proved to be true. And, to add insult to injury, the sergeant threatened to throw us in jail if we continued arguing with the captain-owner-mayor—insulting a French official is a serious offense.

About a year after that incident, I anchored there again, but this time I pulled my dinghy up on the beach and walked to the gendarmerie. The same little sergeant was there. He took one look at me and immediately started ranting in French. From what I could gather, his point was that I had better behave myself or he would run me off the island. Gendarmes are very long in memory and very short in patience.

For those who have the courage, there is a small airport on Terre d'en Haut with regularly scheduled service to Guadeloupe. The runway undoubtedly is one of the world's shortest!

Years ago, we used to walk up to Fort Napoleon—a good, long hike—and "jimmy" our way into the fort, which for some reason was closed to the public. Definitely closed. After we had jimmied our way in four or five times, the gendarmes evidently figured out who was getting in. The next time, we were greeted at the dock by a gendarme who told us that if we went to the fort again, we would be locked up.

Now, though, the fort is open, buses go there regularly, and there are guided tours! It is a magnificent structure that was actually used through World War II, when French troops were stationed there.

The climb to the watchtower at the west end of town is a very strenuous one, but I have been told the view is well worth the effort. Take water.

BAIE DE PONT-PIERRE
(Chart 54; II A-281)

Another good jaunt is an all-day outing over to Baie de Pont-Pierre, where there is a beach that used to be deserted. You can also swim across to the island of Roches Percées and climb to the top. Lying on your stomach and looking straight down over the undercut cliff to the sea 100 feet below, with its awesome display of surge, will take away whatever breath you have left. Today the beach is popular on weekends and during the summer school holidays, but I am told it is quiet during the rest of the year.

In previous editions, and on old charts, you will see a warning about a rock with only four or five feet of water over it in the middle of the channel leading into Baie de Pont-Pierre. This danger no longer exists—French navy divers went out and blew the top off the rock, and there is 12 to 13 feet of water over it. Now anything in Baie de Pont-Pierre that you don't see, you can't hit.

When entering this bay, you are running either dead downwind or with the wind on the quarter and a big Atlantic swell behind you. Thus, there is no room for error. The beautiful French schooner *Jacques Helm* found this out the hard way in the winter of 1992. She was magnificent—a giant, schooner-rigged version of Herreshoff's crowning glory, *Ticonderoga*. Her hull was perfect, her rig superb, and all the deck structures were perfectly proportioned. Most unfortunately, however, the skipper made a terrible mistake while entering Baie de Pont-Pierre and ended up aground on the lee side of the harbor. The wind and swell forced her farther and farther in, until she had to be pulled off by a salvage tug. She was a sad sight being towed from the Saintes to Pointe-à-Pitre. Luckily, the weather was fairly calm when she went up, as otherwise she would have been a total loss! Be advised: Baie de Pont-Pierre is strictly for the skillful and the brave!

West of Bourg des Saintes is an excellent anchorage at the northern end of Anse à Cointe, under Le Pain de Sucre, where you could find complete isolation in years gone by. At night, you could hear monkeys crying in the trees. Ashore was a classic West Indian-style home: a peak-roofed structure with a deep porch on all three sides so the sun never touches the walls of the building. This keeps the interior as cool as if it were air-conditioned. Now the building is a small bar that serves sandwiches, and the beach is public; topless is de rigueur.

When anchoring, sail quite close in, get your anchor well set on the shelf, and give it plenty of scope, as the bottom drops off steeply.

At the southern end of Anse à Cointe is a new hotel, the Boisjoli. It has a nice beach and reputedly a good restaurant—a point of great interest to the yachtsmen anchored here. A bus operates from the hotel to Bourg des Saintes, so you can visit the village without having to endure the 1 1/2-mile dinghy ride, which can be quite rough at times.

From the hotel, a path leads 200 yards southward to Anse Craven, which has a pleasant beach (dress optional) with good swimming. Anchor off Anse Craven only in very settled conditions when the wind is north of east.

When coming from or leaving for Dominica through the Passe des Dames (see Chart 54), make sure you are exactly in the center, since there is shoal water on both sides. Also, keep an eye out for the rock that pops out of 25 feet of water off Les Quilles. Even a shoal-draft boat could be damaged if it bottomed out in the trough of a wave. Otherwise, if approaching Iles des Saintes from the south, pass to windward of Grand Ilet with sheets eased, running through the Passe du Grand Ilet, then head up into the anchorage.

ILES DES SAINTES: TERRE D'EN BAS

(Charts 54, 55; II A-28, A-281, A-3, A-4)

This is a new find. In all the years that I had spent in the Caribbean, I had never visited Terre d'en Bas until 1992. Each time I sailed past Anse des Muriers and Anse Fideling, it was blowing a gale, and I just did not feel like investigating these harbors. Luckily, in 1992, we were in the Saintes specifically to do some heavy-weather shots for *Sailing Quarterly*. The wind died and went almost flat, so with the aid of a dinghy (belonging to Bruce MacLennan, skipper of *Loon*), we went down to Terre d'en Bas and were most pleased with what we found.

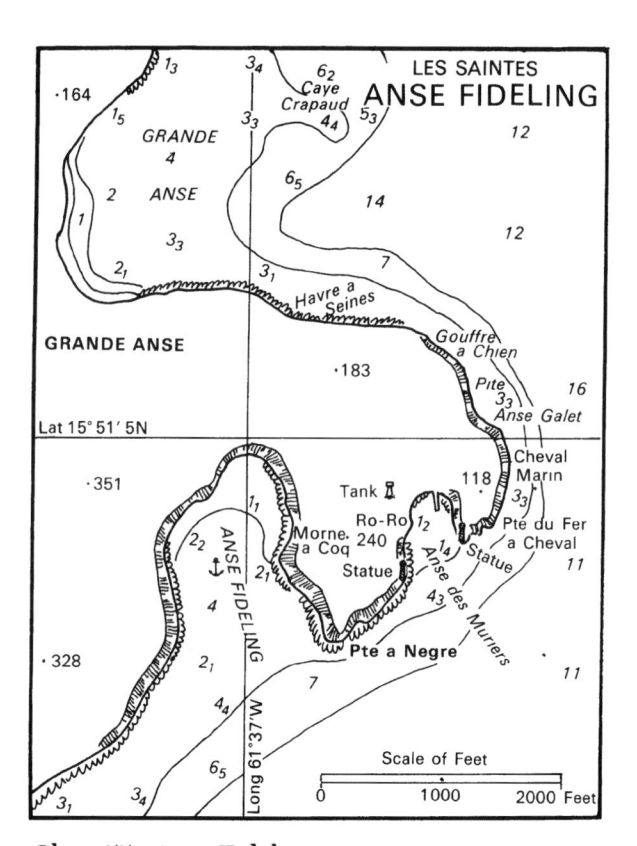

Chart 55 Anse Fideling, Iles des Saintes   Depths in fathoms and feet

In Anse des Muriers, we discovered a small jetty with about seven feet of water at the end of it—where the ferry comes in. At the head of the dock were diesel and gas pumps—obviously used by local fishermen—and a small tourist office staffed at the time by a charming, young, and helpful Guadeloupian girl who spoke a modicum of English.

We did not have time to do an extensive exploration, but we walked along the road toward Grande Anse and spotted a number of houses that obviously were built in the traditional Saintes style. (Ask them if they can make you a lunch and then come back a few hours later to an excellent repast.) We saw one small restaurant and bar, a new supermarket (not very super and not very large) under construction, and a cluster of attractive houses—some completed, some under construction. The situation was much like Terre d'en Haut 20 years ago—completely nontouristy.

The delightful tourist-office staffer told us that the bus fare to the main village on the west side of the island was a mere seven francs. If we had had more time, we would have gone there.

From Anse des Muriers, we went around to Anse Fideling and found a "jewel"—a well-sheltered harbor with a sand bottom and two fathoms at the head of the harbor. In the northeast corner are moorings for the local boats. Clearly, this is a place for a Bahamian moor, to minimize the amount of space your boat occupies and also to make sure that you don't pick up your own anchor when the wind dies. Only two boats were in the anchorage when we arrived. There is no beach, but a set of steps leads from the water's edge up to the road at the north end of the harbor. Snorkeling is good around the edges of the harbor, as the sides are quite steep-to. This would appear to be an excellent place to escape the crowd at Bourg des Saintes—provided the wind did not go around to the south (south of southeast, in fact). In Grande Anse, there is a substantial hotel catering to the sailboard crowd.

As we closed on the Saintes, one of the pleasures of these islands became apparent: For the last 20 years, all the houses have been built in the classic Antillean style, with huge porches and high-peaked roofs. With a setup like that, who needs air-conditioning? In most parts of the Caribbean, air-conditioning is a damned-poor excuse for the mistakes of bad architecture.

MARIE-GALANTE
(Charts 56, 57; II A-28, A-281, A-3, A-4)

Low, flat, and nearly circular, this island for some reason is disdained by both yachtsmen and tourists—which, perhaps, is all the more reason to seek it out. There are three industries on Marie-Galante: sugar, fishing, and cotton. The cotton industry was dying until relatively recently, when demand for long-staple cotton increased drastically. All through the islands where it formerly was grown, cotton fields again are being tilled. It is something of a mixed blessing, however, since the field hands regard picking cotton with as little enthusiasm as they do cutting sugar cane.

One of the distinctive features of Marie-Galante is that the sugar cane is taken to market in ox carts. This is the only place in the Eastern Caribbean where I have seen this mode of transport.

There are three anchorages, of which the first is Capesterre on the southeastern corner (see Chart 56). Caye du Vent, the highest reef, is on the eastern side of the channel, so you should enter the harbor only with the aid of local knowledge—and even then with lots of guts. The Air Guadeloupe sightseeing flight mentioned at the beginning of this chapter provides a spectacular view of this area, and you can spot all the harbors, reefs, and rocks without fear of running aground! On the basis of that flight, I will state categorically that Capesterre Harbor is strictly for small fishing boats that can be pulled up on the beach; it is not recommended for a cruising yacht.

The second anchorage, Saint Louis, probably is fine in the summer months, but in the winter, with the wind from the north, I am not sure it would be comfortable.

Grand Bourg, in the southwest corner of the island, is the main town (see Chart 57). In years gone by, this was an uncomfortable anchorage, as the southeast swell came in over the reef—plus the current sometimes reverses itself and goes to windward, so it meant for a rocky, rolly, and uncomfortable night.

Now, however, a breakwater has been built, creating a completely sheltered basin where you can moor your boat securely in calm water. Thus, Grand Bourg is an excellent base for exploring Marie-Galante, although the draft here is limited to eight feet.

In Grand Bourg behind the break water the entire basin has been dredged out to 8 feet. But it is all loose sand stirred up by the high speed ferries that come in to use the dock. Thus the holding is very poor. If the basin east south east of the ferry pier is full, you can anchor to the west of the ferry pier up as far as the fort. There is 6-7 feet of water quite close to shore.

Marie-Galante is another headquarters for the interesting Saintes fishing boats. Their captains must be fine sailors to be able to fish in the open channel with its strong current and with nothing between them and Africa. Every time we saw French fishermen ashore, they were drunk. My wife said it was because a man would have to get drunk before he could go out and risk his life in one of those little dinghies.

The gendarmes at Grand Bourg are not particularly interested in either entering or clearing you, but while in French waters, it is always best to have a piece of paper with an official French stamp on it. Thus, I advise you to write out a crew list stating where you have come from and where else in Guadeloupe waters you plan to visit, take it to the gendarmes with your passports, and get them to stamp and initial the crew list.

Grand Bourg is misnamed, for it is a sleepy town without much to offer. The cathedral is nothing to write home about; the old wooden interior is presently in dire need of repair. This definitely is a poor parish.

Saint Louis is a most attractive place, with some small grocery stores, small restaurants and bars, a small hotel, and a magnificent small church with three models of sail, cargo, and fishing boats in the rear. At the head of the church is a wonderful sculpture of the Blessed Virgin, the baby Jesus in her arms, with Joseph looking on while a Marie-Galante fisherman, complete with his peaked straw hat, presents them with a bunch of fish. It's obviously locally and lovingly carved out of solid

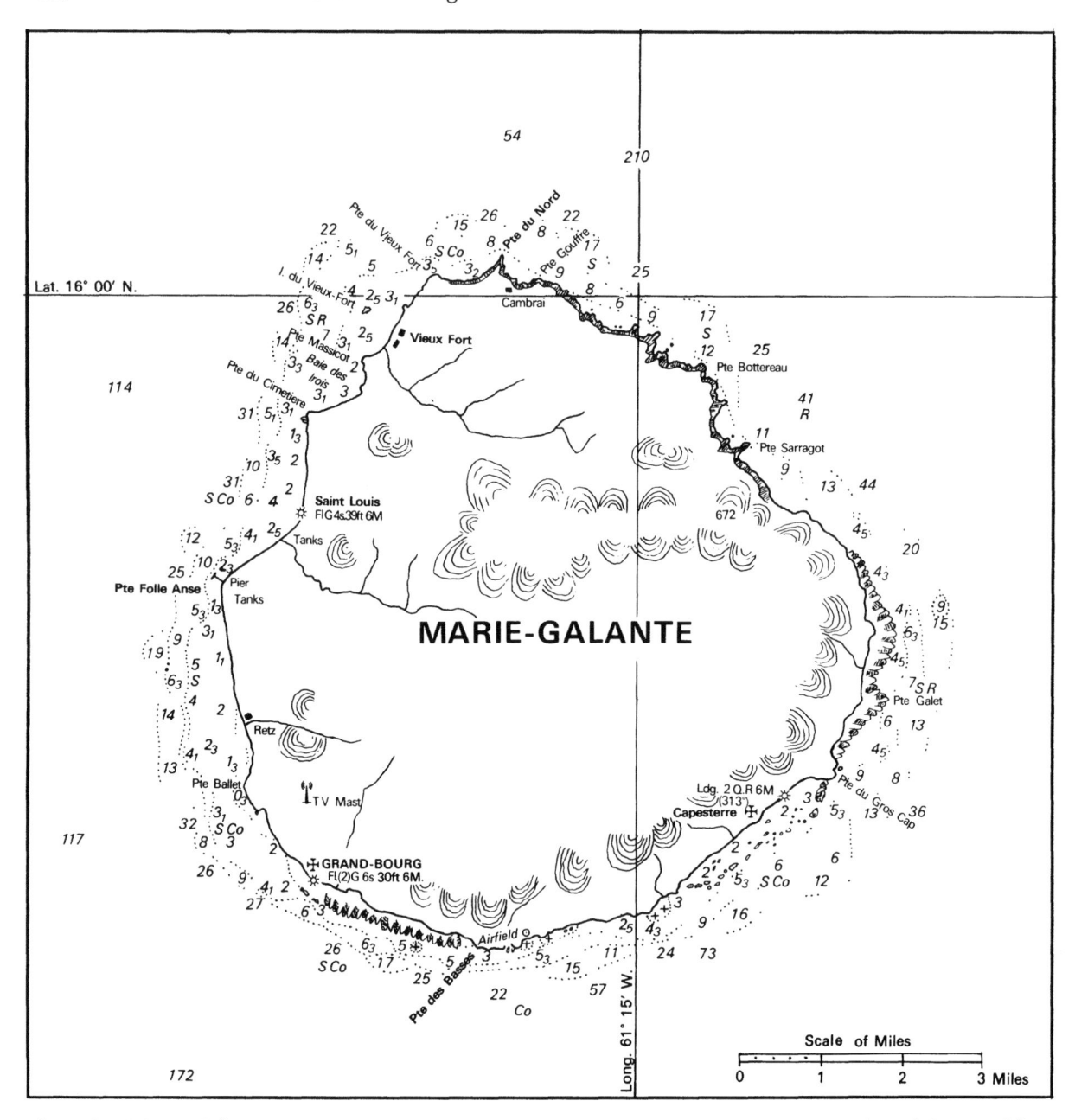

Chart 56 Marie-Galante   Depths in fathoms and feet

blocks of mahogany. This is a church well worth visiting.

Saint Louis looks like an ideal place to spend a few days while you explore Marie-Galante by rented car or taxi, or just by taking bus rides from village to village.

Even though Grand Bourg is not rocky and rolly as it used to be, you can also anchor in most weather anywhere from Pointe Ballet to Pointe du Cimetière, off white-sand beaches that are either deserted or have only a single small fisherman's cottage. The mass of Guadeloupe seems to shelter this area completely from the northwest ground swell.

A string of beautiful white-sand beaches runs from Pointe du Cimetière to Vieux Fort—but, as I have said many times before, beautiful white-sand beaches seldom mean good anchorages. Evidently the surf hooks around the northern part of the island and washes in on these beaches. This probably is true from December through April, but after April, when the wind goes south of east, I suspect that

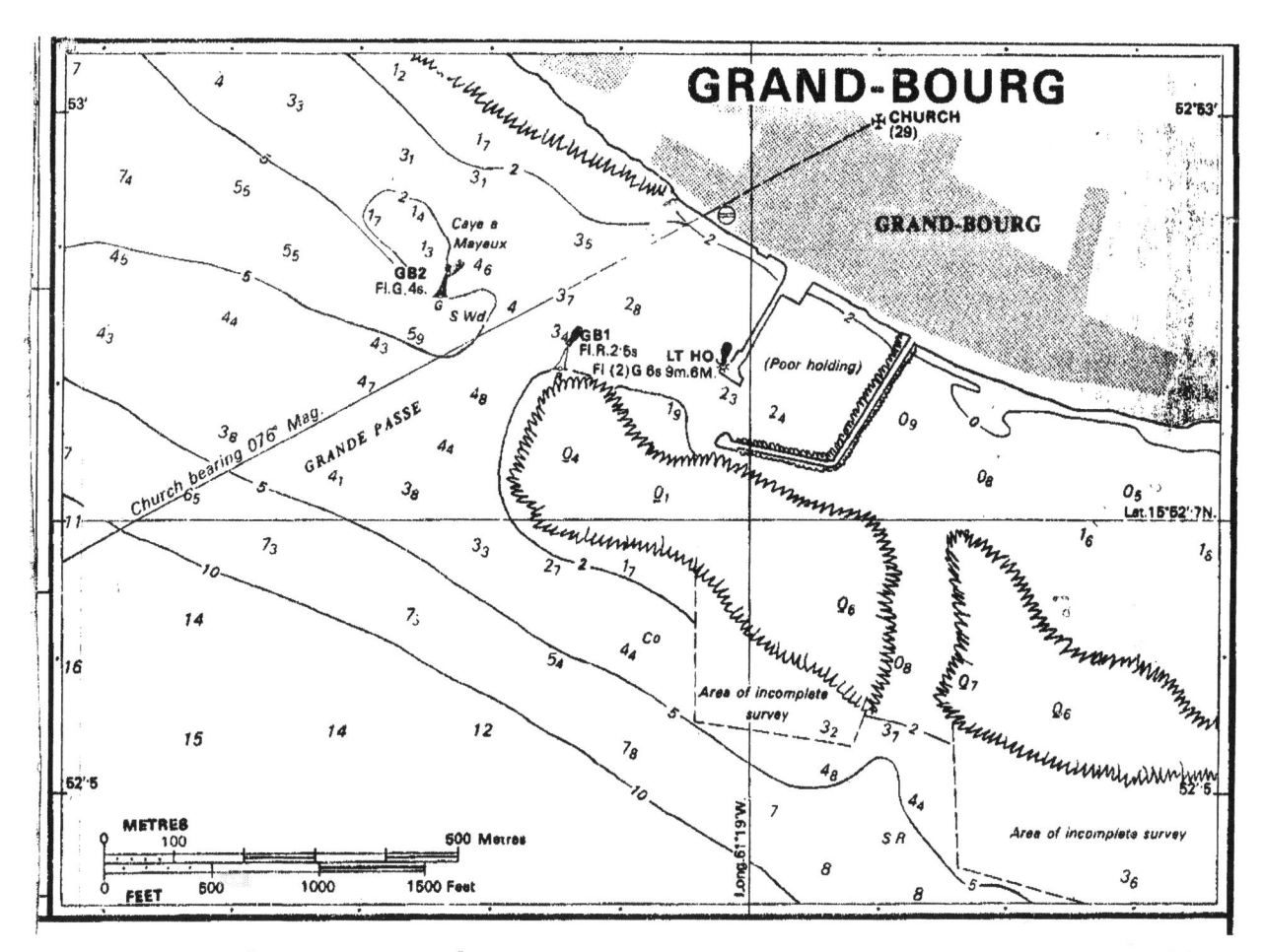

Chart 57 Grand Bourg, Marie-Galante   Depths in fathoms and feet

these beaches might be good anchorages under the right conditions.

We have not visited the village of Vieux Fort, but we did traverse the area in a dinghy. There is no dock, and the only way to reach town would be to land a dinghy on the northernmost beach before the cliffs and walk the few hundred yards to Vieux Fort.

One of the great pluses of visiting Marie-Galante is that you are practically guaranteed to be alone; at worst, you would have only an occasional boat sharing an anchorage with you.

NOTES

9

Dominica

(Imray-Iolaire Charts A, A-29, A-4)

Dominica lies between Martinique and Guadeloupe. High, lush, and rugged, it is a farmer's delight—and a sailor's nightmare. Its central ridge rises to nearly 5,000 feet, with a sheer drop to the sea on both sides. This lofty ridge wrings the moisture from the trade winds, accounting for the 300 or so rivers and streams that cascade down its slopes. So effectively does the ridge block the trades that there is almost a total calm in the lee of the island.

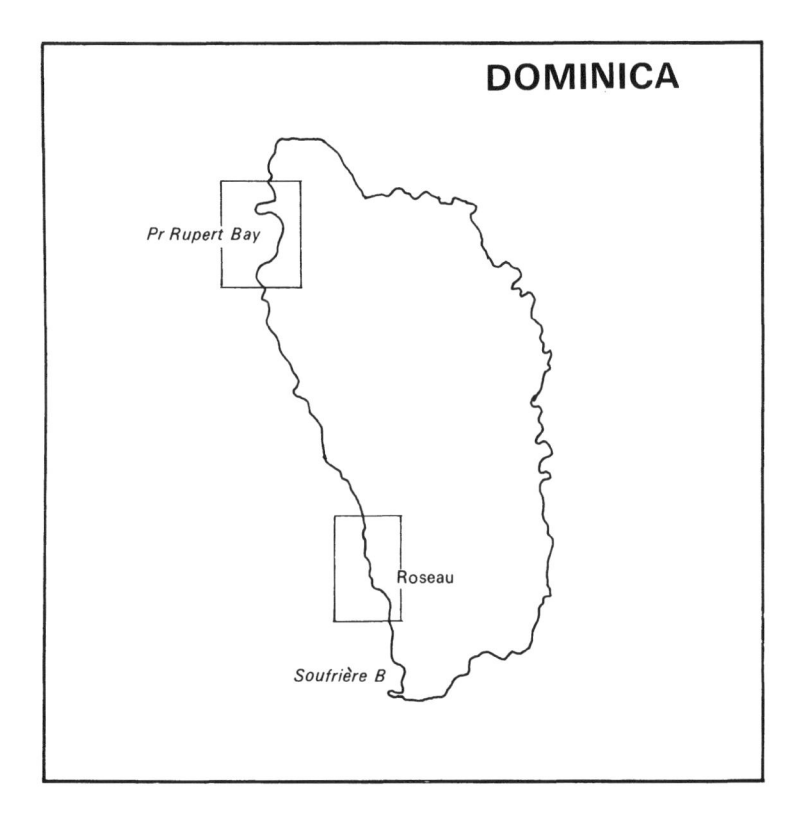

Dominica was discovered in 1493 by Columbus on his second voyage to the New World. During the next century and a half, the local Carib tribesmen successfully resisted every attempt to settle the island. The Caribs entrenched themselves in the mountains, from which they would emerge periodically and make forays against the early settlers, driving them off to neighboring islands. By the Treaty of Aix-la-Chapelle, the colonial powers agreed to declare as neutral the islands of Dominica, St. Vincent, St. Lucia, and Tobago. Peace did not last long, however, as the British and French continued to squabble over Dominica until it was recaptured by the French in 1778. During the American Revolution, the British lost control of their Caribbean territories until Admiral Rodney broke the French hold on the Antilles in the Battle of the Saintes in 1782. After a few years of peace, hostilities were resumed during the Napoleonic Wars. The British acquired permanent possession of Dominica, St. Lucia, St. Vincent, and Grenada by the Peace of Vienna, and Dominica gained its independence in 1978.

Dominica is precariously connected to the outside world by LIAT airlines. The airfield is very poor, and it is small wonder that so few flights land there. A number of good hotels have been built on the island in recent years—some on the beach, some high in the mountains. If you decide to dine in a mountain hotel, take along a heavy sweater. Come sundown, the men will certainly want a jacket, especially if a rain squall comes whistling through.

Roseau, capital of Dominica, is one of the very few towns of any size in the Eastern Caribbean that has not changed a great deal over the years. During the past 40 years, very few new buildings have been put up, and it is still possible to find classic, old West Indian hotels such as The Lodge, run by Mrs. Tavernier. The Lodge has been in continuous operation since 1892. Another classic and beautiful example of West Indian architecture is La Robe Créole restaurant and guest house.

The straw goods in Dominica are the best and cheapest in the Caribbean. There is a large and traditional West Indian market in the main square. Roads are variable. Some are excellent and smooth, some are full of potholes, and others are still under construction and not yet blacktopped—therefore only passable in good weather (and, since Dominica has the heaviest rainfall of any of the islands, many of the roads are muddy much of the time).

All of the roads were badly damaged during Hurricane David, in August 1979. Not only were the roads in dreadful condition in the storm's aftermath, but the hospital had been completely destroyed. Canadians arrived and made minor repairs to the roads and completely rebuilt the hospital. For many years, the new hospital was almost empty, as Dominicans were basically healthy. Then the Canadians decided to do a thorough job of road repairs—with dire consequences. The Dominicans then SPED along the roads, unhindered by bumps and potholes, and the hospital soon became overcrowded because of all the auto accidents!

It looks as though Dominica should install plenty of "sleeping policemen" to solve the problem. If they do, they will have to be smarter than the authorities were in St. Vincent, where there were major problems with speeding vehicles. As a solution, their traffic department installed "sleeping policemen" all over the island and erected signs saying, "Go slow: sleeping policemen." The island's police department, however, took umbrage and insisted that the signs were an insult. So the signs and the "sleeping policemen" were removed. (Perhaps they should have used a bit of imagination and erected signs that said, "Go slow—wide-awake policemen"!)

If you want to explore Dominica—and perhaps avoid a visit to the hospital—it's best to hire a driver or join one of the many organized tours. The Anchorage Hotel runs a varied selection of tours to all corners of the island, and their prices seem reasonable.

The shops in Roseau are fairly good, but the harbor is miserable and the taxi service to the interior is irregular and expensive. Rental cars are available if you are up to the challenge, but if you want to visit the Carib Indian reservations, hire a Land Rover. At the reservations, fine straw baskets are woven so tightly that they can hold water without losing a drop. The Caribs also build sailing canoes, which can be seen in the Antilles as far south as St. Vincent. They may look frail and unseaworthy, but it was in just such boats that the Caribs once traveled throughout the Lesser Antilles. When Columbus arrived, they had conquered all the islands as far north as Puerto Rico, occasionally making raids into Hispaniola and the Bahamas. They were fabulous seamen, fierce warriors, and cannibals to boot. They treated their local enemies, the relatively peace-loving Arawaks, like cattle. The first Europeans frequently found conquered Arawaks penned up in corrals by the Caribs, who would yank them out one by one, kill them, cook them, and eat them.

Because of its ruggedness, Dominica was the last stronghold of the Caribs in their losing battle against the white man. Today they have settled down to a peaceful life on their reservations in the mountains, and they are noted as fine fishermen. Early each morning, they launch their sailing canoes and beat to windward, often against the full force of the winter trades, to fish the bank east of the island. They return in the afternoon and run their canoes through the surf onto the exposed windward shore. The sight of one of these canoes bursting forth from a squall, the crew hanging from a line secured to the masthead, is an impressive one. It gives pause to the modern yachtsman with his trendy electronic aids, zipper-footed Dacron sails, and roller-reefing gear. It seems the Caribs invented the trapeze 300 years before the yachtsmen did!

The climate of Dominica can be summed up in one word—wet. The only difference between the so-called dry and wet seasons is that it rains all of the time during the wet season and it rains most of the time during the dry season. Along the lowlands of the shore, it is hot, but the temperature drops off rapidly as you head upward. The tide is minimal, with the rise and fall less than one foot. The tidal current generally runs north and south, parallel to shore on the east and west coasts, and there usually is a strong westerly current off the north and south points of the island, which seldom is overcome by the flood tide.

If you are anchored at Roseau or Woodbridge and notice the tide running northward, time your departure correctly and you can carry a fair tide all the way to the north end of the island.

In previous editions, I discussed the lack of safety in exploring Dominica, as in the late 1970s a sect called the Dreds threw the island into a state of political turmoil. Exactly how many people were murdered, and how many Dreds were eliminated by the police and the defense force, I am not quite sure, but people did avoid the island—there was absolutely no tourism for a number of years. Now the Dreds are gone and tourism is on the rise, although yachting tourism may be badly hurt by a small band of boat boys—or perhaps I should say boat bums—who operate out of Prince Rupert Bay. (This situation is discussed below.)

If you do sail to Dominica, it is well worthwhile taking a tour of the hinterlands, as the scenery is beautiful and the locals are tremendously friendly and helpful. Small farmers often urge visitors to buy their fresh fruit—at unbelievably low prices. The best way to see the most interesting parts of the island is to hire a knowledgeable local guide. During our visit to Dominica in 1984, we met Joey Magloire in Roseau—he's a Calypso singer and tour guide. Chase him down and have him arrange a tour; it's a good way to spend a day.

I have been informed about an excursion here that sounds very appealing—at least for the young or fairly fit. Anchor off the Sisserou and Anchorage hotels and arrange with one of them for a taxi to Trafalgar Falls. Take along walking shoes, hat, long-sleeved shirt, foul-weather jacket, towels, and soap. When you are dropped off at the foot of the falls, walk upriver to the upper cataract, which, according to Gil Fry, owner of the famous old 72-foot yawl *Escapade*, is the world's best shower. On the left side of the falls, going up, is hot sulfur water, temperature about 110°F, cascading down over a series of rock platforms so arranged that each person can sit and soak in privacy. When you have had enough heat, climb back down and go under the right-hand falls, where you can sit in a clear, cold mountain stream with drinkable water. Sounds pretty good, no?

The coasts of Dominica are steep-to and, for the most part, free of danger. A sail up the windward coast is an exciting experience, although few boats do it, since there are no anchorages. This is dead lee shore, and it is apt to be rough, so keep well off. The scenery is fine on the west coast, too, but the calm in the lee can be frustrating.

Ever since I first arrived in the Caribbean in 1956, there have been continual discussions and arguments about the rocks and shoals off Scotts Head, on the island's southern tip. Finally, in May 1979, I visited the area myself with Carl Armour's son, David, in a Chris-Craft runabout (perhaps not the ideal survey vessel, but adequate). Subsequently, I discussed the problem with Mike Davis, first mate of the *Geest Star*, and have come to the conclusion that the charts are wrong, but not as wrong as we originally thought.

Most yachtsmen (myself included) saw the notation on the chart "seven feet" and interpreted this to mean a *rock* seven feet high. In fact, the "seven feet" relates to the depth of the *water* over the rock, but even this is not strictly accurate. I would say that the rock is only about five or six feet under the water; locals say it breaks in heavy weather. Many boats, unfortunately, have hit the rock while looking for it!

Except for this one spot, the best way to sail the western shore of Dominica is to stay in close at a two-pistol-shot distance. At night, the cold air falling off the mountain will produce a light breeze sufficient to propel a high-performance boat close inshore. Early morning and dusk are pretty much hopeless sailing times. If you plan to sail within the lee of the island, there is no point in setting out before 1100 or noon. During the day, as the land heats up, the hot air rising from the island will draw in the cool air from the sea and frequently give you a light onshore breeze from midmorning to early afternoon. This breeze can only be found very close in; it dies out completely a few hundred yards off.

One word of caution about proceeding along the shore—have your sheets and halyards ready to run. Very violent—albeit brief—squalls occasionally strike in the lee of this island. They consist of cold blasts of air blown down with great ferocity from the mountain passes, and they approach with no warning. Not only is the wind's velocity dangerous, but its angle is, too. Usually, winds are horizontal to the water and will spill out of the sails as a boat is knocked down. But here, the wind blows downward and exerts *greater* force as the boat heels. I have yet to experience one of these clear-air squalls, but I have heard too many hair-raising stories to question their existence.

SCOTTS HEAD
(II A-29, A-4)

When rounding Scotts Head at the southern tip of the island, avoid the rocks mentioned above. Once clear, turn eastward and sail in behind Scotts Head, where there is a sheltered anchorage off the village. In contrast to the rest of this coast, where one tends to roll like mad, this anchorage is usually calm, although it is windswept. According to the chart, the depths are so great that it is almost impossible to anchor, but we discovered that southwest of a line bearing 320° to the northern tip of Scotts Head, you can find an anchorage in six to eight fathoms along the beach. Be sure to use a Bahamian moor, or moor bow-and-stern, since the wind is bound to whistle here, and you might end up on the beach if you set only one anchor. The view is splendid from the top of Scotts Head, and there is good diving and snorkeling off the beach, but the current in this area can be strong; it runs south approximately four hours out of 12, and north the rest of the time. THIS IS NOW A NATIONAL PARK AREA, ANCHORING IS FORBIDDEN.

SOUFRIERE
(II A-29, A-4)

North of Scotts Head is a town familiar to many sailors. Soufrière is not a port of entry, but it used to be the home of the famed Rose's Lime Juice. (Unfortunately, the factory is now closed.) Anchoring is all but impossible—probably the best way to do it is with your anchor in deep water and some stern lines ashore. But this will serve only as a temporary expedient, since at night the area is prone to squalls booming out of the hillsides from every sort of crazy angle.

ROSEAU
(Chart 58; II A-29, A-4)

The port of entry is not in town; it is a mile north at Woodbridge Bay, where the new deepwater dock has been built. Anchor south of the dock on the shelf, where you can find the bottom. Take care, however, as the bottom drops off very steeply.

If you want to do any errands in town after clearing customs, move on down and anchor south of the old jetty, now largely destroyed. The only way to get into town is to row into the old jetty and climb up the ladder that is barely hanging onto the wall by a piece of chain. The jetty was destroyed by Hurricane David in 1979, which flattened the island; I can understand that it has not been rebuilt, since it is not needed for commercial purposes. However, I think it would be worthwhile to fix up the south wall and install a low dinghy landing and steps, since that certainly would encourage yachts to anchor off the town and go ashore to spend money.

The only alternative is to anchor off either the Anchorage or the Sisserou hotel. The Anchorage used to have guest moorings, but the bottom is so steep that oversize boats frequently would drag the moorings off the shelf and into very deep water. Now the best procedure is to anchor temporarily, go ashore in the dinghy, and check with both hotels to figure out which one meets your needs. Then anchor off the hotel you have chosen, run a stern line ashore, and swing the boat around so you are stern-to the shore. That way, with the anchor pulling uphill, there is little danger of dragging. The bottom is rocky, though, so even with a chain leader you may still chafe through your anchor rode. This is a good place to use an all-chain rode.

There is an old warning that holds true for yachtsmen in any unfamiliar anchorage: *Never* hire any local workers until you have checked them out with knowledgeable local yachtsmen, or marina or hotel owners. Generally speaking, the kids who swim out to your boat here are just the ones you should not hire. The most trustworthy ones often are too shy to make the first approach.

Similarly, do not buy fruit and vegetables from small boys who come out to the boat with a canoe full of produce for sale. The food probably was stolen from their neighbors' gardens the night before!

The report I received from the crew of *Phoenix* was that the staff of the Anchorage Hotel was most helpful. The bad news is that the crew made the mistake of not locking the boat when they went ashore. Someone boarded and absconded with a fair amount of jewelry. Many inquiries around town finally pinpointed the culprit, but the police seemed singularly uninterested in tracking down the suspect, arresting him, and recovering the jewelry. The owner of *Phoenix,* who is built like an ex—pro football tackle, was sorely tempted to take the law into his own hands, but he realized that to do so could provoke a massive riot. The crew also recommended NOT walking into town, as the small boys were less than friendly and started pelting them with rocks!

WOODBRIDGE BAY AND ROSEAU ROADS

Ro Tel Call 'Roseau Port Control' VHF Ch 16:12 14
1:17 500

Port Auth ☎ (809) 44-84451
Customs ☎ (809) 44-82222
Anchorage Hotel ☎ (809) 44-82638
VHF Ch 16 (moorings, water, showers)

Caution
Prior permission from the Port Manager is required before anchoring within the area marked by pecked lines in Woodbridge Bay

IF USING JETTY CHECK FOR SURGE. MAY MAKE IT IMPOSSIBLE TO USE.

SOUNDINGS IN METRES

However, the *Phoenix* crew did rent a Jeep and had a wonderful time exploring the interior of Dominica. They enjoyed the island most of the time but said the hassles were enough to make them not want to return in the near future.

If you need any diving done, or any outboard repairs, check with C. M. Prynn, an ex-British naval officer who came up through the hawsepipe, having started his career as an enlisted man. He knows the island well, has the fishermen well organized, and is extremely helpful. His assistant, Elwin, with the aid of a lung, brought up our Seagull outboard, which a crew member had dropped into 120 feet of water. It was so deep that the half-filled fuel tank, which was turned off, was half-collapsed; yet we had it running again that evening. Elwin retrieved the outboard for a reasonable price, which I was happy to pay and he was happy to receive.

The city of Roseau is worth exploring. Some small shops sell straw goods and local artifacts at unbelievably low prices; fruit and vegetables are also very reasonable. The town is very run-down—the result of the devastation caused by the 1979 hurricane. The island economy, which was not too good to begin with, was devastated by the storm. However, there are some excellent examples of traditional West Indian architecture, particularly the churches.

Everywhere along the lee coast (except for Prince Rupert Bay), the anchorage is rocky and open to swells.

The town of Roseau has developed see page 170 for updates.

WOODBRIDGE BAY
(Chart 58; II A-29, A-4)

One mile north of Roseau, Woodbridge Bay is the only natural anchorage in the southern portion of Dominica and is now the clearance port. There are two problems, though: The water is deep, and you must get permission from the harbormaster to anchor there. If you do, then feel your way in to a depth that suits you—or to where you are told to go. But take care; the bottom is very poor holding. Once you feel secure, there are taxis available to town.

Woodbridge Bay has banana docks as well as the deepwater dock. But they are obviously for large shipping and not for small yachts. A river at the south end of Woodbridge Bay has created a shelf that extends out to sea, and an anchorage can be had on the edge of this shelf. Don't go swimming here, however, since the river also serves as the sewer for the town. Further, there is a strong outflow from the river during rainy weather.

LAYOU RIVER
(II A-29, A-4)

Five miles north of Woodbridge Bay, the mouth of Layou River is none too easy to spot. But if you pass close inshore, you will see an opening in the trees, a small village, and surf breaking across the mouth of the river. Anchor north of the river in sand bottom with good holding at two to three fathoms. There is sometimes a swell, and it's essential to keep an eye on the weather. Instead of trying to row through the breakers, wait a while. The canoes probably will come out, and you can arrange a ride ashore, where the beach is black sand. Take along your diving gear. The river has large fish—as well as lots of crawfish that make delicious eating. Take shampoo and any clothes you want to wash, since the Layou offers an unlimited supply of fresh water. After you have done all that, take a stroll along the river bank through the Hillsborough Valley.

If you can land your dinghy through the surf, you can row a fair way up the river, which makes a nice change from sailing the "briny deep." (Be forewarned, however, about the hazards of negotiating breakers—see the discussion about Nevis in chapter 5.) Another advantage of the river trip is that it has not yet been spoiled by the "boat boys." You'll eventually come upon a very pleasant pool that is ideal for swimming, as well as washing bodies, hair, and clothes—and the skipper will have no cause for complaint about overuse of water!

Castaways - One mile north of Layou River one finds another shelf. See Page 170 at the end of this chapter.

PRINCE RUPERT BAY
(Chart 59; II A-29, A-4)

Prince Rupert Bay, at the north end of Dominica, is the logical stop for boats heading south from Iles des Saintes and Guadeloupe, as well as for boats heading north from Martinique, because it's a much better anchorage than Roseau. The town of Portsmouth is really only a village, but basic supplies are available. A wonderful bakery produces not only French bread but also whole-wheat and rye; you can buy fruit at very reasonable prices, and we also spotted a laundry machine. (Considering how much it rains in Dominica, make sure the place has a dryer before you drop off your laundry.)

In the northeast corner of the bay are two beach bar/restaurants and a good anchorage with sand bottom, good holding, and no surge.

Ashore, it is only a short walk to the fort complex (between East and West Cabrit hills) that is in the process of being restored. The restoration is being supervised by Lennox Honeychurch, who knows the

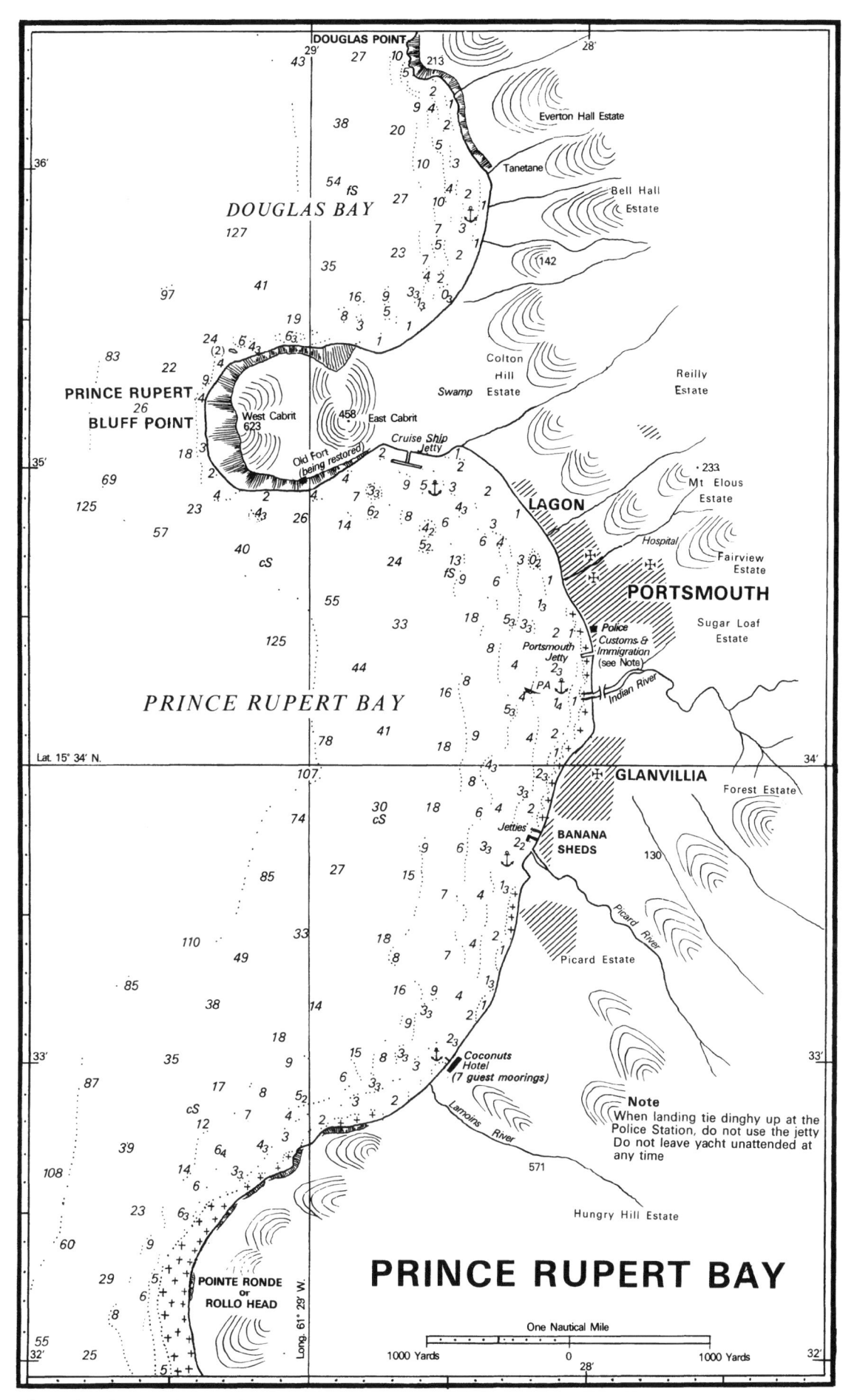

Chart 59 Prince Rupert Bay   Depths in fathoms and feet

island well and has written books about the history of the islands and the fort. A very impressive brochure shows the fort complex, gives its history, and outlines the future plans. Visiting the fort is a must for anyone in the area. The complex is within easy walking distance of the yacht anchorage and offers a spectacular view of the entire harbor.

A new cruise-ship dock has been built below the fort, so it probably is possible to moor a dinghy there, but be sure to carry a stern anchor to hold the dinghy off.

Now we come to the problem with Prince Rupert Bay and its attractive little town of Portsmouth. For a few years, thieving had turned from a minor cottage industry to a major commercial venture. No dinghy was safe tied to a tree on the beach, or even at the main jetty. I never would leave my dinghy anywhere except on the beach in front of the police station. Based on my last experience in Prince Rupert Bay, I wouldn't even leave an anchored boat unattended during the day, let alone in the dark of night.

Our trouble started as we sailed into the bay and were greeted by a bunch of small boats bearing boys who competed to get a line on our boat and who *demanded* to be hired to run errands, guard the boat, act as guides ashore, and so on. Once anchored, we hired a boat boy we didn't need just to get rid of the others—and even that arrangement fell apart the next day, so we paid him off. (One boy we *didn't* hire had a beat-up old dinghy with what looked like a brand-new 6-hp Evinrude on the transom with a remote gas tank; I was very suspicious about the source of that shiny new motor!)

That was only the beginning. One of the finest natural attractions in the whole area is here in Prince Rupert Bay. Let me digress for a moment to quote from a previous edition of this guide:

> The Indian River flows into Prince Rupert Bay, and a dinghy trip up this river is a delightful way to pass several hours. The way is simple. There are no breakers or bars at the mouth, and inside it is wonderfully cool and peaceful, with large trees overarching the stream and shafts of sunlight filtering down. The current is swift enough to require an outboard during the ascent. Don't be discouraged by the old rusted-out bridge. Continue beyond, feeling your way around the various snags and shoal spots, until you reach the first rapids. Here the dinghy can be dragged over the shoals by hand. Farther on, the river will open up into deep pools that are good for swimming or a midday meal. If you have persistence, paddle and drag the dinghy across the second rapids until your way is blocked by a waterfall. This is farther up the river than the average yachtsman penetrates but, according to Zane Mann, well worth the trouble.
>
> On the way back, keep the outboard off. Paddle or pole down quietly, and you will see any number of fabulous birds. It is possible to get close beneath them in their trees. The river is a great way to spend a morning. Start early and take along some supplies.

However, on our last visit to Prince Rupert Bay in March 1984, this wonderful trip was completely ruined by the boat bums. First of all, they told us it was illegal to go up the Indian River except in one of their boats or with one of the boys aboard our dinghy with us. Since we knew this was untrue (later confirmed by the acting superintendent of police), and since the boys' boats are too heavy to be dragged across the rapids below the falls, we started up the river alone in our own dinghy. We had just gotten beyond the bridge when stones started raining down on us—thrown by boys heaving rocks into the air high above the bushes. Rocks began splashing around the dinghy like mortar shells. Since we had a three-year-old child aboard, we turned around and went back—fearing for his life as well as ours. Then, while having a drink at the beach bar, we were abused verbally by the boat bums, who told us never to return to Dominica.

I reported all this to the police, who were cooperative and offered to snag the culprits; I asked them to wait until after we departed, since I was worried that we would be boarded and assaulted during the night. The police and senior Customs officials acknowledged that that had happened in the past.

Fortunately, not everyone has had such bad experiences. Several cruisers I have talked to since then have concurred that the boat boys were a nuisance, but they had found that a few dollars' worth of "cooperation" money eased the way. These sailors reported having a wonderful time on the Indian River in their guides' boats, but they admitted that the boats were too heavy to be dragged up over the rapids, so they missed the upper pools and the waterfall.

Remember that poverty is a serious problem in Dominica, and even the smallest yacht looks like a millionaire's home to some of the boys in Portsmouth. A few dollars to a couple of kids—and a firm insistence that they honor your deal with them—probably will keep your visit to Prince Rupert Bay pleasant.

Incidentally, I wrote to Mrs. Eugenia Charles, the premier of Dominica, after my disastrous experience there, and I received a reply saying that efforts were underway to improve the situation. I suggested, in turn, that the government take the following steps:

1. License the jetty boys.
2. Place signs on the jetty and the bridge stating clearly that it is legal to go up the Indian River in your own dinghy, and also set fees for hiring a boy to take you up in his boat or to go as a guide in yours.
3. Put a window in the west wall of the Portsmouth police station and equip the on-duty officers with binoculars so that they can keep an eye on the yachts in the anchorage.
4. Publish a mimeographed sheet with a sketch of the village, giving information about the markets and other facilities in town, such as rental cars, etc., and also suggesting reasonable fees for hiring the jetty boys for launch service, running errands, and so on.

Things still have not settled down in Portsmouth. During the winter of 1985–86, a yachtsman was murdered. The story goes that they caught the culprit and retrieved most of the stolen money, but that does not revive the yachtsman. One also wonders if the culprit was convicted of murder. If convicted, was he properly hung or did he merely get a comfortable jail sentence? And there have been subsequent murders. Some of the culprits have been caught, and at least one was executed at a public hanging. It has also been reported that a new police officer has been working hard to straighten out the boat boys.

One couple, Jerry and Louise Gable, reported that they and their friends had a wonderful time in Dominica. They hired Eric, who comes equipped with a big pirogue (35+hp). He appeared to be the biggest and toughest of the boat boys, so they were left alone, but Eric's big boat could not possibly ascend the river to its upper reaches, where the pools are. To my mind, the falls and the pools are one of the highlights of Dominica, and they are accessible only in a light dinghy. All we can do now is pray that someday, someone will straighten out the mess.

Even as recently as 1992, I have still had to rely on secondhand information, because a number of threats have been made against my life by Dominicans who have spotted me in other islands. I have been told that the situation has improved somewhat, but I still stress that you should NOT anchor in the northeast corner of Prince Rupert Bay. Instead, go to the southeast corner, where you will find the Coconut Beach Hotel, run by Chris Karam and his sister Liz. They have seven free moorings, free water, 11 feet of water at the end of their dock, a beach bar and restaurant, two public phones, showers, and trash disposal. They can arrange tours and will not let any of the boat boys near the yachts. So there may be some hope!

The hotel is located a mile and a half south of Portsmouth at Lamoins River. The only problem is that since they are on the south side of the harbor, they are more exposed to the swell than they would be in the northeast corner. It is a black cloud that has no silver lining, except that the reputation of Dominica's boat boys creates a steady clientele for the Coconut Beach Hotel—people who want to enjoy the island without being hassled.

In 1992, a couple of boats stopped in Dominica and anchored in the northeast corner. They went to restaurants on shore and explored the old fort complex but ended up being hassled. *Phoenix* hired the biggest and toughest boat boy they could find, and they were left alone for the time the boat boy was there. But after the boat boy departed for another job, the skipper had to go ashore for groceries. He didn't have a lock for tying up his dinghy, and as soon as he left the dinghy, somebody came along and took the boat for a joyride, using up most of the fuel. (Fortunately it was broad daylight and they didn't swipe the dinghy!)

Phoenix reports that my written advice to the officials has gone unheeded—the police station still has no window in its back wall, so they cannot supervise activity in the anchorage. Until some law and order is established here, the Prince Rupert Bay anchorage will never become the popular spot that it deserves to be.

In Dominica, you must leave someone on board your yacht at all times. Locking up the boat is not always the solution, as thieves may break the door and/or the locks, leaving you with a large repair bill plus the cost of whatever items are stolen.

Warren Brown's famous ocean racer *War Baby* (ex—*Tenacious*) also visited Dominica, in January 1992, but they had no problems because they had a large number of crew who managed to chase off the boat boys. But during their two-night stay, three boats around them were robbed! The police really went to work and captured the culprits—and most of the stolen items were retrieved. But for those who were robbed, a relaxing cruise became something of a nightmare.

A cruise-ship dock has now been built under the bluff—promising a large influx of tourists. If these visitors are hassled, the cruise ship certainly will threaten to bypass the island, and perhaps the potential loss of tourism income might provoke the police into rounding up all the boat bums of Prince Rupert bay.

There are honest, industrious boys in Portsmouth who will give you your money's worth in service—as well as men who will give you fascinating sightseeing tours in their trucks or vans. I recommend that before you go to Dominica, check with other sailors in the islands to obtain the names of boat boys and drivers who have been satisfactory. Or check with managers of charter outfits in Antigua or St. Lucia to get a reading on the situation in Portsmouth. If the situation appears to have been sorted out, by all means go there and enjoy the fort area, the Indian River, and the whole north end of Dominica. It's a treat.

Finally, I have been told there is a one-armed outboard mechanic who is fantastic. Not only does he fix outboards, but watching him work is a show in itself.

April 2000 all I can say regarding the above is to double check with the local bare boat managers from Martinique if you are heading north; in St. Lucia, or Guadaloupe if you are heading south, find out as to what the situation is about boat boys and thievery in Portsmouth, Dominica.

ROUSEAU

(Chart 58; II A-29, A-4)

The town of Roseau has developed. Exactly how much I am not sure, but sailing by I noted that there are a couple of new high class hotels in town. Further Old Fort Hotel has now put in a jetty which in calm weather a yacht could moor to. But, care must be exerted here as with very little warning the surge can build up, which would be rather disastrous to a yacht lying alongside the jetty.

Bays North of Prince Rupert Bay

DOUGLAS BAY, TOUCARI BAY

Despite the information in the RCC Pilotage Foundation book, I would definitely NOT visit these bays during the winter (mid-October to early May), as the beaches are subject to ground swells. You might be anchored off one of these beaches when a grounds swell comes in during the night, and your boat would be high and dry on the beach in a very short time.

These bays might serve as viable overnight stops in the summer or daytime anchorages in the winter.

LAYOU RIVER

(II A-29, A-4)

Castaways - one mile north of Layou River one finds another shelf, shallow enough to anchor on and easily spotted by the fact that there are usually a few yachts anchored there and also a big sign painted on the wall saying Castaways. Anchor anywhere on the shelf and try to find a spot of sand clear of the weed to get your anchor to hold. I would advise two anchors, as if you drag the least little bit you will be on the back side of a slope and the next stop for the boat would be Panama.

The sign says Castaways but in the area there appear to be three or four small hotels. Go ashore, take a look around and take your pick.

Unlike Roseau and Prince Rupert Bay, there does not appear to be any of the ubiquitous boat boys to offer their 'services'. (Frequently relieving you of your valuables at the same time.)

Epilogue

Nautical Publications has come out with a new set of Caribbean Charts about which I will make no comments other than as listed below:

Imray-Iolaire charts are not the cheapest Caribbean charts but they are the best value for money.
They are the ONLY charts that are a guide and chart in one as they have on the back sailing and harbour directions compiled by D.M. Street Jr. as a result of his 43 years cruising, exploring and writing about the eastern Caribbean.

1. They are the ONLY waterproof charts that can be used on deck and that can be folded and unfolded ad infinitum to any size you desire.
2. They are the ONLY charts that have been compiled by a mariner who knows the entire area intimately.
3. They are the ONLY charts that have ranges/transits to avoid rocks and shoals.
4. They are the ONLY charts that are regarded so much as standard that they are used by virtually all the bare boat companies and by the U.S. Coast Guard.
5. They are the ONLY charts that have the Way Points carefully placed clear of all navigational dangers.
6. They are available electronically in raster form from: Laser Plot and Live Chart.
   and in vector form from: CMAP & EURONAV.
7. They are the only charts for which you can obtain updates every six months. If every six months you order your updates you can keep your charts up to date for ever.

It is my fond hope that in the year 2101 that this guide will still be available with updates periodically added to the books to keep them current.

I have done the best I possibly could to update this guide to the beginning of the year 2001. For the year 2003 contact Imray and a supplement will be available. It is planned that a supplement will be issued for this guide every two years. Always available from Imray. The costs of these supplements will depend on how much work the author has to put in and how much the current costs are to Imray to produce and mail the supplements.

Index

Anegada, 3, 7
Anegada Passage, 3–4
Anguilla, 3, 7, 9–24
   North Coast, 12–17
   South Coast, 17–20
Anguilla Point, 4
Anse à Bourg, 155
Anse Accul, 148
Anse à Cointe, 156
Anse à Galet, 150
Anse à la Barque, 6, 133
Anse de Colombier, 50, 51–52
Anse de Grand Cul-de-Sac, 52
Anse de Marigot, 52–53
Anse de Petit Cul-de-Sac, 52
Anse de Saline, 53
Anse Deshaies, 6
Anse des Muriers, 156
Anse du Corossol, 47, 51
Anse du Gouverneur, 53
Anse du Public, 47, 51
Anse Fideling, 156–57
Anse Marcel, 37–39
Antigua, 1, 2, 6, 35, 73–119, 127
   Northeast and North Coasts, 98–106
   West Coast, 107–13
Ave de Barlovento, 128
Aves Island, 127–28

Bahamas, 2
Baie de Friars, 36
Baie de Marigot, Guadeloupe, 154
Baie de Marigot, St. Martin, 33, 34–36
Baie de Pont-Pierre, 155–56
Baie des Flamands, 39, 41
Baie Grand Case, 36–37

Baie Mahault, 150
Baie St. Jean, 52
Baileys Cove, 23
Ballast Bay, 66
Banana Bay, 66
Barbados, 63
Barbuda, 4, 6, 73, 74, 75, 96, 114–19, 15?
Baril de Boeuf, 140
Barnakoo Bay, 92
Bas-du-Fort, 129, 143
Basse Terre, 5, 129, 131–33
Basseterre Bay, 62, 63, 64, 68, 69
Bay Rock, 24
Beggars Point, 106
Belfast Bay, 98, 100, 105
Bermuda, 11, 88
Bethesda, 92
Bird Islet, 100
Bird Islet Channel, 98, 105, 106
Bird Islet Reef, 77
Bishop Shoal, 90
Blowing Point Harbour, 17–18
Boat Harbour (Little Harbour), 18–19
Boggy Peak, 76, 77, 95, 97, 100
Booby Island, 68, 69
Boon Channel, 100, 103, 106
Boon Point 106
Bottom, The, 56, 58
Bourg des Saintes, 154, 155, 157
Brimstone Hill, 62, 64
Briscoe Mill, 68

Cade Reef, 75–76, 77, 79, 100, 109
Cades Point, 71
Carlisle Bay, 113, 114
Carrs Bay, 125

171

Caye Verte, 39, 41
Charlestown, 69, 70, 71
Charlotte point, 80
Christian Point, 92
Cistern Point, 98
Clark Point, 106
Clover Leaf, 94
Cockleshell Bay, 66
Cocoa Point, 114, 116–18, 119
Codrington Shoals, 116
Codrington Village, 115, 119
Conk Point, 95, 96, 97
Cook Shoal, 107, 113
Cooper Island, 4
Cove Bay, 17
Cow Rocks, 68, 69
Crabbs Peninsula, 73, 103
Crab Hill Bay, 113
Crocus Bay, 14–16
Crump Island, 98, 105
Cruz Bay, St. John, 7
Curtain Bluff, 100, 114

Deadman's Bay, 21
Deep Bay, 103, 107
Deshaies, 4, 5, 6, 75, 77, 129, 131, 133–34, 136, 144
Désirade, 4, 77
Diamond Bank, 77, 100, 106
Diamond Channel, 76, 77, 100
Dians Point, 98
Dickenson Bay, 6, 106–7
Dieppe Bay, 68
Dodington Banks, 114
Dog Island, 3, 4, 12, 23–24
Dogwood Point, 69
Dominica, 5–6, 107, 121, 132, 161–70
Douglas Bay, 170
Dowling Shoal, 13, 22
Drake Channel, 4

East Codrington Shoal, 116
English Harbour, 4, 5, 6, 74, 75, 76, 77, 79–90, 91, 100, 106, 112, 113, 114, 121, 137, 144
Eustatia Island, 3
Eustatia Sound, 4

Falmouth, 74, 75, 76, 106, 112, 113
Falmouth Harbour, 4, 77–79, 90–91, 100
Fanny's Cove, 94, 95, 97
Ffryes Bay, 113
Ffryes Point, 109, 113
Five Islands, 77, 103, 109, 113
Five Islands Channel, 107
Five Islands Harbour, 109
Flat Cap Point, 16
Flirt Rock, 23
Forest Bay, 19

Fort Amsterdam, 30, 31
Fort Baai, 56
Fort Barclay, 80
Fort Charles, 69
Fort Charlotte Bluff, 80
Fort de France, 5, 144
Fort Oranje, 60
Fort Oscar, 49
Fort Richepanse, 131, 132–33
Freeman Bay, 81, 113
Frégate de Haut, 140
Fullerton Point, 107, 113

Gaynais Bay, 94
Ginger Island, 4, 7
Goat Head Channel, 76, 100, 113
Gorda Sound, 4
Gozier, 145
Grand Anse, 112
Grand Bahama, 2
Grand Bourg, 157, 158
Grand Case, 36
Grand Cul-de-Sac Marin, 5, 77, 129, 134–38, 144
Grande Anse, 150, 156, 157
Grand Etang de Simsonbaai, 31–34
Grand Ilet, 156
Grand Rivière à Goyaves, 134–36
Gravenor Bay, 118
Great Bird Island, 105
Great George Fort, 79
Great Sister, 77, 100
Green Island, 4, 6, 92–94, 96
Grenada, 2, 5, 112, 162
Groot Baai, 31
Gros Ilets, 49, 50
Guadeloupe, 4, 5–6, 48, 49, 73, 75, 77, 121, 129–59, 161
  Bas Terre, 130–31, 136
  Grande Terre, 130, 131, 136, 140
  South Coast, 140–48
Guana Bay, 98, 105
Guana Island, 105
Guana Point, 98
Guard Point, 103
Gun Creek, 7
Gustavia, 46, 47, 50–51

Haut Fond, 154
Hawks Bill Rock, 103, 107
Hells Gate, 58
Hodges Bay, 103
Horse Shoe Reef, 3, 4, 6, 7, 76, 77, 100
Hughes Point, 94
Hurricane Hill, 68

Ile Chevreau, 52
Ile des Saintes, 131
Ile Fourche, 53

Ile Pinel, 39–41
Iles de la Petite Terre, 151–52
Iles des Saintes, 4, 5, 6, 49, 130
    Terre d'en Bas, 156–57
    Terre d'en Haut, 152–56
Ilet à Cabrit, 154
Ilet du Gozier, 145
Ile Toc Vers, 53
Ilots à Goyaves, 133
Indian Creek, 91
Indian River, 168, 170
Indian Town Creek, 97, 98
Indian Town Point, 95, 96, 97, 98, 118
Invisibles, 4
Island Harbour, 16–17

John O Point, 4
Johnson Point, 77, 109
Jolly Harbour, 74, 104, 107, 109–13
Jumby Bay, 103

La Baleine, 50
Ladder Landing, 56, 57
La Désirade, 148–51
La Grande Baie, 144
Lamoins River, 169
La Tortue, 52
La Trinité, 5
Layou River, 166
Ledeatt Cove, 94
Le Gros Loup, 140
Le Moule, 140
Le Pain de Sucre, 156
Les Quilles, 156
Les Saintes, 49
Lime Reef, 41
Little Bird Island, 94, 95, 97
Little Dix Bay, 7
Little Harbour (Boat Harbour), 18–19
Little Sister, 103
Long Bay, 97
Long Island, 98, 100, 103
Lowland Point, 68
Lynch Point 92

Maiden Island, 109
Maid Island, 100, 103
Maid Island Channel, 106
Majors Bay, 66
Mamora Bay, 79, 91–92
Man-of-War (Proselyte) Reef, 28
Marie-Galante, 5, 131, 157–59
Marigot, 25, 34
Martello Tower, 116
Martinique, 1, 2, 5–6, 48, 161
Maundays Bay, 17
Mayagüez, 2
Mercers Creek, 98, 105

Middle Reef, 76, 77, 109
Monks Hill, 79
Montserrat, 121–25
Morne Ronde, 33
Morris Bay (Curtain Bluff), 66, 76, 79, 113–14
Morris Bay (West Coast), 113
Mosquito Bay, 66, 69
Mosquito Bluff, 68
Mosquito Cove, 109, 113
Mosquito Island, 4
Mount Misery, 61

Nags Head, 68
Narrows, The, 68
Necker Island, 3, 4
Necker Island Passage, 3, 28
Nevis, 3, 4, 6, 10, 59, 62, 69–71, 75, 121
Newcastle Bay, 71
Nine Feet Bank, 118
Nonsuch Bay, 6, 92, 94, 98, 100, 106, 118
North Sound, 98–100, 103–6
North Whelk, 100

Old Road Bay, 79, 124, 125
Old Road Bluff, 79, 100, 124
Oyster Pond, 39, 43

Pain du Sucre, 49
Pajaros Point, 6, 7
Palaster Reef, 118
Palmetto Point, 115, 116, 118–19
Parham Harbour, 6, 76, 106
Parham Sound, 98, 100, 103
Passe à Colas, 5, 6, 136, 137–38
Passe Champagne, 148
Passe de la Grande Coulee, 136
Passe des Dames, 156
Passe du Grand Ilet, 156
Passe du Pain de Sucre, 154
Pasture Point, 100
Pearns Point, 109
Pelican Island, 98, 103, 113
Pelican Point, 118
Pelican Rocks, 107
Pelikaan Point, 31
Petite Terre, 5, 6, 150
Petit Havre, 6, 145–46, 148
Philipsburg, 25, 28, 30, 112
Pigeon Beach, 113
Pigeon Islands, 133
Pillars of Hercules, 79
Pillsbury Sound, 7
Plymouth, 124, 125
Pointe-à-Pitre, 4, 5, 6, 130, 131, 133, 137, 140–44
Pointe Ballet, 158
Pointe Basse Terre, 28
Pointe Deshaies, 134
Pointe du Cimitière, 158

Pointe Fouillole, 129, 143
Pointe Mahout, 133
Pointe Nègre, 49
Point Malendure, 133
Port du Moule, 131, 138–40
Port la Royale Marina, 35
Port Lonvilliers, 37
Port Louis, 5, 131, 134, 138
Portsmouth, 5, 169
Presqu'île dela Caravelle, 5
Prickly Pear Cays, 22–23
   North, 23
   West, 22–23
Prickly Pear East, 22, 23
Prickly Pear Island, 100, 103, 106
Prickly Pear reef, 12, 14
Prince Rupert Bay, 6, 163, 166–70
Proselyte (Man-of-War) Reef, 28
Puerto Rico, 2

Rat Island, 94
Redonda, 125–27
Reed Point, 113
Rendezvous Bay, 14, 17, 114
Rickett Harbour, 92, 94, 96
Rivière Salée, 4, 5, 6, 129, 136, 137, 138, 144
Road Bay, 3, 12–14
Road Town, 7
Rocher Crole, 39
Roseau, 5, 6, 107, 163, 164–66
Round Rock, 7
Round Rock Passage, 6, 7

Saba, 9, 56–59
Saba Bank, 3, 58–59
Saba Rock, 4
St. Barthélemy (St. Barts), 4, 6, 9, 11, 12, 27, 45–53, 74, 116
St. Christopher (St. Kitts), 3, 4, 6, 10, 59, 61–69, 73, 75
St. Croix, 3, 7, 74
Sainte-Anne, 146–48
Sainte Marie, 140
St. Eustatius (Statia), 3, 4, 59–61
Saint François, 6, 148
St. John, 7
St. Johns, 35, 58, 74, 106, 107
St. Johns, Antigua, 4
St. Johns Harbour, 107
St. Kitts (St. Christopher), 3, 4, 6, 10, 59, 61–69, 73, 75
Saint Louis, 157–58
St. Lucia, 2
St. Martin (Sint Marten), 1, 3, 4, 6, 7, 9, 11, 12, 13, 18, 25–43, 112
   East Coast, 39–43
St. Martin Rock, 39
St. Thomas, 2, 3, 7, 112

St. Thomas Harbor, 9
St. Vincent, 5, 162
Salt Island, 7
Salt Pond, 22
Sand Bank Bay, 66–68
Sandy Hill Bay, 19–20
Sandy Island, 13, 22, 76, 77, 107
Sandy Point, 18
San Juan, 2
Scilly Cay, 16
Scotch Bonnet, 66
Scotts Head, 5, 164
Scrub Island, 12, 20–22
Sea Island, 23
Seal Island, 12, 13, 23
Seal Island reefs, 12, 14, 23
Seven Stars Reef, 16
Shipstern Point, 103, 107
Shirley Heights, 75, 79
Shitten Bay, 66
Shoal Bay, 16, 17
Shoal Point, 16
Simpson Lagoon, 26
Simson Baai, 31
Sint Marten (St. Martin), 1, 3, 4, 6, 7, 9, 11, 12, 13, 18, 25–43, 112
   East Coast, 39–43
Sir Francis Drake Channel, 7
Snapper Point, 75
Sombrero, 3, 4
Sombrero Light, 3
Soufriere, 164
South Frigate Bay, 64–65
South Side Landing, 56
Spanish Point, 114, 115, 118, 119
Spanish Well Point, 114
Spithead Channel, 95, 96–97
Spring Bay, 23
Stampede Reef, 115–16
Statia (St. Eustatius), 4, 59–61
Submarine Rock, 96
Sugar Loaf, 68

Tartane, 5
Ten-pound Bay, 92–94
Tintamarre, 39, 41, 43
Tonnies Cove, 94
Toucari Bay, 170
Turtle Rock, 79
Tuson Rock, 115, 116, 119

Umbrella Point, 106

Vieux Forte, 158–59
Virgin Gorda, 3, 4, 6–7, 9, 28
Virgin Gorda Sound, 105
Virgin Islands, 2, 28

Warrington Bank, 76
Weatherhills Point, 103
White House Bay, 65–66
Willoughby Bay, 92
Windward Side, 58

Woodbridge, 163
Woodbridge Bay, 164, 166

York Island, 96

AUTHORS GUILD BACKINPRINT.COM EDITIONS are fiction and nonfiction works that were originally brought to the reading public by established United States publishers but have fallen out of print. The economics of traditional publishing methods force tens of thousands of works out of print each year, eventually claiming many, if not most, award-winning and one-time best-selling titles. With improvements in print-on-demand technology, authors and their estates, in cooperation with the Authors Guild, are making some of these works available again to readers in quality paperback editions. Authors Guild Backinprint.com Editions may be found at nearly all online bookstores and are also available from traditional booksellers. For further information or to purchase any Backinprint.com title please visit www.backinprint.com.

Except as noted on their copyright pages, Authors Guild Backinprint.com Editions are presented in their original form. Some authors have chosen to revise or update their works with new information. The Authors Guild is not the editor or publisher of these works and is not responsible for any of the content of these editions.

THE AUTHORS GUILD is the nation's largest society of published book authors. Since 1912 it has been the leading writers' advocate for fair compensation, effective copyright protection, and free expression. Further information is available at www.authorsguild.org.

Please direct inquiries about the Authors Guild and Backinprint.com Editions to the Authors Guild offices in New York City, or e-mail staff@backinprint.com.

Printed in Great Britain
by Amazon